THE MAN WHO KILLED KENNEDY

THE MAN WHO KILLED KENNEDY

THE CASE AGAINST LBJ

ROGER STONE

With Mike Colapietro

SKYHORSE PUBLISHING

Skyhorse Publishing books may be purchased in bulk at special discounts for sales promotion, corporate gifts, fund-raising, or educational purposes. Special editions can also be created to specifications. For details, contact the Special Sales Department, Skyhorse Publishing, 307 West 36th Street, 11th Floor, New York, NY 10018 or info@skyhorsepublishing.com.

Skyhorse® and Skyhorse Publishing® are registered trademarks of Skyhorse Publishing, Inc.®, a Delaware corporation.

Visit our website at www.skyhorsepublishing.com.

10 9 8 7 6

Library of Congress Cataloging-in-Publication Data

Stone, Roger J.
  The man who killed Kennedy : the case against LBJ / Roger Stone, with Mike Colapietro.
     pages cm
  Includes bibliographical references.
  ISBN 978-1-62636-313-7 (hardcover : alk. paper) 1. Kennedy, John F. (John Fitzgerald), 1917-1963--Assassination. 2. Johnson, Lyndon B. (Lyndon Baines), 1908-1973. 3. Conspiracies--United States--History--20th century. I. Colapietro, Mike. II. Title.
  E842.9.S74 2013
  973.923092--dc23
  [B]
                                    2013029015

Cover design by Brian Peterson
Cover photo credit: Public Domain

Paperback ISBN: 978-1-62914-489-4
Ebook ISBN: 978-1-63220-040-2

Printed in the United States of America

To my beloved wife,
Nydia Bertran Stone, who has suffered through my
political enthusiasms, victories, and defeats—all
with good humor and steadfast support.

CONTENTS

CONTENTS

THE MAN WHO KILLED KENNEDY

PREFACE

I recognize that those who question the government's official contentions regarding the assassination of John F. Kennedy are labeled by many in the mainstream media as "nuts," "kooks," and worse. Yet the events of November 22, 1963, have haunted and interested me since the time—as an eleven-year-old boy—I saw the indelible image of John-John saluting his father's flag-draped coffin and wept. My family is Catholic and, although I'm sure my Republican parents voted for Richard Nixon in 1960, they were still proud of our first Roman Catholic president.

I realize that delving into the world of assassination research and a belief in a conspiracy will lead some to brand me as an extremist or a nut, but the facts I have uncovered are so compelling that I must make the case that Lyndon Baines Johnson had John Fitzgerald Kennedy murdered in Dallas to become president himself and to avert the precipitous political and legal fall that was about to beset him.

I feel that I am uniquely qualified to make the case that LBJ had John F. Kennedy killed so that he could become president. I have been involved in every presidential election since 1968 with the exception of 1992, when I sat out Republican efforts and George H. W. Bush—who, as a Reaganite myself, I never had much regard for anyway—went down to ignominious defeat. I first met the then former Vice President Richard Nixon in 1967. In 1968, I was appointed chairman of Youth for Nixon in Connecticut by Governor John Davis Lodge. I later attended George Washington University in Washington, DC by night and worked in the Nixon White House press operation by day. In 1972, I was the youngest member of the senior staff of the Committee to Re-elect the President (CREEP).

Ambassador John Davis Lodge was the brother of JFK's ambassador to Vietnam, Henry Cabot Lodge. John Davis Lodge was a congressman and a member of the House Foreign Affairs Committee. He was also governor of Connecticut, Eisenhower's ambassador to Spain, Nixon's ambassador to Argentina, President Ronald Reagan's ambassador to Switzerland, and my mentor.

It was John Lodge who introduced me to former Vice President Richard Nixon when I was sixteen years old in 1968. Lodge was an old school Brahmin who nonetheless spoke Spanish, Italian, French, and German. He enjoyed a brief career as a B-movie actor in Europe, appearing onscreen with Marlene Dietrich and Shirley Temple.

When Lodge was in his eighties, he served vigorously as the chairman of Ronald Reagan's campaign for President in Connecticut, a post I had recruited him for as the Northeast regional director.

In 1979, we sat in his Westport, Connecticut, home enjoying a cocktail. I knew that JFK had planned to fire ambassador Henry Cabot Lodge upon his return from Dallas on November 24, 1963. I also know that Lodge knew why he had been summoned to see the President.

Lodge had done Kennedy's dirty work coordinating a campaign with the CIA to assassinate Catholic Vietnamese President Diem. I couldn't resist asking John Lodge about his brother.

"Did you ever ask your brother who really killed Kennedy?" I said.

His lips spread in a tight grin. "Cabot said it was the Agency boys, some Mafiosi." He looked me in the eye. "And Lyndon."

"Did your brother know in advance?" I asked.

Lodge took a sip of his Manhattan. "He knew Kennedy wouldn't be around to fire him. LBJ kept him at his post so he could serve his country."

Seven weeks before the JFK assassination, Richard Starnes for the *Washington Daily News* wrote an article titled "'Spooks' Make Life Miserable for Ambassador Lodge" and subtitled "'Arrogant' CIA Disobeys Orders in Viet Nam." The article slammed the

CIA's role in Vietnam as "a dismal chronicle of bureaucratic arrogance, obstinate disregard of orders, and unrestrained thirst for power." The article went on to chronicle the turf war between US Ambassador Henry Cabot Lodge and the CIA. "Twice the CIA flatly refused to carry out instructions from Ambassador Henry Cabot Lodge, according to a high United States source here." The article continued: "'If the United States ever experiences a 'Seven Days in May' it will come from the CIA, and not from the Pentagon,' one U.S. official commented caustically." *Seven Days in May* was a prescient book, read and endorsed by JFK, that gave a fictional chronicle of an attempted military coup in America. John Kennedy was so impressed by that book and its message that he even let them film the movie adaption at the White House while he was away one weekend.

The Starnes' source ominously referencing *Seven Days in May* was probably from someone in the military, and not Lodge, but it is nonetheless significant. Another source told Starnes "They [CIA] represent a tremendous power and total unaccountability to anyone." Starnes continued: "Coupled with the ubiquitous secret police of Ngo Dinh Nhu, a surfeit of spooks has given Saigon an oppressive police state atmosphere."

The Starnes article was a caustic and detailed denunciation of the CIA's authoritarian behavior in Vietnam and its uncontrollability by the Kennedy Administration. "One very high American official here," the article continued, "a man who has spent much of his life in the service of democracy, likened the CIA's growth to a malignancy, and added he was not sure even the White House could control it even longer."

That last quote probably came out of the mouth of Ambassador Henry Cabot Lodge.

The next day on October 3, 1963, Arthur Krock, a columnist for the *New York Times* and a close friend of the Kennedys', wrote a column "The Intra-Administration War in Vietnam" that was based on the Starnes article. The Krock column featured those incendiary quotes that Richard Starnes had collected about the CIA from their opponents in the State Department and the Pentagon. The CIA wanted to keep the Diem-Ngu regime, and the bitter enemy of both the CIA and Diem was Vietnam Ambassador Henry Cabot Lodge who was the point man in the Kennedy Administration for getting rid of Diem and Ngu.

On November 1, 1963, the Diem-Nhu regime was removed in an American-backed coup. Kennedy had been on the fence regarding their removal and he was shocked when Diem and Nhu were both assassinated and not allowed exile. Just as many in the CIA bitterly opposed Kennedy over Cuba policy, there is no doubt that the removal of Diem was a bitter nut to swallow for many in the agency.

Three weeks later there was Dallas. It was then that I decided to write this book.

Nixon introduced me to his former campaign aide, John P. Sears, who would hire me for the staff of Ronald Reagan's presidential campaigns in 1976 and 1980. President Reagan then asked me to coordinate his re-election campaign in the northeastern states in 1984, a slightly broader reprise of my role in his 1980 election.

In my capacity as Reagan's regional political director for the northeast, I helped coordinate thirteen presidential trips, giving me a unique perspective on how the Secret Service interacts with presidential aides during a presidential visit. This perspective, I believe, has given me keen insight into the many anomalies in the way the Secret Service and Vice President Johnson's aides acted in the run-up to President Kennedy's visit to Dallas.

It was in Nixon's post-presidential years that I spent the most time with the former president. *The Washington Post* said I was "Nixon's man in Washington." *New York Times* columnist Maureen Dowd called me "the keeper of the Nixon flame." Nixon had a voracious appetite for political intelligence and gossip; I fed him a steady diet of both. It was also in this period that Nixon asked me to evaluate various speaking requests he received.

I spent hours talking one-on-one with former President Nixon in his office at 26 Federal Plaza in downtown Manhattan, his apartment on the East Side, and later in his modestly appointed townhouse in Saddle River, New Jersey. Nixon was neither introspective nor retrospective in the conversations. "The old man," as staff called him behind his back, was passionately interested in what was happening today and what would happen in the future, but it was difficult to get him to dwell on the past. Generally speaking, when we talked about his peers and the circumstances surrounding the Kennedy assassination, he would grow taciturn, blunt, and sometimes cryptic. When I asked him point blank about the conclusions of the Warren Commission into the assassination of President Kennedy, he said "Bullshit" with a growl, but refused to elaborate.

Nick Ruwe was an advance man who joined the Nixon campaign in 1960 and served as Nixon's chief advance man during his comeback bid for presidency in 1968. Ruwe would become deputy chief of protocol, a position in which he directed the state funerals for former presidents Harry S. Truman and Dwight D. Eisenhower before going on to serve as President Ronald Reagan's ambassador to Iceland. Ruwe liked vodka martinis, unfiltered Camels, Brooks Brothers button-down shirts, solid grenadine ties, and the 21 Club in New York City. Ruwe hailed from an old money family in Grosse Point, Michigan. In 1961, Nixon would send him to Texas to aid in the election of Republican college professor John Tower, who won LBJ's Senate seat in a special election when Johnson resigned to become vice president. Ruwe once told me, "When spending time with RN, speak only when you are spoken to." He would serve as Nixon's chief of staff in his post-presidential years. "If the boss is in a chatty mood, he'll engage you in conversation. Otherwise shut the fuck up, and you'll get along with him fine." Thus, I would often have to wait until the right time to ask the former president the probing questions that piqued my curiosity.

Nixon liked to be alone with his thoughts and often would sit silently for long stretches of time before engaging in spirited conversation. At the same time, I learned that alcohol made our thirty-seventh president loquacious. Nixon's tolerance for alcohol was low, and two martinis would more than loosen his tongue.

Fate would have former vice president and then private lawyer Nixon in Dallas on November 21st and 22nd. It is important to recognize that Richard Nixon was both formally out of power and considered politically washed up in 1963.

I believe, however, that LBJ knew that Nixon was the one man with intimate knowledge of the CIA. He knew that organized crime figures had supported both him and Johnson financially. Because of this, it made him aware that J. Edgar Hoover of the FBI, the Cuban exile community, and right-wing Texas oilmen would be able to figure out that Johnson had directed the plot to murder John Kennedy in order to become president.

Based on my conversations with him contained in this book, Nixon indicated that Johnson was a conspirator and ordered the CIA to deliver all records pertaining to the Kennedy assassination to the White House after his inauguration in 1969 in order to confirm his belief. As we will see later, this request would play a key role in Nixon's downfall in Watergate.

Former Attorney General John Mitchell, who managed Nixon's 1968 campaign, was gracious with his time and memory. I knew he too had spent hours talking to the former president because he had been the only man in Richard Nixon's political career to whom Nixon actually abrogated campaign authority. Even those who were closest to Richard Nixon knew that he was a complicated enigma.

Mitchell lived in a Georgetown mansion with his lady friend Mary Gore Dean in the years after his time in prison following the Watergate scandal. The former attorney general ran a small consulting firm from a Georgetown office.

I first met John Mitchell when I was assigned to a messenger pool as a volunteer for Nixon in the 1968 Republican Convention in Miami Beach. Mitchell would give me envelopes, which carried communications or, in some cases, I suspected, cash. I would deliver them to the intended recipient, questions unasked. He would always pull a ten dollar bill from his own money clip for cab fare. One night around dinnertime, Mr. Mitchell came by the messenger pool, handed me a ten dollar bill, and told me to go across the street to Lum's, a popular beer joint, and buy two beer-steamed hotdogs covered with sauerkraut. He instructed me to slather both with mustard and, with a wink, he said, "eat them both."

When I was on the Committee to Re-elect the President staff in 1972, direct communications with "Mr. Mitchell" as everyone called him, were a violation of the chain of command. I reconnected with the former attorney general during my service in Ronald Reagan's 1976 presidential campaign. Mitchell helped recruit former Kentucky governor Louie Nunn for the small Reagan for President Committee headed by Senator Paul Laxalt. I saw Mitchell pretty regularly from 1976 to 1988.

Mitchell, who had discussed Nixon's thoughts and beliefs regarding the Bay of Pigs and the JFK assassination, helped me interpret many of Nixon's more oblique references to both. Mitchell knew he was revealing truths that, prior to the 1978 House Select Committee on Assassinations (HSCA) hearings, would be viewed as "kooky."

Even then, I was fascinated by the controversy surrounding JFK's murder. "I might write a book about it someday," I told Mitchell. He took out the pipe that had been clenched between his teeth, "Wait until the fiftieth anniversary," he said. I agreed. For those who wonder why I have waited until now to write this book, you now have your answer.

I am grateful to Mitchell for sharing his own conversations with the thirty-seventh president and others in an attempt to figure out what really did happen in Dallas.

Another reason that this book is unique, unlike many books published on the fiftieth anniversary of the JFK assassination is that I do not deify the Kennedys. John and Robert Kennedy were not saints. Both Jack and Bobby Kennedy were well aware of the mob's assistance in the West Virginia Primary in which the campaign they ran against Hubert Humphrey was so vicious that Muriel Humphrey would not speak to either Kennedy again. Bobby Kennedy's pursuit of the mob as attorney general is laudable, but he didn't seem to have much trouble with their substantial assistance in Jack's election.

John Kennedy was also a habitual user of injectible amphetamines. Richard A. Lertzman's and William J. Birnes's incredible book, *Dr. Feelgood*, makes the case that Kennedy was being injected by celebrity doctor Max Jacobson—also known as "Doctor Feelgood"—with a highly addictive liquid mix of methamphetamine and steroids. JFK was hopped up on meth during the presidential debates with Richard Nixon, during the Cuban Missile Crisis, during the Bay of Pigs invasion, and presumably during his many sexual trysts. JFK also arranged for Doctor Jacobson to inject First Lady Jacqueline Kennedy. Methamphetamine and steroids affect mood and judgment.

The Kennedy civil rights record is also a myth. JFK mined for black votes in 1960. His bold call to Dr. King's wife when King was jailed in Selma and Bobby Kennedy's call to the judge in the King case—which lawyer Nixon wouldn't even consider—brought the important endorsement of Dr. Martin Luther King, Sr. and a major swing of black votes against Nixon. Nixon, who had first invited King to the White House and had supported all of the civil rights and anti-lynching bills in the Senate—which LBJ killed—and enjoyed the endorsement of baseball legend Jackie Robinson, would hemorrhage blacks votes in the final days of the 1960 campaign. Yet JFK would drag his feet on civil rights. He would appoint a record number of segregationist federal judges, with Bobby Kennedy brokering the appointments with the Southern titans in the Senate. The open-housing and voting rights acts promised by JFK were late coming and stalled in the Congress when he was killed.

In his excellent book *The Bystander,* author Nick Bryant wrote, "In the summer of 1963, in the wake of the Birmingham riots and hundreds of other protests across the country, John F. Kennedy advanced the most far-reaching civil rights bill ever put before Congress. Why had he waited so long? Kennedy had been acutely aware of the issue of race—both its political perils and opportunities—since his first congressional campaign in Boston in 1946 . . . Kennedy's shrewd handling of the race issue in his early congressional campaigns blinded him as president to the intractability of the simmering racial crisis in America. By focusing on purely symbolic gestures, Kennedy missed crucial opportunities to confront the obstructionist Southern bloc and to enact genuine reform. Kennedy's inertia emboldened white supremacists and forced discouraged black activists to adopt increasingly militant tactics. At the outset of his presidency, Kennedy squandered the chance to forge a national consensus on race. For many of his thousand days in office, he remained a bystander as the civil rights battle flared in the streets of America. In the final months of his life, Kennedy could no longer control the rage he had fueled with his erratic handling of this explosive issue."

John Kennedy played a dangerous game. In the 1960 campaign, he actually ran to the *right* of Richard Nixon. Having been briefed by the CIA about the Eisenhower administration's plan to invade Cuba, he used this knowledge in the presidential debates to attack the Eisenhower administration for not being aggressive enough in their plan to oust Castro. The hapless Nixon had no choice but to charge Kennedy with recklessness or publicly divulge the invasion, thus unmasking the administration's plans. Nixon was boxed. Kennedy attacked the Eisenhower administration to engage in deficit defense spending. Kennedy was signaling to the defense contractors in the military-industrial complex that he would spend for the hardware they wanted. JFK even backtracked to take a harder line in the dispute with Red China over two small islands off the Chinese coast. That is why the military and intelligence establishments felt betrayed when Kennedy sought to cool tensions with the Soviets, secretly withdrew American missiles from Turkey in return for Soviet missiles from Cuba, refused to supply air support for the Bay of Pigs, and planned to withdraw US forces from Vietnam. Kennedy had run as a militant anti-communist.

An excellent monograph by the Center of the Study of Intelligence sums up the way JFK sent false signals to the Military and Intelligence communities and used the formal confidential CIA briefing given him by Allen Dulles himself to out-flank Nixon:

Perhaps the most crucial foreign policy issue raised in the 1960 debates, which derived directly from US intelligence analyses, was the alleged gap between US and Soviet intercontinental missile production. Kennedy charged that the Soviets had "made a break-through in missiles, and by '61 they will be outnumbering us in missiles. I'm not as confident as he (Nixon) is that we will be the strongest military power by 1963." Kennedy added, "I believe the Soviet Union is first in outer space. We have made more shots but the size of their rocket thrust and all the rest. You yourself said to Khrushchev, you may be ahead of us in rocket thrust but we're ahead of you in color television, in your famous discussion in the kitchen. I think that color television is not as important as rocket thrust."

During three of the debates, Nixon attacked Kennedy for his lack of willingness to defend Quemoy and Matsu, the small Nationalist-held islands off the coast of communist China. The extensive discussion of the Quemoy-Matsu issue did not create any direct problem for the CIA, but it led directly to a controversial dispute between the candidates over policy toward Cuba, where a popular revolution had established a Soviet-supported communist government. The politically charged clash had a number of repercussions in the White House and at the CIA.

Kennedy adviser Arthur Schlesinger, Jr. later described the relationship of these China and Cuba issues and the sequence of events in his memoir of the Kennedy administration, A Thousand Days "The Kennedy staff, seeking to take the offensive after his supposed soft position on Quemoy and Matsu, put out the provocative statement about strengthening the Cuban fighters for freedom." The controversial press release, crafted late one evening in the Biltmore Hotel in New York City by speechwriter Richard Goodwin, said "We must attempt to strengthen the non-Batista, democratic, anti-Castro forces in exile, and in Cuba itself, who offer eventual hope of overthrowing Castro." According to Goodwin, the policy statement was not shown to the sleeping Kennedy because of the late hour; it was the only public statement of the campaign not approved by the candidates.

The ill-considered statement on Cuba received wide press play and was immediately attacked. The *New York Times* the next day ran the story as the lead item on the front page with the headline: "Kennedy Asks Aid for Cuban Rebels to Defeat Castro, Urges Support of Exiles and Fighters for Freedom." James Reston wrote in the *Times* that "Senator Kennedy (has) made what is probably his worst blunder of the campaign."

Coming the day before the fourth presidential debate, the statement from the Kennedy camp put Nixon in what he found to be an extraordinarily awkward position. Many years later, Nixon wrote in his memoirs, "I knew that Kennedy had received a CIA briefing on the administration's Cuba policy and assumed that he knew, as I did, that a plan to aid the Cuban exiles was already under way on a top secret basis. His statement jeopardized the project, which could succeed only if it were supported and implemented secretly."

Throughout the campaign, the two candidates had engaged in a spirited exchange about whether the Eisenhower administration had "lost" Cuba, and Nixon knew that the issue would be revived in the final debate, which was to be devoted solely to foreign affairs. Nixon has written that to protect the security of the planned operation he "had no choice but to take a completely opposite stand and attack Kennedy's advocacy of open intervention." And he did attack, saying, "I think that Senator Kennedy's policies and recommendations for the handling of the Castro regime are probably the most dangerously irresponsible recommendations that he has made during the course of this campaign."

Former Kennedy advisors have underscored over the years that the statement on Cuba was released without Kennedy's knowledge by staffers ignorant of the covert action planning under way at the time and was crafted solely to ensure that Kennedy would not again be put on the defensive about Communist expansionism. These same advisers differ among themselves, however, on the key question of whether Kennedy himself knew of the covert action plans. Kennedy speechwriter Theodore Sorensen said in 1993, "I am certain that at the time of the debates, Kennedy had no knowledge of the planned operation." His reference to more assertive action regarding Cuba was put in by one of my assistants to give him something to say.

The assistant was Richard Goodwin, whose memory is quite different. Goodwin asserts that, "As a presidential candidate, he (Kennedy) had received secret briefings by the CIA, some of which revealed that we were training a force of Cuban exiles for a possible invasion of the Cuban mainland." Goodwin and Sorensen have both made clear that they were not in attendance at any CIA briefings.[1]

The US Government's planning for a covert action program intended to undermine Castro had been approved by President Eisenhower in March 1960 and was in progress throughout the period of the presidential campaign. Indeed, Nixon was spearheading the Cuban Initiative. Kennedy would use his CIA briefing to outflank Nixon on the right and falsely signal the generals and spooks at the CIA that he would be okay. This head-fake would help cost him his life and give Lyndon Johnson willing co-conspirators.

I know that there are those who may try to ascribe political motives to my authoring of this book. I am a veteran of eight Republican presidential campaigns and have been a shrill partisan and political operative. Those who read ahead will see that Republicans Gerald Ford, George H. W. Bush, and Arlen Specter are not spared in this narrative. Nor do I pull my punches when it comes to right-wing Dallas oilmen like H. L. Hunt, Clint Murchison, Jr., Sid Richardson, or Senator Harry F. Byrd's cousin, D. H. Byrd. I am not the first person to assert, based on his research, that Lyndon Johnson arranged the murder of John F. Kennedy. I have built on the work of Phillip F. Nelson's *LBJ: The Mastermind of the JFK Assassination*, Barr McClellan's *Blood, Money, & Power*, Glen Sample's and Mark Collom's *The Men on the Sixth Floor*, and Craig Zirbel's *The Texas Connection*. I have interpreted certain events differently from these authors and, in some cases, provided new information to bolster their original claims of Johnson's complicity in Kennedy's death.

This book stands on the research of citizens who have doubted the government's version of events as depicted by the Warren Commission, including:

Vincent Salandria, Mark Lane, David Talbot, L. Flecher Prouty, John Kelin, Jim Marrs, Gaeton Fonzi, Seth Kantor, Harry Livingston, Gary Mack, Jack White, Fred Newcomb, Harold Weisberg, Sylvia Meagher, Penn Jones, Jr., Dr. Charles Crenshaw, Richard Belzer, Jesse Ventura, Peter Dale Scott, Joachim Joesten, David Lifton, Dan E. Moldea, William Turner, Jonn Christian, Russell Baker, James W. Douglass, Edward Epstein, Billy Sol Estes, Peter Janney, Robert Morrow, Edward Harrison Livingstone, Robert J. Groden, John M. Newman, Mark North, Frank Ragano, Gus Russo, Saint John Hunt, Lamar Waldron, and Thom Hartmann.

Special thanks also go to Houston Attorney Douglas Caddy and to author J. Evetts Haley, whose trailblazing early book on LBJ sold more copies in Texas than any book other than The Bible.

NOTE

1. https://www.cia.gov/library/center-for-the-study-of-intelligence/csi-publications/books-and-monographs/cia-briefings-of-presidential-candidates/cia-6.htm.

INTRODUCTION

"I do understand power, whatever else may be said about me," Lyndon Johnson had once remarked. "I know where to look for it, and how to use it."[1]

From the moment Air Force One touched down at Bergstrom Air Force Base in the Texas Hill Country just southwest of Austin in January 1969 on LBJ's last flight from Washington, the power that he had cultivated and grown from Congress, through the Senate, and to the presidency—the power that at times seemed absolute—had begun to dissipate.

Interestingly, the only Republican member of the Texas congressional delegation who went to Andrews Air Force Base to see Johnson off was Houston Congressman George H. W. Bush. Bush's show of respect would be repaid with treachery, as we shall see later.

In the short time that followed his presidency, Lyndon Johnson had fallen into a despondency that would remain with him until his final day. These bouts with depression had come and gone routinely in his life, usually accompanied by heavy drinking, volcanic outbursts followed by dark moods, and long periods of ill health.

The Cutty Sark Scotch now went down with abandon. The girdle he wore as president to strap in his expanding gut was gone, as were the tailored suits. His well-groomed hair, famously brushed back and pasted to his skull with Sta-comb hair tonic, had grown unkempt, almost grazing his shoulders.[2]

Johnson had been hospitalized in early 1970 after complaining of severe chest pains. The diagnosis was angina. His arteries were hardened and narrowed, there was not enough blood getting to his heart, and he was told to lose weight to take pressure off his ticker.[3]

Johnson, however, was not looking to wind back the clock.

In late 1970, he took up smoking again, a habit he had dropped years earlier following a near-fatal heart attack.

"I always loved cigarettes, missed them every day since I quit. Anyway, I don't want to linger the way Eisenhower did," Johnson said shortly before his death. "When I go, I want to go fast."[4]

Without power or the prospect of it, Johnson was killing himself quickly. It was the final determined goal of a man of extreme ambition.

He would reach that goal on January 22, 1973.

Nearing the end, many times short of breath, he clung to an oxygen tank while he continued to smoke. Johnson was experiencing stomach pains due to diverticulitis, small pouches in the lining of the colon or large intestine, and sharp, daily chest pains caused by two completely blocked arteries.[5]

The former president was racked not only with pain in his final days but guilt, undergoing psychotherapy in an attempt to unburden himself from a political past that included as many as eight murders and was ended in shame.[6] Intimates said that Johnson had even smoked marijuana to deal with his demons—the pastime of the counter-culture that had driven him from the White House.

From the moment he assumed the presidency, the ideals of John Kennedy's New Frontier had become Johnson's Great Society.

Despite a legislative lifetime of leading the fight against integration, anti-lynching laws, and voting rights, Johnson championed civil rights, pushing through the Voting Rights Act of 1965, and made the war on poverty a top priority of the administration, although by the end of his time in office, the 1964 Johnson campaign motto "All the way with LBJ" had been cruelly morphed by war protestors to "Hey, hey, LBJ, how many kids did you kill today?"

They were words Johnson couldn't escape. Wherever he went, this reminder of his continued failure in Vietnam followed him. Even in the White House, he could hear the chant from the gates.

In his short retirement, Johnson would coldly recall "young people by the thousands . . . chanting . . . about how many kids I had killed that day," referring to the mantra as "that horrible song."[7]

In the biggest misstep of his presidency, Johnson backed and continued to double down on the war in Vietnam, an initiative made abhorrent with his knowledge that the war was unwinnable.

"Vietnam is getting worse every day," Johnson remarked to his wife Lady Bird in July, 1965. "I have the choice to go in with great casualty lists or to get out with disgrace. It's like being in an airplane, and I have to choose between crashing the plane and jumping out. I do not have a parachute."[8]

In 1967, playwright Barbara Garson wrote *MacBird!*, a political satire which overlaid the Shakespearean tragedy *Macbeth* with the assassination of the nation's thirty-fifth president, John F. Kennedy. *MacBird!* proposed the idea that Johnson engineered the plot carried out on November 22, 1963, in Dallas, Texas.

"People used to ask me then, 'Do you really think Johnson killed Kennedy?'" Garson recalled. "I never took that seriously. I used to say to people that if he did, it's the least of his crimes."[9]

Taken seriously, the supposition that Johnson was behind the plot to kill Kennedy is the key that unlocks the gate to the greatest of Johnson's crimes, the knowing futility of a war that would eventually claim more than fifty-eight thousand American lives.

Admissions and insights divulged in the recent past have begun to show Johnson in a role that was not only complicit but instrumental in the planning, organization, and cover-up of the Kennedy assassination. These confessions have come from business associates, personal acquaintances, law enforcement officials, and top members of the government.

Richard Nixon, no slouch in the use of power, knew Johnson well from their time in the Senate. Of less than modest means like Johnson ("up from dirt" Nixon would say to me), Nixon understood the hunger for power, which consumed Johnson. By 1961, they both resented Jack Kennedy's wealth and privilege and sized him up as a "rich kid whose father bought it for him."

"Johnson was vain, cruel, loud, devious, and driven," Nixon told me.

Many of the same Texas oilmen who wrote big checks for Dick Nixon also wrote big checks for Johnson.

"He liked to squeeze their nuts," Nixon said. "He would tell them the oil-depletion allowance was in trouble unless they coughed up cash—and milked 'em."

"That was the difference between Lyndon and me," Nixon snorted after a very dry martini in his Saddle River, New Jersey home. "I wasn't willing to kill for it . . ." Nixon grew silent and pensive, staring into his martini. I knew from my years as a Nixon loyalist and "Nixon's man in Washington" during his post-presidential years when a conversation with "RN" was over and when not to speak.

Nixon stirred.

"It's a hell of a thing. I actually knew this Jack Ruby fella. Murray Chotiner brought him in back in '47. Went by the name Rubinstein. An informant. Murray said he was one of Lyndon Johnson's boys . . . we put him on the payroll," Nixon's voice trailed off.

What went unsaid was that Nixon had realized the connection between Johnson and the execution of Lee Harvey Oswald. I knew Murray Chotiner had been the éminence grise of Nixon's early political career. Chotiner was a Los Angeles mob lawyer who ran Nixon's first campaign for Congress in 1946 and his 1950 campaign for the Senate. That Chotiner brought Ruby in was no surprise—his mob connections ran deep. Chotiner had strong connections with Meyer Lansky, Bugsy Siegel, and Mickey Cohen. He was also the middleman between Louisiana mob kingpin Carlos Marcello and Nixon.[10]

"Murray and his brother were mob lawyers," said 1968 Nixon campaign manager John Mitchell who went on to become Nixon's attorney general. "He knew all the mob guys and knew damn well that, as attorney general, I couldn't talk to them. He was close to Johnson through Marcello, so it's logical that he brought 'Rubinstein' in."

Marcello held the strings of Jack Ruby, and he was allied with Tampa mob boss Santo Trafficante. According to author Lamar Waldron in his book, *Watergate: The Hidden History*, Trafficante and Marcello would funnel a $500,000 secret campaign contribution to Nixon in 1960 to stop the federal prosecution of Teamsters President Jimmy Hoffa.

Nick Ruwe told me that, on November 24, 1963, he arrived at Nixon's Fifth Avenue apartment—an address he shared with Nelson Rockefeller ironically—to accompany Nixon to a lunch with Mary Roebling, a New Jersey socialite and Nixon family friend at La Cote Basque. It was 12:30. Ruwe came into the room as Nixon turned the TV off. He had just witnessed Jack Ruby shoot Lee Harvey Oswald. Ruwe told me, "The Old Man was white as a ghost. I asked him if everything was all right." "I know that guy," Nixon muttered. Ruwe said that Nixon didn't elaborate. He knew better than to ask questions.

Incredibly, a US Justice Department document provided by the FBI regarding Jack Ruby's connection to Richard Nixon in the late 1940s proved Nixon's recollection was correct.[12]

Some JFK researchers incorrectly discount this document because it has a Department of Justice buck slip, which has an address in Washington, DC with a zip code. Zip codes were nonexistent in 1947. This buck slip is not part of the original record, but was attached in 1978 when the House Select Committee on Assassinations found and filed it as evidence, thus the zip code does not discredit the authenticity of this clear link between Nixon and Ruby . . . and LBJ.

Ruby's service to the House Committee on Un-American Activities is not surprising. In 1950, Ruby would serve as an informant for the Kefauver Committee, a probe of organized crime. According to Luis Kutner, counsel to the committee, Ruby "briefed the Kefauver Committee about organized crime in Chicago," and his "staff learned" that Ruby was a "syndicate lieutenant" who had been sent to Dallas to serve as a liaison for Chicago mobsters.[13]

Thus, Nixon figured out that Lee Harvey Oswald had been silenced by a longtime associate of Lyndon Johnson, linking LBJ directly to the Kennedy assassination. Nixon knew it from the moment he saw Ruby shoot Oswald on national TV along with millions of other Americans. Upon becoming president, he would seek proof.

Johnson himself would be spotted alongside Ruby by Madeleine Brown, LBJ's longtime mistress, and by Carousel Club dancer Shari Angel at the Adolphus Hotel in Dallas only a few months before the assassination. Angel said that the Texas oilman and LBJ crony H. L. Hunt also attended (Hunt would later figure greatly in the Kennedy assassination). In the words of Angel, once billed as "Dallas's own gypsy," "Lyndon Johnson had it done."[14]

Indeed, Lyndon Johnson was prepared to kill to become president. In fact, prior to the Kennedy assassination, he had honed his talent in murder for financial and political gain, as this book will outline.

Johnson's life has been chronicled by Pulitzer Prize winner Robert Caro, who had had access to the same resource materials I used. Caro had had all the pieces of a complex puzzle, but he never put it together. He clearly delineates the motives for Johnson's actions, the means, and the opportunity, but unlike Johnson, Caro would not "pull the trigger."

Johnson was a man of great ambitions and enormous greed, both of which, in 1963, would threaten to destroy him. In the end, Lyndon Johnson would use power from his personal connections in Texas, from the underworld, and from the government—including elements of the CIA, organized crime, and right-wing Texas oilmen desperate to retain the oil-depletion allowance, which JFK wanted to repeal—to escape an untimely end in politics and to seize even greater power. Lyndon Baines Johnson was the driving force behind a conspiracy to murder John Fitzgerald Kennedy on November 22, 1963.

This is the story of why and how he did it.

INTRODUCTION

NOTES

1. Harry McPherson, *A Political Education* (Boston: Little, Brown and Company, 1972), 450.
2. Robert A. Caro, *Master of the Senate: The Years of Lyndon Johnson* (New York: Alfred A. Knopf, 2002), 117.
3. Leo Janos, "The Last Days of the President," *The Atlantic* 232, no. 1 (July 1973): 35–41.
4. Ibid.
5. Ibid.
6. Barr McClellan, *Blood, Money & Power: How L.B.J. Killed J.F.K.* (New York: Skyhorse Publishing, 2011), 274.
7. Robert A. Caro, *Means of Ascent* (New York: Alfred A. Knopf, 1990), xxiii.
8. Michael R. Beschloss, *Reaching for Glory: Lyndon Johnson's Secret White House Tapes, 1964–1965* (New York: Simon & Schuster, 2001), 390.
9. Jane Horwitz, Jane, "She Hopes 'MacBird' Flies in a New Era," *The Washington Post* (September 5, 2006).
10. Don Fulsom, *Nixon's Darkest Secrets: The Inside Story of America's Most Troubled President* (New York: St. Martin's Press, 2012), 43–44.
11. Jim Marrs, *Crossfire: The Plot That Killed Kennedy* (New York: Basic Books, 1989), 269.
12. This document can be found at: coverthistory.blogspot.com/2006/12/many-researchers-believe-that-document.html.
13. Lamar Waldron and Thom Hartmann, *Ultimate Sacrifice: John and Robert Kennedy, the Plan for a Coup in Cuba, and the Murder of JFK* (New York: Carroll & Graf, 2005), 486.
14. "An Interview with Shari Angel," by Ian Griggs, November 19, 1994, www.jfklink.com/articles/Shari.html.

CHAPTER ONE

LYNDON JOHNSON—THE MAN

Secretary of the Senate Bobby Baker, whom Senate Majority Leader Lyndon Johnson called "my strong right arm," predicted on the bitter cold January day of John F. Kennedy's inauguration that the new president would die a violent death and would not finish his first term. Even though the LBJ Presidential Library has done a good job of cleansing Lyndon B. Johnson's public image, he was in fact a crude, vicious, duplicitous, and cowardly man who sometimes lied when it would have been easier to tell the truth. To fully understand LBJ's role in the Kennedy assassination, one must understand Johnson, the narcissist, the bully, the sadist, the man.

Veteran JFK assassination researcher Robert Morrow correctly labels Johnson a "functioning lunatic."

Longtime aides and secret service agents are in agreement that even before his presidency, Johnson was known for doing whatever he wanted, whenever he wanted, simply because he could. The Secret Service, the FBI, and the CIA did a commendable job of covering up Johnson's true persona. And what an evil personality he had: vicious, mean spirited, vengeful, aggressive, arrogant, abusive, sex crazed . . . the descriptions of his vile actions go on and on.

Ronald Kessler is an American journalist who authored nineteen non-fiction books about the Secret Service, the FBI, and the CIA. In

2006, he became the chief Washington correspondent of *Newsmax;* before that he was an investigative reporter for *The Washington Post.* He was one of the first journalists to gain the trust of these organizations to expose the indecent, immoral actions of presidents from Eisenhower to Obama.

Kessler's eighteenth book, *In the President's Secret Service: Behind the Scenes With Agents in the Line of Fire and the Presidents They Protect,* was described by *USA Today* as a "fascinating exposé . . . high-energy read . . . amusing, saucy, often disturbing anecdotes about the VIPs the Secret Service has protected and still protects . . . [accounts come] directly from current and retired agents (most identified by name, to Kessler's credit). . . . Balancing the sordid tales are the kinder stories of presidential humanity. . . . [Kessler is a] respected journalist and former *Washington Post* reporter . . . an insightful and entertaining story."

In this book, Kessler explains that every source he interviewed described Johnson as completely and totally out of control. One unnamed source even stated "if this guy was not president, he would be in a mental hospital." "LBJ is as crude as the day is long" became a common analogy during his time in office.

In Kessler's *In the President's Secret Service,* Agent Taylor recounts escorting Johnson, who was then the vice president, with another agent from the US Capitol to the White House for a 4 p.m. meeting with Kennedy. Due to Johnson's inability to leave the US Capitol on time (he was not ready to leave until 3:45 p.m.) and because of traffic along Pennsylvania Avenue, they were going to be late.

"Johnson said to jump the curb and drive on the sidewalk," Taylor said. "There were people on the sidewalk getting out of work. I told him, 'No.' He said, 'I told you to jump the curb.' He took a newspaper and hit the other agent, who was driving, on the head. He said, 'You're both fired.'"

Fortunately, when Agent Taylor told Evelyn Lincoln, President Kennedy's secretary, that the vice president had fired him, Lincoln informed him—while shaking her head in exasperation—that he was not going to be fired.

Part of Johnson's erratic, reckless behavior stemmed from his reluctance to be vice president. As Robert Dallek, a Pulitzer Prize finalist and American historian specializing in American presidents, explains in his biography *Flawed Giant: Lyndon Johnson and His Times, 1961–1973*, LBJ "had hoped and planned for the presidency, but fate or the limitations of his time, place, and personality had cast him in the second spot. And he despised it."

The book *Protecting the President* by Dennis McCarthy has a lot of anecdotes about what an epic jackass Lyndon Johnson was; how rude and abusive he was with Secret Service agents. McCarthy:

"Johnson had not been very well liked by any of the agents on the detail. He treated us as if we were the hired help on his ranch, cursed at us regularly, and was generally a royal pain to deal with."

Johnson's alienating egoism was not unknown to President Kennedy. "You are dealing with a very insecure, sensitive man with a huge ego," JFK told close aide Kenneth P. O'Donnell.

What Kennedy didn't know was how deeply rooted Johnson's desire was to be top dog. Johnson was used to bending people to his will through intimidation—an art form Washington journalists Rowland Evans and Robert Novak called "the treatment"—but he couldn't control Kennedy. In fact, Kennedy often excluded Johnson from matters concerning foreign policy.

Johnson was jealous of Kennedy's womanizing ways. In *Flawed Giant*, Dallek described that when someone mentioned Kennedy's many affairs, Johnson would bang the table and declare that he had more women by accident than Kennedy ever had on purpose. Due to his insatiable envy, LBJ might have given more women the "Johnson Treatment" than JFK, Harding, and Clinton combined.

These extensive affairs began when Johnson was vice president, but very few of his paramours were around for any great length of time. While Johnson was vice president, one of the women "who held his attention longer than the rest and for whom he exhibited some really deep feelings, was married off, probably because a continued relationship was incompatible with the vice presidency," said George Reedy, White House Press Secretary from 1964 to 1965.

Johnson "filled himself with excessive eating, drinking, and smoking, and an affinity for womanizing—sexual conquests gave him temporary respites from feeling unwanted, unloved, unattended," wrote Dallek.

"He is the only person [president] I have seen who was drunk," said Frederick H. Walzel, a former chief of the White House's Secret Service Uniformed Division.

"Johnson was often inebriated," stated Kessler in his book *In the President's Secret Service*. "One evening when Johnson was president, he came back to the White House drunk, screaming that the lights were on, wasting electricity."

One agent assigned to protect Johnson recounted that the president was "uncouth, nasty, and often drunk." The agent went on to say that after Lady Bird Johnson caught LBJ having sex with a secretary in the Oval Office, Johnson ordered the Secret Service to install a buzzer to warn him of when his wife would be expected to stop by. The agent said that the First Lady was well aware of the buzzer's existence, and was not naive about her husband's many liaisons.

Air Force One crew members had similar experiences with Johnson, who often locked the door to his stateroom and spent hours alone behind closed doors with pretty secretaries, even when the First Lady was aboard.

"Johnson would come on the plane [Air Force One], and the minute he got out of sight of the crowds, he would stand in the doorway and grin from ear to ear, and say, 'You dumb sons of bitches. I piss on all of you,'" Robert M. MacMillan, an Air Force One steward, told Kessler. "Then, he stepped out of sight and began taking off his clothes. By the time he was in the stateroom, he was down to his shorts and socks. It was not uncommon for him to peel off his shorts, regardless of who was in the stateroom."

Johnson didn't care if women were around; he continued his indecent exposure without concern. "He was totally naked with his daughters, Lady Bird, and female secretaries," McMillan recalled.

Lyndon Johnson had absolutely no moral compass or control over his animal instincts. Dallek: "When the wife of television newscaster David Brinkley accepted an invitation to visit Lyndon and Lady Bird at the ranch on a weekend her husband couldn't be there, Johnson tried unsuccessfully to get her into bed."

Sunshine Williams, today a real estate agent in Austin, tells the story of when she was a reporter for a radio station and a young fetching brunette on Election Day of 1964. She interviewed President Lyndon Johnson on the tarmac of the Houston airport; he had liquor on his breath, and he invited her to come to the LBJ Ranch as a guest, although his plane was full, and he would have to kick one of his entourage off to make room for her. Sunshine declined.

When LBJ would get a girl back to the isolated and secluded LBJ ranch, it would inevitably become a game of "survival of the fittest" for the woman as she battled off Johnson's inevitable advances. Austin used to have a music festival called Aquafest, which also crowned a beauty queen. These beauty queens (circa 1969) would be taken to the LBJ ranch to visit the retired President Johnson who would take them on jeep rides to secluded areas and then proceed to make advances on these poor girls.

Whether drunk or sober, Johnson continued his abusive behaviors and apologized for none of it. George Edward Reedy served under him from 1951 to 1965 and was White House press secretary for the last year. In his book *Lyndon B. Johnson: A Memoir*, Reedy was crystal clear describing Johnson's notoriously unbalanced behavior. As president, Johnson was known for driving his staff "to the verge of exhaustion—and sometimes over the verge; for paying the lowest salaries for the longest hours of work on Capitol Hill; for publicly humiliating his most loyal aides; for keeping his office in a constant state of turmoil by playing games with reigning male and female favorites."

Reedy also had full knowledge of the president's sexual escapades with secretaries and aides. "They had to be young, they had to be cheerful, they had to be malleable, and it helped if they were slightly antagonistic to him at the onset. He dearly loved to convert an anti-Johnson liberal with a slightly plump figure and a dowdy wardrobe into a lean, impeccably clad female whose face was masked in cosmetics and who adored the ground he walked on."

Johnson would "screw anything that would crawl, basically," said William F. Cuff, the executive assistant in LBJ's military office.

According to Reedy, the president's flavors of the month—who were often referred to as "the harem" by male staff members— enjoyed many compensations including lavish presents, "travel under plush conditions, attendance at glamorous social functions with the Johnsons . . . expensive clothes, and frequent trips to New York, where a glamorous makeup artist would initiate her into the mysteries of advanced facial makeup, resulting in cosmetics so lavishly applied that they became a mask."

Such an active and careless sexual life certainly had predictable results. Johnson was married to Lady Bird until the day he died; the couple had two daughters, Lynda and Luci. But the philandering politico had three other children outside his marriage. He admitted none.

The first of the known Johnson illegitimate children is Steven Brown, born in 1950 to Madeleine Brown, Johnson's sexual partner across two decades. Steven did not know the identity of his real father until the late 1980s. Until then, he thought his father might be Dallas attorney Jerome Ragsdale—a man charged with watching over one of LBJ's oldest secrets.

Steven Brown sued for paternity in 1987, lost, and died a suspicious death.

LBJ loyalist Jack Valenti would do anything for his boss. The Texas advertising executive joined the Kennedy-Johnson team as a media liaison and later worked as President Johnson's closest aide. But he served a far more important role as a stand-in father for Lyndon Johnson's child.

Valenti had been a long-time bachelor until, in 1962, at the age of forty-one, he married Mary Margaret Wiley, a former receptionist in Johnson's Texas office, who had relocated to Washington. She was remarkably beautiful, and the president enjoyed talking to her for hours. She would be Johnson's mistress and bear him one of at least three illegitimate children.

In fact, Air Force Two pilot Ralph Albertazzie later attested to one of many whirlwind dates the vice president had had with Wiley—from Kansas City to Austin to New York City and back to Washington, all on a whim, all on the taxpayers' expense. She was clearly special—so special that reporter Sarah McClendon alleged that Bill Moyers was brought on as a "religious aide" to prevent the talk of Johnson and his secretary. Sarah McLendon:

> Bill Moyers had just begun handling the press for Lyndon at that time. Moyers, who'd graduated from Southwest Theological Institute in Fort Worth, had been brought to Washington because of another rumor: There had been speculation that LBJ's relationship with his top secretary Mary Margaret Wiley had become an intimate as well as a professional one. Concerned, Lyndon had asked his good friend Harry Provence of the *Waco Tribune* and several other Texas editors to look for someone to prevent that kind of talk. And who better to give the vice presidential staff a more "sanctified" appearance than a young man headed for the ministry? So Moyers was hired on, ostensibly to deal with policy concerning religion and to answer letters that had a religious tone. In actuality, he was a chaperone who would travel with Lyndon and Mary Margaret to show that all was on the up-and-up.

He often chaperoned their dates to discourage speculation.

Many people thought that Jack Valenti was gay and he surprised everyone when he married Mary Margaret. The couple had three children: John, Alexandra, and Courtenay Lynda Valenti (later Warner Bros. studio executive). Mary Margaret gave birth to daughter Courtenay three weeks before the JFK assassination. Courtenay garnered more attention from Lyndon Johnson than any of his other children. Photographs of her playing with the president in the White House were regularly published in the press.

Ironically, the diminutive Valenti, who was 5' 2" in cowboy boots, would have a long-term affair with a married woman who was a close friend of my wife, Nydia Bertran Stone. She said that Jack "had one of the biggest penises she had ever seen. It's almost as big as he is."

Once, as Valenti prepared to end a long day at the White House, he noted to the president that he was eager to get home and play with his daughter. "Your daughter?" Johnson said, with a wry smile.

A 2009 *Washington Post* story detailed declassified files showing that at the same time that Johnson was bedding Valenti's wife, the FBI was investigating whether Valenti, who died in 2007, was gay. Although no proof was ever found, the files offer a new perspective on his marriage to Wiley. Many speculate that he married her to give his beloved president cover for an affair that lasted nine years —and resulted in another daughter Valenti would raise as his own.

A third child thought to be Johnson's progeny is Lyndon K. Boozer, daughter of LBJ secretary Yolanda Boozer. "It was July 19, 1963. Yolanda Garza Boozer had given birth to a boy at the Columbia Hospital for Women in Washington, DC. Her boss, Vice President Lyndon B. Johnson, stopped by to visit the new mother and her husband, a Treasury official."

Secret Service agents attested that Johnson was sleeping with five of his eight secretaries. Based on the fact that he was using his secretarial pool as a harem at the time Boozer gave birth to a boy named after Lyndon, it is not difficult to surmise Lyndon is the son of LBJ. Those who know him say he is a spitting image of the late president.

History has been kind to Lyndon Johnson through all his philandering. One biographer has a very good reason to write a glowing tribute to the former president—Doris Kearns Goodwin had a curiously intimate relationship with the president, especially in his retirement. She had a peculiar relationship with him, which made many tongues wag. *Washington Post* reporter Sally Quinn described this in 1974:

"Johnson was terribly possessive of her time, more and more as he came closer to death. She was seeing many men at this point in her life but had no real attachments until she met Richard Goodwin six months before Johnson's death."

Kearns later admitted that Lyndon Johnson used to crawl into bed with her and just talk, but with nothing else going on. Kearns Goodwin told authors Richard Harwod and Haynes Johnson that Lyndon would confess his love to her, court her aggressively, ask her to marry him, and act jealously about her lovers.

Not suprisingly, Doris Kearns Goodwin has long been the subject of rumors that she was having sex with the subject of her fabulously successful first book *Lyndon Johnson and the American Dream*.

Aside from being a philanderer of the highest order, Lyndon Johnson's sense of humor revolved "chiefly on the contents of toilet bowls," Reedy recounted. Rather than interrupt himself, Johnson would continue his train of thought on the toilet surrounded by his aides. Johnson particularly enjoyed the discomfort this caused among the Ivy League aides of JFK. Ronald Kessler's research confirmed this: "He would sit on the toilet and defecate in front of aides. During press conferences on his Texas ranch that included female journalists, he would urinate in front of them," Kessler noted in his book *In The President's Secret Service*.

If that were not lewd enough, Reedy recalled Johnson's "favorite spectator sport was watching bovine copulation, and he gloried in summoning fastidious males to his bathroom, where conference and excretion could be intermingled."

LBJ was also fond of literally waving his member—which he affectionately nicknamed "Jumbo"—around in public. Perhaps his "pecker humor" combined with the many instances when he would expose himself dubbed him the Secret Service code name of "Volunteer." One time in particular, he exposed himself to Japanese reporters in a bathroom, opining that they probably didn't see "them" that size back in Japan.

In *Flawed Giant*, Dallek writes, "During a private conversation with some reporters who pressed him to explain why we were in Vietnam, Johnson lost his patience. According to Arthur Goldberg, LBJ unzipped his fly, drew out his substantial organ and declared, 'This is why!'"

Mack White, who in 1977 used to work at the LBJ Library where he transcribed oral histories, has a revealing essay about LBJ on the Internet. It is entitled "See the LBJ Robot."

Mack White: "I worked at the library for about a year. It was easy work, and interesting. I would cue up the tapes on a reel-to-reel player, put on a pair of headphones, and, working a foot pedal to rewind, pause and fast-forward, transcribe interviews that had been conducted with people who had known Johnson at different times of his life.

"Most of the interviewees spoke glowingly of him. Even those who were critical of him—Kennedy staffers, most notably—went to some pains to soften their criticism and try to find something nice to say. And yet, despite everyone's best efforts, what emerged from this Citizen Kane-style composite of interviews was not pretty. It was not said in so many words—in fact, was left entirely unsaid—but nothing could obscure the picture: Lyndon Johnson was an overbearing, coarse, ruthless, sociopathic, low-life, power-mad monster. Yes, he was a consummate politician, therefore could charm people when he had to, but the mask could easily slip, and often did."

Stories about LBJ's unhinged and outrageous behavior abound. Marshall Lynam, a top aide to Texas congressman and LBJ friend Jim Wright, tells this one:

". . . Johnson also could be downright cruel. One incident was described to me by a friend of thirty years, a retired US Air Force colonel who flew as an escort officer on a Johnson trip to space installations around the United States. My friend swears he saw Johnson, then vice president, throw a Cutty Sark and soda into the face of an Air Force steward. The reason? The sergeant had failed to use a freshly-opened bottle of soda in mixing the drink."

Though the Secret Service kept most of the president's unruly character relatively unknown to the American public, no one could stop Johnson from being himself in front of the camera. In 1964, LBJ created controversy while taking his beagles, Him and Her, on a walk with the press. A photo was snapped of the president lifting Him up by the ears. The image led to public outrage of animal abuse. Johnson claimed that the move was for the beagles' benefit because "it lets them bark." However, animal lovers were not convinced. He had to apologize to animal rights organizations for his cruelty.

In addition to being a true maniac, Johnson was also known to show no bounds when cursing profusely. Kessler shared some of LBJ's jaw-dropping racial slurs in a book called *Inside the White House*. An Air Force One crew member stated that the president had his own opinions about the Civil Rights Movement, ones that were the complete opposite of his public actions to make America a "Great Society," and he blatantly shared them with anyone in earshot: "These Negroes, they're getting pretty uppity these days, and that's a problem for us since they've got something now they never had before, the political pull to back up their uppityness. Now, we've got to do something about this, we've got to give them a little something, just enough to quiet them down, not enough to make a difference." In a meeting aboard Air Force One, shortly after signing the Civil Rights Act, he was pleased to promise two governors: "I'll have those niggers voting Democratic for the next two hundred years."

Though Johnson may have been "just a country boy from the central hills of Texas," George Reedy likened LBJ's antics to "a Turkish sultan of Istanbul."

And this particular Turkish sultan of Istanbul possessed a staggering ego, which knew no bounds. "To Johnson, loyalty was a one-way street: All take on his part, and all give on the part of everyone else—his family, his friends, his supporters," Reedy explained.

When a truly horrific person, devoid of any redeeming qualities, also harbors scathing jealousy towards the president—enough so to covet his position—this person with a history of no moral compass might, in all likelihood, use his established powers of intimidation to orchestrate the plan to assassinate JFK, and succeed.

Lyndon Johnson's oddly disturbing decisions and complete lack of concern for the future of the country just hours after Kennedy's assassination only solidifies the fact that he had put the plan in motion and covered it up. Investigative journalist Russ Baker discloses several events involving LBJ that cannot be conceived as anything other than incriminating in his book *Family of Secrets*.

"Pat Holloway, former attorney to both Poppy Bush and Jack Crichton, recounted to me an incident involving LBJ that had greatly disturbed him," wrote Baker. "This was around 1 p.m. on November 22, 1963, just as Kennedy was being pronounced dead." As Holloway was leaving the office, he passed through the reception area, and the switchboard operator noted that she was patching Johnson through from Parkland Hospital to Holloway's boss and the firm's senior partner, Waddy Bullion, who was also the vice president's tax lawyer. The operator asked if Holloway wanted to listen in.

"I heard him say: 'Oh, I gotta get rid of my goddamn Halliburton stock.' Lyndon Johnson was talking about the consequences of his political problems with his Halliburton stock at a time when the president had been officially declared dead. And that pissed me off," Holloway recalled. "It really made me furious."

A few days later, on the evening of November 25th, LBJ was speaking to Martin Luther King and said, "It's just an impossible period—we've got a budget coming up." Baker also exposes how Johnson also told Joseph Alsop later that morning: "The president must not inject himself into, uh, local killings," to which Alsop immediately responded, "I agree with that, but in this case, it does happen to be the killing of the president."

On this same day, Johnson also instructed Hoover: "We can't be checking up on every shooting scrape in the country."

These conversations show the epitome of an egomaniac—a sultan—an arrogant, vengeful man unable to exercise the slightest baseline of loyalty or sensitivity. More precisely, he was a cold-blooded murderer who would stop at nothing to survive and seize power.

Even toward the end of his life, Lyndon Johnson stayed true to the principles that he had demonstrated during his time in the White House: "If I can't have booze, sex, or cigarettes, what's the point of living?"

CHAPTER TWO

LANDSLIDE LYNDON

To understand Lyndon Johnson's actions on November 22, 1963, one must first understand how he got to the US Senate in 1948. After a previous failed Senate bid, Johnson's Senate election was stolen with nonexistent votes by a cabal of patrons who knew how to "vote the Mexicans." Whether or not those Mexicans had to have special incentive to vote, stayed home on Election Day, or had been dead for years; if they were needed, their votes were counted. No patron was more effective in getting those key votes to Lyndon Johnson in 1948 than George Parr.

George Parr had been a key figure in Lyndon Johnson's political ascendency. The powerful patron controlled the Democratic political machines, which dominated Duval and Jim Wells counties. His nickname was the "Duke of Duval." Parr would later become the focus of the infamous "Box 13" scandal, which allowed Lyndon Johnson to steal the 1948 US Senate race from former Texas governor Coke Stevenson.

Parr lorded over the large swath of southern Texas, running a political machine inherited from his father Archer in the vein of Boss Tweed's Tammany Hall or Richard Daley's Chicago. It was a system of controlling elections, public officials, the citizens of the county, and their tax money. Above all, Parr knew how to "vote the Mexicans" and would use a combination of violence and bribery to run up vote totals for "his" candidates. Of course, Parr contended that he was simply a rancher who made a little money from oil struck on his land. In truth, if it happened within the boundaries of his rule, it went through Parr, *Patrón*, Boss.

"The niceties of the democratic process weren't part of the immigrant experience," Mike Royko wrote of Daley's Chicago. "So if the machine muscle offended some, it seemed like old times to many more."[1]

For the immigrants in Parr's machine, the system of dependence on a local leader was a custom started long ago in Mexico, and carried generationally into the United States.

Gordon Schendel, writing for *Collier's Weekly* in 1951, reported the vast disparity between living conditions of Parr and that of his vassal-like constituency. Whereas Parr lived in a mansion with, "lushly landscaped grounds," servant quarters, multiple garages, and a private racetrack, those who lived under his hand were domiciled in "extensive treeless, grassless sections of dilapidated one- and two-room shacks crazily crowded together, frequently without plumbing or electricity—which are the prominent eyesores of every south Texas town."[2]

Schendel found no record of Parr ever using his wealth to improve the squalid living conditions of those who lived, voted, and worked for him.[3]

"We had the law to ourselves there," Luis Salas, a deputy sheriff and enforcer who had worked for Parr said. "It was a lawless son-of-a-bitch. We had iron control. If a man was opposed to us, we'd put him out of business. Parr was the godfather. He had life or death control."[4]

At 6'1", and 210 pounds, Salas cut an imposing figure as one of Parr's top soldiers. Salas began work for Parr after fleeing Mexico following a bar brawl in which he had left a man fatally wounded.[5] In Parr's territory, Salas became the main enforcer of the thirteenth precinct of Jim Wells County, the most impoverished Mexican district in Alice, Texas.[6]

The thirteenth precinct would be the focus of the "Box 13" election fraud in Lyndon Johnson's 1948 senatorial bid and intrinsically link Parr, Salas, and Johnson in stealing the election—a matter that would go all the way to the US Supreme Court.

A survey of Johnson's 1948 campaign, prior to its renowned "Box 13" conclusion, highlights the lengths to which he would go to reach a desired goal. As every other political venture in Johnson's career, too much would be at stake to leave the election to chance or virtue, and failure was not an option. Lying, cheating, and stealing are so commonly attributed to politicians that they are clichés. When hung on Lyndon Johnson, each of these acts is given new life.

The image of Johnson as a war hero was one of the main themes of his 1948 campaign; it would follow the common narrative thread strung throughout his life, one of verbose elaborations and outright lies.

To see Johnson, who was never actually in the armed services, embellish a war record of 1942 was to watch one of the great hucksters of American politics in action. Johnson *had* seen action during World War II, as a civilian observer on the Heckling Hare, a B-26 Marauder flown by Lieutenant Walter H. Greer. The mission was an air raid on a Japanese airfield in Papua New Guinea, and out of the eleven B-26 Marauders, only nine would return after staving off heavy enemy fire. The raid would begin and end Johnson's wartime combat experience.[7]

For his part in the air raid, Johnson was awarded the Silver Star, the third-highest award issued to a member of any branch of the United States Armed Forces for combat valor. Johnson, as an observer, would be the only member of the mission to receive a medal, a sentiment he feigned to claim he didn't deserve.

In a letter Johnson drafted, he renounced the decoration. "My very brief service with these men and its experience of what they did and sacrificed makes me all the more sensitive that I should not and could not accept a citation of recognition for the little part I played for a short time in learning and facing with them the problems they encounter all the time." The letter was never mailed.[8]

Similar observer missions had been granted to journalists during the war. Walter Cronkite, accompanying a raid in which seven bombers were lost, wrote that he had "gained the deepest admiration for the bombardiers and navigators, as well as the pilots and gunners on this trip."[9] If the journalist was objective in his retelling, Johnson's recounting would be close to obscene.

When asked shortly after his return if he had engaged in combat, Johnson started to bedeck the truth. "I was out there in May, June, and part of July," Johnson replied. In Johnson's retellings, the actual number of Japanese planes shot down by his squadron (one) had risen to fourteen, and the squadron members had nicknamed him "Raider Johnson."[10]

Johnson began to accept the earning of the Silver Star and worked it into his appearances, going so far as to hold ceremonies where he was receiving the decoration as if for the first time.[11]

The Silver Star would become the most important part of Johnson's attire in the 1948 campaign, and he always made sure it was affixed to his lapel.

"That's the Silver Star. General MacArthur gave it to me," Johnson echoed on campaign stops, often yanking, tugging, or pointing at the pin for effect. "I said that if war was declared, I'd go to war beside them, and I did."[12]

Johnson embellished not only his own war record but spun the war tales of staffers. Petey Green, a sound technician for Johnson's stump stops, had been knocked unconscious in Caserta, Italy, during WWII when a German shell exploded nearby. Green was kept overnight at an aid station, then released. Johnson would weave the Petey Green war story to mythological heights.

"Skull shattered on Monte Cassino. Brains exposed to the raw, icy cold winds sweeping off the Appenines of Italy. For all purposes, a dead man. But he stands here today. Almost normal. Like you and me," Johnson said at a stump speech in Llano. "Almost. But not quite. That skull is not pure bone. A quarter of his head is a silver plate to keep the brains from oozing out. He came back. He's still giving all that's in him. This time on behalf of democracy on the home front. Giving of himself just as freely as he gave those brains he left behind in Italy."[13]

The tale of Petey Green changed from stop to stop. Sometimes the silver plate in Petey's head became gold, steel, or platinum; sometimes Pete lost a quarter of his brain, and other times half. In reality, Green's skull was not only undamaged but completely unmarked.[14]

As Johnson was pumping up his campaign with grandiose falsities, he was attempting to take the air out of his opponents.

Even though Johnson was a man adept at spinning a yarn, his opponent in the Democratic Primary, former Governor Coke Stevenson, was like a character out of the pages of American folklore. Stevenson was a deeply conservative Bourbon Democrat of the Texas variety. Largely a Texas designation, Bourbon Democrats, including Stevenson, favored segregation and were protectors of the petroleum industry and agricultural interests. Stevenson was revered for his integrity, rectitude, and character. He had rooted out substantial corruption as governor and was respected for his honesty.

Stevenson lived an austere life on a ranch in South Llano, a homestead that the former governor lavished with attention and time, a forever-unfinished dream house in the vein of Thomas Jefferson's Monticello.

"The ranch *was* a fortress, or at least a refuge from the world. Since Coke had refused to build even a rough low-water bridge across the South Llano, the only way of reaching it was by fording the river, which was not infrequently too high to be forded. He refused to have a telephone on the ranch. The closest town was Telegraph, a mile across the river, and the "'town' consisted of one building: a store."[15]

At the ranch, land was cleared, cattle were branded, and sheep were sheared, all by Stevenson's hand. Not a day went by on the ranch that Stevenson didn't find something fit for improvement.[16]

He was also a man of definite character. An attorney, Stevenson took a Jeffersonian view of the Constitution, favoring the individual over the institution. He abhorred public spending, taxation, and debt. He was meticulous in his thoughts, and only shared them with conviction, in a "low, slow drawl."[17]

"Coke would never say a word he didn't believe, and that shone through," a fellow attorney recalled. "When he spoke to a jury, the jury believed him."[18]

Stevenson was lovingly given the moniker "Mr. Texas" by the public and "coffee-coolin' Coke" by the media, a term given to symbolize his politics.

"Listen, I'm too old to burn my lips on a boiling cup of coffee," Stevenson would say when asked for an immediate response regarding an issue. "We'll just let that cup cool a while."[19]

The coffee pot and the pipe that he could be seen habitually smoking became indelible to the Stevenson image.

If there was a flaw to Stevenson, it was racism, which as an old Southerner, he carried deep in his bones; he did not withhold his negative feelings toward blacks in Texas. When setting up a Good Neighbor Commission with Mexico, Stevenson was heard to remark, "Meskins is pretty good folks. If it was niggers, it'd be different."[20]

After the US Supreme Court's 1944 decision to eradicate the "white primary," an impediment to the voting rights of blacks, Stevenson derided the decision as a "monstrous threat to our peace and security."[21]

As governor, Stevenson was unflappable. One of his favorite tactics in his fight against government intervention was to "do nothing." During his administration, small-town businesses displaying "No Mexicans" signs were protected by the governor, who said that "businesses are free to establish their own standards."[22]

Johnson would use Stevenson's character against him. Stevenson's heedful thought process and low-key style would be skewed as indecisiveness as Johnson parodied Stevenson's nicknames to exemplify this trait, referring to Stevenson as "Mr. Straddler," "Mr. Do-Nothinger," or "Mr. Calculator."

A song devised by the Johnson campaign parodied Stevenson's non-committal attitude:

My friends, please make me Senator.
I was your calculating governor.
I'm sure you know my steadfast rule
Of always let the coffee cool.

All through my office term just past
Were controversies thick and fast.
And when the matters came to me,
I solved 'em all with 'Leave 'em be.'

You got to let the coffee cool.
Then you'll be safe from ridicule.
Don't ever touch a subject when it's hot.

You got to let the coffee cool,
Courage is for dangerous fools,
Don't never ever touch a boiling pot.

When capital and labor fight
I always find that both are right.
Whenever wets and drys collide
I just wait and choose the winning side.[23]

Johnson also worked mimicry into his public appearances, imitating Stevenson, from his slow, deliberate style to his movement of rocking back and forth on his heels while thinking. Johnson even brought a pipe into the act. The aping of Stevenson's image was clearly devised to show a clodhopping yokel, a backwoods, backward-thinking rube clearly unfit for politics.

Johnson fanned the feathers of his personal war record claiming that, unlike Stevenson, he had served his country. "I didn't sit and puff my pipe when our country was at war."[24]

Johnson pronounced that, during the former governor's administration, Stevenson had handed out a record number of pardons to criminals. This claim was quickly batted down by prison officials, who countered that Johnson had combined the true number of pardons with days allotted to convicts to attend funerals or visit sick family members.[25]

Stevenson would refuse to reply to these and similar charges because he deemed them dirty politics. This only emboldened Johnson's tactics.

Johnson issued a more substantial lie that Stevenson was consorting with heads of labor and receiving payoffs. "Labor leaders made a secret agreement with Calculating Coke that they couldn't get out of me," Johnson said. "A few labor leaders, who do not soil their own clothes with the sweat of honest toil, have met in a smoke-filled hotel room and have attempted to deliver the vote of free Texas workingmen."[26]

The labor ploy was Johnson's way of tying Stevenson to the Taft-Hartley Act, a controversial bill that proposed federal monitoring of labor unions to ensure fair practice. Johnson's allegation that Stevenson was consorting with labor leaders was meant to show that Johnson was strongly opposed to Taft-Hartley. And whereas Johnson would hammer away at this throughout the campaign, it was patently untrue; Johnson himself was accepting money from labor leaders including John L. Lewis and the United Mine Workers.[27]

Even though it came easy for Johnson to devise elaborate lies about himself and his opponent, he was reluctant to meet Stevenson face-to-face, using any and all opportunities to worm out of the possibility of an encounter.

The two candidates were both scheduled to attend the Texas Cowboy Reunion on Fourth of July weekend in Stamford.

Stevenson, a living embodiment of frontier idealism, was asked to lead the horse riders in the parade.[28] Johnson, hearing of Stevenson's grand reception at the event, concocted an escape. Johnson visited Aspermont, Texas earlier in the day but then falsely claimed to reporters present that his helicopter lacked the fuel to fly to Stamford for his joint appearance with Stevenson. When a refueling tanker inauspiciously rolled up, Johnson told his pilot, Jim Chudars, "Tell the driver to go away. He should come back and meet you here in two hours."[29]

Walking away from the tanker back to reporters, Johnson offered an explanation. "Wrong octane," Johnson said, shaking his head. "I swear I don't know what's wrong with my travel team. I don't know why we keep having trouble getting 91 octane gas when we need it."[30]

It was a blatant lie, symbolic of Johnson's character.

"As the truck rolled out of the pasture, all could see clearly printed beneath the Esso Fuel logo: 'Flammable. 91 Octane,'" wrote Joe Phipps, an LBJ campaign worker in his book, *Summer Stock: Behind the Scenes with LBJ in '48.* "But no one, including the reporters, challenged Johnson. They never would. It was almost as if each was ashamed for him in his blatant dishonesty, embarrassed for him in his plain dumbness, even if he was not embarrassed for himself."[31]

Aiding this particular lie was an innovative means of transportation, which Johnson utilized for his campaign: a helicopter—a technological and visual marvel at the time. It is important that, while Stevenson campaigned at a leisurely pace, Johnson barnstormed the state relentlessly by a relatively new mode of transportation. Just Johnson's arrival would guarantee a crowd in rural counties, where no one had seen a "whirlybird." The helicopter thus became an integral part of the Johnson campaign image. "Long Lyndon Johnson, one of Texas's most ebullient congressmen, has introduced the first new gimmick in Texas politics since the hillbilly band and the free barbecue," wrote *Time* magazine. "Out in the bottoms and the back country, the Johnson City Windmill wowed the citizenry."[32]

When asked by the press about the danger of the travel and the concerns of Lady Bird, Johnson wound his response around his war record, stating that his wife "didn't show particular concern when I was flying in B-29s, helping bomb one Japanese island after another into submission three years ago."[33] The helicopter would also assist the campaign in the number of citizens it helped Johnson reach in a short amount of time. Coke Stevenson traveled town to town in a worn-down Plymouth; Johnson could canvass large areas of Texas quickly, sometimes campaigning over a loudspeaker from the air.

"Hello down there," Johnson's voice would bellow over a small town. "This is your friend, Lyndon Johnson of Johnson City. Your candidate for the United States Senate. Just saying good morning."[34]

The hovering transportation not only symbolized a new method of campaigning, but also exemplified Johnson's brand of backdoor politicking. Johnson first utilized the Sikorsky S-51 for fast travel and later he teamed with Bell Helicopter and flew in the Bell 47-B.[35] The Bell Corporation was a better fit, supplying Johnson with campaign money in exchange for political favors. "We're interested in helping him [Johnson] out because helicopters are new, and if we get an important person such as a congressman showing enough confidence to fly in our aircraft, it would help us and the overall industry," founder and owner of Bell Helicopter, Larry Bell, said at the time.[36] Years later, Bell Helicopter would benefit mightily from their association with LBJ, becoming one of the "Johnson" companies to procure big-money Vietnam War contracts. Lady Bird Johnson would make a killing on Bell Helicopter stock.

Johnson's campaign success and political scope was also helped greatly by his control of Texas media in a sixty-three-county area, which included Austin, the state capital. The control gave Johnson a tremendous influence on the message that was delivered to the voting public. In 1943, on purchasing a radio station in his wife's name, KTBC in Austin, Johnson was to exercise his power as a congressman to obtain the necessary license, frequency, and hours of operation, which were all essential to the station's success. Lady Bird acquired the station cheaply. Its value was greatly enhanced in 1945, when the FCC, under tremendous pressure from Johnson, granted KTBC an allowance to quintuple its power, an increase in range that extended the Johnson media umbrella to cover sixty-three counties.[37]

Johnson also traded his political influence for radio advertising. Together with his friend and attorney Ed Clark of Looney and Clark, KTBC obtained high-money advertising contracts with General Electric and Gulf Oil. Speaking of his relationship with Gulf Oil, Clark stated, "I had friends there. I spoke to them about it, and they understood. This wasn't a Sunday-school proposition. This was business."[38] It was a clean arrangement. Corporations with interests in Washington or Texas didn't have to hire a lobbyist or pay a cash bribe. Instead, they paid thousands for advertising on KTBC.

In the early 1950s, the FCC granted Johnson's radio station a television license, and KTBC become the only broadcast television station in Austin, furthering Johnson's political reach and personal enrichment.[39]

Ed Clark would supply Johnson with big business advertising for his radio station and big business money for his campaign—more money than had ever been donated to a politician in Texas.[40] Brown and Root, a Texas construction firm that would later combine with the infamous Halliburton Company, also threw their lot in with Johnson. The company, founded by George and Herman Brown, won the contract to build the Mansfield Dam near Austin in 1937 thanks to the help of Congressman Johnson. With Johnson as a senator, Brown and Root would benefit greatly.

In the closing days of the 1948 campaign, Ed Clark would recall, "Johnson—if he lost, he was going back to being nobody. *They* were going back to being nobody. That was when the chips were down. That was the acid test. That was *it!* All or Nothing."[41]

Having lost his bid in 1941 to jump from the House to the Senate, Johnson knew the 1948 election was it for him. He was frantic, unscrupulous, indefatigable, and prepared to engage in electoral fraud to "win."

Johnson's moneyed campaign of untruths, deception, and technological advance, in the end, still could not topple the popular Stevenson. Even with the collusion of George Parr, who turned over 4,662 votes for Johnson in Duval County compared with forty for Stevenson and 93 percent of the vote in Parr's complete territory, Johnson was behind by 854 votes statewide when the polls were closed. The slim margin quickly elicited desperate measures from Johnson and company. Calls made on Johnson's behalf to several Houston precincts sparked several "revisions," which cut Stevenson's lead in more than half.

George Parr, who had already turned over nearly 100 percent of his territory for Johnson, had also been called. Parr would have to pull another favor for LBJ. The Sunday morning following Election Day, Parr's election officials announced that returns were not in for one of Duval's precincts. When these 427 "uncounted" votes were tallied, Johnson was given a small, short-lived lead in the post-election scramble for votes.[42]

On Monday and Tuesday following Election Day, vote corrections tipped the election back into the hands of Stevenson by 349 votes. Yet again, Parr was called to help. On Friday, more "revisions" came out of Parr's territory, reducing Stevenson's lead to 157. Later that Friday, an amended return out of a box in precinct thirteen proved to be the deathblow to Stevenson: two hundred more votes allegedly cast for Johnson had appeared.

The city of Alice, Texas was in Jim Wells County, where Parr's influence reached. Parr had a strongman in Alice, deputy sheriff Luis Salas. Journalist and author John Knaggs hypothesized the use of Alice to rig the vote as a necessary strategy.

"Parr had used [voted] most of the eligible names in Duval County before he knew Johnson would need more," Knaggs said to John E. Clark in Clark's excellent book on Parr, *The Fall of the Duke of Duval*. "That would explain why he took the chance of using a box in Jim Wells, where he didn't have quite as much control as he had at home, instead of just padding the Duval count a little more. It would also explain why he added all two hundred votes in one box instead of spreading them out over several boxes, which would have been a lot less obvious. By using only Box 13, he limited the number of people who could ever testify what really happened."[43]

Box 13 was stuffed haphazardly, a slipshod job. When voter 841, Eugenio Solis, approached the poll site in the thirteenth precinct, it was close to 7 p.m., closing time. In later testimony, Solis said there was no one else coming to vote when he cast his ballot. The names of two-hundred more phantom voters, 842 through 1041, would later "show up," their names written in one handwriting, a different color ink and strangely listed in alphabetical order. Interviewed later, some of these voters would attest that they did not vote in the election. Others were deceased.

Author Bar McClellan alleged that it was Don Thomas, a lawyer from Ed Clark's firm, who stuffed the box when Salas declined due to fear of retribution. Thomas started writing down names at random from the poll list, then, with time running low, proceeded to write them in alphabetical order. With the poll list exhausted, only then would Thomas begin to add names of the departed.[44] When all the remaining votes were tallied, Johnson would win the election by eighty-seven votes. Upon hearing of the Jim Wells County skullduggery, Stevenson quickly sent investigators to interview residents in Duval County who were listed as having voted, quickly finding in many cases that their county commissioner had voted for them. When word made its way to Parr's agents of enforcement, the investigation was quickly halted.[45]

"We were stopped by sheriff's deputies, one of whom had a submachine gun," Pete Tijerina, a San Antonio attorney and head of the investigation team said. "They said they [had] heard we had guns. We told them we had no guns, but they made us spread-eagle while they searched us. They then told us we had thirty minutes to get out of Duval County. We got out in that time."[46]

Stevenson then sent three attorneys to Jim Wells County to confront Tom Donald, secretary of Jim Wells County's Democratic Executive Committee and the cashier at the Texas State Bank of Alice, who held the poll list for the town. The attorneys brought with them a book on election law, which reiterated that any citizen could view the election tally sheet. When Donald was confronted there and asked to produce the lists, the attorneys were greeted with a readied "No."[47]

Stevenson subsequently took matters into his own hands and went to Alice with Frank Hamer, an old friend and the Texas Ranger who had set up the fatal Bonnie and Clyde ambush. It was now Stevenson's turn to confront Tom Donald at the bank, after which Donald turned over the poll list to Stevenson and his lawyers for a few important moments. In those moments, they memorized some of the added names on the list as well as the noticeable visible discrepancies.

Unfortunately, no amount of evidence could help Stevenson. The case was to go to a federal court less than a month later, but to no avail. The top suspects in the fraud, Luis Salas and Tom Donald, could not appear in court because they were away in Mexico "on business."[48] The altered poll lists had been emptied from their boxes, burned, and blamed on a Mexican janitor. The fix was in, and there was too much invested in Johnson for truth to prevail. Lyndon Johnson was now a senator. For years afterward, he was known in some circles, mockingly, as "Landslide Lyndon" and "Lyin' Lyndon."

Johnson proudly retold a joke that began circulating after the election on countless occasions. It told of a small Mexican boy named Manuel whose father had voted in Alice.

"My father was in town last Saturday, and he did not come to see me," Manuel said

"But, Manuel, your father has been dead for ten years."

"Si, he has been dead for ten years. But he came to town last Saturday to vote for Lyndon Johnson, and he did not come to see me."[49]

Dan Moody, who served as governor of Texas from 1927 to 1931, said "if the district attorney here had done his duty, Lyndon Johnson would now be in the penitentiary instead of the United States Senate."[50]

In 1973, with the stench of the Box 13 scandal still lingering and Parr charged with tax evasion, the Duke of Duval would admit to his attorney that he had spoken with Johnson in the days immediately following election night and determined Johnson would need two-hundred votes to salvage the loss.[51]

On April 1, 1975, helicopters spotted George Parr's Chrysler in a fenced clearing on the southeast corner of his Los Horcones Ranch in Duval County, Texas.[52] Parr had failed to appear for a court date to answer tax evasion charges the day before, and law enforcement officials had been hunting him down. The car was still running, and the Duke of Duval was inside, slumped over with a bullet hole on the right side of his head; a spent round of ammunition had made its way to the floorboard. Parr's dentures were also on the floor, forced out of his mouth by the punch of the gunshot.[53]

In 1977, after Johnson, Parr, and Stevenson had died, Luis Salas would admit to lying under oath and lend context to his role in the "Box 13" scandal. He confirmed that Parr orchestrated the scandal and also divulged that Johnson was present when Parr told Salas what needed to be done. Salas, in his final years, perhaps to clear his conscience, added that he certified the added names.

"Johnson did not win that election," Salas said. "It was stolen for him."[54]

Looking back near the end of his life, Salas was amazed at the level of criminal behavior he was involved in, particularly his role in the "Box 13" scandal.

"Sometimes I wonder why I didn't get the electric chair,"[55] Salas said.

In 1952, Coke Stevenson would get closest to the truth of "Box 13" when Sam Smithwick, another of Parr's deputy sheriffs, wrote him from the state prison in Huntsville pledging his willingness to testify. But mysteriously, Smithwick, serving time for murder, was himself apparently murdered as Stevenson was on his way to the prison to speak with him. En route, Stevenson stopped in Junction to notify prison officials of his arrival time. He was told Smithwick was dead.

"A prison guard found Smithwick at midnight," read the *Valley Morning Star* shortly after his death. "The husky but aging man—he was 64—had twisted a towel, tied it around his neck, and anchored it to the top bunk of the double-decker beds in his cell."[56]

Stevenson would write a letter to the press stating that the murder only strengthened his complaint of election fraud, and in 1956 Governor Allen Shivers would accuse Johnson of having a hand in Smithwick's murder.[57]

Smithwick was the first of a number of people who would perish mysteriously who could be traced directly back to the man who would be president. Johnson would order a chain of murders to protect his Senate seat, cover up corruption, and hide his greed and his adulterous and debauched lifestyle. Johnson's murders would include not only Smithwick but also a married lover of Johnson's sister Josefa, several federal informants, a US Agricultural Department inspector and, ultimately, the President of the United States.

The murder of John Fitzgerald Kennedy would not be Johnson's first.

NOTES

1. Michael Royko, *Boss: Richard J. Daley of Chicago.* (New York: Dutton, 1971), 7.
2. Gordon Schendel, "Something Is Rotten in the State of Texas," *Collier's Weekly* 9 (June 9, 1951): 13–15.
3. Ibid., 70.
4. John E. Clark and George Berham Parr, *The Fall of the Duke of Duval* (Austin: Eakin, 1995), 60.
5. Ibid.
6. Ibid.
7. Caro, *Means of Ascent*, 40–43.
8. Ibid., 51.
9. Walter Cronkite. "'Hell' Pictured as Flying Forts Raid Germany." *Los Angeles Times* (February 27, 1943).
10. Caro, *Means of Ascent*, 49.
11. Ibid., 51–52.
12. Ibid., 229.
13. Joe Phipps, *Summer Stock: Behind the Scenes with LBJ in '48* (Fort Worth: Texas Christian University Press, 1992), 207.
14. Ibid., 209.
15. Caro, *Means of Ascent*, 155.
16. Ibid., 155.
17. Ibid., 149.
18. Ibid.
19. Ibid., 173.
20. Robert Dallek, *Lone Star Rising: Lyndon Johnson and His Times, 1908–1960* (New York: Oxford University Press, 1991), 316.
21. Ibid.
22. George Norris Green, *The Establishment in Texas Politics: The Primitive Years, 1939–1957* (Norman: University of Oklahoma, 1984), 80
23. Dallek, *Lone Star Rising*, 316–317.
24. Caro, *Means of Ascent*, 244.
25. Ibid., 210.
26. Ibid., 224.
27. Lance Morrow, *The Best Year of Their Lives: Kennedy, Johnson, and Nixon in 1948, Learning the Secrets of Power* (New York: Basic, 2005), 277.
28. Caro, *Means of Ascent*, 244.
29. Phipps, *Summer Stock*, 228.
30. Ibid., 229.

31. Ibid.
32. Robert Bryce, *Cronies: Oil, the Bushes, and the Rise of Texas, America's Superstate* (New York: PublicAffairs, 2004), 58.
33. Caro, *Means of Ascent*, 230.
34. Ibid., 220.
35. Bryce, *Cronies*, 57–59.
36. Ibid., 59.
37. Caro, *Means of Ascent*, 100.
38. Ibid., 103.
39. McClellan, *Blood, Money and Power*, 199–120.
40. Caro, *Means of Ascent*, 272.
41. Ibid., 274.
42. Ibid., 314.
43. Ibid., 48.
44. McClellan, *Blood, Money & Power*, 90.
45. Caro, *Means of Ascent*, 322.
46. Ibid., 322-323.
47. Ibid.
48. J. Evetts Haley, *A Texan Looks at Lyndon: A Study in Illegitimate Power* (Canyon, Texas: Palo Duro Press, 1964), 47.
49. Ibid., pg. 399.
50. Haley, *A Texan Looks at Lyndon*, 53.
51. Clark, *The Fall of the Duke of Duval*, 19–20.
52. Ibid.
53. Clark, *The Fall of the Duke of Duval*, 60.
54. Caro, *Means of Ascent*, 388.
55. *The Daytona Beach News-Journal* (July 31, 1977).
56. *Valley Morning Star* [Harlingen, Texas] (April 17, 1952):
57. Dallek, *Lone Star Rising*, 347.

CHAPTER THREE

CURSES

In his first year as attorney general, while investigating corruption in Gary, Indiana, Bobby Kennedy was advised by Edwyn Silberling, his chief of organized crime in the Department of Justice, that one of the city councilmen, a bartender, should be the first indicted, because he had the weakest defense.

"What's wrong with being a bartender?" Kennedy asked, "My grandfather was a bartender."[1]

Robert Kennedy understood his heritage. He and John Kennedy were the sons of Ambassador Joseph P. Kennedy, a cutthroat businessman who had extensive dealings with organized crime. Their grandfather was Boston Mayor John F. "Honey Fitz" Fitzgerald. Neither was known for his integrity. The attorney general was correct in characterizing his grandfather as a bartender, although the context of Pat Kennedy's professional life was historically less blue collar. Born in Boston on January 8, 1858, Pat grew to be an entrepreneur, who sometimes dabbled in business ventures of questionable legality. The one bar in Haymarket Square that he purchased as a young man expanded to three, and Pat Kennedy eventually bought a liquor distribution, which gave him control of spirits sold to his bars and those of his competitors. With the blessing of Mayor John F. Fitzgerald, Pat Kennedy then entered into finance, forming Columbia Trust. Later, Kennedy tried his hand at politics and, in 1886, won five consecutive one-year terms in the Massachusetts House of Representatives. Six years later, he won a seat in the state senate.[2] Kennedy learned the importance of patronage, especially to increase voter turnout and political support. He used his political influence to sway city contracts to bring in more money to his businesses. In 1896, along with Mayor Fitzgerald, Joseph Corbett, and James Donavon, Kennedy formed Boston's Democratic Party Board of Strategy, intent on controlling the city's political fortunes.[3] The Board of Strategy was part of the political machine in Boston, based on ward bosses and cronyism, a system in which favors begot favors, from the city's smallest political unit up to city hall.

The hordes of Irish immigrants who moved into the North End of Boston in the latter half of the 1800s became the fulcrum of the electoral process for politicians like Mayor Fitzgerald. The political system was put in place to help these immigrants, who were oppressed socially, economically, and ethnically. Journalist and historian Henry Adams, whose roots in America could be traced to pre-Revolutionary War times, wrote what others in his more privileged class felt about the Irish: "Poor Boston had run up against it in the form of its particular Irish maggot, rather lower than the Jew, but with more or less the same appetite for cheese."[4]

The machine had grown through the Irish neighborhoods as a way to help their own. Like Parr's system in Texas, it was an in-or-out proposal: Either vote for who the bosses tell you to vote for and you are taken care of, or don't, and good luck. Growing up in the system, Honey Fitz saw the power of the machine firsthand when a friend of the family was left jobless for voting against a system candidate.[5]

When Honey Fitz was elected mayor in 1906, he championed the machine mentality citywide. The job climate during the Fitzgerald era is expanded upon in Gerard O'Neill's *Rogues and Redeemers*, a history of old Irish politics in Boston:

The first Fitzgerald administration was the old North End patronage machine writ large. No holdover city job was safe. By the end, one out of every forty-two residents in Boston held a city job that kept them inside when it rained and finally out of the construction trench. Bartenders and construction foremen were suddenly running the show. The provisional appointment to get around civil service became an art form. There was such a profusion of deputy sealers in the weights and measures department that even an obscure, out-of-the-way agency managed to have its own feather bedding scandal. There were ludicrous new jobs for tea warmers and tree climbers and a new team of watchmen to better watch those warming tea or climbing trees.[6]

Patrick's son, Joseph P. Kennedy, born on September 6, 1888, lived a life that echoed his father in many regards, straddling the worlds of politics and business, using qualities of one to influence the outcome of the other. Joseph Kennedy also made the tactical move of marrying Rose Fitzgerald, daughter of his father's political ally Mayor John Fitzgerald. His increasing knowledge of his father-in-law's bureaucratic affairs raised his own political acumen. Honey Fitz, in becoming Boston's first Irish Catholic mayor, showed him that power could be achieved against the odds. Through his father-in-law, Joseph Kennedy learned the power of the press—Fitzgerald owned the weekly *Republic*, a Boston paper that gave voice to the mayor's political machine. In later years, with Joe's son John running for office, newspapers and magazines would be bought to amass support for the candidate while others were threatened to be bought out and shut down if they didn't fall in line.

Joseph Kennedy began his professional life with the help of Honey Fitz. He was appointed first as the director of the Collateral Loan Company, next, in 1914, to the board of trustees of the Massachusetts Electric Company, and then as assistant general manager of the Fore River Shipyard, a strategic appointment set to coincide with the impending war.

Following the war, Joe Kennedy, once more with the assistance of his father-in-law, acquired a job at the securities firm Hayden, Stone, and Company. It was there that he learned the subtleties of the stock market, that it was important to know a business before investing, and that fortunes could be bluffed. The education would benefit Kennedy, who made his first hefty financial gain in 1924, when he was hired by Walter Howey to stave off a bear raid on the Yellow Cab Company, in which Howey was a major investor. By manipulating the Yellow Cab Stock, Kennedy saved the company and made a great deal of profit for himself. Years later, he would admit that the assignment made him a "very wealthy man."[7]

Kennedy would bring his skills of market massage and business savvy to the motion picture industry, buying the Film Booking Office of America and turning it into a profitable business. Joe approached the motion picture industry like a civil engineer designing a bridge, stressing the importance of a product that was built faster and cheaper than his competition while ensuring that it was structurally sound.

In addition to becoming intimately involved with the economics of his film company, Kennedy also attempted to handle the finances of some of its talent, the most famous being his mistress, Gloria Swanson.

Ambassador Joe Kennedy would brazenly bring Swanson to the family compound in Hyannis Port and the Ambassador's residence in Palm Beach, while his wife, Rose Kennedy, was present. Like their father, Jack and Robert Kennedy both enjoyed a sexual liaison with the reigning movie queen of their time, Marilyn Monroe. The relationships highlight an important difference between that of Joe and his sons: Joe's angle with Swanson was as driven monetarily as it was sexually, using her name to sell his pictures, using her own assets to purchase gifts for the star. To Jack and Bobby, the conquest of Monroe was purely sexual regardless of risk or reward.

"Boy, what an ass!"[8] President Kennedy said as Monroe famously purred her way through "Happy Birthday" to him in a figure-hugging dress.

Joe Kennedy shared with his father Pat a relentless drive for power, an ambition that allowed him, like his father, to prosper through finance and alcohol. Through his father's suppliers, Joe found a foothold in the "import" of Canadian liquor during Prohibition.[9] Bootlegging brought Kennedy a great deal of money and big connections. He once worked out a deal with Al Capone over a spaghetti supper to swap a case of his whiskey for equivalent cases of liquor from Capone's Canadian distillery.[10]

Frank Costello, whose Luciano crime family would later extend coast-to-coast, lording over Carlos Marcello's outfit in New Orleans and Dallas, was counted among Joe's confederates.

"The way he [Costello] talked about him [Joe]," recalled columnist John Miller, "you had the sense that they were close during Prohibition and that something happened. Frank said that he helped Kennedy become wealthy."[11]

A Joe Kennedy mob associate who would be involved in the JFK assassination was Johnny Rosselli, who was the number-two man of Sam "Mooney" Giancana, head of the Chicago Mafia from 1957 to 1966. Born in 1905 in Italy, Rosselli (whose birth name was Filippo Sacco) came of age, like Kennedy, in Boston. Both men were involved with liquor distribution during Prohibition: Kennedy with money, Rosselli with muscle. As a teenager and still unseasoned, Rosselli worked for Kennedy hauling crates of whiskey ashore. Separately, they made names for themselves in the booming motion picture industry. Rosselli, who had spent the early part of the 1920s in Chicago running with Al Capone's outfit, moved to the warmer climes of Los Angeles in 1923 due to an onset of tuberculosis. Kennedy claimed a stake in the motion picture industry with monetary finesse, stock manipulation, and business savvy; Rosselli claimed his by strong-arming unions on behalf of studios, who needed their employees working. Rosselli and other mafiosi would later strong-arm the studios themselves, a shakedown in the form of a pledge to ensure peace with the unions.[12]

Later in life, both men would hover at the outskirts of politics' grandest stage and play a part in the end game of John Kennedy's presidency. Following the use of the Mafia to procure votes for John Kennedy's presidential campaign, Rosselli eventually became another strong link to the underworld which would return to claim the unpaid debts of the Kennedy family. In friendly times, the relationship of Joseph Kennedy and Johnny Rosselli went beyond business. The two men frequently played cards or golf together when Joe had West Coast affairs to tend to.[13] Roselli would emerge later working with the CIA in an assassination plot against Cuban Prime Minister Fidel Castro—a hit squad some of whom would reappear on November 22, 1963. Rosselli would later claim to be one of three gunmen who fired on JFK in Dealey Plaza. He claimed that he had shot from a sewer grate, where he was allegedly concealed. The body of Rosselli would subsequently be found in the mid-1970s floating in an oil drum off the coast of Miami, only days before he was to testify about the assassination for the House Select Committee.

In his life, Joe Kennedy vastly exceeded the business ambitions of his father Pat, expanding from the localism of Boston to a national level and beyond. He had a harder time approaching that success in the political arena.

Joe had dreams of the White House and hoped to be appointed the Ambassador to the Court of St. James, an important and prestigious posting to Great Britain. Realizing the importance of favor in the matter, Kennedy courted Jimmy Roosevelt, son of president Franklin Roosevelt, and he found him work, much the same way Honey Fitz did for him.

Kennedy helped young Roosevelt become president of the National Grain Yeast Corporation of Belleville, New Jersey. Later, he pulled strings in the movie business to get Jimmy a job at MGM Studios as Samuel Goldwyn's assistant.

Courting Jimmy Roosevelt wasn't enough to clinch the ambassadorship for Kennedy. President Franklin Roosevelt, wanting to see the length to which Kennedy would go to get the assignment, ordered that Kennedy drop his pants in front of the president and his son. Kennedy obliged.

"Joe, just look at your legs," Jimmy Roosevelt later recalled his father having said. "You are just about the most bowlegged man I have ever seen. Don't you know that the ambassador to the Court of Saint James has to go through an induction ceremony in which he wears knee britches and silk stockings? Can you imagine how you'll look? When photos of our new ambassador appear all over the world, we'll be a laughingstock. You're just not right for the job, Joe."[14]

Nevertheless, Kennedy did get the appointment to England in December of 1937, but his tenure in the court of St. James would prove to be a disaster. Kennedy was openly pro-Hitler and would pursue an appeasement line. Interestingly, John F. Kennedy himself would write admiringly about Hitler.

"At a time when we should be sending the best that we have to Great Britain, we have not done so," wrote Roosevelt's Secretary of the Interior Harold Ickes. "We have sent a rich man, untrained in diplomacy, unlearned in history and politics, who is a great publicity seeker [Kennedy was the first US ambassador to take along a public relations man to represent him to the press] and who is apparently ambitious to be the first Catholic President of the United States."[15]

As Hitler's forces continued to advance, Kennedy stuck to the ideal of Prime Minister Neville Chamberlain that bending to the demands of the Führer would spare a world war.

"I'm just as convinced that he [Hitler] doesn't want to fight as anybody else is, but I'm not convinced as to how he can save his own situation for his own people," Kennedy remarked to Secretary of State Cordell Hull.

As war with the United Kingdom became imminent, Kennedy even suggested that Roosevelt take a position of appeasement in the increasingly dire situation, which was unacceptable to the president and many others.

"It seems to me that this situation may crystallize to a point where the President can be the savior of the world," Kennedy wrote Roosevelt in September of 1938. "The British government as such certainly cannot accept any agreement with Hitler, but there may be a point when the President himself may work out plans for world peace."[16]

Soon after writing the letter, Kennedy resigned from his position and lost whatever chance he had had for his political aspirations. It would now be up to the Kennedy children to embody Joe's lofty political goals. He did not require his children to succeed in business. He himself had been a tremendous success, and his children would not have to resort to begging, borrowing, or stealing. The elder Kennedy had taken care of that. His children would not work for, but inherit, a mass of wealth and power. For Kennedy, the business of his children would be success in politics.

Rose and Joe's first son, tall, handsome Joseph P. Kennedy Jr. would be introduced to the world by Honey Fitz in a way prophetic of Joe Kennedy's lofty ambitions for the boy.

"I'm sure he'd make a good man on the platform one day," Honey Fitz said to the *Boston Post*. "Is he going into politics? Well, of course he is going to be president of the United States. His mother and father have already decided that he is going to Harvard, where he will play on the football and baseball teams and incidentally take all the scholastic honors. Then he's going to be a captain of industry until it's time for him to be president for two or three more terms. Further than that has not been decided. He may act as mayor of Boston and governor of Massachusetts for a while on his way to the presidential chair."[17]

A number of these predictions from the loquacious mayor were tongue-in-cheek, but the expectations of Joe Jr. would be almost on par with the forecast. Joe Jr., like his three brothers to follow, would attend Harvard and excel scholastically and athletically. While still pursuing an Ivy League education, Joe Jr. was encouraged by his father to run for governor of Massachusetts.

The bar would be set high for all of Joe's children. Failures and character flaws would be closely guarded secrets. Weakness was a source of shame for the Kennedys; they were winners, or they were nothing.

Rosemary, Joe and Rose's third child and first daughter, was a hard lesson to the clan. She was one of the best looking of the Kennedy daughters, but was slow to learn, and her trouble keeping pace with her brothers and sisters led to alleged uncontrolled bouts of rage as she grew older.

Joe Sr.'s answer to Rosemary's embarrassing behavior was an operation, a prefrontal lobotomy, performed in 1941 when Rosemary was twenty-three years old, permanently setting her mind to that of a five-year-old child. The surgery would not correct her behavior; it would erase it.

Years later, it was surmised by Dr. James W. Watts, the surgeon who performed the operation, that Rosemary might not have been mentally retarded.

"It may have been agitated depression," Dr. Watts said. "You're agitated, you're shaky. You talk in an agitated way. All kinds of things go on in the eyes."[18]

It has also been surmised that Rosemary's learning disability was a form of dyslexia. Be it depression, dyslexia, or mental retardation, Rosemary was a failure, not a Kennedy.

"I am still very grateful for your help," Joe Sr. would write to the superintendent at St. Colleta's, an institution in Wisconsin where Rosemary would spend the rest of her life until her death in 2005. "After all, the solution of Rosemary's problem has been a major factor in the ability of all the Kennedys to go about their lives' work and try to do it as well as they can."[19]

John Fitzgerald Kennedy would live most of his life struggling with debilitating illness. He was told at one point that he would be lucky to live to forty years of age, even though the nation, through careful management of public relations, would see him as healthy, vigorous, and undamaged.

Sick throughout his childhood, sometimes to the point of death, John struggled through an obstacle course of affliction. During the 1920s, he was racked with scarlet fever, bronchitis, chicken pox, ear infections, German measles, measles, mumps, and whooping cough.[20]

John's projection of youth and vitality hid darker truths. When in public during his presidential years, Kennedy would wear, under his clothes, a brace that would cover his entire midsection to address the injuries sustained to his back when his PT boat was sunk by the Japanese. He needed pellets of the steroid desoxycorticosterone acetate implanted in his back and thigh muscles every few months. Injections of Procaine, a local anesthetic, every few hours helped him walk without the aid of crutches.[21] A double-fusion spinal surgery in 1954 left John with a metal plate in his back, and during a follow-up operation two months later, he was so close to death that he was delivered last rites by Father John Cavanaugh, personal priest to the Kennedy family.[22] In the late 1950s, Kennedy began taking cortisone shots to control his Addison's disease, which gave his face the puffy look notable in his later years. During his presidency, there was hushed talk of Kennedy having to resort to a wheelchair if elected to a second term.[23]

Following his assassination, it was found that his adrenal glands had wasted away to almost nothing due to Addison's disease.[24]

John and his older brother Joe Jr., in competition to win glory for their nation, and more importantly for their father, would both join the war effort in the 1940s.

John, the commanding officer of a PT boat that was blown in two in the Solomon Islands, became a war hero after saving the surviving crew. This enflamed the competitive nature of Joe Jr.

because it was he who was meant to be the war hero and subsequently use the status to complement his career in politics.

When, on Joe Sr.'s fifty-fifth birthday, with Joe Jr. in attendance, a guest toasted to the "father of the hero, of our own hero," it was not a nod to Joe Jr. but to Lieutenant John F. Kennedy of the United States Navy. Joe Jr. was later found in his room by family friend Joseph Timilty sobbing uncontrollably. "By God, I'll show them," Joe Jr. muttered.

Joe Jr. would end his short life by flying dangerous missions as a Navy pilot, trying to win glory. In August 1944, he signed up for a secret mission code-named "Aphrodite." A PB4Y-1 patrol bomber, Zootsuit Black, was gutted and filled with 21,170 pounds of dynamite. Joe Jr., along with his co-pilot Lt. Wilford J. Willy, were to fly the plane aimed like a guided missile at a German V-1 rocket launching site, parachuting out once the plane was set to be guided by remote control.

Earl Olsen, an electronics officer, discovered circuit problems on the plane prior to the mission, surmising that the arming-firing functions were faulty. Olsen presented his findings to Kennedy before the mission, and Joe Jr. was given the option to delay plans to correct the problems, but he refused.[25] Glory would not wait.

"I think I'm gonna fly it," Kennedy said, "but thanks anyway, Oley, I know you mean well. I appreciate it."[26]

When the remote-control guidance system was switched on over the English Channel en route to the German rocket-launching site, an electrical malfunction set off a spark that ignited the heavily loaded plane, which disintegrated, vaporizing the crew.

"I just had a feeling that plane wasn't airworthy," mechanic Willie Newsome, who removed the turret guns for the plane in anticipation of the mission, would say years later.[27]

Joe Jr.'s death would be the first in a series of tragedies in the Kennedy family, later dubbed by the press as the "Curse of the Kennedys." There was no curse, only a family whose privileged nature and commitment to excel led them to make reckless decisions.

"You cannot live like that," said Kennedy doctor Henry Betts. "You cannot always just repress everything—but with their sense of destiny and feeling that they are different—and they all really feel that they are different—they make a stronger effort at repression than anybody I've ever seen."[28]

With Joe Jr.'s death, John would carry the heavy dreams of Joe Sr., whose political career was destroyed after his failed ambassadorship to the United Kingdom. For John, it would not be a choice.

"I was drafted," said John. "My father wanted his eldest son in politics. 'Wanted' isn't the right word. He demanded it."[29]

It was not without intelligence and charm that John ascended through the ranks of government, but it also was not without Joe Sr.'s money and connections.

"My father used his money to free us," Bobby Kennedy once recalled.[30]

The truth is more complex.

Joe Kennedy did use his money to empower the Kennedy clan, but it was the ways that the money had been obtained that made them, unknowingly perhaps, slaves to their history. And it would be those feelings of freedom to do as they wished that would make the Kennedy brothers victims of their past. If anything was cursed, it was the money and the illusion of freedom it possessed. In reality, the chains were clasped tight, ready to drag either Kennedy down.

When John Kennedy was seeking the highest appointment in the country, it would be Joe's old bootlegging connections that would help secure the election.

Chicago Mafia kingpin "Mooney" Giancana had a hand in Kennedy's success in the 1960 presidential run, persuaded by an intermediary, entertainer Frank Sinatra, with cash and the promise of pardoning future criminal offenses.

Other members of the underworld were recruited. Many of the nation's top mafiosi met Joe Kennedy at Felix Young's restaurant in Manhattan for a dinner meeting during the campaign.

"I took the reservation," said a hostess at Young's. "And it was as though every gangster chief in the United States was there. I don't remember all the names now, but there was John Rosselli, Carlos Marcello from New Orleans, the two brothers from Dallas, the top men from Buffalo, California, and Colorado. They were all top people, not soldiers. I was amazed Joe Kennedy would take the risk."[31] Joe Kennedy understood well the connection between the democratic machines in Chicago, New York, and Buffalo and the mob. Kennedy's organized crime associates leaned on the machine to deliver for JFK.

"If Jack had known about some of the telephone calls his father made on his behalf to Tammany Hall-type bosses during the 1960 campaign, Jack's hair would have turned white,"[32] Kenny O'Donnell later wrote. John and Robert Kennedy were certainly aware of their father's connections to the mob. As attorney general, Robert Kennedy ordered wire taps on some Chicago mobsters, only to learn from the taps that the targets were talking to his father.

John Kennedy was naive to the dangers of the mob and seemed to get a thrill out of consorting with mob associates. His affair with Judith Exner Campbell, whom he met through Sinatra and shared carnally with both Sam Giancana and Sinatra, exemplifies this. Another example would be Tampa mob head Santo Trafficante Jr.'s 1957 run-in with John Kennedy in Havana. Kennedy had no problem accepting Trafficante's offer for a private sex party at one of his hotels, the Commodoro. Trafficante later watched through a two-way mirror as John had his way with three courtesans.[33]

While his father and brother used organized crime to their own ends, Bobby Kennedy was out to end it, due largely to his experience as chief counsel to the US Senate Labor Rackets Committee from 1957 to 1959. Bobby Kennedy had come to believe that the Mafia element would destroy the country if left to continue without proper systems in place to hold it accountable for its actions

"The point I want to make is this," Kennedy wrote in *The Enemy Within*, his literary warning regarding the scale and danger of organized crime. "If we do not on a national scale attack organized criminals with weapons and techniques as effective as their own, they will destroy us."[34]

With more knowledge of how the Mafia already had its hooks in his family and indeed in the government itself, Bobby would have proceeded with more trepidation. Perhaps, but there are indications that Bobby also had knowledge of his father's underworld indiscretions.

When poet and friend Robert Lowell asked Bobby about what Shakespearean character he would most like to be, he picked the one he believed he most resembled: Henry V or Prince Hal. He later read to Lowell the swan song of Henry IV, who Bobby believed most resembled Joe Sr., who he felt resembled one of the "foolish over-careful fathers [who] have broken their sleep with thoughts, their brains with care, their bones with industry," adding that what was left for the Kennedy children was, "the canker'd heaps of strange-achieved gold."[35]

"Henry IV. That's my father," Bobby told Lowell.[36]

As Bobby looked upon Joe Sr. as the father who misused his power to desirable effect, he looked to himself as Hal, the confused boy who tried to find a way to extricate the sins of the father and forge the path of family and country.

The Kennedy brothers could also easily be compared to Icarus, the ill-fated Greek whose waxen wings were forged by his father, Daedalus. Joe Sr. constructed the careers of John and Bobby much like Daedalus constructed the wings of Icarus. The father, as architect, sees the limitations of his construct, but the son perceives the construct as limitless. Much as, against the advice of his father, the sun would melt the wax that fastened the wings tight to Icarus, the Kennedys would also take unneeded risks, flying too high for their wings to carry them.

Bobby, referred to by Adlai Stevenson as "the Black Prince," would stop at nothing to meet his desired ends. When he was given the powers of attorney general in 1960, there were only nineteen indictments of organized crime members; by the time of John's assassination there were over six hundred. The emotional Bobby did not just want to strip the mob of their power. At times, he worked to embarrass them.

During the McClellan Committee's anti-mob hearings in the late 1950s, Bobby certainly had trouble holding back his contempt when faced with top-level mob heads. An exchange between him and an uncooperative "Mooney" Giancana reveals Bobby's ire:

KENNEDY: Would you tell us if you have opposition from anybody that you dispose of them by having them stuffed in a trunk? Is that what you do, Mr. Giancana?

GIANCANA: I decline to answer because I honestly believe my answer might tend to incriminate me.

KENNEDY: Would you tell us anything about any of your operations, or will you just giggle every time I ask you a question?

GIANCANA: I decline to answer because I honestly believe my answer might tend to incriminate me.

KENNEDY: I thought only little girls giggled, Mr. Giancana.[37]

Later, as attorney general, Bobby would attempt to disrupt Mooney at every turn, ordering FBI agents to watch him at restaurants, at his home, and during his leisure, trailing him to and interfering with golf games.[38]

According to Justice Department prosecutor Ronald Goldfarb, Bobby and his aides were considering extreme measures with Giancana. "They said to me what do you think of this idea? The grand jury calls in Giancana, and we offer him total immunity on everything he's ever done in his whole life, as long as he agrees to talk about every crime the Mafia has ever committed. Of course, he can't possibly do that, so he's got to go to jail, and the federal rule is you can only throw someone in jail for contempt for the life of a grand jury, which is eighteen months. But they had a plan:

The day Giancana gets out of jail, they say, we call him back to another grand jury and ask him the same question. This goes on and on. Life imprisonment for Sam Giancana? So I think, oh my God, they're really thinking about doing this—they're going to take the Mafia leaders one by one and put them in jail indefinitely."[39]

Even though Goldfarb saw Bobby's actions as courageous and inspired him to join the fight, he also saw the extreme risk involved in Kennedy's attempt to punish the very people who had helped put the Kennedy brothers in office.

"He was burning the candle at both ends, pressing the mob like he did even after his family had used them for favors," Goldfarb said. "How in God's name he thought he was ever going to get away with this, I don't know. But they were the Kennedys—they came from a family where the father had done all of that, and they still reached the absolute top. I couldn't have slept at night knowing what Bobby did! But these people were different."[40]

Surely Joe knew the dangers of Robert Kennedy's pursuit of organized crime. Perhaps the father had a plan to scale back Bobby's relentless attacks on the Mafia dons, who had helped them obtain power. The old ambassador certainly knew his son Robert's views on organized crime. On Christmas 1956, Joe Kennedy and his son clashed. The elder Kennedy made Bobby aware that he was "deeply, emotionally opposed, and father and son had an unprecedentedly furious argument," said Bobby's sister, Jean Kennedy Smith.[41] Family friend Lem Billings, present at the engagement, concurred. "The old man saw this as dangerous, not the sort of thing or the sort of people to mess around with,"[42] said Billings.

The elder Kennedy was never able to put a stop to his son's meddling with the Mafia. If he had intentions to, they eventually perished. Whatever Joe might have had planned to rectify the darkening situation, it was lost on December 19, 1961, when Joe Kennedy suffered a crippling stroke, which confined him to a wheelchair for the remainder of his years. The stroke paralyzed his body and left him unable to speak.

Frank Sinatra saw the ambassador's stroke as a deathblow to the Kennedys. Ol' Blue Eyes knew of the favors the mob did for the Kennedy presidential campaign and that Joe was the only one who could pay up.

"The tragedy was Joe Kennedy getting a stroke," said Gore Vidal, a Kennedy family friend. "He could have settled the problem with the Mafia in two minutes."

After Joe's stroke, Robert Kennedy pursued Mafia chieftains Carlos Marcello of New Orleans and Santo Trafficante of Tampa. Kennedy's relentless pursuit of the mob would later ensure its involvement in a conspiracy with Lyndon Johnson, elements of the CIA, and Texas oilmen to murder his brother.

When Sinatra had earlier brought up to Jack the damage the attorney general was causing, the president was dismissive, suggesting that Frank "go see dad," who he felt was "the only one who could talk to Bobby."[42]

"Why, oh why," Sinatra asked, "did Joe get that fucking stroke?"

When it came to Sinatra choosing sides, especially following the 1962 perceived slight to Sinatra when President Kennedy chose Republican crooner Bing Crosby's estate for accommodations on a West Coast trip instead of his, the choice was effortless, necessary and possibly mandatory.

"This wasn't a choice for Frank," said Nick Sevano, Sinatra's manager. "He had been raised on the streets with the mob. They were his childhood friends. We understood about politics. We could see that Jack couldn't be seen with Sinatra if Frank was going to the mob, but Jack wasn't important. Frank was loyal to people, and his friends in the mob had been helping him his whole career."[43]

Indeed, liberal Democrat Sinatra would turn on the Kennedys, ultimately endorsing Republican Ronald Reagan for re-election as governor of California in 1970 and going so far as to back Richard

Nixon's presidential election in 1972 after befriending Vice President Spiro T. Agnew.

Dealing with the Kennedys was not a choice for the mob; what was needed was a clear-cut way to do so. They would soon find common associates in the high reaches of government.

"You won't have any trouble finding my enemies," Bobby told a *Life* reporter in 1962. "They're all over town."[44]

NOTES

1. Ronald L. Goldfarb, *Perfect Villains, Imperfect Heroes: Robert F. Kennedy's War Against Organized Crime* (New York: Random House, 1995), 167.
2. Ted Schwarz, *Joseph P. Kennedy: The Mogul, the Mob, the Statesman, and the Making of an American Myth* (Hoboken: John Wiley & Sons, 2003), 27.
3. Ibid., 38.
4. Gerard O'Neill, *Rogues and Redeemers: When Politics Was King in Irish Boston* (New York: Crown, 2012), 17.
5. Ibid., 32.
6. Ibid., 38.
7. Peter Collier and David Horowitz, *The Kennedys: An American Drama* (New York: Summit, 1984), 27.
8. Burton Hersh, *Bobby and J. Edgar: The Historic Face-Off Between the Kennedys and J. Edgar Hoover That Transformed America* (New York: Carroll & Graf, 2007), 322.
9. Schwarz, *Joseph P. Kennedy*, 97.
10. Hersh, *Bobby and J. Edgar*, 24.
11. Ronald Kessler, *The Sins of the Father: Joseph P. Kennedy and the Dynasty He Founded* (New York: Warner, 1996), 34.
12. Charles Rappleye and Ed Becker, *All American Mafioso: The Johnny Rosselli Story* (New York: Doubleday, 1991), 71–72.
13. Ibid., 29.
14. Schwarz, *Joseph P. Kennedy*, 6.
15. Ibid., 238.
16. Ibid., 286.
17. Ibid., 76.
18. Kessler, *The Sins of the Father*, 227.

19. Laurence Leamer, *The Kennedy Women: The Saga of an American Family* (New York: Villard, 1994), 413.
20. Robert Dallek, "The Medical Ordeals of JFK," *The Atlantic Monthly* (December, 2002).
21. Hersh, *Bobby and J. Edgar*, pg. 234.
22. Martin, Ralph, *Seeds of Destruction*, pgs. 196–197.
23. Ibid., 349.
24. Ibid., 256.
25. Schwarz, *Joseph P. Kennedy*, 317.
26. John H. Davis, *The Kennedys: Dynasty and Disaster* (New York: Shapolsky, 1992), 126–127.
27. Gerard Shields, "Mechanic Tells Of Role in Joe Kennedy's Last Flight—Stripped Navy Plane Was Turned Into `Bomb,'" *The Seattle Times* (April 22, 1996).
28. Martin, *Seeds of Destruction*, 166.
29. Ibid., 132.
30. Jeff Shesol, *Mutual Contempt: Lyndon Johnson, Robert Kennedy, and the Feud That Defined a Decade* (New York: W.W. Norton, 1997), 5.
31. Martin, *Seeds of Destruction*, 250.
32. Hersh, *Bobby and J. Edgar*, 283.
33. Martin, *Seeds of Destruction*, 295.
34. Ibid.
35. David Talbot, *Brothers: The Hidden History of the Kennedy Years* (New York: Free, 2007), 135.
36. Ibid.
37. Hersh, *Bobby and J. Edgar*, 177.
38. Talbot, *Brothers*, 138.
39. Ibid., 139.
40. Ibid.
41. Rappleye and Becker, *All American Mafioso: The Johnny Rosselli Story*, 202.
42. Ibid.
43. Hersh, *Bobby and J. Edgar*, 291.
44. Schwarz, *Joseph P. Kennedy*, 414.
45. Talbot, *Brothers*, 91.

CHAPTER FOUR

NEMESIS

It took little effort for Lyndon Johnson to loathe Bobby Kennedy, whose pugnacious behavior created many enemies, including high-ranking members of organized crime and the CIA, as well as director of the FBI, J. Edgar Hoover.

"Bob was the family son of a bitch," said reporter Dave Richardson. "Any time there was anything tough or unpleasant, Bob had to do it."[1]

Agitation in the relationship between Johnson and Bobby Kennedy took root in 1955. Joe Sr., pulling the strings of John's political future, wanted Johnson to grab the Democratic nomination in 1956.

The plan was to have Johnson—a man Joe Sr. knew could be retained for a price—choose John Kennedy, then a senator, as his running mate. The beloved Dwight Eisenhower would surely win, but it would also be a victory for the Kennedys. John would be on the big stage, appreciating his worth and audience, giving him an advantage when entering the 1960 presidential race. The only problem was Johnson. The Texan, tending to his own political futures, declined the offer.

"I did not wish to be a candidate," Johnson recalled telling Joe Sr. in a telephone conversation.

It was politics as usual, but Bobby Kennedy reacted harshly to LBJ's rebuff, taking it as a personal slight.

"Young Bobby was infuriated," said former Franklin Roosevelt aide Thomas Corcoran. "He believed it was unforgivably discourteous to turn down his father's generous offer."[2]

Johnson, as a politician, was full of bluster; Bobby saw the Texan's bluster as bullshit. Johnson, Bobby said, "lies all the time. I'm telling you, he just lies continually about everything. . . . He lies even when he doesn't have to lie."[3] The relationship between the two men worsened in late fall of 1959. Bobby was dispatched by John to the LBJ Ranch to get a bead on Johnson's intentions for the upcoming presidential election. After a long conversation, Johnson assured Bobby he would not be in the running, clearing the path for John. True to Johnson form, this was a lie. Johnson not only planned to run but also thought that the Kennedys were too raw politically and moving forward too quickly. During the trip, Johnson took the opportunity to make a point. Taking Bobby out deer hunting, Johnson neglected to tell him about the powerful kick of the rifle. Upon firing, Bobby was flung backwards to the ground, cutting his forehead on the way down.[4]

"Son," Johnson exclaimed to Bobby, his 6'4" frame casting a shadow over the fallen Kennedy, "You've got to learn to handle a gun like a man."[5]

For Bobby, who at times took politicking personally, trouble with Johnson continued while John and Lyndon were competing with each other for the Democratic Party nomination. "Raider Johnson," who would certainly not stop at the edge of the truth to win, was on the attack. And while there were some valid points in his offensive front, such as Kennedy hiding secret illnesses or buying votes, other claims hinged on the absurd.

"I think you should know that John Kennedy and Bobby Kennedy are fags," said one of Johnson's aides to journalist Theodore White during a phone call. The aide went on to fabricate the existence of photographs showing the brothers dressed in drag at a racy Las Vegas party. The caller promised to deliver the pictures, apparently hoping the tidbit was too tantalizing to wait on hard evidence for publication. Johnson also played up Joe Sr.'s failings as ambassador, pointing to Joe Sr.'s sympathy for British Prime Minister Neville Chamberlain's policy of appeasing Hitler. "I was never any Chamberlain umbrella policy man," Johnson boasted. "I never thought Hitler was right."[6]

The charges had the mercurial Bobby foaming at the mouth. "You've got your nerve," Bobby said to Johnson protégé Bobby Baker. "Lyndon Johnson has compared my father to the Nazis, and John Connally and India Edwards (co-chair of the Citizens for Johnson Committee) lied in saying my brother is dying of Addison's disease. You Johnson people are running a stinking damned campaign, and you're gonna get yours when the time comes!"[7]

Bobby was very good at holding a chip on his shoulder, and the relations between him and Lyndon were irreparable from that point on.

"Anybody who'd ever been against his brother, or who wasn't 100 percent for his brother, was on Bobby's Absolute Shit List, the 'kill list,'" said *Newsweek* Washington editor Ken Crawford.[8]

In the ensuing years, Johnson's character, in Bobby's eyes, would only decay.

"He [Bobby] is, in a strange sort of way, less detached from human actions, more apt to respond directly and vigorously to what he thinks of as bad individual conduct than his brother would," said journalist Murray Kempton. "On the other hand, he lacks his brother's real appreciation for people who were a little older than he was and a little more serious."[9] As it became clear at the 1960 Democratic National Convention in Los Angeles that John Kennedy would win the presidential nomination, Johnson was not anywhere on Bobby's list for vice president and was not at the top of John's either. But once the Kennedy people realized Johnson would help carry the South, both Bobby and John changed their minds, though neither thought Johnson would accept. It seemed logical to the Kennedy camp that, as the most powerful man on Capitol Hill, Johnson would run for re-election as the Senate majority leader. Johnson had power carte blanche when Eisenhower was in office.

Two Texans, Johnson and Speaker of the House Sam Rayburn, "literally ran the country," said journalist Hugh Sidey. "They were the president and the vice president. . . . Christ, [Ike] didn't run the country."[10]

When Kennedy offered the vice presidential nod on the ticket to Johnson, the answer was surprising.

"You just won't believe it. He wants it!" Jack told his brother.

"Oh my God!" Bobby answered.

The elder Kennedy brother was perplexed.

"Now what do we do?"[11] Jack asked.

Southern votes aside, Bobby and Jack were suddenly faced with sharing the ticket with a man neither Kennedy particularly liked or trusted; both realized the choice of Johnson may have been terribly hasty. The Kennedys wavered many times before deciding what to do with Johnson and how to potentially talk him out of accepting his position on the ticket.

"It was the most indecisive time we ever had," Bobby said. "We changed our minds eight times. How could we get him out of it?"[12]

At one point, the brothers decided that Johnson would be ousted and Bobby was sent to Lyndon's suite to deliver the news.

The task for Bobby would be to "get him to withdraw and still be happy."[13]

Bobby went to Johnson's suite twice in futile attempts to get the Texan to withdraw his acceptance. Following the second endeavor, John Kennedy resigned himself to accept Johnson as his choice for vice president, and a phone call was placed.

"Do you really want me?" Johnson asked.

"Yes," replied Kennedy.

"Well, if you really want me, I'll do it,"[14] Johnson replied.

Even after Johnson's acceptance, in a moment of confusion or perhaps of stubborn refusal to accept Johnson as the vice presidential nominee, Bobby again returned to Johnson's suite in an attempt to get Johnson to withdraw.

Thus Johnson "is one of the greatest sad-looking people in the world," Bobby recalled of the moment. "You know, he can turn that on. I thought he'd burst into tears. . . . He just shook, and tears came into his eyes, and he said, 'I want to be vice president, and if the president [JFK] will have me, I'll join him in making a fight for it.' It was that kind of conversation.

"I said, 'Well, then, that's fine. He wants you as vice president if you want to be vice president, we want you to know.'"[15]

There is a darker explanation for how Lyndon Johnson *really* got on the 1960 Democratic ticket: blackmail and intimidation tactics. Anthony Summers interviewed JFK's longtime secretary Evelyn Lincoln, and wrote:

"During the 1960 campaign, according to Mrs. Lincoln, Kennedy discovered how vulnerable his womanizing had made him. Sexual blackmail, she said, had long been part of Lyndon Johnson's modus operandi abetted by Edgar. 'J. Edgar Hoover gave Johnson the information about various congressmen and senators so that Johnson could go to X senator and say, "How about this little deal you have with this woman?" and so forth. That's how he kept them in line. He used his IOUs with them as what he hoped was his road to the presidency. He had this trivia to use because he had Hoover in his corner. And he thought that the members of Congress would go out there and put him over at the Convention. But then Kennedy beat him at the Convention. And well, after that Hoover and Johnson and their group were able to push Johnson on Kennedy. LBJ,' said Lincoln, 'had been using all the information that Hoover could find on Kennedy during the campaign and even before the Convention. And Hoover was in on the pressure on Kennedy at the Convention.'"[16]

Senator Stuart Symington of Missouri was the man whom John Kennedy was courting heavily to be his vice president. Reporter Nancy Dickerson, who was very close to LBJ, interviewed

Symington campaign advisor Clark Clifford about JFK's courtship of Symington and the meetings involved. Dickerson:

"The first was a luncheon at Kennedy's Washington house, where, through Clifford, he offered the vice presidency to Symington, provided Symington's Missouri delegation votes went to Kennedy. Symington turned down the deal. The second conversation, which took place in Los Angeles, was a repeat of the first, and again it was refused. The third conversation was in Kennedy's hideaway in Los Angeles, during which he told Clifford that he was fairly certain of a first-ballot victory and asked if Symington would be his running mate. As Clifford later told me, 'There were no strings attached. It was a straight offer.' The Symington and Clifford families conferred, Symington agreed to run, and Clifford relayed the news to Kennedy.

"Clifford was playing a unique role: He was not only Symington's campaign advisor, but JFK's personal lawyer as well. He is one of the world's most sophisticated men, and he does not make mistakes about matters like this. As he told me, 'We had a deal signed, sealed, and delivered.'"

Seymour Hersh discovered the same thing when he interviewed Clark Clifford and JFK insider Hy Raskin for his book *The Dark Side of Camelot*.

"Johnson was not being given the slightest bit of consideration by any of the Kennedys," Hy Raskin told Hersh. "On the stuff I saw, it was always Symington who was going to be the vice president. The Kennedy family had approved Symington . . ."

"It was obvious to them that something extraordinary had taken place, as it was to me," Raskin wrote. "During my entire association with the Kennedys, I could not recall any situation where a decision of major significance had been reversed in such a short period of time. . . . Bob [Kennedy] had always been involved in every major decision; why not this one, I pondered . . . I slept little that night."[17]

John Kennedy told Clark Clifford on July 13, 1960: "We've talked it out—me, dad, Bobby—and we've selected Symington as the vice president." Kennedy asked Clark Clifford to relay that message to Symington "and find out if he'd run. . . . I [Clark Clifford] and Stuart went to bed believing that we had a solid, unequivocal deal with Jack."[18]

John Kennedy, after what must have been a brutal night of dealing with Lyndon Johnson and Sam Rayburn, told Clifford on the morning of July 14, 1960: "I must do something that I have never done before. I made a serious deal, and now I have to go back on it. I have no alternative." Symington was out and Johnson was in. Clifford recalled observing that Kennedy looked as if he'd been up all night.[19]

In sum, on July 13, 1960, John Kennedy had a deal "signed, sealed, and delivered" for Senator Stuart Symington to be his VP. Then—poof!—in a cloud of magician's smoke, suddenly Lyndon Johnson miraculously and inexplicably appears as the VP selection for JFK by the morning of July 14, 1960, stunning media and inside political observers. This type of black magic sorcery was a staple of LBJ's political career. Two other good examples of black magic would be the 1948 Box 13 ballot box stuffing, which made LBJ the Democratic Senate nominee, and the other one would be the 1952 murder conviction of LBJ's personal hit man Malcolm Wallace, who was convicted of murder "with malice aforethought" and given a mind-blowingly lenient sentence of five years probation with no time in jail for Wallace's conviction of the October, 1951 murder of Doug Kinser in Austin. We shall learn more about Mr. Wallace later.

The JFK assassination itself became the most prime example of LBJ's black magic. Johnson was within days of not just being dropped from the 1964 Democratic ticket, but of being politically executed, personally destroyed, and publicly humiliated by the Kennedys. A *Life* magazine exposé on LBJ's corruption and vast wealth was due to be published within a week. A SWAT team of reporters was combing through LBJ's financial transactions in central Texas. At the very moment when JFK's Dallas motorcade was slowing on Elm Street, Don Reynolds was testifying to a closed session of the Senate Rules Committee about LBJ's kickbacks and corruption.

Then presto! Magically, mysteriously, and tragically, John Kennedy is dead. Lyndon Johnson becomes president, and the media exposés and Senate investigation into LBJ's corruption are deep-sixed.

This was not without the help of H. L. Hunt and the Texas oil industry, which helped navigate, fund, and advise Johnson's career in exchange for prized government contracts and favorable legislation. The oil magnate would later be one of the top financiers of the assassination in Dallas. To Madeleine Brown, he was yet another wealthy Texas businessman in close orbit around her frequent lover, Lyndon Johnson.

"We may have lost the battle, but we are going to win the war," Hunt said to Madeleine Brown after Johnson's loss to Kennedy in the primaries. He believed that Johnson, as vice president, could control the green Kennedy, eventually ascending to commander-in-chief, able to protect and promote Texas oil and other interests through legislation. Richard Nixon later specifically told Maurice Stans and his fundraisers in a memo: "Don't take money under any circumstances from H. L. Hunt."[20]

Following Johnson's acceptance of the vice presidential spot on the ticket, Bobby remarked to Charles Bartlett, a journalist and family friend: "Yesterday was the best day of my life, and today is the worst day of my life."[21]

Kenny O'Donnell, a close friend of both Kennedy brothers and the organizer and director of Kennedy's presidential campaign schedule in 1960, was the most outspoken against the decision, believing that the choice of Johnson compromised the promises that the campaign had made to civil rights groups and labor unions, most of whom were against the Texan.

"You won the nomination as president last night as a knight on a white charger," O'Donnell said to John. "Now, in your first move after your nomination, you're going against the people who backed you."[22]

Kennedy's response would be haunting.

"Get one thing clear, Kenny," John said, angered by the criticism, "I'm forty-three years old, and I'm the healthiest candidate for president in the country, and I'm not going to die in office."[23]

For Johnson and his cronies, who believed he could control the presidency through the vice presidency, it was a rude awakening when he was relegated to an almost dormant position.

"If Jack Kennedy gets elected," Johnson said shortly before Election Day, "you can be sure that the man closest to the president will be the man closest to the Senate. I'm going to be a working vice president."[24] A successful, visible term or two as vice president in Johnson's mind would set him up as the most viable candidate for president, a fate that might not be possible had Johnson remained in the Senate.

The truth couldn't have been any more stark in comparison, and the reality did not take long to sink in. Johnson would be marginalized throughout President Kennedy's first term, and he was humiliated to have to answer to "that little shitass" Bobby Kennedy.[25]

Shortly following the election, President-elect Kennedy visited the LBJ ranch and would be taken on a hunt similar to the one provided for Bobby. Kennedy bagged a deer and was later presented with the stuffed deer head as a gifted trophy. Johnson suggested to Kennedy that it be in the Oval Office, but was slighted when the head was hauled and displayed in the Fish Room of the White House, which today is the Roosevelt Room.

"The three most overrated things in the world are the state of Texas, the FBI, and hunting trophies,"[26] Kennedy said privately.

President Kennedy though, who worked with Johnson in the Senate, recognized the enormous ego of the man and made attempts to temper it. Only a year earlier, as majority leader,

Johnson had ruled over the Senate and the nation. Kennedy, who had worked alongside Johnson, remembered the opulent trappings of the Johnson Senate. Johnson, feeling his office in the Capitol was much too small for his tremendous self-importance, had enlarged his work-space, expanding to other offices like Nero clearing land for his Domus Aurea, until he had, in the words of a reporter, a "seven-room spread of offices."[27]

Robert Caro, biographer of Johnson, details LBJ's additional appropriation of Senate space in his book *Master of the Senate*:

> Grand as this suite was, it was still too far from the Chamber floor for his liking, but on the same level as the Chamber floor, and conveniently near it, was a suite of two huge rooms that had been the staff and meeting rooms of the Senate's District of Columbia Committee. He commandeered that, too. On its high ceilings, above its big crystal chandelier, were frescoes (as soon as he chose the office, painters began touching them up) of boys carrying baskets of flowers and young maidens reclining on couches: a Roman emperor's banquet. Reporters began referring to it as "the Emperor's Room" before coining another name, which stuck: "The Taj Mahal."[28]

Upon seizing this new office, the majority leader hung a life-size portrait of himself reclining against a bookshelf, which greeted people as they entered. The refurbishment, to meet Johnson's standards, had cost taxpayers in excess of $100,000.[29]

Kennedy, anticipating the dark mood of Johnson that would come in his less-powerful position, dispatched aide Kenny O'Donnell to massage the vice president's ego.

"Lyndon Johnson was the majority leader of the United States Senate," Kennedy told O' Donnell. "He was elected to office several times by the people. He was the number one Democrat in the United States, elected by us to be our leader. I'm president of the United States. He doesn't like that. He thinks he's ten times more important than I am—he happens to be that kind of fellow.

. . . Elected officers have a code, and no matter whether they like each other or hate each other. . . . You have never been elected to anything by anybody, and you are dealing with a very insecure, sensitive man, with a huge ego. I want you to literally kiss his ass from one end of Washington to the other."[30]

O'Donnell and President Kennedy had a system for helping Johnson feel important. When Johnson complained to the president, Kennedy would call O'Donnell into his office and scold him in front of the vice president. O'Donnell would be the goat, and Johnson would walk away satisfied.

"Damn it, Kenny, you've gone and done it again," Kennedy said on one occasion while disciplining O'Donnell. "Lyndon, you go ahead and tell him yourself what's happened this time."[31]

President Kennedy also gave Johnson special privileges and assignments to quell his rancor. Johnson was assigned to chair the National Aeronautics and Space Council and also given the benefit of descending the White House stairs with Kennedy to commence formal occasions.

To further ease Johnson's dejection, Kennedy had LBJ make a number of foreign visits including Pakistan, South Vietnam, and Lebanon, representing the United States.

Later, Johnson would recall "trips around the world, chauffeurs, men saluting, people clapping, [and] chairmanships of councils, but in the end, it is nothing. I detested every minute of it."[32]

Johnson was also tasked to command the Committee of Equal Employment Opportunity, but the assignment failed to raise his self-worth in the administration, and constant criticism from the attorney general only amplified the damage done to Lyndon's psyche.

"That man can't run this committee," said Bobby. "Can you think of anything more deplorable than him trying to run the United States? That's why he can't ever be president of the United States."[33]

When Lyndon Johnson embarked upon his vice presidency, he had visions of succeeding John Kennedy and becoming the thirty-sixth president of the United States. As that aim became more of an apparition, Johnson's nemesis, Bobby Kennedy, seemed more and more the likely front-runner for the office. Where Johnson had foreseen himself giving advice to the president, it was Bobby who had John's ear. Where Johnson saw himself pulling the strings of the presidency, it was Bobby who was given the duty and credit of backing the president.

"Nothing big goes on without Bobby being in on it,"[34] a staff member said.

Johnson, who was used to brokering deals with a mix of brute force and Southern charm, was disheartened by the tact of the brothers, believing, with his experience, that they were ignoring a vital asset to help enact legislation.

To his assistant Bobby Baker, Johnson lamented, "those kids . . . from the White House [who] start yelling 'frog' at everybody and expect 'em to jump. They don't have any idea of how to get along, and they don't even know where the power is."[35]

When President Kennedy acknowledged "the second most powerful man in the world,"[36] he was referring to Bobby.

Early in the Kennedy administration, there was already talk of Bobby as John's successor and no talk of the powerhouse who once was Senator Johnson. By the third year of Kennedy's presidency, with Johnson on the vice presidential cutting block, LBJ was an afterthought.

"The public . . . has already forgotten the dynamic Lyndon Johnson who was once master of the Senate," wrote Gore Vidal. "Eight years of vice presidential grayness will have completed his obscurity."[37]

If LBJ thought that Bobby would sympathize with Johnson's exodus from the heights of power to the fringe of the Kennedy administration, he was ill prepared for the insults of the attorney general.

The parties at Hickory Hill, Bobby's large brick mansion in Mclean, Virginia, coursed with bad-mouthing of the vice president.

An incident there early in November 1963 detailed in Jeff Shesol's book, *Mutual Contempt* illuminated the perception of Johnson within the administration:

> The mocking tone of the Hickory Hill gang became so routine, so reflexive, that it was difficult to drop even in Johnson's presence. In November 1963, at a stag party for a recent Kennedy appointee, two mid-level officials stood in animated conversation. Ron Linton, a Kennedy campaign hand now working at the Pentagon, was talking excitedly to John J. Riley, JFK's nominee to chair the Federal Trade Commission, when Linton sensed a third party hovering at his side, awaiting a break in the conversation. Perhaps thoughtlessly, the two men continued chatting. When Linton finally turned his head, he saw the tall figure of Lyndon Johnson walking away dejectedly. "John," Linton said to Riley, "I think we just insulted the vice-president of the United States."
>
> "Fuck 'em," Riley blurted. And Lyndon Johnson, halfway across the room, froze in midstep and wheeled around to face the men. The vice president stood stiffly and stared, indignant and proud. But he said nothing and quickly lost himself in the crowd.[38]

A month earlier at Hickory Hill, Bobby had been presented with a Johnson voodoo doll, imbued with the significance that Lyndon would now further bend to Kennedy's will. Kennedy and his wife Ethel mockingly called Lyndon and Lady Bird "Uncle Cornpone and Mrs. Pork Chop."

Robert Kennedy was not the only Kennedy with misgivings about Lyndon Johnson. Years later, Jackie Kennedy would make a comment during the time period of the House Select Committee on Assassinations investigation into the JFK assassination. One of JFK Jr.'s best friends at the Phillips Academy was Meg Azzoni. In the Spring of 1977, she and John Jr. went to visit his mother, Jackie, while sister Caroline was at Harvard. Meg said "Jackie told John and I at the 'break-the-fast' breakfast, 'I did not like or trust Lyndon Johnson.' No one said another word the whole meal in memorial contemplative silence."[40]

The insults hurled at Johnson during his decline were not the apex of Bobby's plan for Lyndon. Bobby was accumulating intelligence on Johnson's illegal endeavors that he planned to use later to oust and perhaps even send Johnson to jail.

So what did Lyndon Johnson have in store for the Kennedy brothers? Robert Caro has the answer right in front of his eyes, but he is unable to add (a) the fantastic hatred of Johnson and the Kennedys with each other to (b) the machine-gun riddled Warren Report and draw an obvious conclusion.

Robert Caro:

At the end of that long afternoon, after he had stepped down from the chair in the Biltmore corridor on which he stood to make his acceptance statement, he came back into his suite, and closed the door behind him, and cursed Robert Kennedy. He called him, Bobby Baker was to write, "'that little shitass' and worse." Perhaps much worse. John Connally, who during long days of conversation with this author was willing to answer almost any question put to him, no matter how delicate the topic, wouldn't answer when asked what Johnson said about Robert Kennedy. When the author pressed him, he finally said flatly: 'I am not going to tell you what he said about him.' During the months after the convention, when Johnson was closeted alone back in Texas with an old ally, he would sometimes be asked about Robert Kennedy. He would reply with a gesture. Raising his big right hand, he would draw the side of it across the neck in a slowing, slitting movement. Sometimes that gesture would be his only reply; sometimes, as during a meeting with Ed Clark in Austin, he would say, as his hand moved across his neck, 'I'll cut his throat if it's the last thing I do.'

"President Kennedy worked so hard at making a place for me, always saying nice things, gave me dignity and standing,"

Johnson said to reporter Helen Thomas. "But back in the back room they were quoting Bobby, saying I was going to be taken off the ticket."[41]

Bobby smelled blood in the water and was moving to attack.

In 2003, Phil Brennan wrote an article for Newsmax confirming that the Kennedys were going to use the media to politically execute Johnson. At the time, Brennan worked on the Hill and was also writing a column for the National Review under the pseudonym Cato. Brennan had intimate knowledge of both a Senate Rules Committee investigation into LBJ and the RFK media war on LBJ. Brennan:

"A few days later, the Attorney General, Bobby Kennedy, called five of Washington's top reporters into his office and told them it was now open season on Lyndon Johnson. It's OK, he told them, to go after the story they were ignoring out of deference to the administration.

And from that point on until the events in Dallas, Lyndon Baines Johnson's future looked as if it included a sudden end to his political career and a few years in the slammer. The Kennedys had their knives out and sharpened for him and were determined to draw his political blood—all of it.

In the Senate, the investigation into the Baker case was moving quickly ahead. Even the Democrats were cooperating, thanks to the Kennedys, and an awful lot of really bad stuff was being revealed—until November 22, 1963.

Seymour Hersh found out about the "RFK destroy LBJ" plan when he interviewed Burkett Van Kirk, who in the fall of 1963 had been a chief counsel for the Republicans on the Senate Rules Committee led by Senator John Williams, who loved to expose corruption. Van Kirk said that RFK had assigned a lawyer to feed the Rules Committee all the dirt he had accumulated on Johnson's corrupt dealings and financial transactions.

"The lawyer," Van Kirk told Hersh "used to come up to the Senate and hang around me like a dark cloud. It took him about a week or ten days to, one, find out what I didn't know, and two, give it to me." Some of the Kennedy-supplied documents were kept in Williams's office safe, Van Kirk said, and never shown to him. There was no doubt of Bobby Kennedy's purpose in dealing with the Republicans, Van Kirk said, "To get rid of Johnson. To dump him. I am as sure of that [as I am that the] sun comes up in the east."

On November 22, 1963, Lyndon Johnson's political career, reputation, and his life were hanging by a very thin thread . . . and Robert Kennedy was about to clip it with scissors.

At the outset of the administration, a photographer asked him: "Well Bobby, what are we supposed to call you now? Is it Bobby, or attorney general, or general, or sir?"[42]

Kennedy's response would no doubt be agreed upon by enemies of the young attorney general. "Just call me son of a bitch because that's what everybody else is going to be doing."

NOTES

1. Martin, *Seeds of Destruction*, 304.
2. Caro, *Master of the Senate*, 647.
3. Shesol, *Mutual Contempt*, 109.
4. Ibid., 10.
5. Ibid.
6. Ibid., 39.
7. Ibid., 40.
8. Martin, *Seeds of Destruction*, 236.
9. "Bobby Kennedy and Other Mixed Blessings," *Firing Line* (June 6, 1966).
10. Shesol, *Mutual Contempt*, 12.
11. Jeffery K. Smith, *Bad Blood: Lyndon B. Johnson, Robert F. Kennedy, and the Tumultuous 1960s* (Bloomington: AuthorHouse, 2010), 71.
12. Ibid.
13. Shesol, *Mutual Contempt*, 52.
14. Ibid., 53.
15. Ibid., 54.

16. Summers, Anthony, *Official and Confidential: The Secret Life of J. Edgar Hoover*, pg. 272.
17. Hersh, Seymour, *The Dark Side of Camelot*, 124–25.
18. Ibid.
19. Hersh, Seymour, *The Dark Side of Camelot*, 126.
20. Stans, Maurice, *The Terrors of Justice*, 134.
21. Shesol, *Mutual Contempt*, 57.
22. Kenneth P. O'Donnell and David F. Powers, *"Johnny, We Hardly Knew Ye": Memories of John Fitzgerald Kennedy* (Boston: Little, Brown and Company, 1972), 6.
23. Ibid.
24. Shesol, *Mutual Contempt*, 57.
25. Shesol, *Mutual Contempt*, 56.
26. Smith, *Bad Blood*, 86.
27. Caro, *Master of the Senate*, 1018.
28. Ibid.
29. Smith, *Bad Blood*, 60.
30. Shesol, *Mutual Contempt*, 87.
31. O'Donnell, *Johnny, We Hardly Knew Ye*, 7.
32. Shesol, *Mutual Contempt*, 75.
33. Smith, *Bad Blood*, 96.
34. Shesol, *Mutual Contempt*, 74.
35. Ibid., 100.
36. Ibid., 72.
37. Ibid., 111.
38. Shesol, *Mutual Contempt*, 104–105.
39. Smith, *Bad Blood*, 2.
40. Azzoni, Meg, John F. Kennedy Jr. to Meg Azzoni, *11 Letters: Memories of Kennedys & Reflections on His Quest*, p. 52.
41. Arthur M. Schlesinger, *Robert Kennedy and His Times* (Boston: Houghton Mifflin, 1978), 624.
42. Smith, *Bad Blood*, 94.

CHAPTER FIVE

HOOVER

J. Edgar Hoover had been long burrowed in the Justice Department, living off the dirty secrets and information that oozed down from the powers above. To Hoover, who had been director of the Federal Bureau of Investigation almost two full years longer than his new boss had been on the planet, it was a no-brainer to welcome the unseasoned Bobby Kennedy to the position of attorney general.

Hoover had controlled many an attorney general before Kennedy and, through his connections to Joe Kennedy, no doubt thought Bobby's power would be even easier to curb. In the director of the FBI's office was a framed letter from Joe Sr., which detailed the elder Kennedy's strong feeling that Hoover would make a first-rate president of the United States.[1] The director was one of the first to express his approval of John Kennedy's appointment of Bobby to the position of attorney general.

According to former FBI agent Cartha DeLoach, Hoover had informed John Kennedy that he would "need one person in your cabinet who will be loyal to you, who will give good advice to you."[2] That man would be his brother Bobby.

Later, Hoover would intimate to polemic newspaperman George Sokolsky that his recommendation to appoint Bobby to attorney general was "the worst damned piece of advice I've ever given anybody in my life."[3]

If Hoover thought Bobby would come into the appointment as Joe Sr. did to Roosevelt, pants around his ankles, begging, he was mistaken. Hoover's authority would be blunted in the Kennedy administration, and he would be treated by the Justice Department as a byproduct of a bygone age, as antiquated as the John Dillinger death-mask morbidly on display in the anteroom outside of the director's office. Hoover had raised the prestige of his bureau with the capture of big-name criminals, the public enemies, individual Midwest bank robbers developed by circumstances of the Great Depression.

Bobby Kennedy, with his earlier experience as chief counsel on the McClellan Committee, saw that the real problem was organized crime, not the Robin Hood-esque crime sprees of a defunct era. These were not the high-profile heists of Hoover's day. This was a corrupt system with ties to businesses, unions and, indeed, the government.

Before Kennedy was appointed, the Justice Department, in the words of department attorney Bob Blakey, was "a Republican law factory with a staid hierarchy."[4] Kennedy opened the doors of the stuffy department, working personally and personably with his team-oriented staff of young lawyers looking to make a difference.

"He's given it the sense of the public man," said former Deputy Attorney General Byron White.

Bobby's crusade, brought over from the McClellan Committee, would not sit well with the director.

Despite President Kennedy's insistence to Bobby that "you have got to get along with that old man,"[5] the obstinate younger brother would not comply. Hoover was more of an impediment to the new Justice Department than a help.

J. Edgar Hoover would have been of great use to Bobby in the fight against organized crime, as well as helpful in the creation of a nationwide dragnet, which would utilize shared bureau information from across the country to cooperatively attack the mob. Unfortunately, despite extensive evidence to the contrary, the denial of a nationwide syndicate or of organized crime in general was one of the many inconsistencies in the director of the FBI's career.

In November 1957, close to one hundred Mafia members from throughout the country met in Apalachin, New York, at the estate of Joseph "Joe the Barber" Barbara. The meeting was busted up by local police, and fifty of those gathered were arrested. The excuses from the hoods detailing their reasons for attendance were comical.

"Mr. Barbara was sick, and we all came to see him," reasoned one of the apprehended. "We just happened to drop in at the same time."[6]

"I had a problem with one of my windshield wipers, and I decided to get off the highway and drive the sixty-five miles here (Apalachin) to get it fixed,"[7] offered up another.

Among the notable underworld figures in attendance were Santo Trafficante from Tampa, Joseph Civello from Dallas, and Carlo Gambino from New York. The Apalachin meeting provided reasonable evidence for the existence and scope of a nationwide connected syndicate.

"Never before had there been such a concentration of jailbirds, murderers free on technicalities, and big wheels in gambling and dope rackets,"[8] remarked a prosecutor who investigated the case.

"The FBI didn't know anything, really, about these people who were the major gangsters in the United States,"[9] Bobby would lament. It was more probable that the FBI didn't want to know.

For Hoover to acknowledge the existence of the Mafia would undermine the credibility of his institution and would help someone like Bobby, who challenged the director at every step.

To top men in the Mafia, Hoover was a godsend: The top lawman in the country worried more about small-time crooks pilfering pennies from small-town banks than a tightly knit system of criminals working on the big heist.

"Under FBI Director J. Edgar Hoover's watch, the criminal organizations that would become known as La Cosa Nostra, the Mafia, and the Outfit were allowed to operate unimpeded for decades," Sam Giancana, nephew of the famed Chicago mob boss, wrote. "Bureau resources focused instead on high-profile cases like the Lindbergh kidnapping and the apprehension of notorious bank robber John Dillinger—cases that were intended to elevate Hoover's stature, undeservedly, to that of America's quintessential crime buster."[10]

The laws Bobby tried to implement from his first days in the department focused on stymieing the interstate activities of organized crime. As early as May 17, 1961, when Bobby testified before the House of Representatives Judiciary Committee, Subcommittee No. 5, the young attorney general was attempting to halt "the huge profits in the traffic in liquor, narcotics, prostitution, as well as the use of these funds for corrupting local officials and for their use in racketeering in labor and management."[11]

Bobby "got five anticrime bills moved through the Judiciary Committee so quickly that nobody had the chance to read them,"[12] said Justice official William Goeghehan.

Where Hoover's FBI had focused on small independent gangs or crooks, Kennedy's Justice Department was focused on the interconnectivity of criminal activity. "Interstate" was the key word for the new Justice Department, which had previously impeded law enforcement on a local level and now worked also to tackle problems on a national level, laws such as those forbidding the transportation of gambling equipment across state lines or using highways or telephones for the means of racketeering.[13]

"I'd like to be remembered as the guy who broke the Mafia,"[14] said Kennedy.

While Bobby pushed his organized crime agenda, Hoover dragged his feet. Prior to Kennedy's tenure as attorney general, FBI offices in two of the nation's hotspots for organized crime, New York and New Jersey, contained only a half dozen agents assigned to organized crime, with six hundred assigned to the detection and investigation of communism.[15] Hoover contended that the FBI did not pursue organized crime vigorously because the dirty business threatened to contaminate the high standards of the bureau.

"He was concerned that his men would be corrupted," reasoned Howard Diller, a Bureau of Narcotics agent. "This was a nasty business. They could go after communists and kidnappers, but this caused aggravation, and he didn't want any aggravation."[16]

Truth be told, as a gambler, Hoover was friendly with many of organized crime's biggest players. Joe "Joe Bananas" Bonanno, Carlos Marcello, his partner Dub McClanahan, and Johnny Rosselli, when he was more than just a crate hauler for Joe Sr., were more than acquaintances to Hoover.[17]

"I knew Hoover," Rosselli said. "I'd buy him drinks, and we'd talk. It would be fun to be with the director of the FBI like that."[18]

Hoover was also close with mobster Frank Costello. William Hundley, one of Bobby's top aides, met Costello through his friend, Washington, DC trial lawyer Edward Bennett Williams, who represented the New York mob boss. Hundley heard a string of stories from Costello about his relationship with Hoover, relaying their mutual affection for the horse track and their frequent trips there together.

"The *horse* races!" Costello exclaimed. "You'll never know how many races I had to fix for those lousy ten-dollar bets of Hoover's!"[19]

In a conversation caught by FBI electronic surveillance between the "mob's Accountant" Meyer Lanksy, agent Alvin Malnik, and Jesse Weiss, a Miami Beach restaurateur and friend of J. Edgar Hoover, the fears of the Mafia concerning new aims of the bureau were aired:

JW: But Al, you don't see anything in the paper about him; it's all BOBBY KENNEDY
AM: That's all; nothing about him.
JW: They are taking the play away from him.
AM: Hoover is a lost . . .

JW: . . . cause

AM: A lost cause, that's all. A lost cause.

AM: Well, does HOOVER realize this great transformation that's happening within his own organization?

JW: I spoke to him two weeks ago—I was in Washington before he went to California—he goes out to California—he goes out to California every year—he goes to Scripps Clinic in LA JOLLA—couple—goes out there every year—six weeks ago . . . [inaudible] . . . it's like he . . . he told me the same thing . . . shucks, the Bureau is shot, what the hell, he says, but what can I do, he says; the Attorney General is the boss of the Bureau, he runs it . . . dare you to defy it.[20]

With Bobby's entrance, not only the aim but the rigid pretenses of the bureau that Hoover demanded his G-men follow were being challenged by the more whimsically casual work environment that his new boss had brought with him. For years, the lives of the agents inside and outside of the bureau were dictated by the director's peculiarities.

"Ultimately it was not permitted to question even the most outlandish order, drink coffee at work, marry a woman not 'Bureau material,' go bald, or take a left turn with the director in the car," wrote Burton Hersh. "The atmosphere was top-down authoritarian, Mussolini without the chuckles."[21]

Bobby did not adhere to the strict dress code or office behavior that the director of the FBI was accustomed to.

"It is ridiculous to have the attorney general walking around the building in his shirtsleeves," Hoover grumbled to head of the FBI's domestic intelligence division William Sullivan. "Suppose I had a visitor in waiting in my anteroom. How could I have introduced him?"

It would not be long into Bobby's tenure as attorney general before Hoover would refer to Bobby as an "adolescent horse's ass." Hoover, Bobby said, was a "psycho."

Hoover would throw any jab he could. When giving the official FBI tour at the outset of the Kennedy administration, the director had instructed the tour guides to add the line: "Mr. Hoover became the director of the bureau in 1924, the year before the attorney general was born."[22]

In January 1961, during his first month as attorney general, Bobby was paid a visit by Hoover and his associate director and personal companion Clyde Tolson. Burton Hersh, in his book *Bobby and J. Edgar*, describes the scene:

> The director and Tolson came by the attorney general's office by appointment to find Bobby cocked back in his massive red cordovan-leather swivel chair, behind his six-foot-square mahogany desk, shirtsleeves rolled up and his undone necktie dangling in two strips down his narrow chest. Kennedy was tossing darts at a target across the room. As Hoover and Tolson attempted to open up the subject at hand, Kennedy continued to peg dart after dart, picking up the celebrated walnut paneling each time he missed and interrupting their disjunctive exchanges whenever he climbed out of his chair to recover his darts. An inveterate gum-chewer, Kennedy's reedy, singsong voice could be very difficult to understand.[23]

Hoover was infuriated and would begin to compare Bobby to a, "child playing in a Dresden china shop."[24]

The attorney general was also looking to adjust the color of the bureau. Noticing a scarcity of black agents working for the FBI, Bobby circulated a memo to hire a number of black people.

"The only person who didn't respond to the memo was J. Edgar Hoover," said John Seigenthaler, the attorney general's administrative assistant. "I sent a second memo, after which he wrote me saying it was a violation of federal regulations to inquire into the race of government employees. We went back and forth on it, and finally, after we'd found out that the most any division had was one, he wrote back to say he had two, and he gave their names. I showed the memo to Sal Andretta, chief administrator of the department, who'd been there for years, and he said, 'Hell, they're Hoover's drivers.'"[25]

Hoover saw the integration of the bureau as another attempt of Kennedy to exercise his authority and debilitate the standards of the prestigious bureau.

"He wanted to lower our qualifications and hire more Negro agents," Hoover said. "I said, 'Bobby, that's not going to be done as long as I'm director of this bureau.' He said, 'I don't think you're being cooperative.' And I said, 'Why don't you get a new director?'"

The director wasn't going anywhere, but the young attorney general was making noticeable changes in the Justice Department. In the 1960s, 117 black agents were hired; by 1970, there were 122 black agents working for the bureau.[26]

Hoover was frantic that his power was being compromised and that his star-status within the Justice Department was being challenged. He liked to have total control over the bureau; when someone came along to test his high standing, the director would do his best to damage or neutralize his or her position.

In 1934, when Special Agent Melvin Purvis pursued and was given credit for the death of Public Enemy Number One John Dillinger, his instant fame did not sit well with Hoover. Purvis was quickly given the cold shoulder of the bureau, which led to his resignation. Hoover changed the resignation status to, "termination with prejudice."[27] Purvis went on to pursue a variety of failed enterprises, including opening a detective agency. Hoover put out the word to law enforcement not to extend a hand to "Little Mel's" new business, and it floundered. He later also sold his name and likeness to the cereal Post Toasties and found work at a radio station as an announcer. In 1960, he committed suicide with the gun that his fellow agents had presented him with at a party thrown after his resignation.

From the time Purvis left the bureau until after his suicide, Hoover was relentless in his attempt to defer credit from him for the Dillinger killing. Sam Cowley, an agent who commanded the Dillinger squad and had later been shot and killed by "Baby Face" Nelson, was given commendation by Hoover and the bureau.

> "With Purvis out of the bureau and in disgrace, Sam Cowley fit the bill perfectly," wrote Richard Gid Powers. "First, he was dead, so there was no danger that he would turn his glory to personal advantage. Second, by honoring one of its martyrs, someone who had given up his life for the FBI, the bureau would be honoring itself. Third, since Cowley had been Hoover's personal representative on the Dillinger case, any credit Cowley got flowed directly back to Washington without being absorbed by the agents in the field. For these reasons it became permanent FBI policy to tear down Purvis as a glory hound and build up Cowley as the epitome of the corporate G-Man hero."[28]

Bobby Kennedy, however, as Hoover's boss, was very much alive. In another show of authority, Bobby had a direct line installed, which was connected to a buzzer in the director's office, so that he could alert and summon him at will.[29] Hoover was not used to having to listen or deal with someone who would not bend to the will of the bureau, and he did not take the adjustment well.

At one point, with William Hundley in his office, Bobby playfully pushed the buzzer to mobilize Hoover. When Hoover arrived, indignation covered his bulldog face.

"They started arguing about something," Hundley said. "Bobby put it to him, 'How are you coming with hiring minorities and women?' He was tough. Hoover said, 'I can't find any qualified.' They jawed at each other . . . No attorney general had ever done that to Hoover. I couldn't believe it."[30]

By spring of 1961, Bobby was sometimes bringing his bear-like Newfoundland Brumus, all fur and drool, to the office with him. If he beat Bobby to the car in the morning, the hulking Brumus would find himself as assistant to the attorney general for the day. Hoover was simmering when he found that Brumus was marking his territory in Bobby's office and became apoplectic when a pile of dung was spotted outside the director's suite. Hoover called an executive conference to discuss the chances of charges sticking against the attorney general for violating federal code concerning dogs in a government building.[31] "Dog . . . shall not be brought upon property for other than official purposes"[32] read Section 201, Chapter 8, Title 2, of Rules and Regulations for Public Buildings. That the tail-wagger in question also discharged on government property only made the offense more egregious.

Knowledge of pooch legislation aside, there is a reason Hoover had retained his position and power for decades.

Over the previous years, he had used his special files on fellow government employees or persons of particular interest to him to expand and protect the power of his bureau. Hoover, through manipulation or deception, had marginalized the many attorneys general who had come before Bobby Kennedy. In the late 1930s, Hoover neutralized Attorney General Frank Murphy, who had enough documented sexual indiscretions to fill a file. It was under Murphy that Hoover began to bypass the pesky nuisance of having to report to the attorney general and began taking his business directly to the president.

"I was very close to Franklin Delano Roosevelt, personally and officially. We often had lunch in his office in the Oval Room of the White House,"[33] Hoover boasted.

Murphy's successor, Robert Jackson, attempted to penetrate the dominance of the bureau, demanding access to Hoover's secret files. Hoover combated this initiative by opening a new system for the files. When, on March 15, 1940, Jackson ordered Hoover to cease the use of wiretaps by the bureau, Hoover used scare tactics to regain control.

"I spoke to J. Edgar Hoover and asked him whether he was able to listen in on [Nazi] spies by tapping the wires, and he said no; that the order given him by Bob Jackson stopping him had not been revoked," said Treasury Secretary Henry Morgenthau. "I said I would go to work at once. He said he needed it desperately."

The plea for the use of wiretaps in the interest of national security quickly made its way up the ranks to President Roosevelt, who expeditiously rescinded Jackson's order, effectively handcuffing the attorney general.

Roosevelt wrote to the attorney general that the order was not meant to apply "to grave matters involving the defense of the nation."

"You are, therefore, authorized and directed in such cases as you may approve, after investigation of the need in each case, to authorize the necessary investigative agencies that they are at liberty to secure information by listening devices . . . of persons suspected of subversive activities against the Government of the United States, including suspected spies," Roosevelt wrote. "You are requested furthermore to limit these investigations so conducted to a minimum and to limit them insofar as possible to aliens. FDR."[34]

Years later, speaking about Hoover, Jackson would confide in a friend that "he was sorry he hadn't fired him."[35]

In 1943, Attorney General Francis Biddle, objecting to Hoover's custodial detention list, compiled to locate individuals or groups who could become an internal security problem, told the director to trash the file. Hoover, instead, changed the file's name and location.

Whoever tried to subvert the legislative reach of the director found that Hoover had been long prepared for such an action. When President Harry Truman let Hoover know that he would not receive the director's personal phone calls and that all pertinent information would be directed through the attorney general, Hoover gave Truman a whiff of the secret file, which contained dirt on many major government players, including, most likely, Harry himself. Hoover then had his direct line of communication with Truman.

"I do not wish to be the head of an organization of potential black-mailers," Hoover said regarding wiretapping. In truth, however, he had compiled many of his secret files especially for the purpose of blackmail to retain power. Particular to Hoover's blackmailing repertoire were character flaws of a prurient nature. Hoover kept records on operators such as first lady Eleanor Roosevelt, whom Hoover suspected of many sexual indiscretions with both males and females, and on Martin Luther King, whose hotel room the director had bugged. Hoover reveled in the sexual escapades of individuals he had taped, playing them back before selected company. A favorite activity of Hoover's was the viewing of pornography.

Despite his interest in erotica, Hoover took a very strong stance against sexual deviancy, which included, in the director's public estimation, homosexuality. An example of the hypocritical persecution of what he deemed perverse was Hoover's dismantling of the career of President-elect Eisenhower's Chief of Staff Arthur H. Vandenberg, Jr. In late 1952, Hoover reached into his "Sex Deviate" files and pulled out the dirt on Vandenberg. It was reported to Eisenhower that in 1942, there were incidents of a lurid nature between Vandenberg and two enlisted men at Camp Lee, Virginia. Soon after the information was divulged, Vandenberg resigned from his appointment, citing "health reasons."[36]

Shortly after Vandenberg's resignation, Eisenhower issued Executive Order 10450, which outlined the danger that "sexual perversion" as a character trait of a government employee posed to national security.

Years later, letters of Vandenberg's from Dwight and Mamie Eisenhower detailed Ike's remorse.

"I feel very distressed about your health," Eisenhower wrote. "I feel in some respects guilty."[37]

What made Hoover's push against "smut" and what Hoover considered sexual abnormalities more odd was a sexual repression that seemed to dominate his own personal life. His most intimate companion, besides his mother, with whom he lived until her death when he was forty-three years old, was his right-hand man at the bureau, Clyde Tolson. Hoover and Tolson maintained a relationship not unlike that of a gay couple, which led to much speculation.

They were driven to and from work together, ate almost all meals together, and vacationed together.

Before John Kennedy had taken office, there were talks that the new administration would eventually replace Hoover. One of the names being floated as a successor was William Boswell, director of State Department security. Hoover would deal with the problem the way he had so many others—with compiled knowledge of his target's sexual recklessness. Hoover had been keeping a file on John Kennedy's carnal exploits since 1941, when John was an ensign in the Navy and involved with married Danish journalist Inga Arvad. Arvad had ties to Adolf Hitler, with whom she had spent time during the 1936 Berlin Olympic Games. Hitler had deemed Arvad "a perfect Nordic beauty."[38] It has been speculated that Joe Kennedy had implored the FBI to put Arvad under surveillance after learning of her dalliance with his son. Following Joe Sr.'s failed ambassadorship in which he was labeled a Nazi appeaser, an exposé of sexual relations between John and someone who could be suspected a German spy would destroy his son's budding political career. Even though it is true that Joe Sr. opposed the relationship, the FBI certainly would have taken an active interest in Arvad regardless.

The Arvad affair, though, was insignificant in comparison to the president's infidelities with Judith Campbell, who was linked sexually to both Frank Sinatra and Chicago Mafia head Sam "Mooney" Giancana. In February 1960, Kennedy had met Campbell at a Sinatra show at the Sands hotel in Las Vegas. According to Campbell, after their first meeting, she became Kennedy's constant companion.

"He asked me about my day," said Campbell, "whom I saw, what I did, and I'd ask him about the campaign. He seemed very anxious to get together again. I was elated, almost giddy. The world looked wonderful."[39]

Shortly after the New Hampshire primary in March 1960, Campbell, with the help of Sinatra, was introduced to Mooney. The love triangle that ensued was one more connection between the Kennedys and La Cosa Nostra. On December 13, 1961, Hoover alerted the attorney general that the FBI was aware that Giancana had given assistance to the Kennedys in the 1960 presidential campaign. Hoover also revealed critical information that the Kennedys had not made good on their terms, and that the Mafia was planning revenge.

"You got the right idea, Moe, so . . . fuck everybody," Johnny Rosselli had told Giancana, "We'll use them every fucking way we can. They only know one way. Now let them see the other side of you."[40]

Five days later, on December 18, 1961, Joe Kennedy suffered a stroke, which left not only him permanently disabled, but also the line of communication between the Kennedys and the Mafia.

On March 22, 1962, at a planned lunch with the president and his aide Kenny O'Donnell, Hoover laid out his hand.

The director brought his ace to the luncheon: knowledge that the married president was sharing a lover with a mob boss. If played, this information could have instantly destroyed the career and credibility of the president.

Shortly after the meeting, Kennedy canceled his long-planned upcoming weekend stay at Sinatra's Palm Springs mansion—something that Sinatra had taken great pains to prepare for. Kennedy instead opted for the politically safer palatial grounds of older Republican crooner Bing Crosby's estate. He also broke off his two-year relationship with Campbell.

Hoover did not fail to pull out the goods whenever he thought that the Kennedys needed a reminder.

"Every month or so," Robert Kennedy said, Hoover, "would send somebody around to give information on somebody I know or members of my family or allegations in connection with myself. So that it would be clear—whether it was right or wrong—that he was on top of all these things."[41]

Hoover's job was safe, but the Kennedy administration had rendered his power impotent. Hoover would no longer be able to skip the attorney general and go directly to the president on FBI matters. Bobby did that now. Bobby, in an attempt to assuage the director's ego, would arrange for John to occasionally call on Hoover.

Hoover, who had made himself a fixture over the years, was now an ornament, which simply decorated the halls of the Justice Department. Bobby now controlled the power and purpose of the department.

"I started in the department in 1950 as a young man, worked hard, studied, applied myself," Bobby said with a smile. "And then my brother was elected president of the United States."[42]

That was the necessary element, the source of Bobby's power: his brother.

"There's no question that I could do it because of my relationship. They wouldn't have paid attention to me otherwise," Bobby said, "gone over my head to the president . . . because a lot of them in the hierarchy were opposed to it . . . hated the idea."[43]

Hoover, by using his extensive file on John Kennedy, had bought himself more time in the bureau, but with the mandatory US government retirement age of seventy nearing, time was running short. Hoover was sixty-six when John F. Kennedy took office and would be gone by the president's second term. It was Hoover's wish to have the retirement mandate waived, but he knew this was not to be granted by the Kennedy brothers. At one point, in the outset of his term as attorney general, Bobby attempted to mollify his aides in the face of Hoover's obstinate behavior by telling them that Hoover would be retired by 1965.[44]

The choice for the director became simple: It was either them or him. Hoover, instead of reporting information, would begin to discredit or ignore vital intelligence from reliable sources concerning the president's safety at the hands of the Mafia. The information detailed the hows, whens, and whys of the Mafia's plan to dispose of John F. Kennedy. From this intelligence, Hoover regained confidence. By March 1963, the director, who had been disrobed of power throughout the span of the Kennedy administration, slowly learning the plans of the Mafia, in concert with his neighbor and confidant Lyndon Johnson, became bold and obstinate concerning his future in the bureau.

"There had never been any political interference, or misuse of the bureau by any administration since I came here in 1924. . . . There is none now," Hoover said to the press. "I plan to stay and get the job done."

Following the assassination of John F. Kennedy, Hoover would have a strong hand in directing the most important event of his career: covering up the death of a president.

As Lyndon Johnson would later say of the director, "I'd rather have him inside the tent pissing out, than outside the tent pissing in."[45]

NOTES

1. Martin, *Seeds of Destruction*, 305.
2. Hersh, *Bobby and J. Edgar*, 206.
3. Ibid., 207.
4. Goldfarb, *Perfect Villains, Imperfect Heroes*, 28.
5. Hersh, *Bobby and J. Edgar*, 208.
6. Don Glynn, "Area Delegates Attended Mob Convention," *Niagara Gazette* (November 11, 2007).
7. Ibid.
8. Goldfarb, *Perfect Villains, Imperfect Heroes*, 31.
9. Ibid., 47.
10. Sam Giancana, *Mafia: The Government's Secret File on Organized Crime* (New York: Collins, 2007), Foreword.
11. Goldfarb, *Perfect Villains, Imperfect Heroes*, 45.
12. Gus Russo, *The Outfit: The Role of Chicago's Underworld in the Shaping of Modern America* (New York: Bloomsbury, 2001), 410.
13. Goldfarb, *Perfect Villains, Imperfect Heroes*, 64.
14. John H. Davis, *Mafia Kingfish: Carlos Marcello and the Assassination of John F. Kennedy* (New York: McGraw-Hill, 1989), 93.
15. Heymann, *RFK*, 215.

16. Ibid.
17. Hersh, *Bobby and J. Edgar*, 107.
18. Ibid.
19. Davis, *Mafia Kingfish*, 294.
20. Mark North, *Act of Treason: The Role of J. Edgar Hoover in the Assassination of President Kennedy* (New York: Carroll & Graf, 1991), 297-298.
21. Hersh, *Bobby and J. Edgar*, 39.
22. Curt J. Gentry, *Edgar Hoover: The Man and His Secrets* (New York: Norton, 1991), 475.
23. Hersh, *Bobby and J. Edgar*, 239–240.
24. North, *Act of Treason*, 65.
25. Heymann, *RFK*, 196–197.
26. Hersh, *Bobby and J. Edgar*, 337.
27. Ibid., 47.
28. Gentry, *J. Edgar Hoover: The Man and his Secrets*, 177.
29. Hersh, *Bobby and J. Edgar*, 69.
30. Ibid., 219.
31. Ibid., 239.
32. Gentry, *J. Edgar Hoover: The Man and his Secrets*, 476.
33. Ibid., 223.
34. Ibid., 232.
35. Ibid.
36. Dudley Clendinen, "J. Edgar Hoover, 'Sex Deviates' and My Godfather." *The New York Times* (November 25, 2011).
37. Ibid.
38. Gentry, *J. Edgar Hoover: The Man and his Secrets*, 468.
39. Kitty Kelley, "The Dark Side of Camelot," *People* 29, no. 8 (February 29, 1988).
40. North, *Act of Treason*, 116.
41. Gentry, *J. Edgar Hoover: The Man and his Secrets*, 479.
42. Goldfarb, *Perfect Villains, Imperfect Heroes*, 26.
43. Ibid., 49.
44. North, *Act of Treason*, 70.
45. Ibid., 485.

CHAPTER SIX

A THOUSAND PIECES

On November 29, 1963, one week after the assassination of John F. Kennedy, family friend Bill Walton was dispatched to Moscow. With him was a secret message from Bobby and Jackie Kennedy to be delivered to their back channel connection, Georgi Bolshakov.[1] Bolshakov, a Russian intelligence officer and member of the KGB (the principal security agency of the Soviet Union), had held a splintery relationship with Bobby during the Kennedy administration. The two met more than a dozen times on various diplomatic issues between the United States and the Soviet Union, and whereas motives and agendas were held with suspicion, a delicate trust and friendship was developed. Once, at Hickory Hill, Bolshakov challenged Bobby to an impromptu arm-wrestling contest.[2]

Walton intimated to Bolshakov that the Kennedys believed the murder of John was part of a wider, homegrown, conspiracy. "Perhaps there was only one assassin, but he did not act alone," Walton said, relaying the message. "Dallas was the ideal location for such a crime."[3]

Walton went on to discuss Bobby's future in politics and how, if, and when the younger Kennedy could get into the White House, the détente with the Soviet Union would continue.

Bolshakov immediately delivered his report to the Soviet military intelligence agency, and it presumably made its way to Soviet Prime Minister Nikita Khrushchev.

To initiate peace talks between the two Cold War governments, John Kennedy and Khrushchev had to go through similar back channels because each had grown increasingly skeptical of his own government's motives and actions.

"They [government officials]," Bobby professed to Bolshakov, might "go to any length."[4]

The difference between the Kennedy administration and the CIA was stark. An incident that involved Bolshakov, the Kennedys, and a member of the agency is revealing.

"One time, Bob wanted to invite Georgi to a party of government officials on board the presidential yacht, the *Sequoia*," recalled James Symington, Bobby's administrative assistant. "But McCone [John McCone, the CIA director] from the CIA said, 'If he gets on the boat, I get off.'"[5]

The CIA attempted to shape John Kennedy's Cold War strategies. When that tactic had failed, the agency formed its own strategy, independent of the president's wishes. With the approval of National Security Council (NSC) 10/2 in 1948 by President Harry Truman's National Security Council, permission was given to the agency to carry out, "propaganda, economic warfare, preventive direct action including sabotage, anti-sabotage, demolition and evacuation measures; subversion against hostile states including assistance to underground resistance movements, guerrillas, and refugee liberation groups."[6]

Secretary of State George Marshall warned President Truman before the act was passed that the command that it endowed the CIA would be "almost limitless."[7] The act expanded the scope of operations that the CIA could carry out and granted the agency autonomy. Operations could now be "so planned and executed that any US government responsibility for them is not evident to unauthorized persons, and that if uncovered, the US government can plausibly deny any responsibility for them."[8]

The CIA was a conspiracy unto itself.

The agency now had permission to enact operations without the consent of any other government branch, carry them out secretly, and deny their existence if discovered.

The plot for CIA-trained exiles to invade Cuba was a program made possible by NSC 10/2. Later named the Bay of Pigs invasion, initial planning for the operation happened throughout 1959. On November 29, 1959, a reluctant Eisenhower gave the program a green light, which he reaffirmed on January 3, 1960.

Shortly before leaving office, Eisenhower had choice words for the Director of Central Intelligence Allen Dulles. "The structure of our intelligence organization is faulty," he said to Dulles. "I have suffered an eight-year defeat on this. Nothing has changed since Pearl Harbor. I leave a 'legacy of ashes' to my successor."[9]

In his farewell speech, the former five-star general would leave his warning to the American people.

"In the councils of government, we must guard against the acquisition of unwarranted influence, whether sought or unsought, by the military-industrial complex. The potential for the disastrous rise of misplaced power exists, and will persist."

As Eisenhower knew, misplaced power had risen and would make a play with the Bay of Pigs invasion.

The mission was already not without its problems. The Cuban exiles, trained in Guatemala, were discontented because they were not informed of the current political news from Cuba or the kind of future they were being trained to fight for in their homeland. Additionally, the quota was not being filled for the number of exiles intended to be trained.[10]

President Kennedy, as requested after he took office, was filled in on the basic concepts of the invasion along with the new Secretary of State Dean Rusk and Secretary of Defense Robert McNamara. The Bay of Pigs invasion was an inherited operation, which would give John Kennedy quick lessons in foreign and domestic policies. The new president knew the scope of the situation. He also understood that the repressive Castro regime in Cuba was a consequence of the United States support of the Batista regime.

"I believe that there is no country in the world, including the African regions, including any and all the countries under colonial domination, where economic colonization, humiliation, and exploitation were worse than in Cuba, in part owing to my country's policies during the Batista regime," Kennedy told French journalist Jean Daniel. "I believe that we created, built, and manufactured the Castro movement out of whole cloth and without realizing it. I believe that the accumulation of these mistakes has jeopardized all of Latin America. The great aim of the Alliance for Progress is to reverse this unfortunate policy. This is one of the most, if not *the most*, important problems in America foreign policy. I can assure you that I have understood the Cubans."[11]

But speaking of the problems Cuba's nuclear aspirations created in the international community, Kennedy was not sure that Cuban dictator Fidel Castro even "realizes this, or even if he cares about it."[12]

In the early hours of April 17, 1961, a force of 1,400 exiles landed on Playa Giron, a beach in southern Cuba. Fidel Castro's forces easily overtook the rebel invasion, killing two hundred and capturing 1,197 when the invading force, stifled by Cuban air forces, were denied sufficient air support and resupplies of ammunition.

"We are out of ammo and fighting on the beach," the rebel brigade commander called out. "Please send help. We cannot hold."[13]

The invasion was over in two days. Initially considered a failure of the Kennedy administration due to reluctance to send air support, it was later revealed that Soviet forces knew about the attack in advance. The CIA was privy to this information, but neglected to inform President Kennedy.

"There was some indication that the Soviets somewhere around the ninth [of April] had gotten the date of the seventeenth," Jacob Esterline, one of the Bay of Pigs invasion key CIA organizers testified later to the Taylor Commission.[14]

Kennedy friend Charles Bartlett also received preemptive word of the invasion through Castro's former Washington lobbyist, Ernesto Betancourt. Betancourt told Bartlett that the CIA was making a mistake and that Castro knew of the plot.

Bartlett decided to relay this important piece of information to Allen Dulles.

"He said, 'Oh, I don't know about this. I'll look into it and give you a call.' So I get a call about five days later, but by then the boats were already going ashore. Dulles was really the wrong guy to tell."[15]

In an internal investigation performed by the CIA, not released until decades after the operation, blame was lifted from the Kennedy administration after it was revealed that the operation had been poorly managed from the start. Of the many problems detailed, a report found that:

- The agency failed to collect adequate information on the strengths of the Castro regime and the extent of the opposition to it. And it failed to evaluate the available information correctly.
- The project was not staffed throughout with top-quality people, and a number of people were not used to the best advantage.
- The agency entered the project without adequate assets in the way of boats, bases, training facilities, agent nets, Spanish speakers, and similar essential ingredients of a successful operation.[16]

The fallout from the failed Bay of Pigs invasion did not just put an early ugly mark on Cuban-US relations in the Kennedy administration—it completely ruined the relationship between the administration and the CIA. Kennedy saw the CIA as warmongers capable of bringing the world to total annihilation, while the CIA saw Kennedy as a wavering, irresolute panderer.

"The [Bay of Pigs invasion] failure was Kennedy's fault," Eduardo Ferrer, leader of the exile air force, would later say. "Kennedy was a little bit immature, a little bit chicken. Today, 90 percent of the Cubans are Republicans because of Kennedy, that motherfucker."[17]

In late April, Bobby was sensing the damage the Bay of Pigs invasion would have on his brother and was more frequently attuned to the circling war hawks. At a National Security Council (NSC) meeting on April 27, Bobby sharply castigated a council report that recommended invading Cuba.

"This is worthless," Bobby said at the meeting. "You people are so anxious to protect your own asses that you're afraid to do anything. All you want to do is dump the whole thing on the president. We'd be better off if you just quit and left foreign policy to someone else."

In the coming months, the Kennedy brothers would listen less and less to their military advisors and more to themselves. John, particularly, saw that his greatest failure in the Bay of Pigs invasion was not bringing his brother in when the serious decisions needed to be made.

Of the CIA, John Kennedy vowed to shatter the agency, "into a thousand pieces and scatter it to the wind." He asked for the resignation of the Bay of Pig planners: Deputy Director General Charles Cabell, Deputy Director Richard Bissell Jr., and Dulles, who, knowing the Soviets discovered the plan, was either looking to start a war, shame a president, or both.

Having dinner with Richard Nixon on the night the invasion fell apart, asking for a drink, Dulles exclaimed, "This is the worst day of my life!"[18]

Nixon was the right man to cry to. He was the man many wanted to win the 1960 presidential election, a strict opponent of communism who would have carried out the tasks of the CIA diligently.

Instead, Kennedy only feigned compliance to the CIA to get elected; the president's adherence to the CIA agenda began and ended with the Bay of Pigs invasion. He would go on to make silent cuts to the CIA budget in 1962 and 1963 and, according to Kennedy historian Arthur Schlesinger, was "aiming at a 20 percent reduction by 1966."[19]

"Nobody is going to force me to do anything I don't think is in the best interest of the country," John said to war pal and Secretary of the Navy Red Fay. "We're not going to plunge into an irresponsible action just because a fanatical fringe in this country puts so-called national pride above national reason."[20]

The new president's moves surprised and angered many powerful people. This head-fake would help cost him his life and give Lyndon Johnson willing co-conspirators.

Not able to trust his own government, Kennedy would turn to an unlikely ally, Nikita Khrushchev, as a secret partner for peace.

John, an effortless charmer, found it difficult to penetrate the steely personality of the Soviet prime minister when they first met at the June 1961 Vienna Summit.

James Douglass paints a bleak picture of the encounter in his book *JFK and the Unspeakable*:

> The summit meeting with Khrushchev had deeply disturbed Kennedy. The revelation of a coming storm occurred at the end of the meeting. As the two men faced each other across a table, Kennedy's gift to Khrushchev, a model of the USS *Constitution*, lay between them. Kennedy pointed out that the ship's cannons had been able to fire half a mile and kill a few people. But if he and Khrushchev failed to negotiate peace, the two of them could kill seventy million people in the opening exchange of a nuclear war. Kennedy looked at Khrushchev, Khrushchev gave him a blank stare, as if to say, "So what?" Kennedy was shocked at what he felt was his counterpart's lack of response. "There was no area of accommodation with him," he said later. Khrushchev may have felt the same way about Kennedy. The result of their unsuccessful meeting would be an ever more threatening conflict. As Evelyn Lincoln thought when she read what the president had written, "'I see a storm coming' was no idle phrase."[21]

It was no surprise that Khrushchev maintained a frigid presence. Kennedy was only five months in office and two months removed from the failed covert invasion of Cuba. To Khrushchev, Kennedy was surely another politicking functionary whose words meant little compared to his actions. Khrushchev had expressed his objections in a letter to the president written a day after the start of the Cuban invasion.

"It is a secret to no one that the armed bands invading this country were trained, equipped, and armed in the United States of America. The planes that are bombing Cuban cities belong to the United States of America, the bombs they are dropping are being supplied by the American government," Khrushchev wrote. "All of this evokes, here in the Soviet Union, an understandable feeling of indignation on the part of the Soviet government and the Soviet people."

In the coming months, the two men would find they were very much alike, held hostage by their own governments' need to pursue a radical agenda in spite of rational understanding. Perhaps this is what spurred Khrushchev to take a risk by initiating the secret correspondence with Kennedy in late September 1961.

Khrushchev no doubt inferred from their confrontation in June that Kennedy might be someone whom he could get through to, noted by his positive impression of Kennedy's "informality, modesty, and frankness, which are not to be found very often in men who occupy such a high position," which Khrushchev commends at the start of the letter.

Bulshakov delivered the letter to White House Press Secretary Pierre Salinger at the Carlyle Hotel in New York with the specific instruction that it was for the president's eyes only. Certainly, the subsequent history of the world might have taken a remarkably different course if those instructions had not been followed.

At times poetic, the letter expressed Khrushchev's regrets for not pursuing a previous understanding and detailed his desire to do so. The letter stressed that neither he nor the people of his country desired war, and that the world might be on a devastating path. Khrushchev also pointed out that peace and disarmament should be human response, not bureaucratic reaction.

"If, Mr. President, you are striving toward that noble goal—and I believe that is the case—if agreement of the United States on the principles of disarmament is not merely a diplomatic or tactical maneuver, you will find complete understanding on our part, and we shall stint no effort in order to find a common language and reach the required agreement together with you."[22]

Khrushchev closed the letter by reaffirming the importance for a joint effort of the two men to work toward peace.

The letter was bold in its scope and sentiment, and Kennedy's mid-October response was thoughtful and conciliatory, yet guarded—in sharp contrast to the intentions of his government. The letter lacked the strong personal conviction and intelligent emotion of his later correspondence, but got the point across.

The exchange helped facilitate a deeper mutual understanding of the nuclear situation. John Kennedy recognized that he and Khrushchev had "a special responsibility—greater than that held by any of our predecessors in the pre-nuclear age—to exercise our power with the fullest possible understanding of the other's vital interests and commitments."[23]

John let down his guard in his second back-channel letter to Khrushchev. He began to show interest in discovering the makeup of Khrushchev in order to identify with the leader and properly assess the perilous situation.

"I am conscious of the difficulties you and I face in establishing full communication between our two minds," Kennedy wrote. "This is not a question of translation but a question of the context in which we hear and respond to what each other has to say. You and I have already recognized that neither of us will convince the other about our respective social systems and general philosophies of life. These differences create a great gulf in communication because language cannot mean the same thing on both sides unless it is related to some underlying common purpose. I cannot believe that there are not such common interests between the Soviet and the American people. Therefore, I am trying to penetrate our ideological differences in order to find some bridge across the gulf on which we could bring our minds together and find some way in which to protect the peace of the world."[24]

Through a year-long secret exchange of letters now known as the "pen pal correspondence," Khrushchev and Kennedy would attempt to understand each other and their respective countries. They examined the turmoil in Vietnam and Laos and their nuclear dilemma, and they tried to move slowly toward a test ban treaty.

Possibly the most important achievement of the correspondence is the letter exchange that took place during the Cuban Missile Crisis in October of 1962.

The Cuban Missile Crisis grew out of heightened tensions between the United States and Cuba following the Bay of Pigs invasion. Through its U2 spy plane program, the United States discovered that Russia and Cuba had begun building missile-launching sites in the island nation only ninety miles off the Florida coast and that missiles were en route on Russian ships. The thirteen-day nuclear standoff that was the result of a US naval blockade would be the closest the world would come to nuclear devastation.

During the crisis, John and Bobby would sort through the rhetoric of their advisors together and come to hard decisions based on the information available. The military advisors were pushing to attack Cuba, none more passionately than cigar-chomping General Curtis "Bombs Away" LeMay, who was, years later, spoofed as fanatical warmonger Jack D. Ripper in Stanley Kubrick's Cold War film parody, *Dr. Strangelove.*

"This is almost as bad as the appeasement at Munich," LeMay charged, attempting to taunt Kennedy into action. "I just don't see any other solution except direct military action right now. . . . A blockade, and political talk, would be considered by a lot of our friends and neutrals as being a pretty weak response to this. And I'm sure a lot of our own citizens would feel that way too. You're in a pretty bad fix, Mr. President."[25] (LeMay had close relationships with two of Lyndon Johnson's inner circle: Dallas oilmen H.

L. Hunt and Col. D. H. Byrd, the founder of the Civil Air Patrol. Robert Caro has written that the Joint Chiefs were later crying at JFK's funeral. If LeMay was crying, it was probably out of sheer happiness because in his beyond-candid oral history with the LBJ Library, he describes the Kennedys as "vulgar," "vindictive," and "ruthless" with [low] "moral standards," who were "cockroaches" who deserved to be stepped on by President Johnson post JFK assassination.)

When Vice President Johnson was asked for his opinion on weighing the options of talking it out with the Soviets or taking military action, Johnson wavered. "All I know is that when I was a boy in Texas, and walking along the road when a rattlesnake reared up, the only thing you could do was take a stick and chop its head off." At another point in the crisis, Johnson would back the idea of a missile swap, removing US missiles from Turkey in exchange for the Russian missiles from Cuba, a compromise that eventually helped end the crisis.[26] But at the peak of the crisis and with the world on the brink of nuclear war, Johnson sided firmly with the warhawks, telling JFK that he had to do something. The Kennedys later excluded LBJ from the meeting during which the final decisions were made.

The disarming of the Cuban Missile Crisis would also be helped by John Kennedy answering one of two letters sent with Khrushchev's name, the first on October 26 and the second on October 27. The former was in the tone of Khrushchev that John had gotten to know well—one of passion, strength, and understanding.

Assuredly, Khrushchev explained, the weapons positioned in Cuba had the same value that an American weapon would have—purely for defense and not to be used against the United States. These weapons were there to protect the people, not to attack another people. Khrushchev explained that the continued military and economic aid that the Russians provided Cuba during that time was only a humanitarian effort to stabilize the country. Most importantly, the message outlined that the aim of Khrushchev was still peace.

"If you are really concerned about the peace and welfare of your people—and this is your responsibility as president—then I, as the Chairman of the Council of Ministers, am concerned for my people," Khrushchev wrote. "Moreover, the preservation of world peace should be our joint concern because if, under contemporary conditions, war should break out, it would be a war not only between the reciprocal claims, but a world-wide cruel and destructive war."[27]

The second letter was written in a sterile fashion, dealing with facts and devoid of the grim, human realities of the situation. Bobby and his advisors determined that it was not written by Khrushchev and counseled the president to only answer the first letter. Had the private letter exchange between Kennedy and Khrushchev not taken place, the first letter might not have been authenticated, and the crisis might have labored on.

The response to Khrushchev's letter made a few suggestions, the most important being a removal of the Soviet missiles from Cuba in exchange for a vow from the United States to not invade the island nation. The letter worked, and a tentative peace agreement was again at hand. Years later, it would be revealed that over forty thousand Soviet troops and 270,000 Cuban troops were prepared for a potential US invasion.[28]

At the time, John Kennedy had told his teenage mistress Mimi Beardsley who was in the White House on the weekend of highest tensions, "I'd rather my children red than dead."

Following the missile crisis, the conversation between the two leaders would continue, and they would advance the cause of peace, most notably with the Limited Test Ban Treaty in August 1963, which banned nuclear weapons testing in the atmosphere, in space, and underwater forever. In July 1963, President Kennedy discussed his proposed treaty in a nationally broadcast radio and television speech.

"But now, for the first time in many years, the path of peace may be open. No one can be certain what the future will bring. No one can say whether the time has come for an easing of the struggle.

But history and our own conscience will judge us harsher if we do not now make every effort to test our hopes by action, and this is the place to begin. According to the ancient Chinese proverb, 'A journey of a thousand miles must begin with a single step.' My fellow Americans, let us take that first step. Let us, if we can, step back from the shadows of war and seek out the way of peace. And if that journey is a thousand miles or even more, let history record that we, in this land, at this time, took the first step."[29]

On November 22, 1963, as President Kennedy's midnight blue limousine worked its way from Love Field Airport to the ambush site of Dealey Plaza, he carried with him a speech he was to give at the Trade Mart in Dallas later that day. The speech would go unread, but the sentiment was one that he had fostered throughout his final months in office.

In that speech, Kennedy would write of a nation of great power and the responsibility that goes with it.

"That strength will never be used in pursuit of aggressive ambitions—it will always be used in pursuit of peace. It will never be used to promote provocations—it will always be used to promote the peaceful settlement of disputes. We in this country, in this generation, are—by destiny rather than choice—the watchmen on the walls of world freedom. We ask, therefore, that we may be worthy of our power and responsibility, that we may exercise our strength with wisdom and restraint, and that we may achieve in our time and for all time the ancient vision of 'peace on earth, good will toward men. That must always be our goal, and the righteousness of our cause must always underlie our strength. For as was written long ago: 'except the Lord keep the city, the watchman waketh but in vain."[30]

In Kennedy's last months, he became his own man with his own deep convictions, but in doing so, he paid the price to powerful men whose interests were threatened by those convictions. Vice President Johnson used this conflict to his advantage in order to bring the CIA into the assassination compact.

In the wake of Kennedy's assassination, Nikita Khrushchev, a man thought by many to be President Kennedy's enemy, was inconsolable.

"He just wandered around his office for several days, like he was in a daze," a Soviet official told Pierre Salinger.[31] Four years later, Russian intelligence (KGB) would conclude that Lyndon Johnson was complicit in the plot to kill Kennedy.[32]

J. Edgar Hoover wrote a memo on December 21, 1966, to President Johnson about this, and he copied the leadership of the FBI, including Deke DeLoach and William Sullivan. This blockbuster memo remained secret for thirty years until it was forced public by a declassification prompted by the Assassination Records Review Board.

The FBI had a spy, an informant denoted as "NY 3653-S," in the KGB residency in New York City. This informant told the FBI in September of 1965 of an important telegram from the head of the KGB, Vladimir Semichastny, to the KGB NYC residency. Here is how Hoover described it:

> On September 16, 1965, this same source reported that the KGB Residency in New York City received instructions on approximately September 16, 1965, from KGB headquarters in Moscow to develop all possible information concerning President Lyndon B. Johnson's character, background, personal friends, family, and from which quarters he derives his support in his position as president of the United States. Our source added that in the instructions from Moscow, it was indicated that 'now' the KGB was in possession of data purporting to indicate President Johnson was responsible for the assassination of the late President John F. Kennedy.

The first JFK assassination researchers were the Russians and the Cubans. They had a sharp interest in finding out who killed him because they were in grave danger of being framed for the heinous crime both by Lyndon Johnson and US intelligence. In fact, as a diversionary tactic, LBJ told many opinion makers behind the scenes that Fidel Castro had murdered John Kennedy.

Two days before the assassination, Castro was entertaining Jean Daniel, a journalist sent by Kennedy to open a channel of dialogue between the Cuban dictator and himself.

"Suddenly, a president arrives on the scene who tries to support the interests of another class (which has no access to any of the levers of power) to give the various Latin American countries the impression that the United States no longer stands behind the dictators, and so there is no more need to start Castro-type revolutions," Castro said to Daniel. "What happens then? The trusts see that their interests are being a little compromised (just barely, but still compromised); the Pentagon thinks the strategic bases are in danger; the powerful oligarchies in all the Latin American countries alert their American friends; they sabotage the new policy; and in short, Kennedy has everyone against him."[33]

Two days later, Kennedy was assassinated. "This is bad news,"[34] Castro repeated three times when he got the news. "Everything is changed,"[35] Castro announced upon confirmation of the president's death.

On Saturday, the day after the murder of JFK, Castro gave a speech entitled "Concerning the Facts and Consequences of the Tragic Death of President John F. Kennedy" in which he did a fine job of deconstructing the assassination in real time. Castro knew that Cuba was in grave danger of being framed for the crime. And, in fact, that was exactly the line that Lyndon Johnson was pushing behind the scenes with key players whom he needed to manipulate. Castro also correctly surmised that internal American foreign policy divisions played a key role in the JFK assassination.

On December 22, 1963, a month to the day after President Kennedy was assassinated, former President Harry Truman, who as president had signed over enormous power to the CIA, would write an op-ed piece for the *Washington Post* revealing his misgivings concerning the agency. The column outlined Truman's original intent for the CIA as a source for reliable, unfiltered information for the president, and then admonished the agency for working with contrary intent.

"We have grown up as a nation, respected for our free institutions and for our ability to maintain a free and open society," Truman wrote. "There is something about the way the CIA has been functioning that is casting a shadow over our historic position, and I feel that we need to correct it."[36]

Presidential advisor Clark Clifford, when testifying before the Church Commission about the abuses of the CIA in 1975, talked about how expansive the agency had gotten during the Kennedy administration, due in part to the growing conflicts abroad.

"I would hope that possibly, we might be in the posture as time goes on of being able to take the position that the world is in such shape that we are cutting back in intelligence expenditures," Clifford said. "Hopefully détente with the Soviet Union, and possibly Red China, might progress to the point that possibly we could take a public position in that regard."[37]

The CIA did not want peace any more than they wanted a rogue president who would attempt to slowly dismantle the agency. At one point, John said he should have put Bobby at the helm of the CIA instead of the Justice Department. The assignment would have proved effective in reining in the agency, might have prevented the corrupted alliance of the CIA and the Mafia, and could have stopped Vice President Lyndon Johnson from using the services of both on November 22, 1963.

In addition to the KGB who concluded this by 1965, there is yet another high-level political player who came to the eventual conclusion that LBJ was behind the JFK assassination: Senator Barry Goldwater of Arizona, who had opposed Johnson in the 1964 presidential race. In an interview conducted in 2012 at the Dallas JFK Lancer conference, Jeffrey Hoff told of the time that he met Senator Barry Goldwater at a Republican political picnic in Willcox in Cochise County, Arizona, in October, 1973. Hoff had been invited to the GOP picnic by a friend, Louise Parker, who was a "real estate lady" from a prominent Arizona "pioneer" family. She asked Hoff if he wanted to meet Barry Goldwater, and he said yes.

Upon meeting Goldwater, Hoff, who had a keen interest in the JFK assassination, brought up the topic. Goldwater told him that he was convinced that Lyndon Johnson was behind it, and that the Warren Commission was a total cover up. When asked how confident Goldwater was when he was making these statements, Hoff replied Goldwater was "very comfortable" with his belief that LBJ was behind the JFK assassination.

NOTES

1. Talbot, *Brothers*, 30.
2. Evan Thomas, *Robert Kennedy: His Life* (New York: Simon & Schuster, 2000), 179–180.
3. Talbot, *Brothers*, 32.
4. Thomas, *Robert Kennedy*, 208.
5. Talbot, *Brothers*, 31.
6. James W. Douglass, *JFK and the Unspeakable: Why He Died and Why It Matters* (New York: Touchstone, 2008), 33.
7. Ibid.
8. Ibid.
9. Peter Janney, *Mary's Mosaic: The CIA Conspiracy to Murder John F. Kennedy, Mary Pinchot Meyer, and Their Vision for World Peace* (New York: Skyhorse Publishing, 2012), 232.
10. "Inspector General's Survey of the Cuban Operation and Associated Documents," *The George Washington University* 1997, gwu.edu/~nsarchiv/NSAEBB/NSAEBB341/IGrpt1.pdf, 1:22.
11. Jean Daniel, "Unofficial Envoy: An Historic Report from Two Capitals," *The New Republic* (December 14, 1963): 15–20.
12. Ibid.
13. Inspector General's Survey, 1:32.
14. Vernon Loeb, "Soviets Knew Date of Cuba Attack," *The Washington Post* (April 29, 2000).
15. Talbot, *Brothers*, 48.
16. Inspector General's Survey, 1:144.

17. Talbot, *Brothers*, 50.
18. Ibid., 49.
19. Douglass, *JFK and the Unspeakable*, 16.
20. Talbot, *Brothers*, 51.
21. Douglass, *JFK and the Unspeakable*, 12.
22. http://history.state.gov/historicaldocuments/frus1961-63v07/d76.
23. http://history.state.gov/historicaldocuments/frus1961-63v06/d22.
24. Ibid.
25. "Kennedy Assassination Chronicles, vol. 3, no. 3, Current Section: Cuban Missile Crisis: 35 Years Ago JFK on Tape." *Mary Ferrell Foundation* (April–May, 2012), maryferrell.org/mffweb/archive/viewer/showDoc.do?absPageId=222680, 450.
26. Shesol, *Mutual Contempt*, 96–97.
27. http://history.state.gov/historicaldocuments/frus1961-63v06/d65.
28. Dan Fisher, "U.S. Far Off on Troop Estimates in Cuba Crisis," *Los Angeles Times* (January 30, 1989).
29. "Radio and Television Address to the American People on the Nuclear Test Ban Treaty, July 26, 1963," John F. Kennedy Presidential Library & Museum (March–April, 2012), jfklibrary.org/Research/Ready-Reference/JFK-Speeches/Radio-and-Television-Address-to-the-American-People-on-the-Nuclear-Test-Ban-Treaty-July-26-1963.aspx.
30. "Remarks Prepared for Delivery at the Trade Mart in Dallas, November 22, 1963," John F. Kennedy Presidential Library & Museum (March–April, 2012), jfklibrary.org/Research/Ready-Reference/JFK-Speeches/Remarks-Prepared-for-Delivery-at-the-Trade-Mart-in-Dallas-November-22-1963.aspx.
31. Talbot, *Brothers*, 33.
32. "Document Tells Soviet Theory on JFK Death," *Los Angeles Times* (Sept. 18, 1996).
33. Daniel, *Unofficial Envoy*, 15–30.
34. Talbot, *Brothers*, 252.
35. Ibid., 253.
36. *Washington Post* (December 22, 1963).
37. Testimony of Clark Clifford, April 16, 1975.

CHAPTER SEVEN

MOB BOYS

In advance of the 1960 West Virginia primary, the easily recognizable voice of Frank Sinatra echoed in barrooms throughout the state. The lyrics sounded familiar as well, albeit tweaked to promote his candidate for president:

> *K-E-DOUBLE-N-E-D-Y*
> *Jack's the nation's favorite guy*
> *Everyone wants to back Jack*
> *Jack is on the right track*
> *'Cause he's got high hopes*
> *He's got high hopes*
> *1960's the year for his high hopes*
> *Come on and vote for Kennedy*
> *Vote for Kennedy*
> *Keep America strong*

The original version of the song "High Hopes" was written by lyricist Sammy Cahn for the 1959 Frank Sinatra movie vehicle *A Hole in the Head*. The revamped version, written as the Kennedy campaign song, was put on repeat and drummed into the heads of the West Virginia voting public.

"Jesus, we even had to muscle the taverns to convince 'em to play Frank's song *High Hopes* on the jukeboxes," said Mooney

Giancana. "Those hillbillies hate the idea of an East Coast Irish Catholic President."

The reworded tune was one of the Sinatra's contributions to the Kennedy campaign, but his most important job was to sway Giancana's opinion on the sincerity of Joe Sr.

During the campaign, Frank's words were held as bond. Even with Bobby, who had ruthlessly prosecuted mobsters on the McClellan Committee, the assurances of Sinatra and Joe Sr. were taken seriously by Giancana and the Chicago mob.

"There was also trepidation about backing JFK because of Bobby," said George Brady, the godson of Murray "The Camel" Humphreys, a Giancana financial advisor who was thought by some to have pulled the strings of the Chicago mobster. "But on the positive side, Frank [Sinatra] talked him up."[1]

People don't see the real influence in American politics of outside groups like the mob. In the late 1950s, J. Edgar Hoover insisted that domestic communism was the largest single threat to America. To him, organized crime simply did not exist.

Richard Nixon told me that the extent of the mob's involvement in the 1960 election—on both sides—has never really been fully reported. Joe Sr. had a longtime association with New York's urbane gangster Frank Costello, and their bootlegging business proved problematic. Costello and the New York boys had long ties to Nixon and funneled money to his 1946 congressional race and his 1950 Senate election, as syndicated columnist Drew Pearson reported on Oct 31, 1968 in his "Washington Merry-Go-Round" column. Joe Kennedy was forced to go to the Chicago mob through Johnny Rosselli, the Chicago hood. Kennedy also utilized Frank Sinatra to reach out to Chicago mobsters Giancana, Humphreys, Joe Accardo, Jack Avery, and Jake "Greasy-Thumb" Gruzik. In turn, they enlisted New Orleans mob's kingpin Carlos Marcello and Florida's Santo Trafficante. For Joe, who would do anything to secure important votes for his son, Giancana was certainly the man to see.

"Giancana rules the First Ward like a Tartan warlord," wrote reporter Sandy Smith. "He can brush an alderman off the city council with a gesture of his hand—as he did in 1962."[2]

"I think you can help me in West Virginia and Illinois with our friends," Joe Kennedy told Sinatra. "You understand, Frank, I can't go. They're my friends, too, but I can't approach them. But you can."[3]

There is also evidence that the elder Kennedy sought out and convened with Giancana in person. Sinatra was sent ahead, playing the part of cheerleader, extolling the virtues of Kennedy before Joe Sr. went to Mooney to complete the deal.

Joe Kennedy, one of the most successful bootleggers of his era, was known as a rat—his word was not to be trusted. Frank Sinatra was the comeback kid. The singer had begun the 1950s as a falling star, but finished the decade as the top recording artist in the world with an Academy Award. The comeback would be due in no small part to Giancana's associate Johnny Rosselli. When Sinatra bottomed out, Rosselli—so close to Columbia Pictures president Harry Cohn that they wore matching rings[4]—petitioned to deliver Sinatra the role of tough-talking Private Angelo Maggio in Cohn's Pearl Harbor military drama *From Here to Eternity*. The negotiation was later fictionalized with characters Jack Woltz (Cohn), Tom Hagen (Rosselli), and Johnny Fontane (Sinatra) in *The Godfather*.

"The Maggio role, Sinatra wasn't going to get it," said Rosselli associate Joe Seide. "He got it through New York friends, and John Rosselli was the go-between. Johnny was the one who talked to Harry—he was the one who laid it out. That was serious business. It was in the form of look, you do this for me and maybe we won't do this to you. There was none of that stuff about a horse's head, but a lot of 'juice' was directed."[5]

Rosselli was similar to Sinatra in his ties to both legitimate and criminal enterprise. Rosselli, though, with wide knowledge of Joe Sr.'s ruthlessness, was not the man to make a Kennedy pitch to Giancana.

In contrast, Sinatra, who was close to Giancana, was the ideal pitchman to promote the Kennedy image. He would sell the promises of the father to the Mafia much in the way that Joe Sr. would market John to the American public, "like soap flakes." Sinatra figured himself an inside man for the Kennedy family. But it wouldn't be long before the singer, having done the old man's bidding, would be pushed out of Camelot.

"He's got big ideas, Frank does, about being ambassador or something," Rosselli would later tell Giancana. "You know Pierre Salinger and them guys, they don't want him. They treat him like a whore. You fuck them, you pay them, and then they're through."[6]

Kennedy collected sizable contributions from all but Giancana's man Humphreys, a Republican who said Joe Kennedy was "full of shit" and pointed out how Bobby Kennedy had harassed the mob as counsel to the Senate's McClellan hearings on labor racketeering. Instead, Murray "The Camel" sent $100,000 to Nixon while the Midwestern and Southwestern families (with some kicked in from the Bonannos in New York) gave more than a million to Kennedy and pledged their army of enforcers to deliver votes for the ticket.

Mob activity for Kennedy on Election Day would have made the "Duke of Duval" George Parr proud. It included nonexistent voters voting, registered voters being denied the right to vote, and manipulation of the count. Poll watchers for Nixon provided Polaroid photographs of money changing hands for votes outside of polling places. Voters were intimidated and, in many cases, threatened. Bones were broken.

There is no doubt that Sam Giancana and the Chicago outfit stole Chicago for JFK. Giancana later said, "if it weren't for me, Kennedy wouldn't even be in the White House."

But the mob played heavily on both sides.

In his ground-breaking book *Bobby and J. Edgar*, Burton Hersh wrote that Jimmy Hoffa and the Teamsters gave Nixon $1 million while the Eastern mob chieftains like Frank Costello and Meyer Lansky rounded up another million for the Nixon cause.

Richard Nixon had his own arms-length relationship with the mob. Hollywood gangster Mickey Cohen, who was Meyer Lansky's top lieutenant on the West Coast, had funneled money to Nixon's 1946 congressional campaign through Myford Irvine, whose ranch was a big agribusiness in Orange County. He did it again in Nixon's successful bid for the Senate in 1950.

Nixon campaign manager and mob lawyer Murray Chotiner, whose law firm had defended a number of Cohen's underlings for illegal bookmaking, asked Cohen to raise funds for Nixon's 1950 effort.

Cohen convened a meeting at the Knickerbocker Hotel on North Ivar Avenue in Hollywood. He invited several hundred associates from the gambling business; (some flew in from Las Vegas). Cohen later said, "there wasn't a legitimate person in the room." Attending were representatives of Meyer Lansky, Los Angeles mobster Jack Dragna, and representatives of the Cleveland mob including John Scalish and Jewish mobster Bill Presser. Presser's son Jackie would parlay his relationship with Ronald Reagan into the presidency of the International Brotherhood of Teamsters.

Cohen later wrote that the goal for the evening was $75,000 for Nixon's coffers from his crime and gambling associates, and that he ordered the doors locked when the group came up $20,000 short, refusing to let anyone leave until the financial goal was met.

Nixon had met with Cohen as early as 1946 at Goodfellow's Grotto, a fish restaurant in Orange County where the booths were private, and politics could be talked frankly.

Cohen made it clear that the orders to help Nixon in 1950 came from "back East," meaning New York boss Frank Costello and Meyer Lansky, both leaders of the national syndicate.

Ironically, Joe Kennedy Sr., a great friend of Senator Joe McCarthy's and generally distrustful of liberals (even though he had funneled money to presidential candidate Adlai Stevenson through Chicago mobster Jake Arvey), sent $25,000 in cash to Nixon in the same campaign that the Lansky associates funded.

Later, when Cohen was in prison in 1962, Democratic lawyers took a sworn statement from him about his longtime support for Nixon and the thousands of dollars he had raised from his gangland associates. Democrats hoped to leak the affidavit from Cohen to damage Nixon just before the 1962 election for governor of California, in which the former vice president was running against incumbent Democrat Governor Edmund G. "Pat" Brown. Although Cohen's extensive revelations were never leaked, Nixon lost that election when the Cuban missile crisis overshadowed the closing weeks of the campaign—voters rallied behind President Kennedy and swamped Nixon at the polls by more than five percent.

It's unclear if Attorney General Robert Kennedy would have continued his crusade against organized crime if his overbearing father, who had made the original deals with the mob, had not been felled by the debilitating stroke. Clearly, the Chicago boys felt they had bought protection through the hundreds of thousands of dollars (millions in today's dollars) that they had passed to the Kennedy-Johnson campaign and the foot soldiers they had supplied in West Virginia and Wisconsin in the 1960 primaries and in Chicago during the 1960 general election.

Joe Sr. and Giancana met first at Giancana's headquarters in Forest Park, a suburb of Chicago, prior to the primaries and came up with the initial blueprint for capturing the presidency.

"I later heard that Joe Kennedy was asking Mooney and [ward committeeman Pat] Marcy what help they could bring to the election of his son," said Rob McDonnell, an attorney who was on hand for the legendary meeting. "He was obsessed with the election of John Kennedy, absolutely obsessed with it. And I don't know what deals were cut. I don't know what promises were made."[7]

One of the guarantees alleged to have been lined up was the allowance of exiled mobster Joe Adonis to return to the United States. Adonis, a New York mobster close with Charles "Lucky" Luciano, had been deported in 1953 on the charge that he was not a legal citizen.

Joe Kennedy allegedly made another trade-off to assure commitment to his word and ceded a portion of his Cal-Neva resort to Giancana's associates. The resort sat on the California–Nevada border, and in the time before gambling was legal in Nevada, unauthorized games poached by the authorities were pushed across the room and across the border, away from the arm of the law.

Joe Sr.'s portion of the resort was purportedly fronted by Bert "Wingy" Grober.

"Wingy was old Joe's man there," a local recollected in Gus Russo's Chicago mob narrative *The Outfit*, "and he looked after his stake in the joint."[8]

A revealing FBI memo relating the dubious arrangement between Joe Sr. and Giancana was sent to Bobby, the attorney general in 1962:

> Before the last presidential election, Joseph P. Kennedy (the father of President John F. Kennedy) had been visited by many gangsters with gambling interests and a deal was made which resulted in Peter Lawford, Frank Sinatra, Dean Martin and others obtaining a lucrative gambling establishment, the Cal-Neva Hotel, at Lake Tahoe. These gangsters reportedly met with Joseph Kennedy at the Cal-Neva, where Kennedy was staying at the time."[9]

The details of the Cal-Neva arrangement are hazy. It is certain that Sinatra, his manager Hank Sanicola, fellow crooner Dean Martin, and Atlantic City gangster Skinny D'Amato purchased an almost 57-percent majority interest in the resort. John Kennedy had won the Democratic nomination on the day that general particulars of the deal were disclosed, July 13, 1960.

Dean Martin, performing at the Sands that night, briefly silenced the crowd with a revealing joke. "I'd like to tell you some of the *good* things the Mafia is doing,"[10] Dino quipped.

In Giancana's mind, the Kennedys would follow through on their assurances. To him, surely the elder Kennedy, a robber baron with strong ties to the mob, was no different from anyone else in the underworld. There was a code to the Mafia, and certainly Joe Kennedy knew the importance of honoring a pact with someone like Giancana.

"The flower may look different . . . but the roots are the same," Giancana said to his brother. "Never be misled by appearances, Chuck. Once a crook, always a crook. The Kennedys may put on airs and pretend to be blue bloods, but they know and I know the real truth . . . we're cut from the same cloth."[11]

Giancana had been blinded by the assurances of Sinatra, his slender *paisan* from Hoboken, that Kennedy was in his pocket, and Mooney crowed about it to anybody who would listen. Giancana, whose father made his money by selling goods out of a cart, which he pushed through the streets of Chicago's Little Italy, had made it to the top of the Mafia in the city, and now he believed he could own the presidency. Giancana worked hard to deliver Illinois to John Kennedy. In an effort that would have made Honey Fitz proud, Mooney swung the Mafia-controlled wards in Chicago Jack's way at an 8 to 20 percent margin.[12]

"Sam Giancana was always talking about the Kennedys. . . . It was clear that at some point he had met both brothers . . . [Lawford and Giancana] would talk fondly of their shenanigans with the first famiily. . . . they used to talk about the girls Mooney used to produce for the Kennedys. Mooney was proud of it, very proud of his Kennedy connections."[13]

Mooney had not only bought into the promises of the Kennedys, but also into the lifestyle. Sinatra was the perfect broker for such an influence. His career had benefited through associations with the Mafia, and his friendship with Peter Lawford, the brother-in-law of John Kennedy, had bolstered his relationship with the would-be president.

Those who worked for him began to worry about Giancana—stars were clouding the mobster's business sense. Giancana raised his own profile, feasting when he should have been fighting, talking when he should have kept quiet, even when things began to go south quickly with the Kennedys.

"Don't play around with the newspapers," Humphreys told Mooney. "Just stand in the background. That's what I would do, Moe. You stay in the background."[14]

A snapshot of how much Giancana's savvy had gone awry is revealed with the weekend at Cal-Neva he spent with Rosselli, Sinatra, Lawford, and Marilyn Monroe, shortly before the actress's untimely death in 1962. Kennedy had already been president for a year and a half, and the heat was on organized crime. Giancana, while not ignoring the increased assault on the Mafia, also could not resist the celebrity. The story of the weekend of July 27–29, 1963 has been retold many times.

"I developed the film, and some of the pictures, about nine frames, showing Marilyn, on all fours," said photographer William Woodfield. "She looked sick. Astride her, either riding her like a horse or trying to help her up—I couldn't make out which—was Sam Giancana. Frank asked me what I thought he should do with the pictures. I said I'd burn them. He took out his lighter, burned them, and that was the end of it."[15]

Monroe had been distressed because Bobby Kennedy, whom she was involved with at the time, stood her up. He had arranged to meet her at Cal-Neva that weekend, but when the attorney general canceled, Frank and Sam stepped in.

"I was there at the Cal-Neva in '62, when Peter and Frank were there with Monroe," said member of the Genovese crime family Vincent "Jimmy Blue Eyes" Alo. "They kept her drugged every night. It was disgusting."

Monroe was a diversion for the mob. "Because Johnny Rosselli was there that weekend, there was talk of an S&M Mafia orgy to teach Marilyn a lesson for bestowing her famous favors on the

Kennedys," recalled Sinatra valet, George Jacobs. "She was *their* girl, not those Micks'."[16]

The Kennedys could not be controlled as easily. Bobby had no intention of honoring any deals that his father had made, and neither did John. This was shown from the outset of the Kennedy administration—the ties that had been formed with organized crime before the election were promptly cut. Sinatra had done too good a job of talking up the words of the father. Now that Bobby was attorney general, he put all efforts behind expiating the sins of his father by destroying the Mafia.

"Bobby pushed to get Giancana at any cost," said Justice Department attorney Bill Hundley.

The Kennedys did not honor the promise to allow Joe Adonis back into the United States. Adonis would die in Italy, and the attorney general would attempt to deport other mobsters in the United States under illegal status. All bets were off, and it looked bad for the popular crooner.

"Sinatra was an idiot for playing both sides of the field like that," said Skinny D'Amato. "Playing Mooney for a sucker? What? Are you kidding me? If he wasn't so fucking talented, he never would've gotten away with being such a fink. With the boys, when you let 'em down, you got hit . . . and lie to Sam? Forget it. I can't think of anyone else who would've continued to breathe air after telling a story like the one Frank told to Sam."[17]

Sinatra attempted to keep the Kennedys to their word at the end of the election, but to no avail. In a taped conversation between Giancana and henchman John Formosa, Formosa revealed a bit of what Sinatra had told him: "I took Sam's name and wrote it down and told Bob Kennedy, 'This is my buddy, and this is what I want you to know, Bob.'"[18]

It was not long until Sinatra, having done his part, was cut off from the first family.

"The [Kennedys] used him [Sinatra] to help them raise money," said mobster Vinnie Teresa, overheard on an FBI tap. "Then they turn around and say that they're great fighters against corruption. They criticize other people for being with mob guys. They're hypocrites."[19]

Frank would begin to pay back Giancana with his talent and his friends. He and his Rat Pack cohorts would play free shows in venues owned by Giancana. Still, for a while Giancana's "friends" considered exterminating Sinatra for the embarrassment that the singer had caused the mob boss.

"Well, one minute he [Sinatra] tells me this, and then he tells me that," Giancana was overheard telling Rosselli on an FBI recording, "and then the last time I talked to him was at the hotel down in Florida a month before he left, and he said, 'Don't worry about it, if I can't talk to the old man [Joe Sr.], I'm going to talk to the man [President Kennedy].' One minute he says he's talked to Robert, and the next minute, he says he hasn't talked to him. So he never did talk to him. It's a lot of shit. Why lie to me? I haven't got that coming."[20]

Giancana's soft spot for Frank had shown earlier when he had listened to and believed Sinatra regarding the Kennedys' promises—and it would show again when Giancana would call off a contracted hit against the crooner.

"[One night] I'm fucking Phyllis [McGuire]," Giancana recalled, "playing Sinatra songs in the background, and the whole time I'm thinking to myself, 'Christ, how can I silence that voice? It's the most beautiful sound in the world.' Frank's lucky he got it. It saved his life."[21]

Following the election, Giancana was left with promises never to be honored and a loss of respect from those around him.

"Everybody was sorry they got involved in it," wrote Murray Humphreys' wife, Jeanne. "And it all fell back on Mooney. Giancana lost face, and that's when he started going downhill."[22]

This left Giancana with two options: attempt to secure his bet or shut the casino down. Giancana, through two methods, would pursue both options. The first method, in an attempt to get the Kennedys to respect the pact they agreed to, was blackmail. In a method not dissimilar to Hoover's, Mooney collected all the sleazy details that he could on the brothers as a means to rein them in.

"I know all about the Kennedys," Giancana angrily told the FBI early in the administration as the tide began to turn against him, "and one of these days . . . [I am] going to tell all."[23]

To turn the house in his favor, Giancana had, before the election, turned to a man who controlled the inner workings of casinos: his man in Las Vegas, Johnny Rosselli. Rosselli had moved out to Vegas in the early 1950s to look after Mafia interests in the casinos after having served prison time for his extortion of motion picture studios. Before long, if approval was to be granted or something needed to be done in Vegas, Rosselli was the man to see. He arranged the finances for the building and expansion of casinos and also handled the talent that performed within.[24] He also "set up protection for the Sands, the Tropicana, and the Riviera hotels."[25]

It is no coincidence that Jack Kennedy attended a Sinatra concert in February 1960. It is also no coincidence that he met Judy Campbell there. Before Sinatra, Giancana, and Kennedy had their turns with Campbell, she had been a friend and intimate companion of Rosselli.

"Johnny knew Judy Campbell when she was just a kid," said Madeline O'Donnell, niece to Warner Brothers producer Brynie Foy. "Her first husband was Bill Campbell, and Bill Campbell was under contract to Warner Brothers, and they were very young, and they lived in the same neighborhood [as Rosselli]."[26]

Giancana would later take Campbell in as a lover, and she would become his main route of blackmail regarding John Kennedy. Through Campbell, Giancana felt he had all the leverage he needed to get the Kennedys to listen. They didn't.

With the Kennedy blackmail ineffective, Giancana, along with Johnny Rosselli and Santo Trafficante, found members of the government who would be willing to use the Mafia members in their clandestine affairs, including the attempted assassination of a world leader, Fidel Castro.

Giancana, with an unrewarded hand played out in the election of John F. Kennedy, was particularly interested in the replacement of the president with a man who would better honor underworld promises. Working with the CIA put them in contact with that man—the Vice President Lyndon Baines Johnson.

Jeanne Humphreys, wife of Murray "The Camel," reflecting on the Mafia's strong influence in the 1960 election, wrote that "Nixon would have been elected. No assassinations, no Watergate, and most important to the outfit, no Bobby Kennedy as attorney general. The history of the United States from 1960 'til eternity was made by a mobster from Chicago's West Side who wanted to impress a crooner from New Jersey."[27]

NOTES

1. Russo, *The Outfit*, 373.
2. Hersh, *Bobby and J. Edgar*, 299.
3. Ibid., 193.
4. Rappleye and Becker, *All American Mafioso: The Johnny Rosselli Story*, 59.
5. Ibid., 133.
6. Rappleye and Becker, *All American Mafioso: The Johnny Rosselli Story*, 253.
7. Russo, *The Outfit*, 371.
8. Ibid., 377.
9. Ibid.
10. Nick Tosches. *Dino: Living High in the Dirty Business of Dreams* (New York: Doubleday, 1992), 329.
11. Sam Giancana and Chuck Giancana, *Double Cross*. (New York: Warner, 1993), 373.
12. Becker, *The Johnny Rosselli Story: All American Mafioso*, 206.
13. Russo, *The Outfit*, 387.
14. Ibid., 415.
15. Jay Margolis, *Marilyn Monroe: A Case for Murder*. (Bloomington: iUniverse, 2011), 102.
16. Ibid., 102.

17. Russo, *The Outfit*, 423.
18. Goldfarb, *Perfect Villains, Imperfect Heroes*, 137.
19. James W. Hilty, *Robert Kennedy: Brother Protector*. (Philadelphia: Temple University Press, 1997), 208.
20. Rappleye and Becker, *All American Mafioso: The Johnny Rosselli Story*, 234.
21. Russo, *The Outfit*, 423.
22. Ibid., 407.
23. North, *Act of Treason*, 100.
24. Becker, *All American Mafioso: The Johnny Rosselli Story*, 169.
25. Ibid., 167.
26. Becker, *All American Mafioso: The Johnny Rosselli Story*, 208.
27. Russo, *The Outfit*, 403.

CHAPTER EIGHT

CONTACT

In Johnny Rosselli's final interview, Jack Anderson of the *Washington Post* heard a lot about the Kennedy assassination. The key bit of information in Anderson's article was that the Mafia had ordered Jack Ruby's slaying of Oswald.[1] Rosselli had been leaking anonymous confidences to Anderson for some time. Perhaps Rosselli, at seventy-one, felt he had outlived a traditional mob death, or that he was immune to it. Perhaps Rosselli was past the point of giving a damn. He had already testified before the US Senate Select Committee on Intelligence twice the year before concerning his role working with the CIA and was approached about testifying again in the summer of 1976.

Across the years, Rosselli revealed some tightly concealed secrets. He threw hints about the conspirators of the Kennedy assassination lazily into the breeze. There were many accounts of his own involvement. When imprisoned with Joe Bonanno at Terminal Island in the early 1970s, Rosselli told an outlandish story concerning his role in the Dallas ambush.

> "Sam [Giancana] and I both knew I was going to be the one to make the hit," Rosselli said in Bonanno's account. "I had the best chance. My position is in the storm drain on Elm Street, facing the route of the motorcade. The car'll be ten feet from me. There were four of us including the patsy, but Sam and everyone else knew I

was the one who'd have the shot. We had this safe house where all of us got together before two different times. Sam wants to make sure I understand what to do afterward. I even did a dry run the day before. Three blocks to the Trinity River, car was right there. But then it wasn't, Bill. There was no fucking car. I'm standing there on these iron rungs, I watch the cars make the turn, see the guy's head maybe ten feet away. How could I miss, ya know? I don't miss. I saw his head go up. And I'm thinking all the while I'm going like a rat through that tunnel, I was so close, they saw the flash of the muzzle. I'm never gonna make it. My heart's going like a cannon. And then, there's no fucking backup![2]

Perhaps the story was meant to trumpet disinformation or was simply a Rosselli flight of fancy. Either way, it was too close to the truth.

In July 1976, Rosselli had dinner with Tampa mob boss Santo Trafficante at The Landings, a restaurant in Ft. Lauderdale.[3] It is anyone's guess what the two old friends talked about, but more than likely, Trafficante laid the hammer down. Two days later, Rosselli went missing. On August 7, a fifty-five-gallon oil drum was discovered in Dumfounding Bay off the shores of Miami. The drum, punched with holes and weighted down by chains, contained the body of Rosselli. He had been sawed in half and stuffed inside. The drum had become buoyant, filled with gases from the decomposing body.

Rosselli's 1975 Chevy Impala was subsequently found by his brother-in-law, parked at the Miami International Airport.[4] The killers, believing Rosselli's body would never be found, clearly wanted investigators to think that the aging mobster had taken a long trip.

From his early days lugging crates of booze ashore for Joe Sr., Rosselli had spent his life with the Kennedys always close by. Rosselli had rubbed shoulders with the Rat Pack and Marilyn Monroe, all of whom had stood at the gates of Camelot, and he had conspired with the Mafia and the CIA to bust the gates open. Rosselli perpetually hovered between the pinnacle of glamour and the dirt stuck just under the nail. In the end, he was a little too close to all of it.

A year earlier, Rosselli's Mafia and CIA counterpart Sam Giancana went in similar gangland fashion. On the night of June 19, 1975, Giancana was frying sausages in the basement kitchen of his Oak Park, Illinois home. The next day, he was scheduled to meet with US Senate Select Committee members for questioning. Mooney would not make the appointment. Seven rounds from a .22-caliber handgun were fired into the back of his head. The bullets had ripped through Giancana's throat and mouth, which indicated to organized crime lawyer Frank Ragano that the hit had been mob related: The bullets through the throat signified that Giancana had been talking, the bullets through the mouth that he would never talk again.[5]

The handgun was discovered on the side of the road in a nearby suburb. Investigators traced it back to the Miami area, the home of Trafficante and Rosselli. The manufacturer had delivered the weapon to a gun dealer in Miami on June 20, 1965.[6]

Cars from law enforcement agencies that were eternally monitoring the Giancana residence were conspicuously absent at the time of the murder.

"There were cars from the FBI, CIA, and Oak Park Police Department that were always in front of our house, somewhat guarding but watching our home in Oak Park," wrote Antoinette Giancana, daughter of the Chicago mob boss. "On their breaks, only one car at a time would leave, return, and then another car would leave. This staggering arrangement had been going on for months. Joe, the caretaker, told us he saw all three of the cars leave the family property, all at one time on the night of the murder. I believe they were ordered off the property. My father's killer would have entered the house at the basement level, and that basement door was never locked. Just after the three cars had left the property, my father was shot seven times. Not once but seven times. They really wanted to make sure he was dead. Joe went down to see if my father was all right and discovered his body with blood all over the kitchen and made the call to the Oak Park Police Department. Then and only then did all three cars reappear. These three cars all leaving just before my father's killing and all three returning after his death has to be more than a coincidence."[7]

Decades later, Giancana's brother Chuck and nephew Sam would release a book *Double Cross*, which tied "Momo's" complicity in the Kennedy hit more tightly:

"Hey," Mooney said sharply. He leaned forward and knotted his hands into two tight fists. "Forget about the fuckin' G-men. . . . I'm talkin' CIA. They're different. Like night and day. We've been partners on more deals than I have time to tell you about. You should know that by now, for Christ's sake."

"I guess I'll never understand, huh?" Chuck challenged, irritated by Mooney's cavalier know-it-all attitude.

Glowering, Mooney stood up from his chair, cigar in hand, and marched across the room. When he reached Chuck, he lowered his voice and hissed, "Maybe this will help." He fixed Chuck in a steely, impenetrable gaze. "We took care of Kennedy . . . together." He lifted his cigar to his lips and a cruel smile curled like an embrace around it.[8]

The collaboration between the mob and the CIA would not be the first. In 1942, the services of Genovese crime family boss Charles "Lucky" Luciano would be procured to help safeguard American ports during wartime.[9] Luciano, at the time serving a lengthy prison term, was more than happy to assist his country in return for a lighter sentence.

The second CIA-Mafia collusion would be more complex.

Robert Maheu was an ex-FBI agent, who opened his own private investigations firm in 1954. Most famously serving as the public face for eccentric business mogul Howard Hughes from 1955 to 1970, Maheu's services were occasionally tapped by the CIA. He met Johnny Rosselli in the late 1950s and was the perfect middleman to make contact with the mobster. Although Maheu said that he did not know the extent of Rosselli's underworld dealings, it was clear to him that, "he [Rosselli] was able to accomplish things in Las Vegas when nobody else seemed to get that kind of attention."[10]

According to a declassified document, Maheu, working for the CIA, approached Rosselli at the Brown Derby in Beverly Hills early in September, 1960 with a proposition for an overseas assignment: the assassination of Fidel Castro.[11]

Rosselli was, in the words of Maheu, "very hesitant about participating in the project, and he finally said that he felt that he had an obligation to his government, and he finally agreed to participate."[12]

Much like the Bay of Pigs, the operation would involve contact with the exile community in Miami and, with the help of the Mafia's vast interests in Cuba, contacts on the island. Working under the pseudonym "John Rawlston," Rosselli would make Miami contacts claiming he represented a businessman on Wall Street, who wanted help with some properties he had in Cuba. Other mobsters in on the assignment were Sam Giancana, working under the name "Sam Gold" and Santos Trafficante working as "Joe."

Trafficante would be the best person to work inside Cuba. He spoke fluent Spanish and had interest in the Sans-Souci nightclub and casino, the Commodoro hotel, and the Deauville casino in Havana. Trafficante was an opportunist, one of many gangsters, financers and moneymen who bet on Cuba as a tourist spot in the 1950s. Cuba, complete with lush surroundings and lax gambling laws, was not a bad bet. Fulgencio Batista, the Cuban dictator at the time, would match dollar for dollar any hotel investment over $1 million, with the added bonus of a casino license. As the foreign traveler dollars increased, the prospect looked to be fruitful and lasting, and from what Trafficante knew, the young revolutionary Fidel Castro was not a threat.

"There was no question about him taking power," Trafficante said. "They used to—in the papers when you would read about him, you would read like he was some kind of bandit."[13]

Castro did take power, nationalizing every business along the way. The casinos were soon closed, and Trafficante was detained in Trescornia prison for a time, waiting to be sent back to the United States.

The CIA assignment would give the Mafia a chance to reclaim its lost property and offered the unique opportunity to make contacts in Washington. The recruiting, planning, and implementation of the various assassination plots were at times intriguing, at times farcical.

Originally, the idea was to kill Castro in a "gangland style killing," but Giancana, noting the difficulty in finding someone for such an operation, suggested that firearms not be used against Castro. A poison was settled on, something "nice and easy, without getting into any out-and-out ambushing" in the words of Rosselli, something that could be deposited into one of Castro's drinks.[14]

The first attempt in August 1960 failed. Plotters had wanted to inject liquid botulinum toxin, a poison that causes paralysis of the muscles resulting in the inability to breathe, into one of Castro's signature cigars. The dosage was to be so lethal that Castro would only have to touch his lips to the cigar for the poison to take effect.[15]

Other attempts involved poison pills containing botulinum toxin given to Rosselli by the CIA's technical services division. In the early months of 1961, the pills were entrusted to Juan Orta, who Giancana thought would be a reliable accomplice. Orta was a private secretary to Castro and had been receiving kickbacks from the Mafia gambling interests. In a financial bind, Orta could be easily persuaded to act. Unfortunately, he got cold feet before the poison could be used.[16]

The insider tapped by Trafficante to replace Orta was Tony Varona, a Cuban exile leader who had his own interests in overthrowing Castro. Varona was also working with US racketeers, who were funding the anti-Castro movement "in the hopes of securing the gambling, prostitution, and dope monopolies in Cuba in the event Castro was overthrown."[17] The agency, with full knowledge of Varona's motives, went ahead with the mission. Varona was supplied with the pills and $50,000, with a plan to slip the poison into Castro's food at a restaurant he frequented. The plan went awry when Varona discovered that Castro had stopped eating at the restaurant.[18]

The operation would take an interesting turn in February 1962 when the agency discovered that Maheu was working independently for Giancana, wire-tapping the hotel room of comedian Dan Rowan. Giancana's girlfriend, singer Phyllis McGuire, was performing at a Las Vegas nightclub with Rowan, and Giancana heard that he was showing McGuire considerable attention. A suspicious Giancana wanted to know if their relationship extended into the bedroom. When the agency discovered the side project, Maheu faced criminal charges. At the request of the agency, the case was dropped.[19]

Bobby Kennedy, although a big supporter of secret actions by the CIA to undermine Castro's Cuba, was aghast when informed about the CIA's use of the Mafia. The collusion between the two organizations came to light following the illegal use of wiretaps in Rowan's hotel room. The use of organized crime—Bobby's sworn enemy—by the CIA, an organization that Bobby trusted less and less, certainly angered and possibly frightened the attorney general.

"I trust that if you ever do business with organized crime again, with gangsters," Bobby Kennedy told CIA director of security Sheffield Edwards and counsel Lawrence Houston during a May 14, 1962 meeting, "you will let the attorney general know."[20]

The relationship between the CIA and the Mafia, despite the stern warning from the attorney general and the assurances of Edwards and Houston, would not end.

Three months after the Rowan wiretapping incident, CIA agent Bill Harvey took over the reins as Rosselli's case officer. Since November 1961, Harvey had headed up ZR/RIFLE, an assassination plan directed at Castro. This no doubt put Harvey in contact with Operation 40, which was established by then-Director of the CIA Allen Dulles and originally presided over by Vice President Richard Nixon. It was a CIA-sanctioned assassination squad, which made their frustrating debut in the failed Bay of Pigs. The perceived cowardice of President Kennedy in not providing the necessary and promised air support to the mission drove the hatred of Operation 40 members. The group had included E. Howard Hunt, Frank Sturgis (a.k.a. Frank Fiorini), Dave Morales, and Bernard Barker. Some of them would resurface in the Kennedy assassination and again later in the Watergate break-in. Harvey's assignment to interact more closely with Rosselli brought the vital members of the CIA/Mafia assassination compact together.

John Kennedy's first impression of Harvey, who was described to him as "America's James Bond," was no doubt different from what he had imagined. Kennedy was such a James Bond devotee, he once asked Bond author Ian Fleming how he, Fleming, would dispose of Castro. The paunchy, rumpled Harvey, with bulging eyes due to a thyroid problem, was a sharp contrast to the urbane superspy.

Harvey's comparison with 007 was surely derived from his ability to get things done quietly. One example was the Berlin Tunnel operation in 1953, his greatest early accomplishment for the agency. As base chief, Harvey oversaw an operation to dig under southern Berlin and tap into communication wires between Soviet-occupied East Germany and other parts of the Soviet Union.[21] Conducted unassumingly under enemy soil, the tunnel provided the United States with important intelligence on Soviet affairs, both military and diplomatic.

The Kennedy fascination with the CIA, and Harvey in particular, went south quickly. To President Kennedy, Harvey was part of a defective agency. Harvey himself was not enamored with the Kennedys from the start: In private, he referred to the increasingly meddling Bobby matter-of-factly as "that fucker."[22] Harvey, though, was perfect for the CIA–Mafia collusion. It was a cloak-and-dagger operation, which required further secrecy. In a phone call to director of security Edwards in May 1962, Harvey told him that "he was dropping any plans for the use of Rosselli in the future."[23] This claim would be challenged by Harvey, who asserted that he had taken over "a going operation."[24] The phone call was placed to deliberately mislead Sheffield: The operation was continuing, but with different objectives and only a small platoon in the know.

"I wanted everyone else cut out," Harvey would later tell Church Committee investigators.[25]

That same month, a base was built for Rosselli and a military unit assigned to him in Key Largo for the purpose of training snipers.[26]

The back-and-forth accusations within the CIA over who was in charge of what and at what level would be a common theme of the 1975 Church Committee hearings on alleged assassination plots involving foreign leaders. Pennsylvania Senator Rickard Schweiker, a committee member, told Harvey in one exchange: "Mr. Harvey, we've had witness after witness after witness come since you were here last and say that you are in error, and the CIA was operating out of control, and the junior officers were going berserk."[27]

The CIA, and Bill Harvey were acting with power the agency was lawfully granted with the approval of NSC 10/2. Harvey continued the program after he was ordered to shut it down because he believed that it was his right to continue working on it. Harvey even persisted on advancing the mission after he had been removed from the country.

By 1963, Harvey had been exiled to an outpost in Rome by Bobby Kennedy after sending troops, unbeknownst to almost all branches of government, to Cuba for a potential invasion during the missile crisis. Despite being sent away and ordered to stay out of contact with the Florida Castro operation, Harvey was taking many trips back to the Florida Keys to see Rosselli, whose role with the CIA was supposed to have already been terminated. Harvey met secretly with Rosselli, CIA officer David Atlee Phillips, and Operation 40 member David Morales.[28]

Harvey also held separate meetings with Rosselli throughout 1963. On April 18 and 19 of 1963, Harvey and Rosselli chartered a boat and motored off Plantation Key beyond the reaches of surveillance to discuss private matters.

"Regardless of how he may have made his living in the past," Harvey said of his mobster friend, John Rosselli had "integrity as far as I was concerned.[29]

The cooperation of Operation 40 and the Mafia element is integral to the assassination of John Kennedy. They would be necessary to Lyndon Johnson because this was not good ol' boy Texas justice—a more sophisticated plan was needed. The CIA and Mafia element would likewise be dependent on LBJ to effectively control the location, chain of command, and evidence.

"I can just visualize Harvey and LBJ forming a kind of a thieves' compact between them," said Operation 40 agent and Watergate recruiter and organizer E. Howard Hunt. "I think that LBJ was an opportunist, and he would have not hesitated to get rid of obstacles in his way."

"There was no other group that honored, if I can use that term, the clandestine limitations the way the CIA did," Hunt added. "They could do something, turn their back on it, then move on to something else."[30]

Hunt, who was on his deathbed at the time of his confession, said that he was approached to be a "benchwarmer" on the assassination, which was known in certain channels as "The Big Event." Was Hunt in Dallas on November 22, 1963? In 1974, the Rockefeller Commission concluded that Hunt used eleven hours of sick leave from the CIA in the two-week period preceding the assassination. Saint John Hunt, E. Howard's son, remembered his mother informing him on November 22, 1963 that Howard was on a "business trip" to Dallas that day. Later, eyewitness Marita Lorenz testified under oath in a district court case in Florida that she saw Hunt pay off an assassination team in Dallas the night before Kennedy's murder. "One of the things he [E. Howard Hunt] liked to say around the house was let's finish the job," said Saint John Hunt. "Let's hit Ted [Kennedy]."

Saint John Hunt explained that the reason that his father had waited until he was dying to confess was his fear for the lives of himself and his family. Hunt's wife Dorothy had died in a commercial plane crash in Chicago, which killed forty-five people in 1972. Hunt did not believe it was an accident.

"Later on in his life at one of these bedside confessions, tears started welling up in his eyes, and he said, 'You know, Saint, I was so deeply concerned that what they did to your mother they could have done to you children, and that caused the hair on my neck to stand up.' That was the first disclosure from my father that he thought there was something else going on besides sheer pilot error," said Saint John Hunt.[31]

The man who met with Johnson, Hunt believed, to "undertake a larger organization while keeping it totally secret" was CIA official Cord Meyer.

By the time of the assassination, Meyer's ex-wife Mary had become one of John Kennedy's mistresses, making Meyer more easily accessible to Johnson.

"Jack confided to Kenny [O'Donnell] he was deeply in love with Mary, that after he left the White House, he envisioned a future with her and would divorce Jackie," said investigative journalist and author Leo Damore. The writer had been working on a book regarding President Kennedy's affair with Mary Meyer when he died mysteriously of an alleged self-inflicted gunshot wound in 1995.[32]

When he lost his wife to Kennedy, Cord Meyer had nothing left.

A year after Kennedy's death, Mary Meyer was dead, killed by an unknown assassin. In 2001, wasting away in a Washington nursing home, Meyer told author C. David Heymann that the people who killed Mary were "the same sons of bitches that killed John F. Kennedy."[33]

Lyndon Johnson also had many connections to the CIA through Texas oil money. Chief among them was the owner of the Texas School Book Depository building and LBJ oil crony D. H. Byrd, the cousin of Senator Harry F. Byrd, whose political machine dominated Virginia politics from the mid 1920s until 1966.

In the 1960 Democratic primary, Senator Harry Byrd of Virginia crossed over into West Virginia to campaign for Hubert Humphrey at the request of Lyndon Johnson. LBJ wanted to block Kennedy's ascent, but hadn't yet entered any primaries. H. L. Hunt was flooding the state with anti-JFK tracts, tying him to the Pope and Catholicism. In 1964, unlike his Senate Colleague J. Strom Thurmond who bolted the Democratic Party to support Goldwater, Byrd supported the Johnson–Humphrey ticket and accompanied Lady Bird Johnson on a campaign swing through Virginia.

Contrast this with 1960, when Byrd said he would "maintain the golden silence" and withheld his support from Kennedy. In fact, Byrd, along with Johnson, were two of the earliest congressional overseers of the newly created CIA.

Lyndon Johnson had deep intelligence and military ties. Senator Johnson and his top aide Walter Jenkins both had Q clearances, which is a very high-level clearance by the Department of Energy specifically relating to atomic or nuclear materials.

Another connection to help draw the CIA into the plot was oil magnate Clint Murchison. For years, Murchison had colluded the interests of Texas oil with the CIA, FBI, and Mafia elements through his ownership of the La Jolla, California Del Mar Racetrack and the nearby Hotel Del Charro, a resort that entertained and introduced members from all groups. Carlos Marcello and Jack Ruby were also regulars with the Del Mar set.

Harry Hall, a well-connected member of organized crime and Jack Ruby gambling cohort, would join Ruby at the Del Mar to habitually play the odds, in one instance winning an impressive sum of money on the Cotton and Rose Bowls from oilman, LBJ business partner, and JFK assassination moneyman H. L. Hunt.[34]

It would be through Murchison's deep connections that all members with shared interest of a Lyndon Johnson presidency could coalesce.

Murchison could have easily arranged the meeting between Meyer and Johnson to secure the addition of the CIA–Mafia death squad into the fold. Harvey's group of CIA-Mafia hitmen would be indispensable to the assassination because they were professionals. Having a need for the removal of JFK, they would be compliant soldiers and were off the books. Indeed, following the May 14 meeting between the attorney general, Sheffield Edwards, and Lawrence Houston, the small group of assassins had ceased to exist, even to higher-ups in the agency.

The Director of the CIA himself, John McCone, who had replaced Allen Dulles, was unaware of the group.

Murchison, who had deep ties to the vice president, the Mafia, the CIA, and the FBI, would host members from all four groups under his roof the night before John Kennedy was assassinated. Murchison could use many avenues to reach out to the CIA, he had many contacts with the agency, including CIA Oswald groomer George de Mohrenschildt and future director George H. W. Bush. Both worked to protect the oil tycoon's investments in Haiti. A further connection between the CIA, Texas oil, and LBJ, Johnson's right hand man, Bobby Baker, was also assigned to protect Murchison's Haitian business interests.[35]

Another man named by Hunt was CIA assassin David "El Indio" Morales.

"Dave Morales did dirty work for the Agency," said Wayne Smith, who worked with Morales in Havana pre-Castro. "If he were in the mob, he'd be called a hit man."[36]

Hard drinking and violent, Morales was a good fit for the assassination compact. He was a soldier who did what he was told, from being an active member of the 1954 coup in Guatemala to overthrowing democratically elected president Jacobo Arbenz Guzman and the tracking and killing of Ernesto "Che" Guevara.[37] Morales also had a severe dislike for the Kennedys, deeming them traitors because of the failed Bay of Pigs invasion.

"If the son of a bitch [John Kennedy] caused the death of all these people [at the Bay of Pigs], he deserved to die," said Ruben Carbajal, one of Morales' close friends said of how he and Morales felt about the operation. "You should never go around lying to your people. You go back on your word, you ain't no good. My dad taught me that. I don't give a shit who it is. If it was my own father and he lied to me, he deserves to die."[38]

Morales's lawyer Robert Walton had said multiple times that El Indio confessed his guilt in the JFK assassination. Morales told Walton, "I was in Dallas when we got that mother fucker, and I was in Los Angeles [where Robert Kennedy was murdered] when we got the little bastard."[39]

In May 1978, set to appear before the House Select Committee on Assassinations, Morales, like so many other persons of interest, died suddenly before testimony could be given regarding the Kennedy assassination. He quickly succumbed to heart trouble at age fifty-two.

Following his Church Committee testimony in 1975, Bill Harvey would leave behind a cryptic message regarding his knowledge of any CIA wrongdoing in the assassination: "They didn't ask the right questions."

Harvey would be found dead of a heart attack a year later.

JFK assassination researcher James Lesar has commented on Bill Harvey's role as "one of the last remaining, unexplored lines of inquiry in the JFK assassination."[40]

When questioned before the HSCA by Connecticut Senator Thomas Dodd concerning clandestine CIA operations around the time of the Kennedy assassination, Richard Helms, the deputy director for plans of the CIA at the time of the assassination who had intimate knowledge of Operation 40 and their use of Mafioso, was obstinate:

> **MR. HELMS:** The relevance of one plot or another plot and its effect on the course of events I would have a very hard time

assessing and I think you would, too. Suppose I had gone down and told them and said, yes, you know we tried to do this. How would it have altered the outcome of the Warren Commission proceeding?

MR. DODD: Wasn't that really for the Warren Commission to determine?

MR. HELMS: I think that is absolutely correct, but they did not have that chance apparently.[41]

The *Washington Post's* George Lardner reported what Richard Helms said to reporters during a recess from his HSCA testimony:

Helms told reporters during a break that no one would ever know who or what Lee Harvey Oswald . . . represented. Asked whether the CIA knew of any ties Oswald had with either the KGB or the CIA, Helms paused with a laugh and said, 'I don't remember.' Pressed on the point, he told a reporter, 'Your questions are almost as dumb as the Committee's.'

NOTES

1. Jack Anderson, *The Washington Post* (September 7, 1976).
2. Bill Bonanno, *Bound by Honor: A Mafioso's Story* (New York: St. Martin's Press, 1999.), 263.
3. Ragano, *Mob Lawyer*, 325.
4. *Tri City Herald* [Kennewick, Washington] (September 26, 1976).
5. Ragano, *Mob Lawyer*, 325.
6. *Sarasota HeraldTribune*, December 31, 1975.
7. Antoinette Giancana, John R. Hughes, and Thomas H. Jobe, *JFK and Sam: The Connection between the Giancana and Kennedy Assassinations* (Nashville: Cumberland House, 2005), 69-70.
8. Chuck Giancana, *Double Cross*, 457.
9. Becker, *All American Mafioso: The Johnny Rosselli Story*, 153.
10. "AARC Public Library - Interim Report: Alleged Assassination Plots Involving Foreign Leaders," (April 10, 2012), aarclibrary.org/publib/contents/church/contents_church_reports_ir.htm.

11. www.foia.cia.gov/docs/DOC_0001451843/DOC_0001451843.pdf.
12. *Alleged Assassination Plots*, 75.
13. HSCA Report, vol. 5:35.
14. *Alleged Assassination Plots*, 80.
15. "Report on Plots to Assassinate Fidel Castro" (1967 Inspector General's Report), *HSCA Segregated CIA Collection, microfilm* (November 10, 2012), maryferrell.org/mffweb/archive/viewer/ showDoc.do?docId=9983.
16. Central Intelligence Agency, "Family Jewels," foia.cia.gov/docs/ DOC_0001451843/DOC_0001451843.pdf.
17. *Plots to Assassinate Fidel Castro*, 29.
18. *Plots to Assassinate Fidel Castro*, 32.
19. Central Intelligence Agency, "Family Jewels," 46-47.
20. Talbot, *Brothers*, 86.
21. Bayard Stockton, *Flawed Patriot: The Rise and Fall of CIA Legend Bill Harvey*, (Washington: Potomac, 2006), 72.
22. Hersh, *Bobby and J. Edgar*, 310.
23. Ibid.
24. Ibid.
25. Church Committee testimony of William K. Harvey.
26. Stockton, *Flawed Patriot*, 179.
27. Testimony of William K. Harvey, 45.
28. Phillip Nelson, *LBJ: The Mastermind of the JFK Assassination* (New York: Skyhorse Publishing, 2011), 102.
29. Talbot, *Brothers*, 170.
30. The Alex Jones Channel, "Exclusive Interview with E. Howard Hunt: The JFK Cover-Up," youtube.com/watch?v=DbD_u7nUB_c.
31. Paul Joseph Watson, "Son of JFK Conspirator Drops New Bombshell Revelations," *Prison Planet* (May 3, 2009).
32. Janney, *Mary's Mosaic*, 230-231.
33. Richard Gilbride, *Matrix for Assassination: The JFK Conspiracy* (Bloomington: Trafford Publishing, 2009), 204.
34. Dale Scott, Peter, Deep Politics and the Death of JFK, pg. 205.
35. Miller, David, The JFK Conspiracy, pg. 175.
36. Talbot, *Brothers*, 398.
37. Ibid., 399.
38. Ibid., 400.
39. Ibid., 399.
40. Stockton, *Flawed Patriot*, 193.
41. HSCA testimony of Richard Helms.

CHAPTER NINE

THE ROAD TO WATERGATE

Nixon's deep involvement in Operation 40 made him fully aware of a CIA assassination team that included E. Howard Hunt, Frank Sturgis, and David Morales.

Nixon's attorney general John Mitchell told me that he learned in 1971 that Nixon, as vice president, had approved the CIA outreach to organized crime in their plan to kill Castro. The CIA authorized ex-FBI agent Maheu to contact the mob through Johnny Rosselli shortly before Nixon's surprise defeat in November of 1960. The approach by Maheu happened on Nixon's watch and at a time when most believed that Nixon would be the next president. Nixon had his own long-term relationship with Maheu, who had funneled money to his campaign from Hughes. As the point man for the CIA-led operation, it is unlikely Nixon wouldn't have known about the mob recruitment. At the time, Nixon had connections not only to the CIA, but to Hughes and Maheu. They had already come back to haunt him.

Hughes lent $205,000 to Nixon's brother, Don, who established a chain of hamburger restaurants across Southern California called "Nixon Burgers." The vice president's mother, Hannah Milhouse Nixon, pledged the deed on her home as collateral for the loan. News of the loan hit the press so late in 1960 that the issue had little impact.[1]

California Governor Pat Brown and California Democrats successfully resurrected the issue during Nixon's unsuccessful bid for the California governorship in 1962. At one point, Democrat dirty trickster Dick Tuck hung a giant banner in Chinese at a San Francisco Chinatown Nixon rally, which read "Nixon, What About the Hughes Loan?" Nixon spoke as his large audience laughed at his cluelessness. Indeed, Nixon knew Hughes and Maheu well, and he paid a price for doing business with them.

While I will explain why I believe Watergate ended up as a CIA-led coup d'état to topple Nixon, I have always believed that the Watergate burglars broke into the Democratic National Committee headquarters because Maheu had hired Democratic National Chairman Larry O'Brien, an old Kennedy hand, as a secret lobbyist. Someone around Nixon wanted to know if O'Brien had any documentation or knowledge of Nixon's relationship with Maheu and the reclusive Hughes. I am aware of the theory that White House Counsel John Dean may have targeted the Watergate break-in to obtain the records of a call-girl ring that Democrats were using to supply girls for visiting dignitaries and party bigwigs. Dean's girlfriend and later wife, Maureen "Big Mo" Binder, worked for this "escort service." Although I don't reject this theory, I suspect that Nixon's obsession with Hughes, based on the way the Hughes relationship had burned him in 1962, drove the break-in.

Investigative journalist Lamar Waldron makes a compelling case in his book, *Watergate: The Hidden History*, that the purpose of the break-in was to obtain records detailing Nixon's authorization as vice president for the CIA recruitment of mob assassins to assist in the assassination of Fidel Castro. I believe Nixon fully understood that this plan had gone awry and had morphed into the assassination of JFK. The cast of characters involved in both endeavors is more than coincidental. *60 Minutes* producer Don Hewitt would recall an anecdote revealed to him by Senator Howard Baker. Baker asked Nixon who really killed Kennedy. "You don't want to know," Nixon replied tersely.

From the beginning of his presidency, Nixon sought the CIA records that would prove the connection of the Bay of Pig veterans to the Kennedy assassination. Although White House Chief of Staff H. R. "Bob" Haldeman said that Nixon had turned him down when he suggested reopening and gathering the facts surrounding the JFK assassination, Nixon's White House domestic policy advisor John Ehrlichman said that Nixon had requested all of the CIA records on the Kennedy assassination and had been rebuffed by the agency. It is logical that Nixon, a lawyer, would ask Ehrlichman, a fellow lawyer, to obtain the records rather than Haldeman, who was not.

Nixon's effort to obtain the JFK assassination records was an attempt to seize leverage over the rogue agency. This was to be Nixon's "insurance policy" against the CIA. If threatened, Nixon would expose the agency's involvement in Kennedy's death, which took place at the time that he, Nixon, was in political exile without formal governmental influence of any kind.

This is why I believe Watergate was a CIA operation that capitalized on the stupidity and amateurishness of G. Gordon Liddy, CREEP Campaign Director Jeb Magruder, and John Dean, the three Nixon aides who advanced the plans for the Watergate break-in, which leaked to the CIA.

Even without the never-supplied CIA files on the Kennedy assassination, Nixon tried to blackmail CIA Director Richard Helms by using his knowledge of the CIA ties to the Kennedy assassination and the Bay of Pigs to keep a lid on the rapidly expanding Watergate scandal.

Nixon ordered White House Chief of Staff H. R. Haldeman to tell CIA Director Richard Helms that a continued investigation of Watergate would open up "the whole Bay of Pigs thing." It would also induce Helms to tell the FBI to close down the Watergate investigation because it would reveal national security secrets.[2]

"Well, we protected Helms from one hell of a lot of things," Nixon said on June 23, only six days after the break-in. "Of course, this is Hunt, that will uncover a lot of things, and we just feel that it would be very detrimental to have this thing go any further. This involves Cubans, Hunt, and a lot of hanky panky that we have nothing to do with ourselves."[3]

I believe that, in this instance, Nixon was talking about the JFK assassination.

"The president's belief is that this is going to open the whole Bay of Pigs and, ah, because, ah, these people are playing for, for keeps, and that they (the CIA) should call the FBI in, and we feel that. . . . that we wish for the country, don't go any further into this case, period,"[4] Nixon coached Haldeman.

Haldeman would record CIA Director Helms's violent reaction to Nixon's threat. Helms clenched the arms of his chair as his face flushed, and he shouted, "The Bay of Pigs has nothing to do with this! I have no concern for the Bay of Pigs!"[5] In fact, in 1961, Helms had served as deputy director of planning for the Bay of Pigs invasion. He knew the full cast of characters involved in the Cuban invasion, the JFK hit, and the Watergate break-in.

By sending Haldeman to see Helms with the Bay of Pigs threat, Nixon wanted to scare Helms into believing that E. Howard Hunt, under pressure, would spill the beans about the JFK assassination and the ties of many in that plot to the Bay of Pigs.

Indeed, in his own post-Watergate book, Haldeman said, "It seems that in all those Nixon references to the Bay of Pigs, he was actually referencing the JFK assassination."[6]

"In fact, I was puzzled when he [Nixon] told me, 'Tell Ehrlichman this whole group of Cubans [Watergate burglars] is tied to the Bay of Pigs.' After a pause, I said, 'The Bay of Pigs? What does that have to do with this [the Watergate burglary]?' But Nixon merely said, 'Ehrlichman will know what I mean,' and dropped the subject."[7]

National Public Radio correspondent Daniel Schorr, who was on Nixon's enemy list, said that the threat to the CIA was "about some deeply hidden scandal . . . an assassination or something on that order. It was supposed to involve the CIA and President Kennedy."[8]

In fact, Nixon's threat to the CIA's Helms was broader. Nixon was threatening to expose the CIA-mob connections which had paved the way for the Kennedy assassination.

Nixon, a member of four national tickets, knew that there was no information of a political value at the Democratic National Committee, and that information regarding his opponent George McGovern's campaign could only be found at McGovern headquarters. I believe that the Watergate burglars were seeking documents tying Nixon to Maheu and the Howard Hughes loan. Nixon knew that Democratic National Chairman Larry O'Brien lived as a high-paid fixer for Hughes, essentially lobbying without registering for Hughes Aerospace, seeking defense contracts under JFK. He would certainly have been concerned that O'Brien had the proof somewhere.[9]

Watergate is no less a coup d'état by the CIA than the assassination of JFK by a rogue faction of the CIA, working in concert with elements of organized crime and at the direction of Lyndon Baines Johnson. Serving as the youngest member of the notorious Committee to Re-elect the President in 1972, I knew Watergate burglars James McCord, the security director at CREEP, and G. Gordon Liddy, the general consul to the CREEP finance committee by day and seeker of covert intelligence by night.

That anyone would use actual CREEP personnel who could be traced directly to the President's re-election committee in a covert operation shows the amateurish nature of the Watergate break-in. That some burglars carried address books with White House phone numbers in them shows either a stunning ineptness or an effort to take Nixon down. Indeed, the mistakes in Watergate were legion.

It is interesting to note that, although E. Howard Hunt claims he quit the CIA in April 1970, he was immediately hired by a public relations firm representing Howard Hughes's tool company. The firm was, in fact, a CIA front. The Robert R. Mullen Company was

THE MAN WHO KILLED KENNEDY

run by Robert Bennett, the son of Senator Wallace Bennett of Utah, a longtime friend and supporter of Richard Nixon and an elder in the Mormon Church.

Bennett would later write a memo to his CIA case officer, Martin Lukowski. In the memo, directed to Director Helms, he reported that he had deflected reporters at the *Washington Post* and *Washington Star* away from CIA involvement in the Watergate conspiracy. Bennett, who later admitted to being a source for *Washington Post* reporter Bob Woodward, was part of the effort to distract from the CIA's link to the Watergate caper and shift the blame to Nixon.

Although Hunt joined the Nixon Administration in June 1971, he remained a "consultant" to the Mullen Company. While working for the White House, Hunt traveled to Miami to meet with two Cuban exiles with whom he had worked during the Bay of Pigs invasion. These men, Bernard Barker and Eugenio Martinez, accompanied Hunt to a meeting with a woman who claimed to have information about Castro's reaction to the Kennedy assassination. White House counsel Charles Colson told me that Hunt's trek to Miami was at his direction and in response to a letter the woman had written to the president.

"I brought the letter to the president's attention. He sat bolt upright and said 'Send someone down!'" Colson told me. "Nixon had a voracious appetite for information about the Kennedy assassination."[10]

The woman said that Castro had been morose. Hunt reported this back to both the White House and the CIA. The fact that Castro was not jubilant over the death of his rival would, of course, confirm Nixon's suspicion that Kennedy was not murdered by a "communist" as J. Edgar Hoover had insisted to him. Nor had it been a plot by the Cubans, as LBJ had told Nixon in the aftermath. Johnson would repeat this fiction to journalist Leo Janos, Chief Justice Earl Warren, Warren Commission member Richard Russell, and TV journalist Mike Wallace.

The fumbling by Hunt and Sturgis, the incompetence of the Watergate burglary, and the fact that plainclothes units responded almost immediately when a security guard first encountered the burglars pointed to me the strong belief that Nixon was set up by his old Operation 40 colleagues trying to prevent the reopening of their role in LBJ's and the CIA's plot to kill Kennedy.

Hunt, an old CIA hand, would leave a laundry receipt with his name on it in the Howard Johnson motel room lookout post across the street from the Watergate. The experienced operative would also keep an address book with White House phone numbers tying him back to presidential counsel Chuck Colson. The dubious nature of both these mistakes convinces me that Nixon was set up.

White House plumber G. Gordon Liddy's grandiose plan to break into the Democratic National Committee headquarters, the search for files, and the planting of listening devices was no doubt reported to the CIA once Liddy recruited James McCord, Security Director for CREEP and long-time CIA asset. I believe that the company saw the opportunity to remove the threat of Nixon's exposing their role in JFK's murder. It is not coincidental that it was McCord who wrote a letter to the Watergate burglars' trial judge John J. Sirica exposing the cover-up and pointing to higher-ups in the White House and CREEP.

McCord was likely a double agent, who intentionally botched the surreptitious entry into the Watergate. It was McCord who re-taped an office door after security guards had already found it taped and removed the adhesive once. The taping of the door was unnecessary because the door opened, unlocked, without a key. But the tape served its purpose as a clear signal to security. Following the break-in, McCord left tape on some of the doors. McCord also burned all of his files in his home fireplace, with a CIA agent present to witness the paper conflagration.[11]

Nixon first heard about the break-in when he was huddled on the West Coast with his political advisors and staff, including

John Mitchell, CREEP campaign director Jeb Magruder, campaign deputy Robert Mardian, and Mississippi GOP powerhouse and Mitchell confidant Fred LaRue.

The errors made by the Watergate burglars are so manifest that it is clear that the burglars worked for the old Operation 40 gang and purposely botched the job with one more target in their sights: Tricky Dick. Consider how the conspirators expertly left a trail of mistakes as evidence for law enforcement:

The team had a meeting the night before the break-in in a Howard Johnson room booked on the stationary of a Miami firm, which employed Watergate burglar and Operation 40 member Bernard Barker. When Barker was later arrested, he had his hotel room key in his pocket. There, investigators found materials that further incriminated the group.

In lieu of getting the photographs of documents for the break-in developed privately as planned, veteran spy Hunt took them to a commercial camera shop to be developed.

James McCord booked his room opposite the Watergate hotel, at the Howard Johnson, in the name of his company.

On the second night of the break-in, G. Gordon Liddy drove his easily recognizable green jeep recklessly and was eventually stopped by police. After getting pulled over, Liddy proceeded on to the Watergate hotel and parked his jeep right outside.

Neither Hunt or Liddy made any effort through their many contacts to spring McCord from prison before it was revealed that he was linked with the CIA.

After the burglary, Hunt locked a wealth of incriminating evidence in his White House safe, including electronic gear from the burglary, address books, and notebooks with information tying the men involved directly in the break-in.

Before the break-in, each of the burglars was given $100 bills equaling between $200 and $800. All the bills had serial numbers that were close in sequence. When Hunt and Liddy found out that the burglars had been caught, they cleared their hotel room of evidence, but left a briefcase holding $4,600, which by serial number, directly linked it to the money given to the burglars.

Address books taken from Bernard Barker and Eugenio Martinez linked them directly to E. Howard Hunt.

Break-in surveillance man Alfred Baldwin subsequently leaked the story of the burglary, with names, to a lawyer named John Cassidento, a supporter of the Democratic Party.

The double agents involved in the Watergate break-in were not lazy criminals. They were seasoned professionals, skilled in covert operations. The Watergate break-in was simultaneously a botched job and a successful cover-up.

Then there is the question of lawyer Douglas Caddy. For instance, we can only wonder why an experienced spook such as Howard Hunt would have turned to Caddy to represent the burglars at their arraignment. Both Caddy and Hunt were employed by the Robert R. Mullen Company, which the CIA used as a cover—a cover that the agency was desperate to protect. Dragging Caddy into the Watergate affair could only have served to expose that cover (as indeed it did). From a tradecraft point of view, this makes no sense and leads us again to wonder about Hunt's intentions.

In June of 1972, I was working for CREEP as a surrogate scheduler, handling the campaign schedules of the Nixon daughters and cabinet members as well as members of Congress campaigning for Nixon's re-election. The weekend of the break-in, I was housesitting for my boss at CREEP, Herbert L. "Bart" Porter. Porter was a plucky ex-marine who had gone to USC and been recruited by White House chief Haldeman for the Nixon staff. Porter, who was from California, was on the West Coast attending the senior staff meetings. I had just settled in with a takeout pizza and a six-pack of beer when the phone rang.

"Porter residence," I said.

"Is Bart there?" said a gruff voice I recognized as McCord.

"No, he and Mrs. Porter are out of town," I said. "I'm just house-sitting. This is Roger Stone. I work at the Committee [to Re-elect the President]."

"Ok, tell him Jim McCord called. Tell him I'm in the lockup, and tell him the jig is up."

To this day, I am not certain about the import of McCord's words. But even at nineteen years old, I knew the formal denials by presidential spokesman Ron Ziegler and CREEP spokesman DeVan "Van" Shumway that the Watergate break-in was not connected to the White House or the campaign were false.

McCord's letter to Sirica would bust the Watergate cover-up wide open and lead to Nixon's resignation, the indictment of his attorney general, and the prosecution of a number of his top aides. Although Nixon had carefully nurtured the career of Massachusetts Attorney General Elliot Richardson and had rewarded him with two appointments (including secretary of defense and US attorney general) Richardson would appoint Harvard professor Archibald Cox as the special prosecutor in the Watergate matter.

Cox had been solicitor general in the Kennedy administration and a longtime Kennedy hand who was among the Nixon haters. When Cox would not desist in his efforts to secure the Watergate tapes, Nixon fired him in the famous "Saturday Night Massacre." Richardson promptly resigned. So did Deputy Attorney General William Ruckleshaus, who had run unsuccessfully for the Senate in Indiana and been rewarded by Nixon with appointments as assistant attorney general and the first administrator of the United States Environmental Protection Agency. It was ultimately left to Solicitor General Robert Bork to fire Cox.

Incredibly, the man named to replace Cox was Houston lawyer Leon Jaworski. Jaworski was a board member of the M. D. Anderson Foundation, a CIA front company. Jaworski also worked for the Warren Commission, on which he was assigned to investigate a possible connection between Oswald and the CIA. Needless to say, he found none. When Oswald assassin Jack Ruby begged the Warren Commission to get him out of Dallas and fly him to Washington, DC "if they wanted to learn the truth," only three people were present: Chief Justice Earl Warren, Congressman Gerald Ford, and Warren Commission Lawyer Leon Jaworski.[12]

The CIA ensured that secrets of Watergate and the JFK assassination would remain secrets. It was Nixon's power struggle with the CIA and his efforts to pry loose their Kennedy assassination files that caused his downfall. Nixon was taken down by "double agents" who intentionally botched the break-in.

E. Howard Hunt would die in January 2007 at the age of eighty-eight. Hunt named David Atlee Phillips, Cord Meyer, Bill Harvey, David Morales, and Frank Sturgis as being involved in the JFK hit. He also said Lyndon Baines Johnson was the conspiracy's chief organizer.

By March 1974, as the CIA dug their claws deeper into Nixon, more information began to leak out regarding who else the president had crossed. Nixon, it turns out, was making the same mistakes as Kennedy when it came to Big Oil. This is well documented in Russ Baker's book *Family of Secrets*:

> There were news reports that federal officials and members of Congress were looking into possible antitrust violations by people who sat simultaneously on multiple oil company boards. In a December 1973 letter responding to members of Congress, an assistant attorney general had confirmed that the Nixon Justice Department was looking at these so-called interlocking directorates.

Thus, Nixon had crossed the same oil barons who had an interest in the assassination of JFK.

Watergate would clear the way for even more cover-up. Before he himself was driven from office Nixon would install Congressman Gerald Ford as vice president. "Ford was Nixon's insurance policy," Nixon's former 1968 political aide John Sears would tell me. "Nixon thought Ford was so dumb, they'd never impeach him and put Ford in the White House."

Sears would go on to manage Reagan's campaign for the GOP presidential nomination against Ford in 1976 and against Bush in 1980. Ford, who played a key role in the Warren Commission cover-up in the death of JFK would go on to become president and would appoint a Commission headed by Vice President Nelson Rockefeller that would again whitewash the CIA role in Kennedy's death. Incredibly, the Rockefeller Commission chose as its director David Belin, a Warren Commission Counsel and close associate of Arlen Specter. Belin was a vocal proponent of the single-bullet theory.[13]

NOTES

1. Anthony Summers, *The Arrogance of Power: The Secret World of Richard Nixon* (New York: Penguin, 2000), 154, 158.
2. Fulsom, *Nixon's Darkest Secrets*, 129.
3. Gilbride, *Matrix for Assassination*, 198.
4. Jesse Ventura, *American Conspiracies: Lies, Lies and More Dirty Lies that the Government Tells Us* (New York: Skyhorse Publishing, 2010), 87.
5. Lamar Waldron, *Watergate: The Hidden History* (Berkeley: Counterpoint, 2012), 722
6. Fulsom, *Nixon's Darkest Secrets*, 127.
7. H. R. Haldeman, *The Ends of Power* (New York: Dell Publishing, 1978), 187.
8. Fulsom, *Nixon's Darkest Secrets*, 127–128.
9. Waldron, *Watergate: The Hidden History*, 620.
10. Interview with Charles Colson.
11. Jesse Ventura, with Dick Russell, *American Conspiracies*, 214.
12. Ibid., 91.
13. Baker, *Family of Secrets*, 243–244.

CHAPTER TEN

CARLOS

Appearing before the House Select Committee on Assassinations, Santo Trafficante was asked to provide details of his relationship with Carlos Marcello, the New Orleans mob boss. The dodgy Trafficante had concealed his long relationship with Rosselli before the committee, despite having dinner with Rosselli shortly before his testimony. He was equally obscure in his recollection of Marcello.

"Just friendship," Trafficante said. "No business, never had no business dealings with him; no way, shape, or form. I see him once in a while when I go to New Orleans. He's come to Miami, I think, once to appear before a grand jury. I seen him there."[1]

Why would Trafficante have business dealings with Marcello? Throughout his reign as mob boss of New Orleans, Marcello maintained that he was merely a tomato salesman who earned $1,600 a month.[2] In truth, business dealings between the two ranged from a sizable overseas heroin trade through French diplomats[3] and the shared maintenance of gambling interests at home and abroad.

In Bobby Kennedy's crusade to eradicate organized crime, no mob boss was pursued more doggedly than Carlos Marcello. Born in 1910 in Tunis, North Africa to parents of Italian origin, Marcello was brought to the United States as an infant. Though an illegal immigrant, he grew to be one of the most-feared mob bosses in the country, with an iron grip on both New Orleans and Dallas.

Perhaps the attorney general's slow burn for the Louisiana mobster began when Marcello refused to fall in line with other organized crime figures and contribute to the Kennedy campaign. During the 1960 primaries, with his brother campaigning against Johnson, it has been alleged that Bobby reached out to Marcello for a donation. Marcello already had loyalty to Johnson, with whom he maintained a relationship through John Halfen, a Marcello bagman. In typical LBJ fashion, Halfen would ply Johnson with cash, and Johnson would return the contribution in the form of favorable legislation, particularly in relation to gambling law.[4] An estimated $50,000 a year was delivered to Johnson from profits made through Marcello's gambling enterprises.[5] Marcello knew what he was getting from Johnson: favors for cash. With the Kennedys, he was not sure what benefits his loyalty would reap, and he was prudent.

Author Richard Mahoney says it best:

> LBJ's ties to Marcello through Bobby Baker, his chief aide when he was Senate majority leader, went back to the early 1950's. Marcello's Texas "political fixer" Jack Halfen reportedly arranged to siphon off a percentage of the mobster's racing wire and slot machine profits for LBJ's Senate campaigns. Journalist Michael Dorman alleged that in exchange for such contributions, LBJ stopped anti-racketeering legislation. After becoming president, Johnson ordered all FBI bugging (principally of the Mafia) to cease. Part of the reason may have been that a Senate investigation of Bobby Baker's corruption was leading directly to mob connections. Special Agent William F. Roemer, Jr., who had been spearheading the attack on the mob in Chicago, concluded: "If you judge a man by his acts, here was a man [LBJ] who did more to hinder the government agency fighting crime than any other president or leader in our history."

In other words, Lyndon Johnson was "mobbed up" with some of the very people Robert Kennedy was hellbent on destroying. LBJ's stopping of the Mafia wiretaps was not out of some philosophical revulsion at illegal spying and intrusions of privacy. He made sure that the 1964 Democratic national convention and the black activist "Mississippi Freedom Democratic Party" were completely bugged with reports given to him immediately on what was going on at the Atlantic City convention.

Before John Kennedy edged out Johnson for the Democratic nomination, Bobby again would reportedly turn to Marcello for cash, this time at the Democratic convention. Marcello again rebuffed the young Kennedy. Instead, he donated $500,000 to the Richard Nixon campaign.

Bobby did not wait long into the Kennedy administration to act against Marcello by having him deported as an illegal immigrant. The action was also solidified by Marcello's 1938 violation of the Marihuana Tax Act, in which Marcello sold twenty-three pounds of untaxed marijuana and was sentenced to short prison time and a heavy fine. The Justice Department, with Bobby in charge, negotiated with the Italian government to welcome Marcello into their country upon deportation.[6] Marcello, who knew his deportation was imminent, also knew that he could not conduct his business from faraway Italy. His man Carl Noll traveled to Guatemala to broker a deal with a local fixer, who had Marcello's name written into a blank space on the public birth entry ledger in the small town of San Jose Pinula. The ruse worked, and on April 4, 1961, Marcello was deported to Guatemala. Appearing at the Immigration and Naturalization Service in New Orleans, he was briskly handcuffed, taken in a multiple patrol car escort to Moisant International Airport, loaded up, and shipped out.

"You would have thought it was the president going in instead of me going out,"[7] Marcello recalled.

Shortly after his deportation, a local paper in Guatemala, *El Imparcial*, began to expose Marcello's citizenship in Guatemala as fraudulent. Guatemalan President Miguel Fuentes booted Marcello out of the country a short time later.

Burton Hersh, in *Bobby and J. Edgar*, expanded on Marcello's perilous trip back to American soil after his expulsion from Guatemala:

> Marcello's family returned to Louisiana, and he and his lifelong
> friend, the attorney Mike Maroun, started toward San Salvador
> in a battered station wagon. They soon ran into marauding
> soldiers, abandoned the station wagon vehicle, and after a six-
> hour ride on a rickety bus through the ragged, desolate mountain
> country between El Salvador and Honduras these two pudgy,
> aging men in silk Shantung suits were reduced to wandering.
> Starving and increasingly desperate to come upon some vestige
> of civilization, they stuffed the $3,000 they had left between them
> into their crumbling alligator shoes. Fearful that two Indian boys
> they picked up to guide them were about to murder them with
> their machetes, Maroun and Marcello plunged down a thorn-
> ridden ravine, where Marcello tumbled through boulders and
> bayonet grass and broke three ribs.
>
> "If I don't make it, Mike," Marcello said in his Cajun patois
> to his friend and attorney, Mike Maroun, "tell my brothers when
> you get back, about what dat kid Bobby done to us. Tell 'em to do
> what dey have to do."[8]

Marcello, bruised and battered, made it to Honduras and, with
the help of forged documents, reentered the United States on May
28, 1961.[9] One bruise would never heal.

Marcello's lawyers had been working up a case for wrongful
deportation before the wheels of his plane touched the ground in
Guatemala. Marcello, upon his return, would fight the Kennedys
in the courtroom claiming that it was the administration that had
secured forged documents confirming his Guatemalan birth and
"that had the true facts been revealed, Guatemala would not have
accepted him as a deportee."[10] It was a deft strategy that held up
the courts.

Italy did not want Marcello because he had claimed to be
a Guatemalan citizen, a claim he vehemently refuted in the

American courts. He had a lawsuit in the civil court of Rome in a previous case that had declared him "not to be a citizen of Italy and to enjoin the Italian Government from issuing a travel document to him."[11] Guatemala also no longer wanted him. Marcello used the system against itself and played dumb in relation to the entire deportation. He claimed "he was never in Guatemala previously, is unfamiliar with its customs and language, and asserts that the statute authorizing his deportation there as construed and applied to him is unconstitutional in that it violates due process and the prohibition against cruel and unusual punishment."[12]

Marcello cited the Fifth Amendment and Eighth Amendment and Section 243(a) of the Immigration and Nationality Act, which stated that the country of deportation would have to be one from where "such alien last entered the United States" or was "the country in which he was born."[13]

As Bobby was attempting to issue a second deportation order, Marcello was looking to question the legality of the first, which gave him time to plot strategy outside the halls of justice.

In late 1962, pieces of Marcello's contribution to the Kennedy assassination plot began trickling out through FBI informant Edward Becker. In September 1962, during a New Orleans business meeting at a Marcello-owned swamp property called Churchill Farms, Baker heard an inebriated Marcello begin to let bits of the conspiracy slip out upon mention of Bobby Kennedy's name.

"Livarsi na petra di la scarpa!" Marcello screamed in Italian, which translated to "Take the stone out of my shoe!"[14]

"Don't worry about the little son of a bitch," Marcello yelled. "He's going to be taken care of."

"But you can't go after Bobby Kennedy," Becker said. "If you do, you're going to get into a hell of a lot of trouble."[15]

"No, I'm not talkin' about dat," Marcello said, intimating more details. "Ya know what they say in Sicily: If you want to kill a dog, you don't cut off the tail, you cut off the head. The dog will keep biting you if you only cut off its tail, but if the dog's head is cut off, the dog will die, tail and all."[16]

Marcello then told his plans to get a lone nut to take the fall, "the way they do in Sicily."[17]

Hoover no doubt learned about the meeting, and surveillance on Becker would increase though the fall of 1962.[18] Hoover, after learning about the Marcello meeting through Becker, made a strong effort to discredit the informant.

In late October 1962, a bureau report declared that Becker "allegedly made up 'stories' and invented rumors to derive 'possible gain' from such false information."[19]

Years later, Becker would reflect on what he learned from Marcello. "Remember Carlos had said in front of me at Churchill Hills that he was already thinking of hiring a nut to do the job, the way they do in Sicily? Well, that's the way the Mafia works in Sicily. Sometimes they entice some half-retarded illiterate kid into making a hit for them. Then they knock the kid off before he can talk."[20]

The "half-retarded illiterate kid" would, like Marcello, Giancana, Rosselli, and Trafficante, have connections to both the Mafia and the CIA. Lee Harvey Oswald's uncle, Charles "Dutz" Murret, whom the HSCA found to be "a surrogate father of sorts" to Oswald, had been an underworld gambling figure and an associate to the Marcello crime family.[21]

It was also discovered that Oswald was connected to David Ferrie, who worked as a pilot for Marcello up until the Kennedy assassination. Oswald had been in a unit of the Civil Air Patrol in which Ferrie was an instructor.

The Civil Air Patrol counted oilman D. H. Byrd as one of its founders. Byrd, along with owning the building that housed the Texas School Book Depository from where the shots that killed JFK were allegedly fired, was a close friend of and shared business interests with Lyndon Johnson.[22]

Ferrie was also a link between the CIA and the Mafia. He was reportedly involved in a CIA training camp for Cuban exiles outside of New Orleans in the summer of 1963.[23]

On the day of the president's death, Ferrie was in a New Orleans courthouse with Marcello waiting on a verdict concerning Carlos's deportation.

Following the assassination of John Kennedy, many roads left unexplored by the Warren Commission would lead a clear path to Marcello. He is the one character in the Kennedy assassination conspiracy with connections to all the major players. Oswald, Ruby, Texas oil, the CIA and, most importantly Lyndon Johnson all had direct ties to Marcello.

In 1979, Marcello admitted to FBI informant Joseph Hauser that he had also played a role in the CIA operations to assassinate Castro.

The HSCA would report in its findings that, even though the national crime syndicate as a whole was not involved in the assassination, a splinter group consisting of a "crime leader or a small combination of leaders" could have devised the plot.[24]

The committee also detailed "credible associations relating both Lee Harvey Oswald and Jack Ruby to figures having a relationship, albeit tenuous, with Marcello's crime family or organization."[25]

When Marcello was brought before the HSCA, he denied any knowledge of or involvement in the Kennedy assassination. He also denied ever making any threats against President Kennedy.[26]

By the mid-1970s, with the government getting ever more curious concerning the relation of Marcello to the CIA, it would no doubt begin to touch on Marcello's connection to the Kennedy assassination. Giancana and Rosselli were set to testify, and from all indications from Jack Anderson's reportage, Rosselli was not shy about his involvement.

A plaque that hung from the door of Marcello's office at the Town & Country Motel in New Orleans conveyed his thoughts on the matter:

THREE CAN KEEP

A SECRET

IF TWO ARE DEAD[27]

The relationship between the underworld and the government was the key to devising and realizing a crime where the judge and jury, prosecution and defense, accuser and accused would be one and the same. The last thing needed was a man who could control the parameters of the crime, the crime scene, the evidence and the investigation. No man was in a more desperate position to do so by November 1963 than the vice president of the United States.

In 1979, I signed on to run Ronald Reagan's campaign for president in New York, among other Northeastern states. I was given a card file that supposedly held Governor and Mrs. Reagan's "friends in New York" who might be solicited for help. Among them was a card for Roy M. Cohn, Esq. with the law firm of Saxe, Bacon and Bolan. I called Cohn's office to make an appointment.

Cohn had his own dust-up with the Kennedys. He had tangled with Bobby when both were on the committee staff of Senator Joseph R. McCarthy. As attorney general, RFK would push New York US Attorney Robert Morgenthau to indict Cohn twice. Cohn, essentially representing himself, had been acquitted both times. I knew he hated the Kennedys.

On the appointed morning, I arrived at Cohn's law firm brownstone on the Upper East Side. I cooled my heels for about an hour. Finally I was told to go to a second floor dining room where Mr. Cohn would meet me. He was wearing a silk dressing gown. His heavy-lidded eyes were bloodshot, most likely from a late night of revelry. Seated with Cohn was his client, a heavy-set gentleman, who had been meeting with Cohn.

"Meet Tony Salerno," said Roy.

I was face to face with "Fat Tony" Salerno, at that time the boss of the Genovese Crime family. In October 1986, *Fortune Magazine* would call the seventy-five-year-old Salerno America's "top gangster in power, wealth, and influence." Salerno served as consigliore, underboss, and acting boss of the Genovese family.

"Roy says we are going with Reagan, and that's all right by me," said Tony. Salerno said he had eschewed presidential politics since 1960 when "Jack Kennedy took our money and our votes and then fucked us."

I couldn't resist.

"Who really killed JFK?" I asked Fat Tony.

"It was Carlos and LBJ," the gangster replied. "He got what was coming to him."

Cohn simply nodded his head to affirm Salerno's claim and they both laughed.

Salerno's comments are intriguing in light of the fact that Clint Murchison Sr., an inner circle LBJ oilman from Dallas, had a close business relationship with the Genovese family. Vito Genovese and his family owned twenty percent of the Murchison Oil Lease Company, as a Senate Committee discovered in 1955. Clint Murchison also had close business ties with Carlos Marcello, a mafioso with a fantastic hatred of the Kennedys.

In 1963, Clint Murchison was the preeminent business and behind-the-scenes political leader in Dallas. His son Clint Murchison Jr. was a founding owner of the Dallas Cowboys in 1960. Clint Murchison Sr. also had friendships at the highest level nationally. In the summer of 1963, he hosted John J. McCloy, the chairman of the Council on Foreign Relations from 1953 to 1970 and longtime high-level foreign policy establishment player, on his Mexican ranch, where they hunted whitewing doves together. McCloy biographer Kai Bird: "That summer, McCloy relaxed more than he had for many years. He hunted whitewings with Clint Murchison on the Texas oil man's Mexico farm."

After Allen Dulles and Gerald Ford, John McCloy was one of the key architects of the cover-up perpetrated by the Warren Commission.

Ernestine Orrick Van Buren, a longtime secretary of Murchison, wrote a biography about him entitled *Clint*. Van Buren relates that Murchison suffered a huge disappointment with the Democratic nomination of John Kennedy for president in 1960 and was in "cold disbelief" when Lyndon Johnson joined the ticket as VP to JFK.

Van Buren:

> In December 1963, soon after Lyndon Johnson became president following the assassination of John F. Kennedy, there was a soft rap on the bedroom door where Clint was napping. It was Warren Tilley, butler at Gladoak Farms. "Washington calling, Mr. Murchison. The President [LBJ] wants to speak with you."
>
> A brief silence followed. Then through the closed door came the muffled voice of Clint Murchison. "Tell the president I can't hear him." Clint resumed his nap.

What kind of person takes a nap instead of answering the call of the president of the United States? Maybe someone who is more important than the president.

NOTES

1. HSCA Testimony of Santos Trafficante.
2. Goldfarb, *Perfect Villains, Imperfect Heroes*, 76.
3. Scott M. Deitche, *The Silent Don: The Criminal Underworld of Santo Trafficante Jr.* (Fort Lee: Barricade, 2007), 120.
4. Hersh, *Bobby and J. Edgar*, 252.
5. Davis, *Mafia Kingfish*, 154.
6. Goldfarb, *Perfect Villains, Imperfect Heroes*, 74.
7. Hersh, *Bobby and J. Edgar*, 255.
8. Ibid.
9. Ibid.
10. Jack Wasserman and Paul L. Winings. *Carlos Marcello, Petitioner v. Robert F. Kennedy, Attorney General of the United States, et al. U.S. Supreme Court Transcript of Record with Supporting Pleadings* (Making of the Modern Law Print Edition, n.d.), 5.

11. Ibid., 2.
12. Ibid.
13. Ibid., 4.
14. North, *Act of Treason*, 200.
15. Davis, *Mafia Kingfish*, 122.
16. Ibid.
17. Ibid., 122.
18. North, *Act of Treason*, 200.
19. Ibid., 221.
20. Davis, *Mafia Kingfish*, 231.
21. "HSCA Final Assassinations Report," *History Matters*, June 2012, history-matters.com/archive/contents/hsca/contents_hsca_report. htm, 170
22. Baker, Russ, *Family of Secrets*, 97–98.
23. Waldron and Hartmann, *Ultimate Sacrifice*, 171.
24. HSCA Fina Report, 166.
25. Ibid., 169.
26. HSCA Final Report, 172.
27. Hersh, *Bobby and J. Edgar*, 180.

CHAPTER ELEVEN

RELATIONSHIPS

By 1963, Bobby Kennedy and the Justice Department were closing in on Vice President Johnson. Johnson was wealthy far beyond what life as a civil servant could afford him, paid by unscrupulous dealings with associates. By President Kennedy's second term, Bobby wanted to ensure that Johnson would not only be out of office but also facing possible imprisonment. John Kennedy, who remained publicly devoted to Johnson, was covertly plotting to replace him. According to plan, Kennedy would not have to drop Johnson. With Bobby's help, Johnson would be a victim of his own undoing.

Shortly before his trip to Dallas, President Kennedy sat down in the rocking chair in his personal secretary Evelyn Lincoln's office. He spoke to her about the considerable governmental changes that he planned to implement in his second term and how Johnson was not the right man to help advocate these transitions.

"I am going to Texas because I have made a commitment," Kennedy told Lincoln. "I can't patch up those warring factions. This is for them to do, but I will go because I have told them I would. And it is too early to make an announcement about another running mate. That will perhaps wait until the convention."[1]

When asked by Lincoln about his choice for a running mate, Kennedy replied, "At this time, I am thinking about Governor Terry

Sanford of North Carolina. But it will not be Lyndon."[2] And there were several reasons why.

Twin scandals were consuming the careers of two of Johnson's closest affiliates: Billy Sol Estes and Bobby Baker. And the vice president was linked to their corruption.

Bobby "Little Lyndon" Baker had served as secretary for the majority in the Senate as well as Johnson's personal secretary. When he entered the Senate in 1948, Johnson sought Baker out. He had worked in the Senate for six years and knew the ins and outs of the upper house and its occupants.

"Mr. Baker, I understand you know where the bodies are buried in the Senate," Johnson remarked in their initial telephone call. "I'd appreciate it if you'd come to my office and talk with me."[3]

The relationship was mutually beneficial. Johnson had the energy and ambition, and Baker had the insider's edge to propel their alliance through the Senate.

Baker, whom Johnson sometimes referred to as "my son," was an errand boy. Calls were made on Johnson's behalf, notes were taken, and hands were shaken. Baker would be brought to receptions with Johnson to taste the majority leader's drinks, making sure they were weaker than those of the people he was trying to subdue politically.[4] In his years in the Senate and for the majority of his time as vice president, Johnson was in contact with Baker daily, considering him an invaluable protégé.

Through Johnson, Baker learned the art of politics and the science of moving money.

At the time, a number of influential Texas politicians and businessmen would meet regularly at the Houston Lamar Hotel.[5] The confab took the moniker "Suite 8F," named after Herman Brown's hotel room, where they convened. His company, Brown and Root, had supported Johnson's political campaigns and helped to make him a wealthy man in exchange for government contracts and favorable legislation.

The group favored a "healthy business climate, characterized by a minimum of government regulations, a weak labor movement, a tax system favorable to business investment, the use of government subsidies and supports where needed to spur development, and a conservative approach to the expansion of government social services."[6] Ultimately, the proceedings were an unhealthy collusion of greedy business owners and self-serving politicians.

These men were, in the words of Johnson's long-time mistress Madeleine Brown, "the great, white fathers of Texas. Primarily, it was your oil people, your high rollers."[7] And she should know.

Madeleine Duncan Brown's twenty-one-year relationship with Johnson, which produced a son, provides a view to a side of Johnson that his wife and daughters never saw. It was a life that Johnson kept hidden, and for a good reason: the fiery redhead was a prostitute.

As a young girl, Brown spent her evenings with the richest and most powerful men in Texas. When asked many years later about the company she kept, she told researcher Casey Quinlan that she was an advertising executive by day and a call girl by night.

Starting in 1948, the Dallas single mother answered the frequent call of Lyndon Johnson, then just a Texas congressman with the mark of destiny. They wouldn't meet for long—usually a half hour, according to Brown, and often at Johnson's Driskill Hotel suite in Austin. There is strong indication that she traveled with Johnson on occasion, too, but most of their meetings were short, sweet, and purely physical.

"I was wild and full of fire. He had a certain amount of roughness about him, and maybe that's what I liked, you know. He commanded," Brown told *People Magazine* in August 1987. "I've been told that every woman needs to act like a whore in bed, and I guess that's what I did."

Johnson family confidant Jesse Kellam organized the trysts, and Brown was sworn to secrecy. In April 1950, soon after Johnson had ascended to the US Senate, she told him she was pregnant. Angry at first, the senator watched as Brown grew heavy with his child and quietly made arrangements. When Steven Brown was born, the mother and her sons were set up in a house with a maid and plenty of credit cards. The support continued for many years, but LBJ would never admit paternity.

Brown remembers seeing J. Edgar Hoover while with Lyndon on their second date together in Austin. She asked Lyndon about it, and it was the first time he warned her with a phrase that he would often repeat: "He told me little girls shouldn't have big eyes and big ears, and they didn't see, hear, or repeat anything." She fulfilled his wishes until the late 1980s, when she made herself available for assassination researchers. Soon after, her son Steven sought paternity redress from the Johnson estate. He died under mysterious circumstances in 1990.

Brown's interviews are laced with blushing admissions that she was a wild child, kinky in bed, and ready to go whenever a hat was dropped. She worked Jack Ruby's Carousel Club for a time, a Dallas nightclub notorious for hookers. Her stories about the Texas rich and powerful of the JFK era also ring true. Texas oil barons were known to consort with call girls.

Madeleine Duncan Brown had been a high-dollar prostitute, and Lyndon Baines Johnson was her favorite john. And her stories about whom she saw and overheard while servicing Johnson ring true to this day. In fact, it is her intimate memories that fill in many of the gaps in the Kennedy assassination.

Members of Suite 8F included oil barons Clint Murchison and H. L. Hunt, as well as David Harold Byrd, the owner of the building that housed the Texas Book Depository, and Johnson attorney Ed Clark—names that would be standard roll call in Johnson's political business deals. All these men would factor into and stand to benefit from the succession of Kennedy to Johnson. Known as a "shadow government,"[8] the men of Suite 8F could bend business, politics, and power to their will.

Brown claimed she saw the Suite 8F group together the night before the Kennedy assassination, at a party in Murchison's Dallas mansion. Other guests she claimed to have seen at the party were Richard Nixon, who saw the meeting only as a social function, and FBI Director J. Edgar Hoover, who, as a semi-regular attendant of Suite 8F gatherings, knew the more sinister intentions of the gathering.

"He hobnobbed with those people," Brown said of Hoover, "particularly Clint."[9]

Hoover had been friends with Murchison for many years, accepting free vacations to his California estate, Hotel del Charro, to curry favor. Staying at the Murchison's hotel, Hoover would rub shoulders with Big Oil, the CIA, and the Mafia. He would frequent the local Del Mar racetrack also owned by Murchison. Similar to Johnson's relationship with Murchison, Hoover's was mutually beneficial.

"Hoover alerted his Del Mar buddies Clint Murchison and Sid Richardson to forthcoming regulatory agency—and Supreme Court—decisions, through their Washington lobbyist Tommy Webb," Curt Gentry wrote in *J. Edgar Hoover: A Man and the Secrets*. "In return, in addition to picking up the tab for Hoover's and Tolson's annual southern California vacations, the two Texas wheeler dealers (Murchison and Richardson) gave the FBI director tips on oil stocks and, on more than a few occasions, complimentary stock."[10]

The relationship between the construction firm Brown and Root and Lyndon Johnson, which started in 1937 with the building of the Marshall Ford Dam, would be a blueprint for the Suite 8F crowd.

Prior to the construction of the Austin-area dam, Brown and Root, a company founded by brothers Herman and George Brown with Dan Root, was a small construction business primarily building roads to accommodate the rapidly growing use of automobiles.[11] With their business dwindling in the Depression era, Brown and Root turned to former Texas state senator and behind-the-scenes player Alvin J. Wirtz to help secure the dam project.[12] Wirtz, who would later become a Suite 8F member, used his government influence and persuasion to acquire the dam project for Brown and Root, a company that had never built a dam before.[13] As Brown and Root became more connected with the government, they were frequently awarded big contracts for which they were not the best qualified.

"To be road builders, you have to know about concrete and asphalt," George Brown said at the time. "You have to learn something about bridges. Once you learn these things, it's only a step, if you're not afraid, to pour concrete for a dam. And if you get into the dam business, you'll pick up a lot of information about power plants. . . . each component of a new job involves things you've done before."[14]

The dam project caught a snag when Brown and Root found out that it was not being built on land owned by the federal government, which made its construction unlawful. Wirtz in turn got the twenty-eight year old Lyndon Johnson, who was looking for support in his run for US Congress, to petition the president for his allowance to continue construction.[15]

Franklin Roosevelt, impressed by Johnson and his voracious support for the New Deal, gave the project his blessing.

"Give the kid the dam," directed the president.[16]

It would later be said that the life and career of Johnson was built on the Marshall Ford Dam. The same was true of Brown and Root and their business of plying politicians with favors and money to get government contracts.

It was, in the words of Johnson, "a joint venture . . . Wirtz is going to take care of the legal part, and I'm going to take care of the politics, and you're going to take care of the business end of it . . . The three of us together will come up with a solution that will improve the status of all three of us."[17]

In 1947, Brown and Root founded Texas Eastern Transmission. For a $143 million cash investment, the company had bought the "Big Inch" and "Little Inch" pipelines, which had been laid during World War II and carried oil from Texas up to the Northeastern United States.[18] Interest in Texas Eastern Transmission was bought by many of the Suite 8F crowd including Ed Clark, the attorney known as the "secret boss of Texas," a man Barr McClellan connected to many a Johnson crime.

When Johnson reached the Senate, Brown and Root pushed him to help put an end to federal regulation of the oil industry. Deregulation would privatize the business for Texas Eastern Transmission, allowing them to dramatically raise the prices on natural gas, reaping a huge profit for the company and its investors. In order for the deregulation to become reality, Johnson would have to rid the Federal Power Commission (FPC) of its head, Leland Olds, a strict enforcer of the Natural Gas Act of 1938.

"This [Olds's defeat] transcended philosophy, this would put something in their pockets," said former Texas Governor John Connally. "This was the real bread-and-butter issue to these oilmen. So this would prove whether Lyndon was reliable, that he was no New Dealer. This was his chance to get in with dozens of oilmen—to bring very powerful rich men into his fold, who had never been for him, and were still suspicious of him. So for Lyndon this was the way to turn it around: *take care of this guy.*"[19]

Johnson, in his plan to rid the oil industry of Leland Olds, would chair the subcommittee investigating Olds's renomination to the FPC in 1949. Helping Johnson dig dirt on Olds was Alvin Wirtz, who along with representing the interests of Johnson and Brown and Root, was also a Texas oil lobbyist. The key to the attack on Olds was painting him as a communist by using articles written by the FPC head that were printed in communist magazines through a newswire twenty years before.

"Yes, unbelievable as it seems, gentlemen, this man Leland Olds, the man who now asks the consent and approval of the senate to serve on the Federal Power Commission, has not believed in our constitution, our government, our congress, our representative form of government, our churches, our flag, our schools, our system of free enterprise,"[20] said Texas Congressman John Lyle to the subcommittee.

Following the hearings, the character of Olds was effectively damaged, his career was ruined, and Texas oil had the deregulation they needed and the politician they wanted in Lyndon Johnson.

Getting in bed with Big Oil helped Johnson with cash and connections. While campaigning for a Senate seat in 1948, he advocated for the oil-depletion allowance. When he won, Johnson and House Speaker Sam Rayburn fought any legislation against what amounted to a massive tax break.

The depletion allowance was a loophole for Texas oilmen to avoid paying heavy taxes on income. It was "a special provision of the federal income tax under which oil producers can treat up to 27.5% of their income as exempt from income tax—supposedly to compensate for the depletion of oil reserves. In effect, this provision gave the oil industry (and a few others) a lower tax rate than other industries."[21]

John Kennedy, when campaigning for president, realized the importance of upholding the depletion allowance. It went hand-in-hand with putting Johnson on the ticket to elicit the Southern vote. Furthermore, Joe Kennedy had been a big supporter of and prospered from Big Oil. A strong stance against the allowance could have easily killed Kennedy's chances of victory.

"I am not kidding when I say we are lost," John Connally told Lyndon Johnson during the 1960 presidential campaign. "If Kennedy comes out for the repeal—or anything that can be interpreted that way—there is no power on earth that can save us."[22]

Kennedy, while campaigning, wanted to make "clear my recognition of the value and importance of the oil-depletion allowance. I realize its importance and value. . . . The oil-depletion allowance has served us well."[23] His words assured Big Oil and the men of Suite 8F.

Like the Mafia and the CIA's cold warriors, the oilmen would see a very different and unexpected man when Kennedy became president. On January 24, 1961, less than a week after his inauguration,

President Kennedy presented a bill to Congress that "called into question both the principle and the rates of the fiscal privileges, the improper use of tax dollars, and the depletion allowance."[24]

There is no doubt that Kennedy saw a danger in Big Oil's massive profits gained through beneficial legislation.

"Now is the time to act," said Kennedy. "We cannot afford to be timid or slow."[25]

Once again, Kennedy would make powerful enemies who would require his exit from office to continue their flow of massive subsidized wealth.

In stark contrast to the Kennedys, Johnson was always about helping those who helped him. In the years following the Marshall Ford Dam project, Brown and Root had also got involved in military projects, beginning with building boats for the Navy.

"We didn't know the stern from the aft—I mean the bow—of the boat," George Brown later said.[26]

Four days after the death of President Kennedy, Johnson signed National Security Action Memorandum 273 (NSAM 273), setting the stage for increased assistance to the South Vietnamese, which would not only be a military effort but a "political, economical, social, educational, and informational effort."[27]

The signing of NSAM 273 nullified President Kennedy's own memorandum, NSAM 263, set "to withdraw the bulk of US personnel by the end of 1965." Kennedy's view of the turmoil in Vietnam was realistic. "I don't think that unless a greater effort is made by the government to win popular support that the war can be won out there," Kennedy said in an interview with Walter Cronkite on September 2, 1963. "In the final analysis, it is their war. They are the ones who have to win it or lose it. We can help them, we can give them equipment, we can send our men out there as advisers, but they have to win it, the people of Vietnam, against the communists."[28]

Where Kennedy saw a futile effort and an unforgivable death toll, Johnson saw opportunity and a commitment to his donors. During the Kennedy administration, in keeping good relations with the war hawks, Johnson was provided with intelligence reports on Vietnam that were held back from JFK.[29]

Johnson had "a charm based on pure self-interest," said journalist Murray Kempton, "which makes him, in a sense, the only truly Marxist materialist political figure we have ever had."[30]

Four months later, after signing NSAM 273, Johnson initiated NSAM 288, signing into action an American takeover of the activities in Vietnam. And in August of 1964, the Gulf of Tonkin Incident, two separate confrontations perceived as North Vietnamese aggression against American ships, would give Lyndon Johnson the impetus needed to push the Vietnam War to a full launch. In reality, the Gulf of Tonkin Incident was full of bent truths and fabrications. During the first confrontation on August 2, it was discovered later (and not initially reported by the Johnson administration) that the destroyer USS *Maddox* had fired first. The second confrontation, on August 4, was not a confrontation at all.

"For all I know, our Navy was shooting at whales out there," Johnson would later say of the incident.[31]

Along with Raymond/Morrison-Knudsen and J. A. Jones Construction, Brown and Root, by then a subsidiary of Halliburton, were given roughly ninety percent of construction projects in Vietnam.[32] Working under the acronym RMK–BRJ, these companies dubbed themselves the "Vietnam Builders."[33]

Speaking about the need of construction in Vietnam, Secretary of Defense Robert McNamara would explain that military involvement "in a country of this sort requires the construction of new ports, warehouse facilities, access roads, improvements to highways leading to the interior of the country and along the coasts, troop facilities, hospitals, completely new airfields, and major improvements to existing airfields, communications facilities, etc."[34]

Over a billion dollars was paid to the companies for the construction projects, sparking the interest of Donald Rumsfeld, then a young congressman, who pushed for a probe into the "thirty-year association between LBJ as congressman, senator, vice president, and president"[35] and Brown and Root.

Seeing the potential for malfeasance, Rumsfeld said "under one contract between the US government and this combine, it is officially estimated that obligations will reach at least $900 million by November 1967 . . . Why this huge contract has not been and is not now being adequately audited is beyond me. The potential for waste and profiteering under such a contract is substantial."[36]

Bell Helicopter, the company that contributed to Johnson's 1948 Senate campaign with money and transportation, also found fortune in Vietnam. It was given a contract to mass-produce the signature UH-1 Huey gunship helicopter for transporting troops and supplies as well as performing reconnaissance work.[37]

"We went from shipping fifty helicopters to shipping two hundred helicopters per contract order," said a former Bell employee. "That was a huge jump." The employee added that "Vietnam made Bell."[38]

A note written from George Brown to Johnson in his early years as a congressman is revealing of Johnson's loyalties:

Dear Lyndon,

In the past I have not been very timid about asking you to do favors for me and hope that you will not get any timidity if you have anything at all that you think I can or should do. Remember that I am for you, right or wrong, and it makes no difference whether I think you are right or wrong. If you want it, I am for it 100 percent.[39]

It was a model for success that would continue for decades. In 1995, Halliburton would hire former congressman and Washington insider Dick Cheney. To benefit the company, Cheney would provide the ability to "open doors around the world and to have access practically anywhere. . . . There was a lot that he could bring in the way of customer relationships."[40]

NOTES

1. Evelyn Lincoln. *Kennedy and Johnson* (New York: Holt, Rinehart and Winston, 1968), 204–5.
2. Ibid.
3. Bobby Baker and Larry L. King, *Wheeling and Dealing: Confessions of a Capitol Hill Operator* (New York: Norton, 1978), 34.
4. Caro, *Master of the Senate*, 336.
5. Dan Briody, *The Halliburton Agenda: The Politics of Oil and Money* (Hoboken: John Wiley & Sons, 2004), 121.
6. Ibid., 133–34.
7. Ross, Gaylon, "The Clint Murchison Meeting" YouTube video, 1:21:24, posted by "Se7ensenses," May 26, 2011, youtube.com/watch?v=POmdd6HQsus.
8. *Houston Chronicle*, August 4, 2003.
9. Ross, Gaylon, "The Clint Murchison Meeting" YouTube video, 1:21:24, posted by "Se7ensenses," May 26, 2011, youtube.com/watch?v=POmdd6HQsus.
10. Gentry, *J. Edgar Hoover: The Man and his Secrets*, 383.
11. Briody, *The Hallibuton Agenda*, 25.
12. Ibid., 37–40.
13. Ibid., 40–43.
14. Ibid., 44.
15. Ibid., 47.
16. Ibid., 54.
17. Ibid., 61.
18. Caro, *Master of the Senate*, 246.
19. Ibid., 248.
20. Ibid., 254.
21. James G. Hepburn, *Farewell America* ([Vaduz]: Frontiers, 1968), 217.
22. Bryce, *Cronies*, 91.
23. Ibid., 92.
24. Hepburn, *Farewell America*, 235.
25. Ibid.

26. Briody, *The Halliburton Agenda*, 85.
27. "LBJ Library: NSAM 273." May, 2012, lbjlib.utexas.edu/johnson/archives. hom/nsams/nsam273.asp.
28. Douglass, *JFK and the Unspeakable*, 189.
29. Baker, *Family of Secrets*, 99.
30. *Firing Line*, June 6, 1966.
31. Joseph C. Goulden, *Truth Is the First Casualty: The Gulf of Tonkin Affair: Illusion and Reality* (Chicago: Rand McNally, 1969), 160.
32. Prata Chatterjee, *Halliburton's Army: How a Well-Connected Texas Oil Company Revolutionized the Way America Makes War* (New York: Nation, 2009), 23.
33. Ibid., 24.
34. Ibid., 25.
35. Ibid., 27.
36. Ibid.
37. Bryce, *Cronies*, 106–7.
38. Ibid., 107.
39. Briody, *The Halliburton Agenda*, 63.
40. Bryce, *Cronies*, 188.

CHAPTER TWELVE

WHEELER DEALERS

I f there was one thing Bobby "Little Lyndon" Baker could learn from Lyndon Johnson, it was to put one's personal welfare above the good of the nation. Brown and Root had lifted Johnson through the ranks of government. With the presidency, the company and the politician would be among the few beneficiaries of war in Vietnam.

From Suite 8F and dealing directly with Johnson, Baker made the connections and learned the tricks that would define his career. He watched as Johnson shook down television executives for better advertising rates or accepted prodigious amounts of money from multiple benefactors for his own personal use.[1] Baker kept this knowledge close, to protect a man he revered.

During the height of a scandal that would consume Baker, Johnson was more than happy to accept Baker's silence concerning his questionable business affairs.

The business venture that would spark the investigation into Baker's questionable finances was Serv-U, a Washington vending machine business, which Baker had started with his friend Fred Black. Serv-U came under fire from Ralph Hill, the president of Capitol Vending, who charged that Baker was obtaining his vending machines by offering assistance in the acquisition of defense contracts, a twist on an old Johnson ploy.[2] The fire spread quickly, and more of Baker's questionable actions began to surface, including allegations that he furnished prostitutes for politicians at a social club located in a hotel near the Senate offices.

One senior senator recalled that "girls were solicited on government telephone lines, taken to the place, and entertained the prospective customer."[3]

On October 7, 1963, Baker resigned as secretary of the US Senate majority. By the end of the month, the buzzards were circling over Johnson. The vice president's reaction was first to panic. Then, he severed all ties to Baker.

When asked for a response concerning the growing scandal, Johnson refused to issue a comment.[4]

On the morning of November 22, 1963, as the presidential motorcade made its way through Dallas, the Bobby Baker scandal had shifted focus to the vice president. For a man who had begun his public service career devoid of money, Johnson, as a civil servant, had become rich beyond comprehension. That morning, Don Reynolds, a Baker associate, told the Senate Rules Committee about an insurance policy that he had arranged for Johnson. He testified that, at the suggestion of Baker, he had given the Johnson family a stereo set that cost over $500 and bought $1,200 worth of advertising on the radio and television station owned by Johnson's company.[5] More damaging in his testimony was the admission that Reynolds had seen Baker with a suitcase containing $100,000 to be delivered to Johnson—a payoff for steering a government contract to General Dynamics.[6] This *same* Don Reynolds told the FBI in 1964 an eyebrow-raising comment uttered by Bobby Baker on Inauguration Day, January 20, 1961, just as Kennedy was being sworn into office. As reported by Jay Epstein in the December, 1966 issue of *Esquire*, Baker, to whom LBJ famously referred as his "right arm," said "Words to the effect that the SOB [John Kennedy] would never live out his term, and that he would die a violent death."

"I had been too recently a member of the club, and too keenly felt a kinship with LBJ and others, to turn rat," wrote Baker years later. "You may say that I was honoring the code of the underworld if you will, but I didn't want to hurt my friends. That's the context in which I thought of it."[7]

Baker soon found out that Johnson was much less of a friend. From the time of his resignation to only a few months before Johnson died, Lyndon cut communication with his former personal secretary in order to save his own career. His one conversation with the Johnson family during the "Bobby Baker Scandal" would come when Lady Bird phoned to assure Baker that the family still loved and stood by him.

"I was thinking. LBJ's right there by her side, but he won't talk to me because he wants to be able to say that he hasn't," Baker wrote. "I knew Johnson was petrified that he'd be dragged down; he would soon show this by attempting to make light of our former relationship and saying that I had been more the Senate's employee than his own."[8]

As Johnson attempted to separate himself from Baker, Bobby Kennedy put the puzzle together.

Reporters from *Life* magazine had been sent out the week before the assassination to fill in the gaps of the Johnson fortune. They found corruption on a scale that could ruin Johnson's career. The feature story, which would focus on Johnson's dealings with Baker, would run without a byline. The person with his hand buried the deepest in the story was the attorney general.

"It was all coming from Bobby," said former *Life* editor James Wagenvoord. "It was going to blow Johnson right out of the water. We had him. He was done. Bobby Baker had taken the fall for Johnson. Johnson would have been finished and off the 1964 ticket, and would have probably been facing prison time."[9]

With the death of the president, the article would never see the light of day. In its stead, the issue's focus was the Zapruder film. Following the assassination, *Life* had bought the rights to it and fashioned the truths shown in this key piece of evidence to keep in line with the official story.

Wagenvoord would also witness an FBI agent drop off material further incriminating Oswald: a newsreel of Oswald handing out pro-Castro fliers in New Orleans.[10]

"An hour later [after the film arrived at *Life*], the fat lady sang an encore. Jack Ruby shot Oswald,"[11] said Wagenvoord.

Johnson went on to be president, and Baker went on to jail.

In September 1972, three months after Baker was released from jail for his crimes, former Johnson aide Walter Jenkins sent word to him that the Johnson family wanted to invite him for a weekend at the ranch. Baker accepted.

"Well, Mr. Johnson isn't in the best of health. He's been seeking out old friends lately," Jenkins said. "I think he's mending fences."[12]

What Baker was treated to was not an apology for not coming to his aid and breaking communication with his loyal friend, but a final Johnson pity party. Johnson talked to him about how he would have helped him, but the media and Bobby Kennedy would have "crucified"[13] him, adding how tough it was to be president.

Baker asked for another bit of help. Nixon man Bebe Rebozo was putting pressure on Bobby to dole dirt about politicians, and a call from LBJ could help smooth it out. Johnson wouldn't consider it.

"If Bebe Rebozo told President Nixon I was sticking my nose into it, or, uh, if the press got a hold of it, then it'd be in big black headlines, and I don't think it would help either one of us," Johnson told Baker.

For Baker, whose admiration led him to name two of his children after Johnson, the brush-off was insulting.

"I rethought just about everything he'd told me during the afternoon and evening, realizing that most of it had touched on how people had let him down; not a word of his own faults or failures; not a word of his own backing and filling,"[14] Baker wrote.

Upon leaving the LBJ Ranch that weekend, Baker glimpsed the guestbook, which had last been signed by Johnson attorney and company man Abe Fortas a few days before.[15] In a final slight to

Baker, he had not been asked to sign the book that Johnson had always carefully maintained.

"So the prodigal son had not returned all the way home," Baker wrote. "He was welcomed only by the back door."[16]

During the years of the Kennedy administration, the money-making schemes of fellow Texan and Suite 8F member Billy Sol Estes would also threaten Johnson. If Bobby Baker was a glad-handing politician looking for a con, Estes was a con-man looking for a glad-handing politician. Both contributed to the desperate measures that Johnson would take in Dallas.

When, in 1953, the US Junior Chamber of Commerce named him one of the ten outstanding young men in the United States, Estes said that to be successful, "you had to walk out on a limb to the far end—for that's where the fruit is. If it breaks, you learn how far to go next time."[17]

The quote would be symbolic of Estes, who often went too far out on the limb, overstretching and overselling his business deals until he was brought up on fraud charges in 1962.

In the mid-1950s, Estes began selling anhydrous ammonia, a low-cost farm fertilizer made marketable by its easy application and availability. It was through the sale of anhydrous ammonia that Estes incurred a sizable debt to his distributor, Commercial Solvents. The company overlooked Estes's $555,000 debt, and with the aid of Billy's smooth talking, provided him $125,000 more for the purchase of additional ammonia and with $225,000 for him to start a business in grain storage.[18] Federal money rolled in, and Estes was able to slash the prices of his ammonia, cutting the cost of the competition and forcing them out of the industry.

"If you shatter an industry," Estes said, "you can pick up all the pieces for yourself."[19]

Estes then used his salesmanship to sell imaginary anhydrous ammonia storage facilities to West Texas farmers, who took out mortgages on unseen tanks and leased them back to him. Estes made over $30 million on the scam.[20]

In 1958, Estes also began conducting business with the federal government, obtaining subsidies to support his grain storage. It was through this government contact that Estes and Johnson began working together. He, like Baker, was treated as a personal friend to Johnson. The two hunted quail together, and Estes was given an invitation to John Kennedy's inauguration.[21] He would contribute a lot of money to Johnson personally and politically, while Johnson helped Estes secure cotton allotments for a scheme in which he grew the cotton on allotments illegally whittled off farmers.[22] When regulations were tightened, Estes would look to the vice president's top aide, Cliff Carter, for relief.

"Am moving my family to Washington this week so call on me in the vice president's office as we can serve you,"[23] Carter wrote to Estes on December 27, 1960, as he was preparing for the Kennedy administration.

By that time, it was typical Johnson: money for favors.

"During that time, daddy had been supplying Lyndon with large infusions of cash, not only for his own political needs, but for people Johnson himself chose to help," Estes's daughter Pam wrote. "Since these transactions were all cash, there is no reliable way of knowing how much money went to Johnson or what became of it."[24]

By 1960, the US Department of Agriculture was looking into Estes's scams. Henry Marshall, an inspector with the department, led the investigation as Johnson campaigned for the White House.

In January 1961, Estes had the manager of Billy Sol Enterprises, A. B. Foster, write to the newly-elected vice president's aide, Carter, to help stamp out the spreading blaze.

"We would sincerely appreciate you investigating this and seeing if anything can be done,"[25] Foster wrote. Of course, Johnson would have interest in quashing the examination of his deals with Estes, which would no doubt spark interest into many of Johnson's other deals with Texas businessmen.

Two days before the Kennedy inauguration, Estes, Carter, and Johnson met at Lyndon's Washington home and determined that Marshall would have to be "taken care of for good."[26]

On June 3, 1961, Marshall was found dead on his farm in the grass alongside his Chevy Fleetside. Shot five times in the chest and left abdomen with a .22 bolt-action rifle, the case was impossibly determined to be a suicide by the sheriffs on the scene. It was a verdict rendered without blood samples gathered or fingerprints taken from the truck or murder weapon.[27] Carbon monoxide was also found in Marshall's body—a hallmark in LBJ's Texas justice murders.

It was a death that would follow famed Texas Ranger Clint Peoples long into retirement. For Peoples, no sense could be made of the bizarre nature of the crime. Aside from the evidence, which convinced the ranger that it was a murder, Marshall did not seem to be a man who would take his own life.

Years later, Marshall's brother Robert related that Henry had no monetary or personal reasons to kill himself.

"He and his wife lost their first two kids, and this little boy (Donald Marshall) came along, and he was the happiest person in the world," Robert Marshall said. "He had everything to live for."[28] The case was reopened in May, 1962. Marshall's body was exhumed and examined, and the case was put before the Robertson County grand jury. The doctor who conducted the autopsy upon exhumation on May 22, Joseph A. Jachimczyk, backed Peoples's claim of a homicide. "Based on my preliminary autopsy examination," Jachimczyk said. "I believe this was not a suicide."[29]

Jachimczyk found that, if Marshall had used his shirt to seal off the exhaust pipe and administer carbon monoxide, there would have been soot on the shirt. But no soot was found. The doctor also found that the bruise on Marshall's head could not have occurred from a fall but from a harder blow.

Jachimczyk found that "if in fact this is a suicide, it is the most unusual one I have seen during the examination of approximately fifteen thousand deceased persons."[30]

The case was garnering attention in Washington, particularly from the attorney general. "I talked to John Kennedy one time and I talked to Robert Kennedy ten or twelve times," said Judge W. S. Barron. "He [Bobby] would just ask questions—how we were getting along, what we'd found, things like that."[31]

Nolan Griffin was a gas station attendant, who recalled a man stopping to ask for directions at the approximate time of the murder. The man, in Griffin's recollection, "wore dark-rimmed glasses, had dark hair, and a scarred, dark face."[32] The description led to "Mr. X," an artist's rendering that was circulated in the national media.

The police brought in a man who they claimed had been positively identified by Griffin. The man would later pass a polygraph test and be cleared of wrongdoing, which effectively discredited Griffin's testimony. Griffin would say later that the police were wrong and that he had been tricked by county attorney Bryan Russ and Sheriff Howard Stegall.

"When I was talking to Howard," Griffin said, "he handed me a pen, and Bryan shoved a paper under me and asked me to sign it. I didn't know what it was, didn't read it or anything. They were my friends, and I just did what they asked me to. A minute or so later, they got up, shook my hand, and I left."[33]

The trick worked, and all the fuel was taken out of Griffin's story.

"I never positively identified the man," Griffin said. "All I did was sign my name when they shoved that thing under me."[34]

Estes would be called to testify, but spent the majority of the inquiry clinging to the Fifth Amendment. The case would be rendered inconclusive, and the strange death of Henry Marshall would be shelved for a decade. Ranger Peoples, though, continued his dogged investigation.

In a report sent to Texas Rangers chief Homer Garrison in July 1963, Peoples's detailed the improbable elements of the death, which he said pointed more likely to homicide.

Our investigation reveals that, for Mr. Henry Marshall to have committed suicide, the following acts would have had to occur:

- The first act of Mr. Marshall would have been to take carbon monoxide. (The pathologist's report reveals that 15 percent carbon monoxide was present at time of autopsy one year later and that 15 percent would have been lost from embalming processes. A lethal dose consists of 40 percent.)
- Mr. Marshall would have had to dispose of the facilities with which the carbon monoxide was administered.
- Mr. Marshall received a serious brain injury on the left side of his head from a fall and a cut over his left side of his head from a fall and a cut over his left eye, causing the eye to protrude.
- Severe bruises with skin breakage on the back of his hands.
- Blood left on the right and left sides and the rear of the pickup truck.
- Mr. Marshall would have had to cut off the motor on the pickup.
- Absence of blood inside of the pickup after the motor was cut off.
- Absence of blood on the front of Mr. Marshall's shirt.
- The shirt of the deceased was open, with no bullet holes in front.
- Nitrites present only on the tail of Mr. Marshall's shirt (back side).
- A deep dent present on the right side of the pickup caused by some type of instrument other than a human hand or head, which was placed there on this date.
- Due to the lack of blood on the front of the shirt but considerable amounts present around the pickup creates another mystery.
- The investigation revealed that it was difficult for Mr. Marshall to straighten out his right arm, which was due to a prior injury, and it would have been necessary for him to pull the trigger with his left hand.[35]

Peoples went on to ascertain that all of the gunshot wounds were fired in a straight manner, which would have required composure and balance, a skillful feat that would have been impossible given the incapacitating damage that three of the shots inflicted: "one severing the aorta and two paralyzing."[36] The Texas Ranger contended that this was one of the "very, very few"[37] murder cases that he had been unable to solve and that he, like many others involved in the case, learned there were higher powers at work.

Johnson would be safe in the confines of government, and Estes would be sacrificed in the same vein as Bobby Baker. In April 1962, Estes was indicted by a Federal grand jury on fifty-seven acts of fraud.[38] At the time, Bobby Kennedy ordered seventy-six FBI agents to sort through the Estes scandal.[39] The Department of Agriculture and other sectors of the government were also being investigated for jobs and gifts received from Estes. The inquiry, no doubt, made Johnson, who had not only accepted money but had been cut into some of Estes's business opportunities, very nervous.

At the Estes trial, Johnson made sure that he was protected, hiring personal attorney John Cofer to serve his interests. Cofer had previously represented Johnson in the "Box 13" scandal. The attorney made certain that Estes never took the witness stand to ensure that nothing was said about his associations with Johnson.

"I don't believe that Johnson wanted Daddy convicted," wrote Estes's daughter Pam concerning the intentions of the vice president. "However, his order of priorities and those of Cofer were to protect Lyndon Baines Johnson and to prevent Daddy's conviction if possible. But, if not, to get the verdict overturned, and, if that didn't work, get Daddy to go to prison all by himself without making any waves. And that is exactly what happened."[40]

Before Estes was convicted, he was offered a deal by Bobby Kennedy: freedom in exchange for evidence and testimony against LBJ.

"I didn't take that deal," Estes told the *Houston Chronicle*. "I'd have been free for thirty minutes. Then, I'd have been dead. There were already some others who had gone that route."[41]

In 1971, after serving more than six years in prison, Estes was no more ready to start handing over names of those who had been in high places than while he was locked up.

"I can't see that there would have been any honor in doing time with big-name people," Estes said. "I know I was betrayed by some of them. I got my business and my politics all mixed together. As they say in Texas, I got my tit in a wringer. That won't happen again."[42]

Peoples, still certain that Marshall's death was a homicide, hounded Estes for the truth. In 1979, he escorted Estes to La Tuna Federal Prison in El Paso to serve four more years in prison for tax fraud. During their flight from Dallas-Fort Worth International Airport, Peoples asked about the Marshall murder.

"You may be assured . . . that Henry Marshall very definitely did not commit suicide," said Estes. "He was murdered."

"Billy Sol, which direction should I have been looking?" asked Peoples.

"Well, you know I cannot say too much because I am in the penitentiary. However, you should be looking at the people who had the most to lose," answered Estes.

"Should I have been looking in the direction of Washington?" Peoples asked.

"You are now very definitely on the right track," said Estes.[43]

By the mid-1980s, Estes was ready to talk.

In 1984, he dragged the death of Marshall back into questioning before the Robertson County grand jury. He charged that Johnson and Cliff Carter were intimately involved with the death of Marshall and that Johnson had given the order. The testimony of Estes was rejected on the basis that many of the major players in the story were dead and could neither confirm nor deny the charges. The accomplishment of the testimony was two-fold: It changed the death of Marshall from suicide to death by gunshot, and it brought into light bespectacled Johnson hit man, Malcolm "Mac" Wallace.

At one point, Wallace, a former marine who had been the president of the University of Texas student body, had strong political aspirations. In 1946, Wallace was an organizer for Homer Rainey's campaign for governor.[44] Wallace eventually became indebted to

Johnson, and the closest he would ever get to political office would be in administering of carnage for Johnson and his Texas business associates. Wallace was the Mr. X at the gas station asking Nolan Griffin for directions.

Described as a "hatchet man"[45] for Johnson by Lyndon's mistress Madeleine Brown, Wallace was an important link in many of the murders connected to Johnson. Estes's lawyer, Douglas Caddy, revealed Wallace's and Johnson's complicity in Texas-style justice in a letter to Stephan S. Trott at the US Department of Justice:

> My client, Mr. Estes, has authorized me to make this reply to your letter of May 29, 1984.
>
> Mr. Estes was a member of a four-member group, headed by Lyndon Johnson, which committed criminal acts in Texas in the 1960's. The other two, besides Mr. Estes and LBJ, were Cliff Carter and Mack Wallace.
>
> Mr. Estes is willing to disclose his knowledge concerning the following criminal offenses:
>
> Murders
> 1. The killing of Henry Marshall
> 2. The killing of George Krutilek
> 3. The killing of Ike Rogers and his secretary
> 4. The killing of Coleman Wade
> 5. The killing of Josefa Johnson
> 6. The killing of John Kinser
> 7. The killing of President J. F. Kennedy[46]

Of the seven names listed, three stood out: Henry Marshall, Johnson's sister Josefa, and President John Kennedy. Johnson's sister Josefa had become a political liability to Lyndon. An employee at a local brothel, Josefa was branded as a "working girl."[47] On Christmas Eve, 1961, Josefa died under mysterious circumstances, and despite state law, no autopsy was performed on the body.[48]

George Krutilek was one name not so easily recognizable. He was Estes's business associate and accountant. Seven days after the arrest of Estes on fraud charges, on April 4, 1962, Krutilek was found dead in his car. Two days earlier, Krutilek had been interrogated by FBI agents about the Estes affair.[49] In a crime scene that resembled Marshall's, his death was also ruled a suicide by carbon-monoxide poisoning.

When Marshall's body was found, it was theorized that, in an initial attempt to kill himself, he had pulled his shirt over his head to form a hood and endeavored to inhale fumes from the exhaust pipe.[50] More likely, Wallace attempted to kill Marshall with carbon-monoxide to make it look more like suicide. At some point, there was a struggle: There were bruises on Marshall's face, hands and arms. Mac used the bolt-action rifle to finish the job.[51]

Two other of Estes's associates, Harold Eugene Orr and Howard Pratt, were also found dead of carbon monoxide poisoning in 1964. Orr owned the Superior Manufacturing Company of Amarillo and had played a key role in Estes's fraudulent dealings. There was some fear that Orr, who was sentenced to ten years in prison, would open up to authorities for a lighter sentence, but he never made it to prison. Two days before he was to begin serving his sentence, he was found dead in his garage.[52] It was ruled accidental, with the claim that Orr had been changing the exhaust pipe on his car. The tools found scattered around his body were unfit for that type of automotive repair.[53]

Barbara Orr, Harold's wife, maintained her belief that her husband had been murdered. "I never did believe that Harold killed himself, but what good does it do to bring it out now?"[54] Barbara asked years later.

These deaths, all occurring in the span of a few years, had a strange similarity both in the way they occurred and their connection to Estes.

"They were all carbon monoxide poisonings," Peoples said concerning the deaths of Orr, Krutelik, and Pratt. "But I didn't look into it in any depth. They were off in another district, and the authorities were handling it."[55]

Another name on the list was John Kinser, the owner of the Butler Pitch and Putt Golf Course in Austin. Years earlier, in 1951,

Wallace shot Kinser several times in his pitch-and-putt office during a daytime argument. It has been speculated that the killer's actions stemmed from a bitter love triangle between Kinser, Johnson's sister Josefa and Wallace—or that Kinser was involved with Wallace's estranged wife, Mary Andre DuBose Barton.[56] In truth Kinser had knowledge of Lyndon's sister Josefa's indiscretions and was trying to blackmail Johnson.[57]

When he was arrested for the murder, Wallace slipped to Austin police investigator Marion Lee that "he was working for Mr. Johnson and [that's why] he had to get back to Washington."[58] Wallace, at the time of the shooting, was an economist working for the Department of Agriculture in Washington, a position secured for him by Senator Lyndon Johnson.[59]

After learning that Wallace had connections with Johnson's family and other prominent state political figures, Clint Peoples remarked, "I knew that I had to put every bit that I had into the investigation because the smell of politics was all around there."

During the ten-day trial in February 1952, Wallace was defended by Lyndon Johnson's personal attorney John Cofer, who had previously represented LBJ in the "Box 13" scandal and who would, years later, defend Billy Sol Estes. Wallace was found guilty of murder, sentenced to five years in prison, but with a suspended sentence. Years later, Peoples would say that in his fifty years of law enforcement, he had never seen such a thing happen.[60] In a review of Texas jurisprudence, this author has found no other examples of any Texas citizen convicted of murder receiving a suspended sentence.

Only three months following the suspended sentence verdict, Wallace would get a job with Temco, a defense contractor in Dallas owned by Suite 8F member and owner of the Texas School Book Depository building, D. H. Byrd,[61] a major contributor and fundraiser for Vice President Lyndon Johnson.

Incredibly, Byrd, a big game hunter whose living room was stuffed with taxidermy of the wild game he had shot, had the sixth floor window of the Texas School Book Depository removed and sent to his home as a trophy following the assassination of President Kennedy.

Temco, later known as TLV, would get a major federal defense contract from Johnson's defense department at the same time convicted murderer Malcolm Wallace went to work for the firm as an "economic consultant."

Glen Sample and Mark Collum in their book *The Men on the Sixth Floor* unearthed a May 13, 1984 *Dallas Morning News* article that reports an incredulous Clint Peoples finding from a Navy intelligence officer about Wallace's new job.

"I was furious that they would even consider a security clearance for Wallace with the background he had," said Peoples. "I asked him [the intelligence officer] how in the world Wallace could get the security clearance, and he said 'politics.' I asked who could be so strong and powerful in politics that he could get a clearance for a man like this, and he said 'the vice president.'"[62]

Five years later, in 1957, still a free man, Wallace's record was wiped clean.

In 1960, during Lyndon Johnson's bid for the presidential nomination, Wallace would be a frequent hanger-on. Lucianne Goldberg, a campaign worker, had seen Wallace at functions at least three times, always in the company of LBJ aide Cliff Carter.

"I just knew him and remember him because that was sort of what we were all about—remembering everybody you meet, because you never knew where they were going to end up,"[63] Goldberg said in her recollection of meeting Wallace in the hospitality suite of the Mayflower Hotel in Washington. Goldberg would later remember seeing Wallace at the Ambassador Hotel, the home of Johnson's campaign headquarters.

"I'd be sitting at my desk, and there'd be a lot of people milling around, and I'd see him with his thumbs hooked into his belt the way those [Texas] guys do."[64]

Wallace would never realize his political ambitions, but he would certainly play a part in seeing that Johnson realized his.

After the assassination of President Kennedy, a fingerprint was found on a cardboard box in the sniper's nest on the sixth floor of the Texas School Book Depository. It could not be linked with Oswald, any other employee of the Texas School Book Depository, or any law enforcement officer who had handled the box. Wallace's print from his previous conviction and the one found on the box were a match, according to fingerprint expert A. Nathan Darby, former head of Austin's police identification unit. Darby was the most experienced certified latent print examiner in America, with more than thirty-five years of military forensic and police experience. An initial comparison found a match between the two prints on fourteen *unique* points while Darby ultimately ascertained that the two prints had thirty-two matching points,[65] far exceeding the requirement for identification and conviction.

"I'm positive," said Darby. "The finger that made the ink print also made the latent print. It's a match."

In comparison, "the Dallas police found only *three partial finger-prints of Oswald on only two of the boxes* in the area."[66]

Robert Caro, who through four volumes of a planned five-volume biography of Lyndon Johnson painstakingly recreated the life and character of Johnson, has painted a picture of a man who holds power and monetary gain over all else. Caro shows the duplicitous nature of the man, the animalistic drive, and the treachery of his political and business deals. Still, his biographies miss a key part of the Johnson makeup: Mac Wallace.

In a 2012 correspondence, Doug Caddy, Billy Sol Estes's lawyer, revealed a confrontation he had had with Caro in the mid–1980s and the forces still at hand in burying the truth:

When Barr McClellan's book, *Blood, Money, & Power: How LBJ Killed JFK*, was about to be released in 2003, both Barr and I independently received about a half dozen phone calls from someone who was vitally intent in stopping its publication or limiting its impact. The person who called always remained unidentified, and the phone number from which the call was made was later found to be non-existent. In one of the phone conversations with me, the person in response to my bringing up Robert Caro hopefully covering LBJ's involvement in JFK assassination, told me that "We are not worried about Caro. He is on board." I was disappointed to hear this because I took it to mean that Caro may downplay LBJ's involvement in his forthcoming final volumes on the biography of LBJ. In 1985 or 1986, Robert Caro gave an address at the University of Houston on the subject of urban planning. I attended his speech accompanied by my father. After the speech, I approached him when he was answering questions posed by about a half dozen attendees gathered around him. I decided to pose my own question to him, asking, "Do you plan to cover the role of Mac Wallace in your biography of LBJ?" Caro looked startled and shaken and grabbed me by the lapels of my business suit, saying "Who are you? How can I get in touch with you?" I gave him my business card, which he examined on the spot and pocketed it. However, I never heard anything more from him.[67]

Caro helps to wipe away the blood and bury the bodies littering Johnson's path to power by failing to mention Wallace. Johnson used Wallace to keep secrets protected and to stop the cancer which grew from his own more loathsome characteristics. Baker and Estes acted like Johnson: Wallace was the solution to the way Johnson acted. Baker and Estes served their time for their indiscretions; Wallace was there to ensure Johnson never would.

In 1971, Wallace would be disposed of in a fashion similar to his victims. A stuffed tailpipe caused carbon monoxide to permeate the interior of the car that he was driving, causing him to lose control and crash near Pittsburg, Texas.

The death of Wallace did not deter Texas Ranger Clint Peoples in his attempt to find answers in the strange death of Henry Marshall, its connection to related deaths, their connection to Wallace, and his connection to Estes and Johnson.

In 1992, Peoples was also killed in an untimely automobile accident. Madeleine Brown remembered the "accident" in her interview with author Robert Gaylon Ross:

> I'm really gunshy talking about this because Clint Peoples was really killed. Clint was going on camera to verify the things that I said and my friend Billy Sol Estes, and anyway, I called Clint, it was on a Friday, I distinctly remember that, and I said, "Clint, I understand you are going on a recorder with Billy Sol and me. They were gonna do it as the end of a movie." I said, "I have a sick sister," and I couldn't make arrangements to go, and I said "I'll tell you what I'll do, Clint. I'll come next Friday, and I'll even buy lunch. Then you can be a kept man." I really liked Clint. Well, on the Tuesday following my conversation, Clint was run off the road in Waco, Texas and ultimately died, passed away from his injuries.[68]

Billy Sol Estes, who died on May 14, 2013, rebuffed my many attempts to interview him. He had long stopped speaking publicly about the strange deaths or his knowledge of them, praying as he got older in years for a more spiritual solution to the murders.

"I think there's still a God in heaven, and I think that God will straighten history out," Estes said. "I've decided that none of us can do it down here."[69]

I did have access and the full cooperation of Billy Sol Estes's personal attorney Douglas Caddy, who supplied interviews, source materials, and remembrances for this book. I can understand Estes's reluctance to give interviews in his later years. By the time I asked him in 2012, he had already identified Lyndon Johnson as the ultimate perpetrator in the murder of President Kennedy and had implicated him in seven other murders on record, in interviews and with many credible media outlets.

Both Bobby Baker and Billy Sol Estes were self-described wheeler dealers, operators, hustlers; both were in deep with Johnson, made money from his political influence, and eventually paid for it. Both overreached for personal gain, possibly believing that their leader could exonerate them. Johnson used them for his own wealth until they became a liability. Then, they were promptly cut off the tree and left to rot.

It had been Lyndon Johnson's great obsession to become president of the United States. But it would not be until he was threatened with the prospect of prison that he needed the office of the presidency to cloak his indiscretions.

It was not a lapse in reason when Kennedy family friend Bill Walton said, in reference to the assassination, "Dallas was the ideal location for such a crime."[70] For Johnson—with members of the Houston-based Suite 8F group, organized crime figures connected to Dallas, and state and federal government operatives—Dallas was home turf. It was a perfect ambush point because many involved knew the environment intimately, making facts surrounding the assassination easy to manipulate. The point was made clear by Billy Sol Estes's daughter Pam in her book *Billy Sol: King of the Texas Wheeler-Dealers:*

> Lyndon Johnson was not about to be ruined by such tactics by two upstarts from Massachusetts. He proved to have more influence than they counted on. In going through all the mounds of trial and investigation testimony, there appeared to be little curiosity about the large gifts Daddy had provided for the Democratic Party and Lyndon Johnson personally.
>
> A year and a half later, after John Kennedy was shot while riding down the streets of Dallas in an effort to mend his Texas political ties, Daddy said, "It looks like Lyndon won after all."[71]

NOTES

1. Baker, *Wheeling and Dealing,* 82–86
2. Caro, *Passage of Power,* 277.
3. Nellor, *Washington's Wheeler Dealers,* 5.

4. North, *Act of Treason*, 322.
5. *Gettysburg Times*, January 13, 1964.
6. Janney, *Mary's Mosaic*, 307.
7. Baker, *Wheeling and Dealing*, 185.
8. Baker, *Wheeling and Dealing*, 182.
9. Janney, *Mary's Mosaic*, 307.
10. Ibid., 308.
11. Ibid.
12. Baker, *Wheeling and Dealing*, 261.
13. Ibid., 308.
14. Ibid., 270.
15. Ibid., 276.
16. Ibid.
17. "Investigations: Decline and Fall," *Time* (May 25, 1962), n.p.
18. Ibid.
19. Ibid.
20. Ibid.
21. North, *Act of Treason*, 152.
22. McClellan, *Blood, Money and Power*, 125.
23. Bill Adler, "The Killing of Henry Marshall," *The Texas Observer* (November 7, 1986), n.p.
24. Pam Estes, *Billy Sol: King of Texas Wheeler-Dealers* (n.p.: Noble Craft, 1983), 47.
25. Spartacus Educational website, «Famous Crimes: Henry Marshall,» entry by John Simkin, September 1997–June 2013, www.spartacus.schoolnet.co.uk/JFKmarshallH.htm.
26. McClellan, *Blood, Money and Power*, 156.
27. Adler, "The Killing of Henry Marshall," n.p.
28. George Kuempel, "Cause of Death Changed from Suicide to Murder," *Dallas Morning News* (August 14, 1985).
29. Adler, "The Killing of Henry Marshall," n.p.
30. Ibid.
31. Ibid.
32. Ibid.
33. Ibid.
34. Ibid.
35. James M. Day, *Captain Clint Peoples: Texas Ranger: Fifty Years a Lawman* (Waco: Texian, 1980), 133–34.

36. Ibid., 134.
37. Ibid., 131.
38. North, *Act of Treason*, 140.
39. "Investigations: Decline and Fall," May 25, 1962, n.p.
40. Estes, *Billy Sol*, 66.
41. Mark Collom and Glen Sample, *The Men on the Sixth Floor* (Garden Grove: Sample Graphics, 1997), 120.
42. Kent Demaret, "Billie Sol Estes May Face New Fraud Charges, But He's Never Up the Creek Without a Paddle," *People* 11, no. 16 (April 23, 1979).
43. Ibid., 135.
44. Adler, "The Killing of Henry Marshall," n.p.
45. Madeleine Brown, *Texas in the Morning: The Love Story of Madeleine Brown and President Lyndon Baines Johnson* (Baltimore: Conservatory, 1997), 79.
46. Collom and Sample, *The Men On the Sixth Floor*, 150–51.
47. McClellan, *Blood, Money and Power*, 105.
48. Ibid., 167.
49. Haley, *A Texan Looks at Lyndon*, 137.
50. Adler, "The Killing of Henry Marshall," n.p.
51. Ibid.
52. Haley, *A Texan Looks at Lyndon*, 137.
53. Ibid., 138.
54. *The Reading Eagle* [Reading, PA], March 30, 1984.
55. John Gonzalez, "1962 Death of Estes' Accountant to Be Probed," *The Dallas Morning News* (March 29, 1984).
56. Ibid.
57. McClellan, *Blood, Money and Power*, 107.
58. *Dallas Times Herald*, April 6, 1984, n.p.
59. Day, *Captain Clint Peoples: Texas Ranger*, 81.
60. Ibid., 82.
61. Collom and Sample, *The Men on the Sixth Floor*, 167.
62. Ibid, pg. 169.
63. Adler, "The Killing of Henry Marshall," n.p.
64. Ibid.
65. McClellan, *Blood, Money and Power*, 328.
66. Craig I. Zirbel, *The Texas Connection: The Assassination of John F. Kennedy* (Scottsdale: Wright & Co., 1991), 209.

67. Education Forum Q&A with Douglas Caddy: educationforum.ipb-host.com/index.php?showtopic=18833&st=0&gopid=247779.
68. Ross, Gaylon, "Madeleine Brown Interview, www.youtube.com/watch?v=POmdd6HQsus.
69. Kuempel, "Suicide Ruling Changed to Murder." *Dallas Morning News,* August 14, 1985.
70. Talbot, *Brothers,* 32.
71. Estes, *Billy Sol,* 69.

CHAPTER THIRTEEN

LOCATION

Why Dallas? It is important to understand LBJ's control of law enforcement and local government in Dallas County when Kennedy arrived in town for the parade. At the time, the Mayor of Dallas was Earle Cabell, the brother of Charles Cabell, whom JFK had fired from the CIA after the disaster of the Bay of Pigs invasion in which CIA-trained Cuban exiles attempted to invade the island. The mayor and his brother hated JFK. They were Johnson men.

The mayor helped LBJ secure the loyalty of Dallas Police Chief Jesse Curry. Strangely, Curry would appear at Johnson's sleeve for all of the days in the aftermath of the president's murder. It was clear that Johnson, through Curry, was controlling the Dallas Police Department.

Over one thousand deputies of the Dallas County Sheriff's Department were called to their department auditorium on the morning of November 22 and told expressly, "You are in Dealey Plaza as observers. No matter what you see or hear, take no law enforcement action. You are there in respect for the presidency of the United States as observers and not law enforcement officers."

This would explain the strange actions of the Dallas Police Department in the aftermath of the president's shooting. The Texas School Book Depository building was not sealed as a crime scene, and the building was swarmed by reporters, thrill seekers, and tourists creating mayhem. The entire building was never searched. The search of the sixth floor was bungled: No evidence was photographed as found, most was marred with the fingerprints of police handlers, and the legally required "chain of evidence" documentation of strict evidence control was willfully violated.

Likewise, LBJ's relationship with Secret Service Director John Rowley is also underestimated by many of those examining the JFK murder. They both served in the National Youth Administration under Roosevelt and were friends beginning in the forties. There is no other way to explain the serious lapses in Secret Service protocol during Kennedy's trip to Dallas on November 22, 1963. The 120-degree turn to get to Dealey Plaza where the president's limousine would drop below 40 MPH was against all Secret Service mandates. Agents were directed not to ride on the limousine bumper; the two agents normally assigned to walk beside the car at the rear axle were called off. A stunning and widely available Internet video shows agents being pulled from their normal positions by superiors. It is quite simple to conclude that Rowley was in Johnson's pocket. And then one must examine the alleged shooter, Lee Harvey Oswald.

Oswald was hired by the Texas School Book Depository on October 16, 1963, just two days shy of his twenty-fourth birthday. Thirty-seven days following his start of the job, President Kennedy was gunned down. After Oswald allegedly shot dead Dallas police officer J. D. Tippit, he was taken into police custody and within hours was named the lone assassin.

A big challenge to conspiracy theorists who question a lone gunman theory is Oswald's acquisition of the job only a month before the assassination. In fact, Oswald's job came through Ruth Paine, with whom Oswald's estranged wife Marina was staying. The Oswalds were introduced to Paine by none other than George de Mohrenschildt, who we shall see was Oswald's CIA handler.

"Even the presidential motorcade that drove beneath the sixth floor window where Oswald was, that motorcade wasn't even determined until November 18, just four days before the assassination," said Vincent Bugliosi, author of *Reclaiming History:*

The Assassination of John F. Kennedy. "Does any rational person believe that the CIA or the mob would conspire with Oswald to kill the president within four days of his coming to Dallas?"[1]

The faulty argument hinges on the major assumption that the conspirators had no authority concerning the route of the motorcade. Indeed, the route is only revealed to the public on the morning of November 22 when the *Dallas Times Herald* prints the map in its morning newspaper.

Interestingly, Oswald could only have known of the president's route via the *Times Herald*, but he traveled from Irving, Texas so early that he could not have seen the newspaper until he arrived in the city and made the instant decision to murder John F. Kennedy.

The Warren Commission claims that he brought the alleged murder weapon, a bolt-action rifle, from Irving in a long, brown paper bag. Of the five people who said they saw Oswald that morning, three said that he had no brown paper bag. Two people, nineteen-year-old Buell Wesley Frazier and his sister, claimed that they saw Oswald with a package, but it was almost a foot shorter than the length of a disassembled Mannlicher-Carcano bolt-action rifle.

Bugliosi is correct in his claim that a route was determined on November 18. Dallas Police Chief Jesse Curry, chief of the Dallas Secret Service office, Forrest Sorrels, and Secret Service advance man Winston Lawson met on that day to conduct a dry run of the drive from Love Field to the Trade Mart. Upon reaching Dealey Plaza, Curry pointed down Main Street.

"And afterwards there's only the freeway,"[2] Curry said to the two Secret Service agents.

Farewell America, a 1968 book published in France under the pseudonym James Hepburn detailed the trial run when it reached Dealey Plaza, an open area of downtown Dallas boxed in by tall buildings and expressways:

> But instead of turning right into Houston Street in the direction of Elm Street, as the motorcade did on November 22, Curry turned left in front of the Old Court house, and neither Lawson

nor Sorrels followed the parade route past that point, where they would have been obliged to make a 90-degree right turn into Houston Street, followed 70 yards later by a 120-degree turn to the left into Elm Street. Had they done so, it might have occurred to them that the big presidential Lincoln would be obliged to slow down almost to a stop in order to make that second turn. This type of double turn is contrary to Secret Service regulations, which specify that when a presidential motorcade has to slow down to make a turn, "the entire intersection must be examined in advance, searched, and inspected from top to bottom." Curry, however, brought the reconnaissance to an end at the very point where it became unacceptable (as well as unusual) from the point of view of security.[3]

The original route had been mapped out by Kennedy advance man, Jerry Bruno, who had wanted a luncheon at the Women's Building following the motorcade. The HSCA 1979 report on the motorcade states that the "Secret Service initially preferred the Women's Building for security reasons, and the Kennedy staff preferred it for political reasons."[4] The route for the Women's Building would have had the motorcade pass by Dealey Plaza briefly at a high rate of speed, "without taking any turns in or around the Plaza."[5]

Johnson's man, Texas Governor John Connally would not have it. Connally argued passionately with Bruno for the Dallas Trade Mart as the venue for the luncheon. Located on the Stemmons Freeway, the Trade Mart would force the route through Dealey Plaza—the kill site. Connally's unwavering position on the Trade Mart, the only point of contention in Kennedy's five-city tour of Texas, ignited a quarrel between the Kennedy and Johnson people.

"The feud became so bitter that I went to the White House to ask Bill Moyers, then deputy director of the Peace Corps and close to both Connally and Johnson, if he would try to settle the dispute for the good of the president and his party," Bruno wrote in a November 14 journal entry. "On this day, [Kennedy scheduler] Kenny O'Donnell decided that there was no other way but to go to the mart."[6]

The next day, Bruno affirmed in his journal the White House approval of the Trade Mart and Connally's unusual behavior preceding it.

"I met with O'Donnell and Moyers, who said that Connally was unbearable and on the verge of cancelling the trip. They decided to let the governor have his way."[7]

Bruno had not seen anything like it in his three years as advance man for the president.

"Either we select the stops and run the trips, or the president can stay home," Connally told Bruno. "We don't want him."[8]

Johnson accessory Cliff Carter also attempted to force the Trade Mart as the luncheon location. Carter, according to Bruno, "kept insisting that Connally was the best man for Kennedy in Texas, and he should be allowed to run the whole trip."[9]

Never had local hosts been so adamant on a specific location, and the stance was made especially questionable considering the security challenges of the Trade Mart.[10] Due to the concerns for the president's safety in Dallas, the city itself had been questioned as a suitable location for campaigning.

"Dallas was removed and then put back on the planned itinerary several times," wrote Evelyn Lincoln. "Our own advance man urged that the motorcade not take the route through the underpass and past the Book Depository, but he was overruled."[11]

Connally and Carter were simply acting on the wishes of their man Lyndon. Connally and Johnson went back a long way politically. The governor had served as Johnson's administrative assistant and for decades worked as his campaign director. When Johnson asked for something, Connally delivered.

"Look at John Connally," Johnson said. "I can call John Connally at midnight, and if I told him to come over and clean my shoes, he'd come running. *That's* loyalty."[12]

223

As a member of Suite 8F and as a Johnson campaign stalwart, Connally learned from many of the vice president's business connections.

Working Johnson's 1948 Senate bid, Connally collected money from Brown and Root, oil tycoons and other business interests, and a lot of money passed through his hands. "A hell of a lot," said Connally. "I'd go get it. Walter [Jenkins] would get it. Woody would go get it. We had a lot of people who would go get it, and deliver it. . . . I went to see [Taylor oil baron] Harris Melasky three or four times. . . . *I handled inordinate amounts of cash.*"[13]

Later, Connally benefited from these associations. In the 1950s, he became an attorney for Sid W. Richardson, an oil executive and co-owner of the Del Mar Racetrack. He ran Richardson's business ventures in Texas and Jamaica and later became an executor of Richardson's estate.[14]

In 1969, after leaving the governorship of Texas, Connally was named to the board of directors for Brown and Root,[15] the company that had financed Johnson's political career and the main beneficiary from the war in Vietnam. Subsequently, President Nixon appointed Connally to his foreign advisory board.[16] The plum appointment symbolized the continued patronage between the government and big business.

Nixon also appointed Connally as secretary of the treasury and tried to dump Vice President Agnew to maneuver Connally onto the 1972 *Republican* ticket.

Concern for Connally's safety would prod Johnson into an argument with Kennedy during the early evening hours of November 21. Johnson had been summoned to the Kennedy suite at the Rice Hotel in Houston. The argument that unfolded focused on the seating arrangement of the motorcade.

Senator Ralph Yarborough, the leader of the liberal wing of the Democratic party in Texas, was bitterly playing into Johnson's hand. Yarborough, who believed Johnson had worked with Connally to exclude him from planning the president's trip, refused to

Johnson aide Bobby Baker said in 1961 that JFK would not live out his term.

Warren Commission member Congressman Gerald Ford would change autopsy reports to hide the truth.

The LBJ "treatment" was intimidating.

LBJ knew how to use power to his advantage.

Nixon knew who really killed Kennedy.

Nixon told me: "Lyndon and I both wanted to be president. The difference was I wouldn't kill for it."

My attempts to ask George Bush about his whereabouts on November 22, 1963, have been unsuccessful.

LBJ on Bobby Kennedy: "I'll slit his throat if it's the last thing I do."

Lawyer Roy Cohn and his mob client "Fat" Tony Salerno
told me in 1979 that "Lyndon did it."

Richard Nixon recognized Jack Ruby
as a Johnson associate whom he met
in 1947.

Jacqueline Kennedy wrote: "I never liked
Lyndon Johnson and I never trusted him."

Robert Kennedy said LBJ
was "an animal."

LBJ would try to get protégé and
Governor John Connally switched
out of the Presidential car—
November 22, 1963.

ride in the same car as the vice president. Johnson, with knowledge of the conspiracy to assassinate the president, was clearly using this as leverage to ride with Connally the following day. Kennedy, though, was adamant about Johnson riding with Yarborough as a sign of party solidarity. In order to protect his friend Connally, LBJ wanted Yarborough in the president's limousine and Connally moved to the vice president's car in the motorcade. The president and vice president argued bitterly over the seating.

Jackie Kennedy, in a neighboring room, heard the argument and walked in just as Johnson stormed out, "like a pistol."[17]

"He sounded mad," Jackie said to John.

"That's just Lyndon," Kennedy responded. "He's in trouble."[18]

Jackie then impulsively relayed to John her distaste for Governor Connally.

"But, for heaven's sake, don't get a thing on him because that's what I came down here to heal," Kennedy replied. "I'm trying to start by getting two people in the same car. If they start hating, nobody will ride with anybody."[19]

President Kennedy later gave strong instructions of the Dallas motorcade arrangements to White House aide Larry O' Brien.

"I don't care if you have to throw Yarborough in the car with Lyndon. But get him there."[20]

Along with control over the route, it was essential that the powers within had dominion over the security detail in Dealey Plaza. "Assistant Chief Batchelor would coordinate the security pre-operation among various elements and agencies," Police Chief Curry said. "As [advance man] Lawson suggested the speeds and timed the route, Assistant Chief Batchelor wrote down the number of men to be assigned at each intersection."[21]

On the day of the assassination, there were no Secret Service agents assigned to the Plaza. The area remained unchecked by security—an engineered snafu.

"This is the greatest single clue to that assassination," said former Air Force intelligence officer L. Fletcher Prouty. "Who had the power to call off or drastically reduce the usual security precautions that are always in effect whenever a president travels? . . . The power source that arranged that murder was on the inside. . . . They had the means to reduce normal security and permit the choice of a hazardous route. It also has had the continuing power to cover up that crime."[22]

It was "a freak of history that this short stretch of Elm Street would be the assassination site, and the Texas Book Depository Building was virtually ignored in the security plans for the motorcade,"[23] Chief Curry later added.

That "freak of history" was meticulously planned. That the kill zone was abandoned by the Secret Service was a detail enacted by James Rowley, head of the Secret Service and close friend of the vice president. Rowley would also have a hand in the reaction time of the Secret Service protecting the presidential limousine, the expeditious cleaning and reconstruction of the vehicle following the hit, and the ordering of John Kennedy's body from Parkland Hospital before an autopsy could be conducted. On his return to Andrews Air Force Base from Dallas, Rowley would be the first person to greet and confer with President Johnson.[24]

Johnson would become increasingly frantic in the waning hours preceding the November 22 motorcade from Love Field. Following the plane ride from Houston to Ft. Worth later that evening, Johnson attended the party at Clint Murchison's mansion. The gathering, attended by Murchison, J. Edgar Hoover, Richard Nixon, H. L. Hunt, and assassin Mac Wallace, was alleged by Johnson's mistress Madeleine Brown. It was later confirmed by May Newman, an employee of the Murchison family.

"They were having a big party for a very special guest that was coming from Washington to go to the party by the name of Bulldog, which I found out later was J. Edgar Hoover,"[25] Newman recalled. Critics who question the validity of the party have been quick to point out that Hoover was back at work at the Justice Department late the next morning. Hoover could not have attended the party, it is contested, because he could not have gotten back to work in time.

But Hoover had many private jets at his disposal, including those of the oilmen, and could have flown to and from Dallas at any time necessary.

The event took an ominous turn with the arrival of Johnson.

"It must have been eleven o'clock, the party was breaking up at that time, and it shocked everyone that he came in," said Brown. "Of course I was thrilled to see him. Normally I knew his agenda when he was in Texas, but that night I did not know that he was coming. They all went into this conference room."[26]

Behind closed doors, the intentions of the gathering became clear: These men had not assembled for a party, but to plan a funeral.

Hoover, Murchison, Hunt, and Johnson had a shared urgency— they were all fighting for their livelihood. In two years' time, if the Kennedys still maintained power, Hoover would be retired, Johnson would be incarcerated, and Big Oil would be significantly minimized. Hunt famously said about the Kennedys that there was "no way left to get these traitors out of our government except by shooting them out."[27] This meeting was a final review to confirm the plan set in place to do exactly that.

When Johnson emerged from the private meeting, he was apoplectic.

Grasping Brown's arm, he growled into her ear, "After tomorrow those SOBs will never embarrass me again. That's no threat, that's a promise."[28] Calling Madeleine Brown the next morning from his hotel, a simmering Johnson repeated the ominous threat.[29]

The countdown was in its final hours.

With Hoover committed to the plot, Johnson had keenly scanned the political horizon to see if anyone else would be smart enough to figure out that there had been a coup d'état. One man worried him, a man as cunning, daring, and driven as he himself. A man whose ambition to be president burned just as brightly as his own: former Vice President Richard Nixon.

Johnson knew that Nixon had his own connections to mob boss Carlos Marcello. In 1960, Marcello had declined to contribute to the Kennedy–Johnson ticket and made a $500,000 donation to the Nixon campaign instead.[30] It is reasonable to assume that Johnson was concerned that Nixon was in a position to "hear things."

Madeleine Brown insists that Nixon, who was in Dallas the week of the assassination for a Pepsi-Cola company board meeting, also met LBJ privately on the afternoon of November 21 at a suite at the Adolphus Hotel in Dallas. Neither Johnson nor Nixon ever publicly acknowledged the Adolphus Hotel meeting or what was discussed. In fact, during the conversation, a seed was planted with Nixon that was intentionally designed to mislead him.

To misdirect Nixon, Johnson told him of his concern for the president's safety due to the atmosphere of hate in Dallas. Johnson warned Nixon of the dangerous right-wing cauldron that boiled in the city. Only weeks before, US Ambassador to the UN and former presidential candidate Adlai Stevenson had been attacked in the street by an angry mob, which spat on him and knocked him to the ground.

Johnson had tried to use this line before. On November 4, 1960, he and Lady Bird were in Dallas at the Adolphus Hotel to rally support for Kennedy when the two were confronted by a right-wing mob holding signs that read LBJ SOLD OUT TO YANKEE SOCIALIST and BEAT JUDAS. Johnson alleged that conservative Republican Congressman Bruce Alger organized the riot (a claim Alger later vehemently denied). Using the protestors to his advantage, Johnson turned the event into an extravaganza.

"LBJ and Lady Bird could have gone through the lobby and got on that elevator in five minutes," said D. B. Hardeman, an aide to House Speaker and Texan Sam Rayburn, "but LBJ took thirty minutes to go through that crowd, and it was all being recorded and photographed for television and radio and the newspapers, and he knew and played it for all it was worth. They say he never learned how to use the media effectively, but that day he did."[31]

Johnson would later cite the same congressman who he claimed ginned up the "mink coat mob" to intentionally misdirect Nixon, setting him up for the death of the president, which took place only a day later. Johnson first thanked Nixon for a statement that the former vice president had released in Dallas urging the courteous treatment of the president. The vice president then asked him to contact Congressman Alger, who Johnson said had been whipping up right-wing enmity in Dallas, to suggest Alger tone it down.

With this clever deflection, LBJ laid the groundwork for Nixon's subsequent conclusion that a right-wing cabal had killed JFK. He even enlisted him in a solution.

In fact, Johnson sent Nixon on a wild goose chase—Alger attended the Murchison party only hours after Nixon and Johnson had met privately at the Baker Hotel. Although a virulent right winger, Alger carried water in Washington for the same oil barons who funded LBJ's ambitions.

After his midday conversation with Johnson, Nixon stopped by early at Murchison's right-wing bash and was no doubt peppered with anti-Kennedy sentiment. LBJ arrived at the party long after Nixon had left, and his ploy to amplify right-wing hatred in Dallas had worked. It is not surprising that Nixon dialed Hoover in the hours after Kennedy's death to ask if JFK had been killed by "one of the right-wing nuts."

Shortly following Kennedy's death, Nixon was "very shaken," said writer Stephen Hess. "He took out the Dallas morning paper, which had a story about the press conference he had had the day before. He had talked about how the people of Dallas should have respect for their political adversaries. . . . He was saying to me in effect, 'You see, I didn't have anything to do with creating this.' He was very concerned that Kennedy had been assassinated by a right-winger, and that some-how, Nixon would be accused of unleashing political hatred."[32]

Clearly the former vice president was stunned when Hoover told him a left-leaning communist was the sole gunman.

The coincidental timing of Nixon's trip to Dallas and the assassination is made a bit more suspicious by the conflicting stories that Nixon told of how he had learned of the assassination. One version had him in New York, taking a cab from the airport following his return from Dallas. "We were waiting for a light to change when a man ran over from the street corner and said that the president had just been shot in Dallas," Nixon told *Readers Digest* in 1964. Another version also occurred in the cab ride, but the cab driver "missed a turn somewhere, and we were off the highway . . . a woman came out of her house screaming and crying. I rolled down the cab window to ask what the matter was, and when she saw my face, she turned even paler. She told me that John Kennedy had just been shot in Dallas."[33]

A third story had the former vice president returning from his trip to his New York apartment when the building doorman informed him of the assassination. Nixon's confusion as to his whereabouts could be attributed to LBJ's misdirection.

Lyndon Johnson would later try, in vain, to derail Nixon's 1968 comeback bid by calling a halt to the bombing in Vietnam and for three-party talks with North and South Vietnam. In fact, the Paris Peace Talks with the North Vietnamese had yielded no development to justify Johnson's gambit. As Election Day neared, Nixon's carefully crafted comeback was stalled while Vice President Hubert Humphrey, the Democratic nominee, was gaining. Johnson figured that the peace feeler could give Humphrey a two-point bump as Democrats who had supported McCarthy or RFK came home to him.

It is important to stress that Johnson's announcement was pure politics poorly cloaked as foreign policy. Nixon saw it as a political maneuver to deny him the presidency a second time. Johnson knew that Nixon was boxed into publicly supporting his "peace talks" proposal.

That is why Nixon launched a back-channel dialogue through campaign manager John N. Mitchell and Anna Chennault, the notorious dragon lady whose husband, Claire Chennault, had founded the Flying Tigers airline after their wartime exploits. Chennault was in touch with the South Vietnamese ambassador and passed a discreet message to President Thieu that the South should hold out for a better deal and refuse the three-party talks.

Unfortunately, J. Edgar Hoover and the FBI learned of Chennault's back channel and advised Johnson, who was furious. An angry Johnson called Nixon to confront him, but Nixon denied any knowledge of the maneuver. Nixon aide H. R. Haldeman later remembered that Nixon, he, and traveling aide Dwight Chapin dissolved in hilarious laughter after hearing Nixon's side of the conversation with Johnson and seeing him hang up.

Thieu, sensing a double-cross from LBJ, was happy to comply. His announcement deflated the last-minute swing to Humphrey, and Nixon had the final successful chess move in his rivalry with Johnson.

Nixon avoided risk and played it safe in the final weeks as his claim to a "secret plan" to end the Vietnam conflict without revealing any of the specifics began to hurt him with voters. His own polling showed Humphrey gaining rapidly, and he knew that the last-minute dagger from Johnson could be fatal. In the end, Nixon moved to counter Johnson's potentially fatal thrust.

Liberal critics would later charge Nixon with treason because Johnson's maneuver was cloaked in US government policy. Nixon knew that LBJ was no closer to peace in Paris, and that it was a gambit. Johnson himself muttered that Nixon's private diplomacy was "treasonous."

If Nixon was confused on the day of the assassination, Johnson was angered and impatient. According to a *Dallas Morning News* report that day, Nixon questioned Johnson's future in the Kennedy administration. According to Nixon, Johnson had lost his biggest asset to the administration: the Southern states. Johnson was now "becoming a political liability in the South, just as he is in the North."

Reading through the paper that morning in Dallas though, one would see that Johnson was certainly not alone in the South.

Kennedy had been handed an advertisement taken out in the *Dallas Morning News*. The ad, bordered in black, symbolic of an announcement of mourning, questioned many of the president's policies, domestic and abroad. It was paid for by an organization calling itself "The American Fact-Finding Committee," whose most prominent member was Nelson Bunker Hunt, the son of oil magnate and Suite 8F member H. L. Hunt.

The ad intended to voice the views of Dallas, expounding that the city was:

- A CITY so disgraced by a recent Liberal smear attempt that its citizens have just elected two more conservative Americans to public office.
- A CITY that is an economic "boom town," not because of federal handouts, but through conservative economic and business practices.
- A CITY that will continue to grow and prosper despite efforts by you and your administration to penalize it for its non-conformity to New Frontierism.
- A CITY that rejected your philosophy and policies in 1960 and will do so again in 1964—even more emphatically than before.[34]

President Kennedy jokingly incorporated his romanticized love of spy lore with the gravity of the ad in an attempt to put Jackie at ease, whose mood had taken a downward turn upon viewing it.[35]

"You know, last night would have been a hell of a night to assassinate a president," Kennedy said. "I mean it. There was the rain, and the night, and we were all getting jostled. Suppose a man had a pistol in his briefcase."

Pointing his fingers like a gun, Kennedy then pulled an imaginary trigger.

"Then he could have dropped the gun and the briefcase and melted away in the crowd."[36]

At 11:38 a.m. on November 22, Air Force One, carrying the president and his wife, touched down at Love Field. Kennedy was ebullient, staring out the window of the plane at the throngs of Dallas well-wishers.

"This trip is turning out to be terrific," the president said to Kenny O'Donnell. "Here we are in Dallas, and it looks like everything in Texas is going to be fine."[37]

The morning, which had begun drizzly and overcast, had cleared for sunshine.

"Kennedy weather,"[38] aide Larry O'Brien called it.

Lyndon and Lady Bird arrived on Air Force Two a few moments later.

Johnson, after a long night, was looking at an even longer day ahead. That he was viewed as "dour and perfunctory"[39] that morning is no surprise.

Dour and perfunctory were two attributes that Johnson embraced in his long, powerless time as vice president. The previous months, with charges and potential jail time now on the horizon, only dampened his mood. Johnson was, by this time, an afterthought in the world of politics.

That morning, he already knew that the laughter at, indifference to, and charges against him would disappear. Despite the clearing weather forecast, Kennedy did not give the order to remove the top off of the presidential limousine. That order was given by Johnson aide Bill Moyers, who claimed to be echoing the wishes of the president. Moyers ordered his assistant Betty Harris to "get that Goddamned bubble off unless it's pouring rain."[40]

Descriptions of the removable top following the assassination would give the erroneous impression that it resembled a clear, plastic bubble, which was not bulletproof and did not pose an impediment to assassination. In fact, the top was more box-shaped, and, aside from the side windows and a small decorative rear window, was covered in black vinyl, which would make it impossible for a sniper to see through from a high vantage point. Its removal was essential to a clear shot.

Moyers, with a vital role in the assassination, would later use his considerable media influence and political connections to quickly extinguish any connection of Johnson to the killing of

Kennedy. *The Guilty Men*, a program that aired on the History Channel in November 2003, postulated that Johnson was *the* major player in the assassination. Moyers quickly enlisted the help of ex-Presidents Gerald Ford and Jimmy Carter as well as Johnson's widow Lady Bird to move against the History Channel. The incident "is a strange one," wrote Bruce Weber of *The New York Times*, "not least because of the people involved, who seem to have brought a great deal of thunder to bear on a controversy that might well have disappeared of its own accord. But it was important, Mr. Moyers said, to put the public record straight."[41] Indeed, Moyers wants anything but the truth. "Gerry Ford was always up Lyndon's ass," Nixon told me. Ford had been House Minority Leader during Johnson's presidency. Perhaps that's why it's not surprising that Ford was among those who called on the History Channel not to air the nine-part series.

The Men Who Killed Kennedy included *The Guilty Men* and had aired in the United Kingdom to critical acclaim. The series pointed the finger directly at LBJ.

Before leaving Love Field, Johnson's secret service ally, Director James Rowley, had one more measure enacted to ensure a clear shot from all sides: The police motorcycles were moved from the side of the presidential limousine to the rear. B. J. Martin, a motorcycle officer in the motorcade testified that "they instructed us that they didn't want anyone riding past the president's car, and that we were to ride to the rear, to the rear of his car, about the rear bumper."[42]

With the clock nearing noon, the twenty-two-car motorcade, extending more than a half-mile, began the nine-and-a-half-mile trip from Love Field to the Trade Mart. Jesse Curry and two secret service agents rode in the lead car. Curiously, two members of John Crichton's Army Reserve unit—Deputy Police Chief George L. Lumpkin of the 488th Military Intelligence Detachment and Lieutenant Colonel George Whitmeyer, the East Texas Army Reserve commander—rode in the "pilot car" of the motorcade, a quarter mile ahead of the lead. It has been reported that the men bullied their way into the motorcade at the last minute. Crichton, a close friend of Lyndon Johnson and Texas oil tycoons, who was also a comrade and the 1964 running mate of George H. W. Bush, will be fleshed out in his relation to the assassination later in this narrative.

Five cars back was the presidential limousine, code named SS-100-X by the Secret Service, which carried Governor Connally and his wife, Nellie, in the jump seats. President Kennedy was seated directly behind the governor with Jackie on his left.

"Mr. President, remember when you're riding in the motorcade downtown to look and wave only at people on the right side of the street," presidential aide Dave Powers told Kennedy before the motorcade began rolling. "Jackie, be sure that you look only at the left side and not to the right. If both of you ever looked at the same voter at the same time, it would be too much for him."[43]

Following the presidential limousine was the "Queen Mary," the Secret Service follow-up car carrying six agents and Kennedy aides Powers and O'Donnell. The next car was a rented 1961 Lincoln convertible, in which Johnson, Lady Bird, and Senator Yarborough occupied the back seat, while Rufus Youngblood, the Secret Service agent assigned to the vice president, rode in the front. Lady Bird, seated between the vice president and the senator, acted as a buffer between the two feuding politicians.[44]

As the motorcade snaked through downtown Dallas, Johnson's peculiar temperament continued. He did not bother to look at the crowds that lined the streets but only "stared glumly, straight ahead."[45] At one point during the motorcade, Kennedy stopped the procession to shake hands with an onlooker. Johnson was visibly annoyed by the interruption.[46]

When the motorcade turned into Dealey Plaza, onto Houston from Main Street, a perfect unobscured shot on the presidential limousine was offered to Mac Wallace, who was situated on the sixth floor of the Texas School Book Depository. Wallace would have to forgo that clean shot because it would have stopped the procession before it reached the ambush site. Wallace would also have to hold when the motorcade took the 120-degree turn on to Elm Street. At this point, the presidential limousine was slowed to a crawl, allowing the clearest and shortest range shot to a sniper situated on the sixth floor of the depository.

As the "Queen Mary" made the turn onto Elm Street, O'Donnell, concerned about the day's agenda, inquired about the time.

"It's just 12:30," Powers said. "That's the time we're due to be at the Trade Mart."

"Fine," said O'Donnell. "It's only five minutes from here, so we're only running five minutes behind schedule."

Precisely after this exchange, O'Donnell and Powers heard shots ring through Dealey Plaza and saw the violent reaction by the injured President.

The first shots were fired as the vice-presidential limousine was making its turn onto Elm Street. Officer B. J. Martin, one of the police officers assigned to the presidential escort, later heard reports from officers in the motorcade who were treated to the curious sight of Johnson crouched down in his seat, reacting *before* any shots were fired. "According to the guys who were escorting his car in the motorcade, our new president is either one jumpy son of a bitch or he knows something he's not telling about the Kennedy thing. . . . he started ducking down in the car a good thirty or forty seconds before the first shots were fired."[47]

Parade-goers who lined the street offered a similar recollection. "Wasn't that rather odd that Johnson was on the floor before the shot sounded?" one witness recalled.[48]

The witness claims were validated by a photograph taken by Associated Press photographer Ike Altgens, who captured the vice-president's Lincoln as it turned onto Elm Street one to three seconds after the first shot was fired.[49] In the picture, Lady Bird and Senator Yarborough are seen clearly, riding and smiling to the crowd. The picture allows a clear viewing lane to Johnson's seat, but the vice-president is nowhere to be seen. In his place, onlookers are seen to the left and back of the Lincoln.[50]

Johnson would later combat the story of his pre-emptive duck and cover by claiming that Agent Youngblood immediately shoved Johnson and then jumped on him to protect him. This account was disputed by Senator Yarborough. "It just didn't happen. . . . It was a small car. Johnson was a big man, tall. His knees were up against his chin as it was. There was no room for that to happen."[51]

Yarborough also claimed to smell gunpowder as the shots rang out. "I thought, 'Was that a bomb thrown?' And then the other shots were fired," he told assassination researcher Jim Marrs. "And the motorcade, which had slowed to a stop, took off. A second or two later, I smelled gunpowder. I always thought that was strange because, being familiar with firearms, I could never see how I could smell the powder from a rifle high in that building."[52]

At least four shots hit the presidential limousine. The first shot hit Kennedy in the upper-right shoulder area of the back; the bullet lodged there "a short distance . . . the end of the opening could be felt with a finger,"[53] according to the FBI autopsy report.

"My God, I am hit," shouted the president.[54]

The next bullet fired on the presidential limousine came from the front and penetrated him at the base of the neck. As the Zapruder film clearly shows, the president then balled up his fists and moved them to the area close to his throat.

"Kenny, I think the president's been shot," Powers said to O'Donnell.[55]

"What makes you think that?," O'Donnell asked, making the sign of the cross.

"Look at him!" Powers answered. "He was over on the right, with his arm stretched out. Now he's slumped over toward Jackie, holding his throat."[56]

Governor Connally, who heard what he believed to be shotgun fire, also sensed something was wrong.[57] He turned to his right to try to catch a glimpse of the president over his shoulder. Struggling to get a good look on the right side, he was attempting to turn in the opposite direction when he was hit. Over a decade later, Nellie Connally recalled the events sharply:

I heard a noise that I didn't think of as a gunshot. I just heard a disturbing noise and turned to my right from where I thought the noise had come and looked in the back and saw the President clutch his neck with both hands. He said nothing. He just sort of slumped down in the seat. John had turned to his right also when we heard that first noise and shouted, "No, no, no," and in the process of turning back around so that he could look back and see the president. I don't think he could see him when he turned to his right—the second shot was fired and hit him. He was in the process of turning, so it hit him through this shoulder, came out right about here. His hand was either right in front of him or on his knee as he turned to look, so that the bullet went through him, crushed his wrist, and lodged in his leg. And then he just re- coiled and just sort of slumped in his seat. I thought he was dead. When you see a big man totally defenseless like that, then you do whatever you think you can do to help most, and the only thing I could think of to do was to pull him down out of the line of fire, or whatever was happening to us and I thought, if I could get him down, maybe they wouldn't hurt him anymore. So, I pulled him down in my lap.

At that moment, the presidential limousine rolled into alignment with the grassy knoll: the kill zone. Earlier in the day, Dallas resident Julia Ann Mercer saw a green Ford pickup truck illegally parked on the curb at the base of the knoll, partially blocking the road.[58] The truck was labeled "Air Conditioning" and had a Texas license plate. One "heavy-set, middle-aged man"[59] occupied the driver's seat while another, "a white male, who appeared to be in his late twenties or early thirties and wearing a gray jacket, brown pants, and a plaid shirt,"[60] who was at the rear of the vehicle "reached over the tailgate and took out from the truck what appeared to be a gun case," according to Mercer.[61] The brown case had a handle and appeared to be 3.5 to 4 feet long. The man then walked up the grassy hill, case in hand. Mercer added that this was all carried out in the presence of three Dallas police officers, "standing, talking near a motorcycle on the bridge ahead."[62]

Lee Bowers Jr., a railroad towerman, who had a clear view of the area behind the grassy knoll, saw three suspicious vehicles just before the shooting moving through the railroad yards, which had been sealed off by Dallas police. The first vehicle, a station wagon with out-of-state plates curiously adorned with a Goldwater bumper sticker moved through the area approximately twenty minutes before the shooting "as if he were searching for a way out or was checking the area, and then proceeded back though the only way he could, the same outlet he came in."[63] The second vehicle, a black 1957 Ford with a sole occupant who, while casing the area, seemed to "have a mic or telephone or something. . . . He was holding something up to his mouth with one hand, and he was driving with the other."[64] The third vehicle, a Chevrolet Impala, showed up minutes before the assassination and was driven in a similar suspicious fashion.[65] Bowers lost track of the car, but he saw two men who completely fit Mercer's earlier description near the fence on the knoll just before the shots were fired.[66] According to Bowers, "These men were the only two strangers in the area. The others were workers whom I knew."[67]

Just following the kill shot on President Kennedy, J. C. Price, watching from the Terminal Annex building in the plaza, saw a man with khaki pants, who fit the description of the younger man supplied by both Mercer and Bowers, running away from the area behind the picket fence.[68] The three witnesses would be ignored by the official investigation in the coming months. Bowers, along with S. M. Holland, James L. Simmons, reporter Cheryl McKinnon, Ed Hoffman, and others saw puffs of smoke, which indicated to them that a gun had been fired, rising above the picket fence on the knoll. Hoffman had also seen two men behind the fence; one held a gun.

Compounding the evidence of a shooter on the knoll was an acoustical analysis of a Dictabelt recording from a motorcycle microphone in the presidential motorcade—an integral part of the HSCA investigation. Dr. James Barger, a scientist from the acoustical consulting firm Bolt, Beranek, and Newman concluded that there were at least six sounds on the tape, which were likely gunshots, and at least one was fired from the grassy knoll.[69] Following Barger's analysis, Mark Weiss, a professor at Queens College, and his research associate, Ernest Aschkenasy, both experienced acoustical analysts, were commissioned by the HSCA to reconstruct the Dictabelt using microphones placed throughout Dealey Plaza and live-fire tests from the Texas School Book Depository and the grassy knoll.[70]

"The principle behind the acoustic reconstruction was based on the timing of shock waves and their reflections off of buildings and structures in Dealey Plaza," wrote Paul G. Chambers in *Head Shot*. "When a projectile exceeds the speed of sound, as in a rifle shot, it produces a shock wave, a pressure wave, commonly known as a sonic boom. An example is the cracking of a whip: The tip briefly exceeds the speed of sound to produce the characteristic snap. The pattern of shock waves with time is called an acoustical signature, which differs from one sound source to another due to echoes and reflections off of structures in the area. These echoes create characteristic patterns that can be used to determine the origin of shock waves."[71]

Each microphone location would produce a "unique sound travel pattern, or sound fingerprint."[72] When the recording was compared to the Dictabelt tape, researchers were able to gain a strong indication as to where the shots were fired from. The test was able to verify a 95-percent certainty that a rifle shot had been fired from the grassy knoll.

This was the area of Dealey Plaza that onlookers and police alike believed to be the location of the assassin. Many ran there after the shooting. Of the ninety people asked by the police, FBI, or the Secret Service where they thought the shots had come from, fifty-eight said the grassy knoll. This overwhelming evidence pointing to the knoll as the strategic kill location[73] was suppressed.

The shooter, positioned behind the picket fence on the knoll, was insurance that President Kennedy would not leave Dealey Plaza alive. Unlike the shots fired from the depository, the proximity of the fence to Elm Street made the final blast a turkey shoot. With

Kennedy lined in his sight, the assassin, no doubt a trained assassin from Operation 40, dropped the hammer and hit Kennedy in the right side of the head towards the front.

As seen clearly on the Zapruder film, which was not shown to the public until 1975, the final shot jarred Kennedy's head back and to the left. This was an important piece of evidence, which was intentionally misinterpreted for years following his murder. The deception was aided in part by Dan Rather, then a green newscaster who worked at a Texas television station.

Rather was the only reporter to view the Zapruder film the day after the assassination. In this situation, he was an all-important set of eyes from the fourth estate, a voice the public could trust. He issued an erroneous, purposely falsified statement concerning the film. Following the final shot, the head of Kennedy, in Rather's angled report, "went forward with considerable violence,"[74] a description that anyone with eyesight in the fifty years following the assassination would find to be a blatant lie.

In 1993, CBS anchorman Dan Rather confessed to Robert Tannenbaum, the former deputy chief counsel of the House Select Committee on Assassinations: "We really blew it on the Kennedy assassination."

"I could see a piece of his skull coming off," Jackie said a week after the assassination to journalist and historian T. H. White. "He was holding out his hand—and I could see this perfectly clean piece detaching itself from his head. Then, he slumped in my lap; his blood and brain were in my lap."[75]

Powers and O'Donnell watched helplessly from the "Queen Mary" as their friend and leader died violently.

"While we both stared at the president, the third shot took the side of his head off," O'Donnell wrote. "We saw pieces of bone and brain tissue and bits of his reddish hair flying through the air. The impact lifted him and shook him limply, as if he were a rag doll, and then he dropped out of our sight, sprawled across the back seat of the car. I said to Dave, 'He's dead'."[76]

Appearing before the Warren Commission, O'Donnell would testify that he had heard the shots coming from behind him. But years later, he would admit to longtime Massachusetts Congressman and Speaker of the House Thomas "Tip" O'Neill that he actually heard shots coming from the knoll.

"That's not what you told the Warren Commission," O'Neill said.

"You're right," O'Donnell replied. "I told the FBI what I had heard, but they said it couldn't have happened that way and that I must have been imagining things. So I testified the way they wanted me to."[77]

With the hit on the president complete, the limousine sped to Parkland Hospital to perform fruitless last minute procedures in an attempt to save John F. Kennedy.

"I have read stories where I screamed and he screamed and all these things," said Nellie Connally. "There was no screaming in that horrible car. It was just a silent, terrible drive."[78]

NOTES

1. Vincent Bugliosi, *Reclaiming History: The Assassination of President John F. Kennedy* (New York: W. W. Norton & Company, 2007).
2. Hepburn, *Farewell America*, 352.
3. Ibid., 352–53.
4. Politics and Presidential Protection: Staff Report, HSCA, second session, 1979: 508.
5. Ibid.
6. Ibid., 518.
7. Ibid.
8. Steven M. Gillon, *The Kennedy Assassination—24 Hours After: Lyndon B. Johnson's Pivotal First Day as President* (New York: Basic, 2009), 16.
9. Ibid.
10. Zirbel, *The Texas Connection*, 188.
11. Nelson, *LBJ: The Mastermind of the JFK Assassination*, 374.
12. Caro, *Means of Ascent*, 118.
13. Ibid., 274.

14. Richard Severo, "John Connally of Texas, a Power in 2 Political Parties, Dies at 76," *The New York Times* (June 16, 1993).
15. Briody, *The Halliburton Agenda*, 170.
16. Bryce, *Cronies*, 103.
17. Zirbel, *The Texas Connection*, 191.
18. William Manchester, *The Death of a President* (New York: Harper & Row, 1963), 82.
19. Ibid., 82–82.
20. Ibid., 20.
21. Harrison Edward Livingstone and Robert J. Groden, *High Treason: The Assassination of JFK & the Case for Conspiracy* (New York: Carroll & Graf, 1998), 135.
22. Ibid., 134.
23. Nelson, *LBJ: The Mastermind of the JFK Assassination*, 379.
24. Ibid., 429.
25. Turner, Nigel. "The Men Who Killed Kennedy." History Channel.
26. Ross, Gaylon, "The Clint Murchison Meeting," YouTube video, 1:21:24, posted by "Se7ensenses," May 26, 2011, youtube.com/watch?v=POmdd6HQsus.
27. Nelson, *LBJ: The Mastermind of the JFK Assassination*, 321–22.
28. "LBJ's Mistress Blows Whistle on JFK Assassination," YouTube video, 5:14, posted by "onedeaddj," November 22, 2006, www.youtube.com/watch?v=79lOKs0Kr_Y.
29. "LBJ's Mistress Blows Whistle on JFK Assassination," YouTube video, 5:14, posted by "onedeaddj," November 22, 2006, www.youtube.com/watch?v=79lOKs0Kr_Y.
30. Hersh, *Bobby and J. Edgar*, 253.
31. David Pietrusza, *LBJ vs. JFK vs. Nixon: The Epic Campaign That Forged Three Presidencies.* (New York: Union Square Press, 2008), 387.
32. Summers, *The Arrogance of Power*, 262.
33. Fulsom, Don. "Richard Nixon's Greatest Coverup: His Ties to the Assassination of President Kennedy."
34. *Dallas Morning News*, November 22, 1963.
35. Manchester, *Death of a President*, 121.
36. Ibid.
37. O'Donnell, *Johnny, We Hardly Knew Ye*, 28.
38. Manchester, *Death of a President*, 122.
39. Gillon, *The Kennedy Assassination: 24 Hours After*, 23.
40. Nelson, *LBJ: The Mastermind of the JFK Assassination*, 393.
41. Bruce Weber, "Moyer and Others Want History Channel Inquiry Over Film That Accuses Johnson," *The New York Times* (February 5, 2004).
42. Nelson, *LBJ: The Mastermind of the JFK Assassination*, 387.
43. O'Donnell, *Johnny, We Hardly Knew Ye*, 28.
44. Gillon, *The Kennedy Assassination: 24 Hours After*, 25.
45. Ibid., 27.

46. Ibid.
47. Nelson, *LBJ: The Mastermind of the JFK Assassination*, 471.
48. Fred T. Newcomb and Perry Adams, *Murder from Within: Lyndon Johnson's Plot Against President Kennedy.* (Bloomington: AuthorHouse, 2011), 49.
49. Nelson, *LBJ: The Mastermind of the JFK Assassination*, 477.
50. Ibid., 478.
51. Ibid., 473.
52. Marrs, *Crossfire*, 16.
53. James H. Fetzer, *Assassination Science: Experts Speak Out on the Death of JFK.* (Chicago: Catfeet, 1998), 98.
54. Edward Jay Epstein, *Inquest: The Warren Commission and the Establishment of Truth* (New York: Viking, 1966), 49.
55. O'Donnell, *Johnny, We Hardly Knew Ye*, 29.
56. Ibid.
57. "HSCA Testimony of John and Nellie Connally." June 2012, jfkassassination.net/russ/m_j_russ/hscacon.htm.
58. Mark Lane, *Rush to Judgment: A Critique of the Warren Commission's Inquiry* (Greenwich: Fawcett Publications, 1967), 29.
59. Ibid.
60. Ibid., 30.
61. Ibid.
62. Ibid.
63. Marrs, *Crossfire*, 76.
64. Ibid.
65. Ibid.
66. Lane, *Rush to Judgment*, 31.
67. Ibid.
68. Ibid., 32.
69. G. Paul Chambers, *Head Shot: The Science Behind the JFK Assassination* (Amherst: Prometheus, 2010), 118.
70. Ibid., 121.
71. Ibid.
72. HSCA Final Report, 73.
73. Lane, *Rush to Judgment*, 37.
74. Marrs, *Crossfire*, 68.
75. Gillon, *The Kennedy Assassination: 24 Hours After*, 49.
76. O'Donnell, *Johnny, We Hardly Knew Ye*, 29.
77. John Kelin, *Praise from a Future Generation: The Assassination of John F. Kennedy and the First Generation Critics of the Warren Report* (San Antonio: Wings, 2007), 214.
78. Warren Commission Testimony of Nellie Connally.

CHAPTER FOURTEEN

LYNCHPIN

Surely one of the main thoughts that plagued Johnson following the assassination was the whereabouts of Malcolm Wallace and the shooters. Had Wallace fled from the depository unnoticed? Had the CIA and Mafia conspirators firing from behind the fence on the grassy knoll gotten away successfully? Unlike the other murders that Johnson had guided, this one had many pieces that could not easily be lawyered away.

In the early hours after the death of Kennedy, Johnson uttered more than one ridiculous cornpone morsel promoting a cabal.

"We've all got to be careful," he said at one point. "This could be a worldwide conspiracy to kill off all our leaders."[1]

It was a necessary move. Parkland Hospital was frantic when the Kennedys and the Connallys arrived and was insulated from news of the goings on in Dealey Plaza. If a conspiracy was unearthed in the unfolding madness, it would be Johnson who would have the power to direct the outcome. Once Oswald was in police custody, Johnson would order his minions to hush any talk of a conspiracy.

Johnson aide Cliff Carter placed multiple calls to Dallas District Attorney Henry Wade to this end. It "would hurt foreign relations if I alleged a conspiracy," said Wade, "whether I could prove it or not . . . I was to charge Oswald with plain murder."[2]

Wade added that, "Johnson had Cliff Carter call me three or four times that weekend."[3]

If Johnson was, on the surface, overwrought with the reality of the events that had unfolded that afternoon, there is also evidence that he was putting on an act—inside, he was coolly calculating.

Attorney Pat Holloway, whose boss Waddy Bullion was Johnson's tax lawyer, overheard a conversation between Bullion and Johnson that fateful afternoon. In Holloway's estimation, Johnson, in typical style, was less worried about the tragedy of the day and more concerned about personal business interests and how they might affect him personally.

Johnson talked to Bullion "not about a conspiracy or about a tragedy," said Holloway. "I heard him say: 'Oh, I gotta get rid of my goddamn Halliburton stock.' Lyndon Johnson was talking about the consequences of his political problems with his Halliburton stock at a time when the president had been officially declared dead. And that pissed me off. . . . It really made me furious."[4]

Finances aside, Johnson was also concerned with validating his presidency. The moment when the final rifle blast had shattered John Kennedy's skull, Lyndon Johnson was the new president. It was the formalities of the position, though, that he immediately sought to wrap himself in, requiring the power and safety that the presidency now afforded him.

Johnson would later try to distance himself from the eagerness that he showed in taking full and unabashed command of his new office. On most counts, he would use Kenny O'Donnell as his front, possibly believing that O'Donnell was too grief stricken to challenge or recognize the facts as they happened. The new chief executive certainly knew that the approvals of a close Kennedy confidant would bolster his credibility as president.

Johnson claimed that O'Donnell had told him of Kennedy's death at 1:20 p.m. "He's gone,"[5] O'Donnell was claimed to have said. In reality, Secret Service Agent Emory Roberts had told Johnson of Kennedy's death seven minutes earlier.[6]

The importance of Johnson's claim is minute, but revealing of the total control the new president sought over the official story.

The next disputed account with O'Donnell concerned Air Force One.

"I figured that Johnson, who had flown to Texas separately from the Kennedys on Air Force Two, the second 707 jet plane in our party, which was identical to Air Force One, would be taking off for Washington immediately," O'Donnell recalled.[7]

In O'Donnell's recollection, he and Johnson had agreed that LBJ would fly immediately back. It was Johnson's assertion that O'Donnell twice insisted that the unseasoned president use Air Force One for the return flight to Washington, with Johnson's qualification that he would wait for Mrs. Kennedy and his predecessor's body before taking off.

To O'Donnell, this version of events was "absolutely, totally, and unequivocally wrong."[8]

"He [Johnson] never suggested that he might wait at the airport for Jackie and the body of President Kennedy before he left for Washington. If he had made such a suggestion, I would have vetoed it. . . . He never discussed with me whether he should use Air Force One instead of Air Force Two, a question which would have seemed highly unimportant at the time."[9]

The importance in Johnson's using Air Force One to fly back to Washington had nothing to do with the significance of the plane because whatever plane the active president flies is designated Air Force One.

"When the President was killed and we were going to fly him back, President Johnson refused to fly in Air Force Two because he said the communications were not the same as Air Force One, which of course was not the case," said Kennedy's Air Force aide, General Godfrey McHugh. "He just wanted to be on Air Force One. But they were identical."[10]

One difference in the Boeing 707 that Johnson insisted on using was its interior decoration. Kennedy had used the Boeing known as 26000 as his personal plane for just over a year, flying in it for the first time in early November 1962 to attend the funeral of former First Lady Eleanor Roosevelt in New York. The cabin was festooned with Kennedy family memorabilia.

"There are two things the president adores," Jackie had told General McHugh. "One is 'Hail to the Chief,' he adores that song, and he adores Air Force One."[11]

As uncomfortable as the surroundings must have been for Johnson, they were necessary. It was not Johnson's desire to immerse himself in the personal effects of Kennedy or the adornment of presidency that made him use Air Force One. It was the necessity for oversight of the most important piece of evidence: the body of the dead president.

The Secret Service urged LBJ to rush to Air Force One and its security "because we don't know if this is a conspiracy and the new president could also be subject to attack." But Johnson was in no hurry because he knew that the only conspiracy afoot was the one he was directing.

At 1:26 p.m., President Lyndon Johnson left Parkland Hospital for Love Field. As he boarded the plane, he told James B. Swindal, the Air Force colonel who had commanded Air Force One for Kennedy, that they would not leave for Washington without the remains.

Other key pieces of evidence were already in the process of being rendered unusable to investigators. Johnson aide Cliff Carter had collected John Connally's clothes from Ruth Standrige, the head nurse of emergency rooms at Parkland. Carter then gave them to Texas Congressman Henry Gonzalez, who put them in his office closet in Washington, DC.[12] The clothes were then given to Nellie Connally, who washed them with cold water. When found, they showed signs that they had been cleaned and pressed.[13]

SS-100-X, the 1961 Lincoln Continental limousine that carried Kennedy to his death, was also in the process of being intentionally destroyed as evidence at Parkland. First, a Secret Service agent ordered the top be put on the car to obscure interior viewing. An orderly was then asked to get a bucket of water.[14]

"A guard was set up around the Lincoln as Secret Service men got a pail of water and tried to wash the blood from the car," said *Time* reporter Hugh Sidney.

After hurriedly cleaning up the body fluids and other bits of relatable evidence, the limousine was driven back to Love Field against the wishes of some Dallas Police investigators, loaded onto a cargo plane, and flown back to Washington to be parked in the White House garage.[15]

A few days following the assassination, the limousine was driven by Carl Renas, the head of security for the Dearborn Division of the Ford Motor Company, to Hess and Eisenhart in Cincinnati, Ohio to replace a chrome molding strip damaged in the shooting.[16] Hess and Eisenhart was the specialty-car company that had a hand in the car's original design and engineering. During the transfer of the vehicle, Renas noticed that the molding strip had been hit with "a primary strike" and "not a fragment."[17] He was told by the Secret Service to "keep his mouth shut."[18]

Renas was not the only one who noticed the damage to the interior of the car. During the Warren Commission hearings, Secret Service agent Roy Kellerman, who rode in the front passenger seat of SS-100-X in the Dallas motorcade, used the example of the damage in an attempt to sway the commission into considering that there were more than three shots fired at the motorcade. He was responding to questioning from commission counsel Arlen Specter:

SPECTER: Do you have anything to add, Mr. Kellerman, on the total number of wounds in relationship to your view that there were more than three shots?

KELLERMAN: Well, let's consider the vehicle.

SPECTER: Fine. What about the vehicle would you consider relevant in this regard?

KELLERMAN: The windshield itself, which I observed a day or two after the funeral here, had been hit by a piece of this missile or missiles, whatever it is, shell.[19]

Kellerman noticed an indentation on the chrome molding of the windshield upon examining the car on November 27 in the White House garage. He wanted to look at the car because the trajectory of the shots as he remembered them were different from the official record that was starting to form:

KELLERMAN: I wanted to look this car over for—let me go back a bit. When this car was checked over that night for its return to Washington, I was informed the following day of the pieces of these missiles that were found in the front seat, and I believe aside from the skull, which was in the rear seat, I couldn't conceive even from elevation how this shot hit President Kennedy like it did. I wanted to view this vehicle, whether this was a slant blow off of the car, whether it hit the car first and then hit him, or what marks are on this vehicle, and that is what prompted me to go around and check it for myself.
FORD: Had anybody told you of this indentation prior to your own personal investigation?
KELLERMAN: Not of the windshield. No, sir.
FORD: You were the first one to find this indentation?
KELLERMAN: I believe I am the first one who noticed this thing up on the bar.[20]

Later in his testimony, Kellerman, led by commission members to the conclusion of three shots fired, still believed otherwise, offering up a damning piece of evidence.

"Gentlemen, I think that if you would view the films yourself, you may come up with a little different answer."[21]

In December 1963, the White House inexplicably approved plans to have the limousine rebuilt and reupholstered for President Johnson, destroying the evidence for future inquires.

The body of the former president would be harder to control.

The medical staff at Parkland Hospital had already discovered too much about Kennedy's injuries in their futile attempts to resuscitate and stabilize him. When Kennedy was brought into Trauma Room One on a gurney, Dr. Charles Crenshaw observed the wounds of the fallen president.

"I was standing at about the president's waist, looking at his general appearance, still unbelieving," wrote Crenshaw. "Blood was seeping from the wound in his head onto the gurney, dripping into the kick bucket on the floor below. Then I noticed a small opening in the midline of his throat. It was a bullet-entry wound. There was no doubt in my mind about that wound, as I had seen dozens of them in the emergency room."[22]

Dr. Malcolm Perry performed a tracheotomy to aid Kennedy's breathing and talked about the entrance wound at a recorded press conference hours after the assassination :

Q: Where was the entrance wound?
PERRY: There was an entrance wound in the neck.
Q: Which way was the bullet coming in the neck wound? At him?
PERRY: It appeared to be coming at him.[23]

The entrance wound in the throat was seen by more doctors at Parkland, including Paul Peters and Ronald Jones, but not mentioned on the official autopsy.

Crenshaw and other Parkland doctors also noticed a large wound at the back of the president's head, above and behind his right ear, consistent with an exit wound.

Jim Sibert, an FBI special agent tasked with watching the autopsy at Bethesda Naval Hospital, maintained that the head wound was in the "upper back of the head."[24]

Tom Robinson, the mortician who prepared Kennedy in the casket for funeral, when interviewed by HSCA staff members Andy

Purdy and Jim Conzelman, echoed the claims of a large wound in the back right side of the head:

PURDY: Approximately where was this wound (the skull wound) located?
ROBINSON: Directly behind the back of his head.
PURDY: Approximately between the ears or higher up?
ROBINSON: No, I would say pretty much between them.[25]

More than forty witnesses described the exit wound in the back of the head; strong correlations existed in both the extent and area of the damage they detailed.[26] According to the official record asserted later by the Warren Commission and the HSCA, the witnesses were mistaken in what they saw. The wound in Kennedy's head had, according to the Warren Commission, "entered through the right rear of the president's head and exited from the right side of the head, causing a large wound."[27]

Upon re-examination by the HSCA with the aid of a forensic pathology panel, it was found that "President Kennedy was struck by two, and only two, bullets, each of which entered from the rear. The panel further concluded that the president had been struck by one bullet that had entered in the upper right of the back and exited from the front of the throat, and one bullet that had entered in the right rear of the head near the cowlick area and exited from the right side of the head, toward the front. This second bullet caused a massive wound to the president's head upon exit."[28]

This description was the antithesis to most first-hand accounts. When photographs from the autopsy were later released, many would see different wounds from the ones that they had borne witness to. The questionable photographs showed that, at the autopsy, the back of Kennedy's skull was intact.

"To virtually every eyewitness, these photographs are perplexing," wrote Dr. David Mantik, a medical doctor who has studied much of the medical evidence produced from the assassination.

"They show a completely intact right posterior skull, which is in absolute conflict with the medical records of numerous Parkland physicians. Even on the widely broadcast *Nova* television program on PBS in 1988 involving four Parkland physicians, the placement of their hands well behind the right ear to locate the large skull defect is in gross conflict with the posterior head photographs. This conflict persists in the memories of ancillary personnel at Bethesda and even with the measurements and descriptions of the pathologist themselves. The autopsy protocol specifically describes the skull defect as extending in the occiput. The photographs, however, show the defect far above the occipital bone. The pathologists were never asked if these photographs were accurate. In fact, on the one question they were asked based on the photographs (regarding the posterior entry wound), they disagreed by four inches!"[29]

The medical staff at Parkland anticipated performing an autopsy of Kennedy. Instead, the body was seized by the Secret Service. An autopsy at Parkland would be impossible to control and could not commence.

Agent Roy Kellerman, who moments earlier had watched the death of the man whom he was employed to protect, sprang into action. He was on orders from Director Rowley: The body had to be expeditiously transported to Air Force One. Johnson had maintained that he would not leave for Washington otherwise.

Parkland doctor James Crenshaw thought it odd that the Secret Service was more interested in protecting the former president considering that he was dead. If an autopsy was performed without proper guidance and at a public hospital, the truth about Kennedy's injuries would be harder to suppress.

An argument quickly ensued between Kellerman and Dr. Earl Rose, the Dallas medical examiner.

"There has been a homicide here," Rose said. "You won't be able to remove the body. We will have to take it down to the mortuary for an autopsy."[30]

"There must be something in your thinking here that we don't have to go through this agony," Kellerman answered. "We will take care of the matter when we get back to Washington."

Rose would not have it—it would be against the law for the Secret Service to take the body. The order, though, was coming from someone who now believed himself above the law.

"No, that's not the way things are. You're not taking the body anywhere,"[31] Rose said.

John Kennedy's personal physician, George Burkley, who accompanied him on all trips, spoke for the well-being of the former First Lady.

"Mrs. Kennedy is going to stay exactly where she is until the body is moved. We can't have that . . . he's the President of the United States."[32]

"That does matter," replied Dr. Rose. "You can't lose the chain of evidence."

Rose knew that moving the body from Parkland would compromise not only the autopsy, but the entire investigation.

He sought out Theron Ward, a justice of the peace, who tried to tell the Secret Service agents about the questionable legality of assuming control of Kennedy's body.

Kellerman, though, was leaving with the body without regard of the law.

"You are going to have to come up with something a little stronger than you to give me the law that this body can't be removed,"[33] Kellerman said.

The Secret Service agents, by then brandishing pistols, made their way out of Parkland with the body.

Shortly before 2 p.m., as the Secret Service agents were forcing their way out of Parkland to expedite the return to Washington, President Johnson, with the body of Kennedy secured and en route, was in no rush to leave Dallas. The president felt the need to take the oath of office to validate his title.

A call placed by Johnson from Air Force One to Robert Kennedy became another bone of contention in the official story.

Kennedy had heard of his brother's death only forty minutes before and only a few moments earlier he received a second phone call from J. Edgar Hoover.

"The president's dead,"[34] Hoover said apathetically before hanging up.

Johnson's call concerned a different matter.

"First, he expressed his condolences," Kennedy said. "Then he said . . . this might be part of a worldwide plot, which I didn't understand, and he said, 'A lot of people down here think I should be sworn in right away.'"[35]

Johnson wanted to know the particulars about the oath: who could administer it and how and where he should take it.

The attorney general was aghast. Not only were his brother's wounds still fresh, but the man whom Bobby resented was quick to step in and on the Kennedy's shoes. Johnson could have found someone other than Bobby to answer questions about the oath, but Bobby Kennedy served the same purpose that Johnson sought in his previous encounters with O'Donnell. If he had the approval of the attorney general, the slain president's brother, Johnson would seem to the American people and perhaps to himself like less of a tyrant.

Kennedy was "taken aback at the moment because it was just an hour after . . . the president had been shot and I didn't think—see what the rush was. And I thought, I suppose at the time, at least, I thought it would be nice if the president came back to Washington—President Kennedy . . . But I suppose that was all personal."[36]

Bobby showed restraint. "I'll be glad to find out and call you back,"[37] he told Johnson.

In Johnson's skewed rendition of history, Bobby urged him to take the oath as soon as possible. According to Johnson, Bobby suggested "that the oath should be administered to me immediately, before taking off for Washington, and that it should be administered by a judicial officer of the United States."[38]

In truth, the oath was a formality and could be administered at any time, but Johnson was not taking any chances. O'Donnell was certain that Johnson wanted to take the oath on the ground in Dallas because "he was afraid somebody was going to take the thing away from him if he didn't get it quick."[39]

Johnson chose Judge Sarah T. Hughes to administer the oath. Hughes had been waiting at the Trade Mart for the presidential motorcade and told Johnson she could be there in ten minutes.[40] There was significance in this as well: JFK had blocked Hughes from a judicial promotion even though Johnson had pushed her.

As Johnson made phone calls to arrange the ceremony, Jackie Kennedy arrived with members of Kennedy's staff and the former president's body. O'Donnell was anxious to get the plane in the air and JFK's body back to Washington. But this was not the intent of Johnson, whom the Kennedy staff assumed had left at least a half-hour prior on Air Force Two.

"Tell O'Donnell he's not commander-in-chief anymore," a press aide shouted. "President Johnson is on the plane."[41]

Godfrey McHugh was bewildered by the holdup. "Mrs. Kennedy was getting very warm, she had blood all over her hat, her coat . . . his brains were sticking on her hat. It was dreadful,"[42] McHugh said.

McHugh, pleading his case to pilot James Swindal, was told that the flight was delayed for reasons concerning the transfer of Johnson's luggage from Air Force Two and the swearing in of the new president.

"I only have one president, and he's lying back in that cabin,"[43] McHugh yelled, referring to the body of President Kennedy.

"McHugh said that Lyndon Johnson had been—and I remember the word that he used—obscene," recalled Bobby Kennedy. "It was the worst performance he'd ever witnessed."

Johnson, sensing that those who surrounded him had begun to question their new boss's authority, put on a virtuoso performance. He went to hide in private, so the occupants of Air Force One could find him, acting as if he were losing his mind in this tragedy. If the incessant, insensitive demands could not be met out of his new authority, they might be met out of pity.

When McHugh went to look for Johnson, he found the new president holed up in the bathroom.

"I walked in the toilet, in the powder room, and there he was hiding, with the curtain closed," said McHugh. Johnson was feigning delirium. "They're all going to get us. It's a plot. It's a plot," Johnson said. According to McHugh, Johnson "was hysterical, sitting down on the john there alone in this thing."[44]

McHugh proceeded to slap Johnson, prompting the president to "snap out of it."[45]

Johnson righted himself, and, as Sarah Hughes arrived, the new president had one more inconvenience for the Kennedy party. Once again summoning O'Donnell, Johnson asked for Jackie to stand in for the swearing-in ceremony.

The conversation is well detailed in *RFK* by C. David Heymann:

> Once Judge Hughes arrived, the new president addressed Ken O'Donnell. "Would you ask Mrs. Kennedy to come stand next to me?"
>
> "You can't do that!" O'Donnell cried. "The poor kid has had enough for one day. You just can't do that to her, Mr. President."
>
> "Well, she said she wanted to do it."
>
> "I don't believe it."
>
> But when O'Donnell found the now-former first lady, she agreed to stand by her husband's successor. "At least I owe that much to the country," she whispered. In her pink wool suit stained by blood and gore from Jack's shattered skull, she watched as Lyndon Johnson raised his right hand to take the oath as the thirty-sixth president of the United States.[46]

Jackie may have had her own reasoning for standing in on the ceremony. When asked by Lady Bird before the ceremony if she wanted to change her blood-stained clothing, Jackie was adamantly against it.

"I want them to see what they have done to Jack,"[47] Jackie said. But what they had done to Jack would never be seen.

The results of the autopsy were made to correspond with the official story in play. While Air Force One was in flight to Washington, the White House Situation Room informed the passengers that there was no conspiracy. Only four hours after the president had been murdered, they had their man in custody: Lee Harvey Oswald.[48]

"That is conclusive evidence of high-level US governmental guilt," wrote Philadelphia attorney Vincent J. Salandria. "The first announcement of Oswald as the lone assassin, before there was any evidence against him, and while there was overwhelmingly convincing evidence of conspiracy, had come from the White House Situation Room. Only the assassins could have made that premature declaration that Oswald was the assassin."[49]

On arrival in Maryland at Andrews Air Force Base, John Kennedy's body was quickly loaded into an ambulance and taken to Bethesda Naval Hospital. At Bethesda, although Bobby Kennedy authorized a full autopsy,[50] it would be a carefully scripted farce.

Under military supervision, three pathologists—J. Thorton Boswell, James J. Humes and Pierre A. Finck—"moved" certain wounds and disregarded others to fit the narrative. The exit wound at the back of his head would now be an entrance wound.

The neck wound would be disregarded, and the pathologists would not track the bullet hole in the upper back. When brought to testify during New Orleans District Attorney Jim Garrison's criminal trial against Clay Shaw in 1969, Dr. Finck would admit the pressure put on him by the military present:

Q: This puzzled you at the time, the wound in the back and you couldn't find an exit wound? You were wondering about where this bullet was or where the path was going, were you not?
FINCK: Yes.
Q: Well, at that particular time, doctor, why didn't you call the doctors at Parkland or attempt to ascertain what the doctors

at Parkland may have done or may have seen while the President's body was still exposed to view on the autopsy table?

FINCK: I will remind you that I was not in charge of this autopsy, that I was called—

Q: You were a co-author of the report though, weren't you, Doctor?

FINCK: Wait. I was called as a consultant to look at these wounds; that doesn't mean I am running the show.

Q: Was Dr. Humes running the show?

FINCK: Well, I heard Dr. Humes stating that—he said, "Who is in charge here?" and I heard an army general, I don't remember his name, stating, 'I am.' You must understand that in those circumstances, there were law enforcement officers, military people with various ranks, and you have to co-ordinate the operation according to directions.

Q: But you were one of the three qualified pathologists standing at that autopsy table, were you not, doctor?

FINCK: Yes, 'I am.'

Q: Was this army general a qualified pathologist?

FINCK: No.

Q: Was he a doctor?

FINCK: No, not to my knowledge.

Q: Can you give me his name, colonel?

FINCK: No, I can't. I don't remember.[51]

James Curtis Jenkins, a technician who was at the autopsy table, saw a shot that had blown off a portion of the back of Kennedy's skull. To his dismay, this finding did not appear in the autopsy report. "I found out that he was supposedly shot from the back. I just, you know, I just couldn't believe it, and I have never been able to believe it."

George Burkley, John Kennedy's personal physician, present with both the medical staff at Parkland and the pathologists at Bethesda, was never to be called to testify in front of any of the official investigations and never questioned by the Secret Service or the FBI.[52]

When asked in 1967 if he agreed with the Warren Commission report as to the number of bullets that entered the president's body, Burkley's response was simple: "I would not care to be quoted on that."[53]

Burkley was never brought before the Warren Commission because his testimony was one of many that could only damage the story being massaged from on high. The Commission would also not permit its members or witnesses who testified to view photographs or X-rays. Instead, the Commission used sketches that provided a likeness of the integral evidence.

"The doctors almost begged for the production of the photographs during their testimony, especially Dr. Humes," assassination researcher Harold Weisberg said. "And finally, after this happened three or four times, the Commission asked, 'Well, would your testimony be any different if you had the pictures here?' What was the poor doctor going to do? Say he testified incompetently? Or falsely? Obviously, he just said 'No. But—' But he did put a 'but' in, and he insisted that the pictures would have been best. And he insisted that pictures and X-rays are basic and normal to an autopsy—apparently, everybody's autopsy but that of a president."[54]

The orders, as many of the others that day, had come from above.

"This was a political assassination, and there was a lot of power behind it," said Vincent Salandria, one of the earliest Kennedy assassination researchers in 1967. "A *lot* of power. If you want to find the men behind it, you have to raise your sights. You have to screw your courage way up high. You have to look even higher than J. Edgar Hoover and the FBI."[55]

NOTES

1. Nelson, *LBJ: Mastermind of the JFK Assassination*, 412.
2. Ibid., 485.

3. Ibid., 372.
4. Baker, Russ, *Family of Secrets*, 132.
5. Gillon, *The Kennedy Assassination: 24 Hours After*, 80.
6. Ibid., 82.
7. Ibid., 89.
8. Manchester, *The Death of a President*, 234.
9. Pat Speer to The Education Forum, October 25, 2012, educationforum. ipbhost.com/index.php?showtopic=19632
10. Gillon, *The Kennedy Assassination: 24 Hours After*, 90.
11. Ibid.
12. Warren Commission Testimony of Ruth Jeanette Standridge, March 21, 1964.
13. Newcomb and Adams, *Murder From Within*, 138.
14. Ibid., 131.
15. Ibid., 132.
16. Charles A. Crenshaw, *Trauma Room One: The JFK Medical Coverup Exposed* (New York: Paraview, 2001), 81.
17. Ibid.
18. Ibid.
19. Warren Commission Testimony of Roy H. Kellerman.
20. Ibid.
21. Ibid.
22. Crenshaw, *Trauma Room One*, 62.
23. Crenshaw, *Assassination Science*, pg. 45.
24. Aguilar, Gary L. MD, "The HSCA and JFK's Skull Wound", March 30, 1995.
25. Ibid.
26. Ibid.
27. HSCA Final Report, 41.
28. Ibid., 43.
29. Fetzer, *Assassination Science*, pg. 109.
30. Gillon, *The Kennedy Assassination: 24 Hours After*, 119.
31. Ibid.
32. Crenshaw, *Trauma Room One*, 89.
33. Gillon, *The Kennedy Assassination: 24 Hours After*, 119.
34. Manchester, *Death of a President*, 257.
35. Gillon, *The Kennedy Assassination: 24 Hours After*, 112–13.
36. Ibid., 113.
37. Manchester, *Death of a President*, 269.

38. Ibid., 271.
39. Gillon, *The Kennedy Assassination: 24 Hours After*, 132.
40. Ibid., 118.
41. Heymann, *RFK*, 348.
42. Ibid., 125.
43. Manchester, *Death of a President*, 316.
44. Gillon, *The Kennedy Assassination: 24 Hours After*, 127-28.
45. Christopher P. Andersen, *Jackie After Jack: Portrait of the Lady* (New York: William Morrow, 1998), 11.
46. Heymann, *RFK*, 348–49.
47. "Selections from Lady Bird's Diary on the Assassination." June 10, 2012 pbs.org/ladybird/epicenter/epicenter_doc_diary.html.
48. Kelin, *Praise from a Future Generation*, 5.
49. Ibid.
50. Talbot, *Brothers*, 16.
51. Clay Shaw trial testimony of Pierre A. Finck.
52. Ibid., 16–17.
53. Oral history interview with Admiral George G. Burkley; 10/17/1967. jfkassassination.net/russ/testimony/burkley.htm.
54. Kelin, *Praise from a Future Generation*, 280.
55. Kelin, *Praise from a Future Generation*, 338.

CHAPTER FIFTEEN

PATSY

"When a rich man dies, he is loaded with his possessions like a prisoner with chains," Lee Harvey Oswald once said. "I will die free; death will be easy for me."[1]

The proclamation couldn't be further from the truth.

William Bobo. That was the name assigned to the gravesite of Oswald. The fictitious name was procured to ward off the media and potential grave robbers. Bobo, slang for fool or sucker, couldn't have been more appropriate.

It would be argued that Lee Harvey Oswald adopted more than one alias during his life. He allegedly used the name A. Hidell to order the Italian carbine used to kill the president. O. H. Lee was reportedly the name he was registered under in the boarding house at 1026 North Beckley Ave, his last residence.

More interesting than the names attributed to Oswald would be imposter Oswalds who had taken his.

The pretenders had used Oswald's name and identity from as far back as 1961 when a group of men in New Orleans claiming affiliation with the anti-Castro group "Friends of Democracy" attempted to buy a volume of Ford trucks, using the name "Oswald" on the purchasing documents.[2] In September 1963, another Oswald appeared at the Dallas-area apartment of Cuban exile Sylvia Odio. This Oswald ranted to Odio about the Cubans being gutless for not assassinating Kennedy following the Bay of Pigs.[3] On November 9, 1963, on a day spent with his wife Marina at her friend Ruth Paine's house, Oswald impostors were seen in several areas. One Oswald applied for a job at the Dallas Southland Hotel, while another recklessly test-drove a car at a Dallas Lincoln Mercury dealership.[4] A third Oswald cropped up at the Sports Drome Rifle Range in Dallas. This Oswald displayed excellent marksmanship to witnesses and a repugnant temperament.

On a recorded phone conversation the day following the assassination, J. Edgar Hoover told Lyndon Johnson that he knew of an imposter Oswald in Mexico City.

"We have up here the tape and the photograph of the man who was at the Soviet Embassy using Oswald's name," said Hoover. "That picture and the tape do not correspond to this man's voice, nor to his appearance. In other words, it appears that there is a second person who was at the Soviet embassy down there. We do have a copy of a letter which was written by Oswald to the Soviet embassy here in Washington, inquiring as well as complaining about the harassment of his wife and the questioning of his wife by the FBI. Now of course, that letter information—we process all mail that goes to the Soviet embassy. It's a very secret operation. No mail is delivered to the embassy without being examined and opened by us, so that we know what they receive. . . . The case, as it stands now, isn't strong enough to be able to get a conviction. . . . Now, if we can identify this man who was at the . . . Soviet embassy in Mexico City. . . . This man Oswald has still denied everything."[5]

Contained in this phone conversation is not only the knowledge by Hoover of Oswald being impersonated, but knowledge of a conspiracy that would subsequently not be pursued by Hoover or Johnson. Hoover and the FBI had known about Oswald since the late fifties.

"A file concerning Oswald was opened," Hoover wrote to the Warren Commission, "at the time, newspapers reported his defection to Russia in 1959, for the purpose of correlating information inasmuch as he was considered a possible security risk in the event he returned to this country."[6]

What is more alarming is that Hoover had personally known and written to the State Department's Office of Security concerning the possibility of an Oswald identity theft as early as June 1960.

"Since there is a possibility that an imposter is using Oswald's birth certificate," Hoover wrote, "any current information the Department of State has concerning subject [Oswald] will be appreciated."[7]

The FBI wasn't the only agency keeping tabs on Oswald. The CIA also had a particular interest in and an extensive file on the young defector. After Oswald was murdered in cold blood, many of these files, when requested by the Warren Commission, were withheld or manipulated, leaving a puzzling paper trail. Oswald, according the agency, was of no interest to the CIA. Subsequent discoveries in the matter found documents on him scattered and deposited in varied nooks throughout the agency.

Jane Roman, a retired CIA officer who signed many of the agency's documents concerning Oswald prior to the assassination, was interviewed by journalist Jefferson Morley and former US Army Intelligence officer John Newman. The interview was an attempt to add framework to the agency abyss in which the truths of Oswald lied. The query began with Roman's denying knowledge of Oswald prior to the assassination. Newman then furnished copies of CIA cables that Roman had signed in regards to Oswald from 1959 till the time of the assassination.[8] From that point, Roman admitted to pre-assassination knowledge of Oswald and agreed to answer questions. Newman and Morley were particularly interested in the mysterious actions of the agency while Oswald was in Mexico City in late September to early October 1963.

Newman read off to Roman the wide variety of agency names that were signed to agency routing slips in September 1963.

"Is this the mark of a person's file who's dull and uninteresting?" Newman asked. "Or would you say that we're looking at somebody who's . . . ?"

"No, we're really trying to zero in on somebody here," Roman replied.[9]

Newman then unearthed a document dated October 10, 1963 composed by Charlotte Bustos, an employee on the agency's Mexico desk. The document stated that the "latest HDQS [headquarters] info [rmation]"[10] concerning Oswald was a report from May 1962. Roman had signed off on this document, which purported that the agency had no previous reports on Oswald for over a year, but only a few days prior Roman had signed reports on him.

It's not even a little bit untrue," Newman said. "It's grossly untrue."[11]

It was at this point in the interview that Roman admitted to a few agency truths held close to the chest on Oswald.

"Problem, though, here," Newman said pointing to the words "latest HDQS info."

"Yeah, I mean I'm signing off on something that I know isn't true,"[12] Newman admitted.

"And I'm not saying that it has to be considered sinister, don't misunderstand me," Newman added later. "It is one thing if I don't say anything, I tell you 'You don't have a need to know.' But if I tell you something that I know isn't true, that's an action [that] I'm taking for some reason . . . I guess what I'm trying to push you to address square on here is, is this indicative of some sort of operational interest in Oswald's file?"

"Yes," Roman replied. "To me, it's indicative of a keen interest in Oswald held very closely on a need-to-know basis."[13]

It was at this point in the query that Roman, using her operational knowledge of agency workings, released a stunner.

"There wouldn't be any point in withholding it [the recent information about Oswald]," she answered. "There has to be a point for withholding information from Mexico City."

"Well, the obvious position which I can't contemplate would be that they [meaning the people with final authority over the cable] thought that somehow . . . they could make some use of Oswald,"[14] Roman added.

Oswald's CIA contact in Dallas was George de Mohrenschildt, who claimed to be an oil geologist and consultant. He was prompted to contact Oswald by Dallas CIA man J. Walton Moore.[15] From October of 1962 until April of 1963, de Mohrenschildt was a close friend to Lee and Marina Oswald, watching over them.

De Mohrenschildt, in his Warren Commission testimony, talked of helping the Oswalds out and spending a good deal of time with them. It is suspect that an educated, worldly man such as de Mohrenschildt would meet and maintain relations with Oswald, a man whom, to the Warren Commission, de Mohrenschildt considered to be "a semi-educated hillbilly. And you cannot take such a person seriously. All his opinions were crude, you see."[16] Before he died in 1977, de Mohrenschildt's assessment of Oswald had changed considerably.

"In my opinion," de Mohrenschildt wrote, "Lee was a very bright person, but not a genius. He never mastered the English language, yet he learned such a difficult language! I taught Russian at all levels in a large university, and I never saw such a proficiency in the best senior students, who constantly listened to Russian tapes and spoke to Russian friends. As a matter of fact, American-born instructors never mastered the Russian spoken language as well as Lee did."[17]

Also greatly altered in de Mohrenschildt's statements was Oswald's motive for the assassination. The reasoning given to the Warren Commission was one of social status. "In my opinion," de Mohrenschildt stated, "if Lee Oswald did kill the president, this might be the reason for it: that he was insanely jealous of an extraordinarily successful man, who was young, attractive, had a beautiful wife, had all the money in the world, and was a world figure. And poor Oswald was just the opposite. He had nothing.

He had a bitchy wife, had no money, was a miserable failure in everything he did."[18]

Later, de Mohrenschildt again re-characterized Oswald as a man of political idealism not at all envious of material possession. "Lee, an ex-Marine, trained for organized murder, was capable of killing, but for a very strong ideological motive or in self-defense."

This could not be a possible motive for Oswald in the assassination of President Kennedy. De Mohrenschildt, as well as Oswald's wife Marina, knew that Oswald had a great appreciation for Kennedy, especially the president's efforts in mending the politically divisive relationship with Russia. Once in conversation, the topic between de Mohrenschildt and Oswald turned to Kennedy's work to end the Cold War.

"Great, great!" exclaimed Lee. "If he succeeds, he will be the greatest president in the history of this country."[19]

Why the changing feelings on Oswald? De Mohrenschildt said he was initially pressured by Albert Jenner, assistant counsel to the Warren Commission, into answering in a particular way, but also felt he had given an unfair evaluation of Oswald. "It would not have made him a hero to have shot a liberal and beloved president, especially beloved by the minorities," wrote de Mohrenschildt, "and Marina was not such a bitch, while Jacqueline was not so beautiful."

What is likely is that de Mohrenschildt, shortly before his death, felt guilty about the initial portrait that he had painted of the man whom he had been assigned to oversee. Evidence suggests that de Mohrenschildt was procured to develop Oswald for his role in the assassination.

In April 1963, following his grooming of Oswald, de Mohrenschildt traveled to Washington, where he convened with CIA officials and sought a meeting with Vice President Johnson.

A letter written to de Mohrenschildt on April 18 from Lyndon Johnson's office adds details to his trip to Washington:

Dear Mr. Mohrenschildt:

Your letter has come in the vice president's absence from the office. . . . I would like to suggest that you see Colonel Howard Burris, Air Force aide to the vice president, when you come to Washington. Should Mr. Johnson happen to have any office hours here during your stay, we will be happy to see if a mutually convenient time can be found for you to meet. . . .

With warm wishes,
Sincerely, Walter Jenkins, Administrative Assistant to the Vice President.[20]

Why was de Mohrenschildt seeking council with Vice President Johnson? Besides de Mohrenschildt's connections to the CIA and Texas Oil, he also had connections to other Johnson associates. Following his mysterious death, the unlisted phone number of Colonel Burris was found in de Mohrenschildt's address book.[21] As Johnson's military advisor, Burris accompanied Johnson to Vietnam in 1961, where the two convinced Prime Minister Ngo Dinh Diem to petition JFK for the training of sixteen thousand more US troops, a request that the president denied.[22]

The decision to request more troops was not made in a vacuum—it was a result of Johnson's evolved relations with the intelligence community that had shunned Kennedy. According to Burris himself, "Johnson had back-channel sources at the CIA, which kept him apprised of such matters."[23] Burris was an integral link in this "back channel."

For Burris to be interacting personally with de Mohrenschildt adds another integral connection between oil, intelligence, and LBJ. For a man depicted as a lone nut, Oswald had made a very interesting friend in the older de Mohrenschildt. Indeed, de Mohrenschildt told the Warren Commission of a business trip that he had taken to Mexico City in 1959 "on behalf of Texas Eastern Corp."[24] for the purpose of entertaining members of the Mexican Government in relation to a natural gas contract.

Texas Eastern Corporation was the Texas Eastern Transmission Company, the major oil-pipeline firm owned by Johnson's main contributors, Brown and Root. De Mohrenschildt had many similar business and political associations in Texas. He was also close friends with D. H. Byrd, owner of the Texas School Book Depository building. In 1950, de Mohrenschildt started an oil investment firm with Eddie Hooker, George H. W. Bush's roommate at Phillips Academy in Andover, Massachusetts. This odd connection between Bush and de Mohrenschildt did not stop there: years after the assassination of President Kennedy, in 1976, a desperate de Mohrenschildt wrote a plea for help to Bush, who at that time was the director of the CIA.

The letter was an obvious attempt to call the dogs off in a time when, with the HSCA hearings, new inquiries into the assassination were being opened and people who had been involved were dying. Bush, though, in an important government position, took the time to answer back, perhaps as a precaution, deflecting the accusations of surveillance intrusions on de Mohrenschildt and his wife as paranoia.

"My staff has been unable to find any indication of interest in your activities on the part of federal authorities in recent years," wrote Bush. "The flurry of interest that attended your testimony before the Warren Commission has long since subsided. I can only suspect that you have become 'newsworthy' again in view of the renewed interest in the Kennedy assassination and, thus, may be attracting the attention of people in the media."[25]

Despite the assurance of Bush, de Mohrenschildt's situation worsened. In conversation with Dutch journalist Willem Oltmans in 1977, de Mohrenschildt's long-held secrets began to leak.

"I feel responsible for the behavior of Lee Harvey Oswald . . . because I guided him," de Mohrenschildt said. "I instructed him to set it up."[26]

De Mohrenschildt was unraveling, filled with guilt over his past associations and no doubt filled with fear. He pleaded with Oltmans to get him out of the country. The journalist complied and took him to Holland. It was during that trip that de Mohrenschildt revealed more of his sensitive assassination knowledge.

"On the trip, via Houston and New York, de Mohrenschildt purportedly began dropping small pieces of information," wrote Russ Baker in *Family of Secrets*, an investigative indictment of the Bush dynasty. "He claimed to know Jack Ruby. And he began providing fragments of a scenario in which Texas oilmen in league with intelligence operatives plotted to kill the president."[27]

De Mohrenschildt then reportedly provided names of those implicated in the plot to the Dutch media. Knowing his time was short, he was talking. A month later, back in the United States, the HSCA continued the investigation of de Mohrenschildt, but it wouldn't last long. During the second day of interviews, de Mohrenschildt was found in the room where he was staying dead of a gunshot through the head. The death was later deemed to be a suicide.[28]

De Mohrenschilt's death came only hours after he intimated to investigators that the CIA had approved his contact with Oswald.[29] At the time of his death, a tape recorder was running nearby, the audio of which was studied and described later by assassination researcher Mark Lane:

> They claimed he committed suicide. But if you listen to the tape, you hear this: You hear a little noise, then you hear silence and you hear 'Beep-Beep-Beep-Beep-Beep,' a little more noise, and then you hear the shot. The 'Beep-Beep-Beep-Beep-Beep' was a security system on medium mode. One mode is, if it's on fully armed and someone opens a door or a window, a siren goes off, and the police are notified. On another mode, it's off entirely. But on the *medium* mode, it goes 'Beep-Beep-Beep-Beep' to show that someone has opened the door and come into the house. Just before de Mohrenschildt was shot, that's what happened.[30]

In *I am a Patsy! I am a Patsy!* his unpublished memoir written shortly before he died, de Mohrenschildt wrote that he believed Oswald was "probably innocent of the Kennedy assassination."[31]

The use that the CIA had made of Oswald would almost replicate the use they would attempt to make out of another ex-Marine, Thomas Arthur Vallee. Parallels between the two men are striking. Like Oswald, Vallee, while in the Marines, was assigned to a U-2 base in Japan, where CIA operations were being held. Following their time in the Marines, both Oswald and Vallee trained Cuban exiles at CIA camps: Oswald at Lake Pontchartrain and Vallee in New York.[32] Vallee subsequently moved from New York to Chicago in August of 1963, where he was employed as a printer in a warehouse at 625 West Jackson Boulevard. The warehouse was on President Kennedy's motorcade route on November 2.

"Vallee's location at IPP Litho-Plate actually gave him a nearer, clearer view of the November 2 Chicago motorcade than Oswald's so-called 'sniper's nest' did of the November 22 Dallas motorcade," wrote James W. Douglass in *JFK and the Unspeakable*. "Oswald's job was on the sixth floor, whereas Vallee's work site, three floors lower than Oswald's, put him in the culpable position of having an unimpeded shot at the president passing directly below him. At the same time, the unidentified snipers in the Chicago plot could have shot Kennedy from hidden vantage points and then escaped, leaving Vallee to take the blame."[33]

Kennedy was traveling to Chicago to attend the Army–Navy football game, but at the last minute, the trip was cancelled. Almost immediately thereafter, Vallee was arrested by intelligence officers of the Chicago police.[34]

Word of the plot had come from an FBI informant named "Lee" on October 30. The next day, a landlady called the Chicago police with information that four men were renting rooms from her, and, in one of these rooms, she had discovered four rifles with telescopic sights.[35] The men were questioned but never arrested. Chicago too had its patsy, in what looked to be a dry run of the actual assassination in Dallas.

Dallas, though, was given attention on all levels by the conspirators. Even Oswald's Russian bride, Marina, was made presentable for the lone gunman theory. Marina Oswald, who spoke no English, was not pleased with the interpretation assistance of Ilya Mamantov, the interpreter assigned to her by the Dallas Police Department. Many years later, she would say that she despised the man. Interestingly, Mamantov, a geologist with Sun Oil, received a call to interpret for her five hours after the assassination from spy-cum-oil baron, George H. W. Bush crony, John Crichton.

Oswald was certainly groomed to be the fall guy. Following the kill shot on President Kennedy, the initial location and temperament of Oswald described by witnesses does not match up with that of a man who has just killed the president. Only a minute after the assassination, he was encountered by the Book Depository superintendent Roy Truly and Dallas police officer Marrion L. Baker. Oswald, in the second floor lunchroom, four floors down from where the shooting had taken place, was calmly sipping on a Coke. The incident was recounted in subsequent Warren Commission testimony with commission member Hale Boggs of Louisiana:

TRULY: [Immediately after the shooting] I saw a young motorcycle policeman run up to the building, up the steps to the entrance of our building. He ran right by me. And he was pushing people out of the way. . . . I ran up and . . . caught up with him inside the lobby of the building. . . . I ran in front of him . . . I went up on a run up the stairway. By the time I reached the second floor, the officer was a little further behind me than he was on the first floor . . . a few feet. . . . I ran right on around to my left, started to continue on up the stairway to the third floor, and on up . . . I suppose I was two or three steps before I realized the officer wasn't following me. . . . I came back to the second-floor landing. . . . I heard . . . a voice coming from the area of the lunchroom . . . I ran over and looked in this door . . . I saw the officer almost directly in the doorway of the lunchroom facing Lee Harvey Oswald. . . . He was just inside the . . . door . . . two or three feet possibly. . . . The officer had his gun pointed at Oswald.
BAKER: As I came out to the second floor there . . . I caught a glimpse of this man walking away from this—I happened to see

him through this window in the door. . . . He was walking away from me about twenty feet away . . . in the lunchroom [. . . drinking a Coke]. I hollered at him at that time and said, 'Come here.' He turned and walked straight back to me . . .

REP. BOGGS: Were you suspicious of this man?

BAKER: No, sir, I wasn't.

REP. BOGGS: Was he out of breath? Did he appear to be running or what?

BAKER: It didn't appear that to me. He appeared normal, you know.

REP. BOGGS: Was he calm and collected?

BAKER: Yes, sir. He never did say a word or nothing. In fact, he didn't change his expression one bit.

TRULY: The officer turned this way and said, 'This man work here?' And I said, 'Yes.' . . . [Oswald] didn't seem to be excited or overly afraid or anything. He might have been startled, like I might have been if somebody confronted me. But I cannot recall any change in expression of any kind on his face. . . . Then we left . . . Oswald immediately and continued to run up the stairways . . .[36]

Oswald was next seen by Book Depository clerical supervisor Mrs. Robert Reid. She saw Oswald walking through her second-floor office. Oswald, still nursing the Coke, was in Reid's estimation "just calm. . . . He was moving at a very slow pace. I never did see him moving fast at any time."[37]

Oswald left the Book Depository shortly after the confrontation with Reid at approximately 12:33 p.m. and headed to his rooming house.

"Because of all the confusion, I figured there would be no work performed that afternoon, so I decided to go home," Oswald told investigators while in custody.

The housekeeper, Earlene Roberts, was watching reports of the assassination on television when she saw Oswald enter the house at approximately 1 p.m. While Oswald was in his room, Roberts saw a police car stop in front of the boarding house and lay on the horn. Mrs. Roberts, who knew several policemen, did not recognize the officer.

"And who was in the car?" asked Commission lawyer Joseph Ball.

"I don't know," Mrs. Roberts replied. "I didn't pay any attention to it after I noticed it wasn't them, I didn't."[38]

The police car left, and Oswald emerged from his room and exited the house after three or four minutes. He then, allegedly, walked nine-tenths of a mile to Tenth Street and Patton, where he shot and killed Officer J. D. Tippit. After allegedly killing Tippit, Oswald was diverted from his path, which was a direct route to Jack Ruby's apartment, and proceeded to the Texas Theatre, where he was quickly arrested by Dallas police.

"I can't, in my mind, firmly make myself believe that he might not have been trying to get to Ruby's apartment," said Jesse Curry in an interview following his years as Dallas police chief. "You know he was in close proximity to it, and I know he didn't leave his house with the idea of going to the Texas Theatre. There again, after he shot Tippit, I think in his fright he just thought the movie house was the place to hide."[39]

Curry never earnestly pondered the Oswald–Ruby connection, at least not publicly "because I never really seriously admitted that there was a conspiracy. But there's been coincidental things that have happened here to lead one to believe that there could have been a conspiracy after all. . . . There might have been a connection between the two that we never established. And if there was, it was more than a local thing, I believe. I think if there was a collusion between those two, it involved probably an international conspiracy."[40]

Curry's leap from a "local thing" to an "international conspiracy" might have been his way of distancing his police force and his country from the assassination when, in truth, members of both would be needed to carry out an operation of this caliber. Had

Curry known Ruby, he would have seen a gateway between his world and the underworld.

NOTES

1. George De Mohrenschildt, "I Am a Patsy! I Am a Patsy!" jfkassassination.net/russ/jfkinfo4/jfk12/hscapatsy.htm.
2. North, *Act of Treason*, 62–63.
3. Ibid., 313.
4. Ibid., 354.
5. Michael R. Beschloss, *Taking Charge: The Johnson White House Tapes, 1963–1964* (New York: Simon & Schuster, 1997), 23.
6. John M. Newman, *Oswald and the CIA* (New York: Carroll & Graf, 1995), 19.
7. Ibid., 144.
8. Jefferson Morley, "What Jane Roman Said," August 10, 2012, history-matters.com/essays/frameup/WhatJaneRomanSaid/WhatJaneRomanSaid_1.htm.
9. Ibid.
10. Ibid.
11. Ibid.
12. Ibid.
13. Ibid.
14. Ibid.
15. Baker, *Family of Secrets*, 99.
16. Warren Commission testimony of George de Mohrenschildt.
17. De Mohrenschildt, "I am a Patsy! I am a Patsy."
18. Warren Commission testimony of George de Mohrenschildt.
19. Ibid.
20. Baker, *Family of Secrets*, 107.
21. Nelson, *LBJ: Mastermind of the JFK Assassination*, 506.
22. Gilbride, *Matrix for Assassination*, 166.
23. Nelson, *LBJ: Mastermind of the JFK Assassination*, 506.
24. Warren Commission testimony of George de Mohrenschildt.
25. Ibid., 270.
26. Ibid., 273.
27. Ibid.

28. Ibid., 277.
29. Nelson, *LBJ: Mastermind of the JFK Assassination*, 341.
30. Richard Belzer, *Hit List* (New York: Skyhorse Publishing, 2013), 236–37.
31. De Mohrenschildt, "I am a Patsy! I am a Patsy!
32. Douglass, *JFK and the Unspeakable*, 205.
33. Ibid., 206.
34. Ibid., 213.
35. Edwin Black, "The Plot to Kill JFK in Chicago," *Chicago Independent* (November, 1975).
36. North, *Act of Treason*, 388–389.
37. Ibid., 390.
38. Kelin, *Praise from a Future Generation*, 86.
39. Seth Kantor, *The Ruby Cover-up* (New York: Kensington Publishing, 1978), 385–86.
40. Ibid.

CHAPTER SIXTEEN

RUBY

Dallas nightclub owner Jack Ruby arrived at Dallas police headquarters at just after 7 o'clock on the evening of November 22, after the assassination. He quickly made his way to the third floor and toward room 317, the Homicide Bureau Office where Lee Harvey Oswald was being held and interrogated for the alleged killing of President Kennedy and Dallas Police Officer J. D. Tippit.[1] In the office, Oswald would maintain a categorical denial of killing either, a steadfast claim he stuck to since being arrested at the Texas Theatre at 1:45 p.m. The interviews with Oswald conducted by Secret Service agent Thomas J. Kelley were mostly lost. At the instructions of Johnson's Secret Service cohort James Rowley, the interrogations were not recorded.

Later, to the Warren Commission, Rowley would claim the failure to properly question Oswald was an error caused by the confusion and time constraints caused by the assassination.

"I don't know whether we had tape recorders," Rowley said, "but I think you must recognize, under the situation at that time, that Mr. Kelley was rushed down there, and even if he had the funds to rent a tape recorder, I don't think he would have had the time to do so. Furthermore, I don't think that he would have anticipated the type of confusion that he encountered as he described it to you, nobody would have."[2]

What little did come out of the interrogations provided a picture of a less-than-complacent Oswald.

"I insist upon my constitutional rights," Oswald said while detained in the room, "the way you are treating me, I may as well be in Russia."[3]

Outside the room, Ruby was looking for an opportunity. He attempted to enter but was turned away by the guard on duty; he was friendly with many officers in the department, but the guard assigned to the homicide bureau door, Clyde F. Goodson, could not identify him when later shown pictures.[4]

One who could identify Ruby was detective August Mike Eberhardt, who was in the burglary and theft bureau, across the hall from the homicide office. Ruby had worked as an informant for Eberhardt on a case of check forgery and narcotics trafficking. There were at least two other detectives whom Ruby knew personally who were in the room as well.[5]

Ruby opened the door to the burglary and theft bureau office and walked in with a greeting and a handshake for Eberhardt. He had brought corned beef sandwiches and coffee for the reporters and officers and told Eberhardt, notebook in hand, that he was there as a translator for the newspapers.

"Of course, I knew that he could speak Yiddish,"[6] Eberhardt said.

Ruby had purposes beyond delivering deli sandwiches and assisting Israeli newspapers—he needed access to Oswald. He found out after hanging around for five to ten minutes that he could not get as close as was necessary, and he left.

"Well, he said that he—he called me by my middle name he said, 'It is hard to realize that a complete nothing, a zero like that, could kill a man like President Kennedy was,'" Eberhardt recalled. "He said that 'it is hard to understand how a complete nothing,' that is what he referred to him as, 'a complete nothing could have done this,' and then he left, and then I didn't notice where he went."[7]

Oswald was hardly a complete nothing, but Ruby most certainly wished he was. The alleged killing of Kennedy by Oswald had set into motion a chain of events that Ruby would have to follow through to the end.

Ruby's disposition following the assassination of President Kennedy was irregular to say the least—like that of a man who knew that he was doomed.

Reporter Seth Kantor saw Ruby at Parkland Hospital in the emergency room area before his appearance at Dallas police headquarters. Ruby tugged on the back of Kantor's coat to get his attention. In the estimation of Kantor, Ruby was "miserable. Grim. Pale. There were tears brimming in his eyes."[8]

Ruby asked Kantor if he thought it would be a good idea if he shut down the Carousel Club, the nightclub that Ruby ran and owned, for the next three days. Kantor told Ruby that he thought it would be a good idea and then hurried ahead to complete his story.[9]

Ruby denied both the run-in with Kantor at Parkland Hospital and his appearance outside of Oswald's interrogation room later that evening. The Warren Commission accepted his version of the story and concluded that Kantor and the detective must have been mistaken. If Ruby had been at the locations at the times witnesses gave, it would lend credence to the argument that his subsequent slaying of Oswald on national television, with almost an entire police force on hand, was premeditated.

Even though the association between Oswald and Ruby is murky, it is crystal clear that both men had connections with Carlos Marcello. In August 1963, Oswald was arrested for public disturbance. The person who arranged for bail was "an associate of two of Marcello's syndicate deputies."[10] The HSCA found that one of those deputies, Nofio Pecora, had received a telephone call from Ruby on October 30, 1963.[11] Did Oswald know Ruby? According to witnesses, Oswald had been at the Carousel Club in the months before the shooting—at least once in the company of Ruby.

Carousel patron Wilbur Waldon Litchfield positively identified Oswald as a man who came into the club, entered Ruby's office, and approximately twenty minutes later, walked out with the nightclub owner. Upon walking out the office, Litchfield got a close look at Oswald, who passed within two feet of him.[12] Carousel entertainer Bill Demar and stripper Karen Carlin also remembered Oswald attending the club. Demar told the Associated Press that he was positive that the man he had seen was Oswald.[13]

Rose Cheramie, who warned Louisiana authorities about the Kennedy assassination plot and Jack Ruby's involvement as early as November 20, also had seen Oswald in Ruby's club.[14]

In the mid-1970s, comedian Wally Weston also recalled Oswald showing up at the Carousel Club on at least two occasions.

Oswald, according to Weston, "walked up in the middle of the club, right in front of the stage [where Weston was performing] and for no reason, he said, 'I think you're a communist.' I said, 'Sir, I'm an American. Why don't you sit down?' He said, 'Well, I still think you're a communist,' so I jumped off the stage and hit him. Jack was right behind him when I hit him. He landed in Jack's arms, and Jack grabbed him and said, 'You—I told you never to come in here.' And he wrestled him to the door and threw him down the stairs."[15]

Weston said that he had withheld this information for such a long stretch of time due to fear. "So many people connected with it [the assassination investigation] died or disappeared."[16]

The Oswald whom Weston saw in the Carousel Club had all the personality traits of the Oswald imposters who were seen in Dallas and other locales before the assassination: tempestuous, violent, and overtly communist.

Jack Ruby's temperament could also swing wildly. Once, at a previous establishment owned by Ruby, the Silver Spur Club, Willis "Dub" Dickerson, a musician who worked for Ruby, was blocking an aisle with his chair. Ruby told him to move, and Dickerson told Ruby to "go to hell."[17] A fight ensued in which Ruby had Dickerson pinned against the wall. With Ruby's left hand holding back his face,

Jack proceeded to knee Dickerson repeatedly in the groin. Dickerson reacted by biting down on one of Ruby's fingers, mutilating it. The tip of the finger would subsequently be amputated.[18]

These were the types of businesses Ruby owned and ran. He would frisk strippers who he thought were pinching booze and had been known to submit them to lie-detector tests if he suspected them of providing customers with personal services.

"This isn't a goddamn bedroom,"[19] Ruby once told one of his girls.

The clubs were known for their rough-and-tumble clientele as well.

"Jack had seven fights a week," said Barney Weinstein, a club owner who competed with Ruby. "I've had three fights in thirty years."[20]

The violent nature of the clubs was the product of an owner who had grown up around criminal elements. Ruby was raised in Chicago, the son of Polish immigrants. He grew up fighting in Jewish street gangs, in the Air Force, and eventually in his clubs. In 1939, he was implicated in the murder of Leon Cooke, head of the Chicago Waste Handlers Union for which he worked as an organizer.[21] Ruby's picture would appear in connection with the murder in the *Chicago Tribune*, but the arrest record on him disappeared.[22] Ruby's official title was union secretary, but he worked as a bagman.

Ruby's life played out as a low-level mob associate until he died of cancer in prison in 1967. In 1947, when he moved from Chicago to Dallas, he was an associate of Paul Roland Jones, a member of the Chicago mob outfit who was also a payoff man to the Dallas Police Department. Following a ten-year period of no communication between the two, Jones would appear the week before the assassination.

Even though the Warren Commission determined that Ruby had no credible ties to the mob, it was found later by the HSCA that this conclusion had been in error.

"The Committee also established associations between Jack Ruby and several individuals affiliated with the underworld activities of Carlos Marcello," noted the HSCA Final Report. "Ruby was a personal acquaintance of Joseph Civello, the Marcello associate who allegedly headed organized crime activities in Dallas; he also knew other individuals who have been linked with organized crime, including a New Orleans nightclub figure with whom Ruby was considering going into partnership in the fall of 1963."[23]

In another intersection of crime, oil, and politics, Civello represented Marcello at the Murchison mansion the night before the assassination.

Ruby had ties to at least eight members of the Marcello crime family, the most prevalent of these being Civello. Bobby Jean Moore, a former hired hand of Civello who also periodically played piano at Jack Ruby's Vegas Club, went to the Oakland FBI office a few days after the assassination. Moore had heard a colleague of Ruby on television discounting the mob ties of the Dallas nightclub owner. Moore told the FBI that he "came to suspect that [Joseph] Civello and his partner Frank LaMonte were engaged in racket activities," and that he "came to believe Civello and LaMonte were importing narcotics."[24]

Moore also informed the FBI that Jack Ruby "was also a frequent visitor and associate of Civello and LaMonte."[25]

Joe Campisi, the proprietor the Egyptian Lounge, a notorious organized crime hangout, was another Dallas mob associate close to Ruby. He was good friends with the Marcello brothers; he golfed and gambled with them often. Every Christmas, Campisi would send the family 260 pounds of homemade sausage.[26] Campisi was Ruby's first visitor in jail after the slaying of Oswald. The two men had a ten-minute long conversation not recorded by the Dallas police.[27] Ruby also had dinner with a member of the Marcello crime family the night before the assassination.[28]

Ruby had ties not only to Marcello but was networked like the mob itself. He had connections to Trafficante in Tampa through a friend to Trafficante associate Norman Rothman, and he helped Rothman with Cuban gun smuggling.[29] Publicly, Trafficante said that he did not know Ruby, but he knew that the man was a mob functionary.[30] When Melvin Belli, Ruby's Los Angeles defense attorney, later represented Trafficante attorney Frank Ragano in a libel suit, Santo had choice words for Ragano: "Whatever you do, don't ask him about Jack Ruby. Don't get involved. It's none of your business."[31]

Ruby was also close with Lewis McWillie, known as a "Mooney Giancana underling."[32] Ruby had gone with McWillie on several mysterious trips to Cuba in 1959, a record he lied about to the Warren Commission considering "transportation records show that he was there twice in 1959, and CIA files report him there at least twice more after it became illegal for Americans to travel to Cuba."[33] Ruby was in Cuba to assist the release of Trafficante from Triscornia—a mission to protect the interests of organized crime.

"It *is* a bad sign," Sam Giancana said to his brother Chuck concerning the Mafia's fortunes in Cuba. "Marcello's worried about his drug rackets . . . We could lose a lot down there besides gambling and Santo Trafficante. But I'll get him out. . . . Ruby's workin' on it. It's gonna cost me, though, because Castro knows Santo was real close with all the old guard. I may have to go down to Havana myself. What the hell, I got investments to protect, right?"[34]

When pressed by the HSCA to recollect the visit from Ruby, Trafficante again reinforced his denial of knowledge concerning Ruby.

"There was no reason for this man to visit me," Trafficante professed. "I have never seen this man before. I have never been to Dallas. I never had no contact with him. I don't see why he was going to come and visit me."[35]

In the time leading up to killing Oswald, Ruby owed the government in excess of $39,000 on income and excise taxes. On November 19—three days before the murder of JFK—Ruby appeared at the office of his tax attorney Graham Koch and told him of a contact who would furnish Ruby the money to settle his debt. He then signed a power-of-attorney, giving the lawyer control over Ruby's monetary issues with the government.[36]

It was the CIA who developed Oswald as a patsy, and the mob who used Ruby to eliminate him.

The mercurial Ruby had ingratiated himself with the police department for years, providing the officers information and company; he also supplied drinks and dates through the Carousel Club. There were at least seventy officers whom Ruby knew by name.[37]

Members of the Dallas Police Department helped Ruby gain access to the police headquarters basement to kill Oswald in clear view of the entire world. Oswald was scheduled to be transported to a maximum security cell at the Dallas County Jail in an armored van that was to be backed into the basement. He was expected to be moved at approximately 10 a.m., but it would not be until the moment that Ruby arrived on the scene that Oswald was paraded to his death.

Ruby was at a Western Union office close to the police station sending $25 to one of his nightclub strippers at shortly after 11:00 a.m. The transaction was completed at 11:17 a.m., and Ruby proceeded to the police station with a loaded snub-nosed handgun in his right hip pocket.[38]

"It just seemed like an act of God that Ruby got in there," Police Chief Jesse Curry remarked. "I've thought about it a thousand times. We backtracked and walked the distance. We investigated from every possible angle."

It is laughable to think that it would be difficult for Ruby to gain access to the station that morning. Even though he was not a police officer, Ruby would walk in and out of the police station regularly. But it is ridiculous to believe his explanation that, while out running errands, he had taken along a loaded gun, which he hadn't planned on using that day and, in a flash of passion, shot Oswald who was led out to reporters at the exact time that he arrived because "someone owed this debt to our beloved president."[39]

In the words of FBI informant Edward Becker, "He [Ruby] was the ideal guy to get Oswald. As I see it, the original game plan was to knock off Oswald in jail. The Marcellos knew who Jack Ruby was, don't kid yourself. They knew he had contacts in the police department, that he could get into the city jail at the right time. . . . As for Ruby, he probably was happy as hell to get the hit. Now he could do something big for Uncle Carlos. It's ridiculous to say that Ruby's job on Oswald was emotional, spur of the moment. Listen, that was a professional job if there ever was one. Ruby just rolled in there like he had twenty years' experience at it. Beautiful."[40]

Subsequently, there has been speculation that Dallas police did not help Ruby access the station. Instead, the Dallas policemen were a bumbling, Texas-sized version of the Keystone Kops.

"So the Dallas PD came in, and at that point, they were a bunch of rednecks and didn't know what they were doing," Bill O'Reilly said recently while promoting his book *Killing Kennedy*. "Obviously, they let Oswald get killed."

In truth, it was not the incompetence but the corruption of the Dallas police force that led to Oswald's slaying.

The two officers most likely involved in aiding Ruby's entrance and execution of Oswald were L. D. Miller and W. J. "Blackie" Harrison, both of whom had gone out for coffee at the Deluxe Diner on Commerce Street in Downtown Dallas on the morning of Oswald's public execution. Miller, who admitted to never going out socially with Harrison prior to that morning, could not remember a single thing the two had talked about at the diner.[41] Harrison was equally evasive upon questioning.[42]

The only thing certain about Harrison's and Miller's trip to the diner is that a call was placed to them with information pertinent to the Oswald transfer.

Later, another call was placed to Ruby's apartment from an unlisted number.[43] Both Harrison and Miller returned to the station moments after the call. Upon their return, just before 11:00 a.m., at a time close to the transfer of Oswald, Harrison went alone to the station subbasement to purchase cigars from a vending machine. Also in the subbasement were four public telephones, any of which could have been used to transmit updated information to Ruby concerning the transfer of Oswald. Dallas Police Lieutenant Jack Revill, was questioned by Connecticut Senator Christopher Dodd in a 1978 HSCA hearing committee about the coincidental timing of Oswald's transfer and Ruby's arrival at the station:

> **MR. DODD:** Prior to the shooting of Lee Harvey Oswald, in fact only minutes before, Jack Ruby sent a money order from the Western Union office. Did the special unit consider the possibility that Jack Ruby had utilized the sending of this money order to make his entrance to the basement and that the subsequent shooting of Oswald seemed a fluke or coincidence of timing?
> **MR. REVILL:** We discussed it, yes, sir.
> **MR. DODD:** What did you conclude?
> **MR. REVILL:** If that be the case, then Ruby had to have had assistance from someone in the police department. To know exactly what time Oswald was to be transferred.
> **MR. DODD:** Did the inspection unit assume that for Jack Ruby—I guess you have answered that by your response to your last question—you would have assumed he would have had to have assistance? Did you examine, or how thoroughly did you examine whether or not there was a possibility of such assistance.
> **MR. REVILL:** We interviewed everyone that had been assigned to the basement. We interviewed members of the news media in an effort to determine if there was complicity between Ruby and any member of the police department or anyone else for that matter, and we were unsuccessful in that endeavor.[44]

When Oswald was being moved into the basement to be loaded into the van, Ruby was standing directly behind Harrison and lunged past him to shoot and kill Oswald as he was walked into the throng of reporters and officers.

The Warren Commission would later ask Dallas police inspectors to examine their own force in regard to a possible collusion between the department and Ruby. The idea that the Commission would expect a potentially corrupt police force to investigate itself was ridiculous, but useful. It would follow the same protocol of self-examination with the CIA, the Secret Service, and the FBI.

"It would be have been like asking the Chicago White Sox baseball team of 1919 to examine charges that some of its players had conspired with gamblers to throw the World Series,"[45] wrote Seth Kantor.

Both Harrison and Miller were uncooperative when questioned by Warren Commission assistant counsel Burt Griffin.

MR. MILLER: I still don't understand the reason of it. Are you going to use this thing to try to prosecute me?

MR. GRIFFIN: No.

MR. MILLER: What are you going to use it for?

MR. GRIFFIN: We have no authority to prosecute anyone except for perjury before the Commission. Now, we—our instructions are—let me get a copy of the resolutions. Let me suggest that we handle it this way. I have got a copy here of the resolutions, Executive Order signed by President Johnson, and the joint resolutions of Congress. The rules of the Commission and a memorandum dated March 20, 1964, from Mr. Rankin, who is the general counsel of the Commission authorizing Mr. Hubert and me to administer your oath and take your deposition. Now, I think that what I prefer to do here so that you can be sure what you want to do, and I don't want to put you under any pressure. Now, I would like to give you this and have you try to find another room out here and look at this, and read it over, and think about this and ponder it as long as you want, and I want to give you assurance that I am going to call another—I am going to call officer Montgomery in here and proceed with him. I am not going to tell him that I have not completed your deposition or anything like that. I want to be sure that, as far as anybody is concerned whatsoever, what has transpired here is completely routine so that any decision you make, I can give you as much assurance as possible—

MR. MILLER: All I wanted to know is the purpose of the thing.[46]

The morning that Harrison was to take a lie-detector test concerning the Oswald slaying, a rumor floated in police ranks that he was heavily sedated on tranquilizers to prevent an accurate test reading; the results would be inconclusive.[47]

Ruby was held in the Dallas county jail after he had killed Oswald, but pleaded with the Warren Commission and Earl Warren in particular on multiple occasions, to be moved to a place where he felt safe enough to tell the true story.

"Is there any way of you getting me to Washington?" Ruby asked on one occasion.

"I don't think so," replied Warren.

"It is very important," said Ruby.[48]

The members of the Warren Commission certainly had the authority to move Ruby whenever and wherever they wanted, particularly if they thought that Ruby was in danger and that his testimony was altered due to threats of harm. They had Ruby right where they wanted him.

"I may not live tomorrow to give any further testimony . . . and the only thing I want to get out to the public, and I can't say it here, is with authenticity, with sincerity of the truth of everything, and why my act was committed, but it can't be said here,"[49] Ruby asserted. He then intimated to Warren that his family was in danger.

Ruby, rotting in jail, once believed himself to be a networked friend of the mob and the Dallas Police Department. But after he had killed Oswald, Ruby himself assumed the role of patsy. A short time after his death, the *Dallas Times-Herald* reported that Ruby had admitted in a note smuggled out of prison that he was "part of a terrible political frame-up."[50]

In the years following Ruby's slaying of Oswald, only one reporter, Dorothy Kilgallen, was granted a private interview with him. Kilgallen had voiced strong speculations about the Kennedy assassination, especially concerning the connections of Oswald and his killer.

"It appears that Washington knows or suspects something about Lee Harvey Oswald that it does not want Dallas and the rest of the world to know or suspect," Kilgallen wrote in February 1964. "Lee Harvey Oswald has passed on not only to his shuddery reward, but to the mysterious realm of 'classified' persons whose whole story is known only to a few government agents. . . . Why is Oswald being kept in the shadows, as dim a figure as they can make him, while the defense tries to rescue his alleged killer with the help of information from the FBI? Who was Oswald, anyway?"[51]

Kilgallen had more pieces of the assassination puzzle, including that Texas oil barons—Lyndon Johnson moneyman H. L. Hunt in particular and Carlos Marcello—were involved in the plot. Following her interview with Jack Ruby, Kilgallen announced to friends that the information she was privy to in the Ruby interview was game-changing, and that she was "about to blow the JFK case sky high." The new information was to be released in a book Kilgallen was writing titled *Murder One*, which she hoped would finally reveal elements of the conspiracy and cover-up integral to the assassination.

The book, however, would never be released. Kilgallen would be found dead in her New York City apartment on November 8, 1965, the result of an accidental overdose in the early hours of the day. The cause of death was a potent mix of alcohol and barbiturates, but, as so many who died in connection to the assassination, Kilgallen's abrupt passing was suspicious. The death was made to look natural, but clues that she had been murdered and her body had been moved postmortem were abundant. Her body was found in a bed that she never slept in, positioned next to her was a book that she had already read, and the room was cooled by an air conditioner that she never used in the evening hours.[52] Kilgallen's final clothing choices were also bizarre: The reporter was outfitted as if she were ready for a night on the town.

"She was dressed very peculiarly, like I've never seen her before," a friend who had discovered her body said. "She always [was] in pajamas and old socks, and her make up [would be] off, and her hair [would be] off."[53]

Gone were the revelatory notes that Kilgallen had taken from her interview with Ruby, never to be found. It could only be speculated as to what they revealed, but perhaps some of the public statements to reporters that Ruby made following his incarceration could shed some light on what they contained.

"I wish that our beloved President Lyndon Johnson would have delved deeper into the situation, hear me, not to accept just circumstantial facts about my guilt or innocence and would have questioned to find out the truth about me before he relinquished certain powers to these certain people," Ruby told the Warren Commission. "I have been used for a purpose,"[54] he added.

It was not the last time that Ruby would bring up President Johnson.

"Everything pertaining to what's happening has never come to the surface," Ruby told reporters. "The world will never know the true facts of what occurred, my motives. The people that have had so much to gain and had such an ulterior motive for putting me in the position I'm in will never let the true facts come above board to the world."

"Now these people are in very high positions, Jack?" a reporter asked.

"Yes," replied Ruby.

Ruby later added context to his statement.

"I want to correct what I said before about the vice president," Ruby said.

"The vice president?" a reporter inquired.

"When I mentioned about Adlai Stevenson, if he were vice president, there would have never been an assassination of our beloved President Kennedy," Ruby answered.

"Would you explain again?" the reporter asked.

"Well, the answer is the man in office now," Ruby coldly replied.[55]

NOTES

1. Kantor, *The Ruby Cover-Up*, 96.
2. Warren Commission testimony of James J. Rowley.
3. "The Last Words Of Lee Harvey Oswald", compiled by Mae Brussell," May, 2012, ratical.org/ratville/JFK/LHO.html.
4. Kantor, *The Ruby Cover-Up*, 98.
5. Ibid., 96.
6. Warren Commission testimony of August Mike Eberhardt.
7. Ibid.
8. Kantor, *The Ruby Cover-Up*, 89.
9. Ibid.
10. HSCA Final Report, 170.
11. Ibid., 170.
12. North, *Act of Treason*, 345.
13. Ibid., 361.
14. Nelson, *LBJ: Mastermind of the JFK Assassination*, 364.
15. Kantor, *The Ruby Cover-Up*, 390–91.
16. Ibid., 391.
17. Bugliosi, *Reclaiming History*, 1117.
18. Ibid.
19. Garry Wills and Ovid Demaris, *Jack Ruby* (New York: New American Library, 1968), 6.
20. Ibid., 13.
21. Dan E. Moldea, *The Hoffa Wars: The Rise and Fall of Jimmy Hoffa* (New York: Shapolsky, 1993), 152.
22. Kantor, *The Ruby Cover-Up*, 199.
23. HSCA Final Report, 171.
24. Davis, *Mafia Kingfish*, 157.
25. Ibid.

26. Ibid., 449.
27. Ibid.
28. Ibid.
29. Deitche, *The Silent Don*, 157.
30. Ibid., 160.
31. Ibid.
32. Deitche, *The Silent Don*, 156.
33. Ibid., 102.
34. Giancana, *Double Cross*, 388.
35. HSCA testimony of Santos Trafficante.
36. Kantor, *The Ruby Cover-Up*, 62.
37. Davis, *Mafia Kingfish*, 156.
38. Kantor, *The Ruby Cover-Up*, 139.
39. Warren Commission testimony of Jack Ruby.
40. Davis, *Mafia Kingfish*, 232.
41. Warren Commission testimony of L. D. Miller.
42. Warren Commission testimony of W. J. Harrison.
43. Kantor, *The Ruby Cover-Up*, 126.
44. HSCA testimony of Jack Revill.
45. Ibid., 118.
46. Warren Commission testimony of L. D. Miller.
47. Kantor, *The Ruby Cover-Up*, 127.
48. Ibid., 29.
49. Ibid., 27.
50. *The News and Courier* [Charleston, SC] (Sept. 27, 1978): 14-D.
51. Belzer, *Hit List*, 79.
52. Ibid., 82–83.
53. Ibid, pg. 88.
54. Warren Commission testimony of Jack Ruby.
55. Dreamslaughter2. "Jack Ruby Talks." YouTube, January 25, 2011, youtube.com/watch?v=omnpQBa1Euc.

CHAPTER SEVENTEEN

POPPY

No one acted more curiously than future President George H. W. Bush on the day President Kennedy was shot. For over twenty years, Bush claimed he couldn't remember where he was on that day. In fact, he went out of his way to create an alibi and dissemble about where he really was on November 21 and 22, 1963.

I have a unique experience with George H. W. Bush: I helped bar his assent to the presidency in 1980. It would be a major mistake to assume Bush's unfailingly polite, friendly, affable, and sometimes goofy style as benign. Don't fall for the vapidity and obfuscation. Underneath it lie consuming political ambition, steely determination, boundless energy, and remarkable physical discipline for relentless travel to pursue his political goals. Barbara Bush brings a vindictive streak; she remembers everyone who was *not* for her husband. Despite his "nice guy" image, George Bush is high-handed, secretive, and fueled by an incredible sense of entitlement.

He is also disciplined and extremely well organized. He was a model candidate, traveling relentlessly, shaking hands, writing notes, and building his friends list. He was always collecting: people, addresses, supporters, and money. Only Richard Nixon was a more indefatigable campaigner.

I met George Bush when I was Young Republican National Chairman and he addressed the group's national leadership conference. He was cordial. I heard later that my introduction of him as "George Herbert Walker Bush" was taken as a slight, as if I was mocking his four-part patrician moniker. I wasn't.

I grew up in Connecticut's Fairfield County when the Bushes still lived in Greenwich. I saw Senator Prescott Bush speak to the 1966 Republican state convention. I rooted for George Bush in his 1970 campaign for the US Senate. Then, I had only three posters in my room: Jim Buckley (New York) for Senate, John Lupton (Connecticut) for Senate, and George Bush "He Can Do More for Texas." I also knew the seeds of a family feud with Lowell Weicker, which would play out in the 1980s.

Bush was not a conservative, but, like Nixon, he knew when he had to sound like one. He always accommodated the "kooks" as Harris County GOP chair and even worked with them. He treated every one with bonhomie. He knew the buzz words and dutifully repeated them: UN, Gun Owners, Civil Rights. Post election in 1988, he famously swept a copy of Bill Buckley's *National Review* off a coffee table in his Kennebunkport, Maine home and said "well we don't need this shit anymore."

I had the chance to observe George Bush up-close when I worked against him in the Northeast during the 1980 presidential campaign. The states that I handled for Ronald Reagan had GOP establishments still dominated by the Eastern moderates and were thought to be Bush strongholds. In fact, Bush's campaign manager James A. Baker would later tell me that I was "a pain in the Bushes' ass."

Baker admitted that Bush was counting on delegate votes in New York and New Jersey, where Reagan swamped him, seizing all the delegates. In Bush's native Connecticut, Reagan victories in three congressional districts forced Bush to split the thirty-five delegates down the middle.

"Barbara hates your ass," Lee Atwater told me. He was Bush's campaign manager, later Republican National Chairman and my friend of twenty years.

When I saw presidential candidate George W. Bush, whose campaign for governor I had financially supported at a fundraising reception in New Jersey, he told me "My father always said you stole those New Jersey delegates from him."

Secretary to the Eisenhower cabinet and New Jersey Republican National committeeman Bernard "Bern" Shanley, who ran for the Senate in New Jersey, told me "the Bushes hate you." As a soldier in the service of Ronald Reagan, I still wear their scorn proudly.

Bush's 1980 campaign was hampered when it hired his long-time mistress, Jennifer Fitzgerald, as his scheduler. Fitzgerald hoarded information; power struggles plagued the campaign. Barbara Bush once famously exploded at Fitzgerald in the back of a limousine when she touched Bush's knee. Senior campaign aides plotted to remove Fitzgerald, and eventually Bush's savvy campaign chief James A. Baker III gave Bush a "her or me" ultimatum. Fitzgerald would leave the campaign, only to be hired later to handle the vice president's schedule (she was kept in the vice president's ceremonial Capitol Hill office rather than the White House). Fitzgerald let it be known that she had a trove of love letters from the vice president and wouldn't be going anywhere.[1]

George Bush was checking into political obscurity when he was defeated for president in 1980 after losing two US Senate races. Only his elevation to the vice presidency by Ronald Reagan gave him a chance to become president. His unwillingness to defend Reaganomics, which had given the nation its largest economic boom in history, was a stunning display of disloyalty to the "Gipper."

Perhaps it was because George H. W. Bush has no fixed ideology that he was underrated within his own party. Nixon and Kissinger considered Bush a lightweight; in his book *Being Poppy*, Richard Ben Cramer would say that Nixon believed Bush "lacked the killer instinct." In the House, Bush was so active for birth control that his colleagues would nickname him "Rubbers." In his 1970 Senate race, he said "I realize this is a politically sensitive area. But I believe in a woman's right to chose. It should be an individual matter. I think, ultimately, it will be a constitutional question. I don't favor a federal abortion law as such." He would switch to oppose abortion to run for vice president with Reagan. Deriding Reagan's tax cuts as "voodoo economics," Bush himself ran on a no-new-taxes pledge in 1988—a pledge he would promptly break.

George H. W. Bush is the son of US Senator Prescott S. Bush. As did his son, Prescott graduated from Yale where he had been a member of the secret Skull and Bones society. He was an investment banking partner at Brown Brothers Harriman, a golfing partner of Eisenhower, and a pillar of the Eastern Establishment.

A tall imposing man and heavy drinker, Prescott was a man whose wrath you didn't want. He narrowly lost the US Senate seat in 1950 when it was revealed in the heavily Catholic state of Connecticut that he and his wife had contributed to Planned Parenthood. In 1952, Prescott would win a special election to fill the seat of Senator Brien McMahon, who died unexpectedly. He was friendly with John Foster and Allen Dulles, Wall Street lawyers who represented Brown Brothers.

In 1952, George Bush served as Co-Chair of Citizens for Eisenhower–Nixon in Midland County, Texas, where he had relocated to work for Dresser Industries and later founded the Zapata Petroleum Company and Zapata Offshore. In his masterful book, *Family of Secrets*, author and reporter Russ Baker established that both Dresser and Zapata had been used as covers for CIA business.

According to a CIA internal memo dated November 29, 1975, Zapata Petroleum began in 1953 through Bush's joint efforts with Thomas J. Devine, a CIA staffer who had resigned his agency position that same year to go into private business, but who continued to work for the CIA under commercial cover.[2]

George Bush, known to his Ivy League friends as "Poppy," may have been associated with the CIA as early as 1953. Fabian Escalante, the chief of a Cuban counterintelligence unit during the late 1950s and early 1960s, describes a plan called "Operation 40" that was put into effect by the National Security Council and presided over by Vice President Richard Nixon. Escalante said that Nixon, as operation director or "case officer," had assembled an important group of businessmen headed by George Bush and Jack Crichton, both Texas oilmen, to gather the necessary funds for the operation. Operation 40, a group of CIA assassins, was subsequently brought into the Bay of Pigs invasion. Interestingly, CIA official Fletcher Prouty delivered three Navy ships to agents in Guatemala to be used in the invasion. Prouty claims that he delivered the ships to a CIA agent named George Bush. Agent Bush named the ships *Barbara J, Houston,* and *Zapata.*[3]

In 1963, George "Poppy" Bush was serving as Chairman of the Harris County (Houston) Republican Committee and was warming up for a 1964 US Senate bid. There, he presided over a rift in the local GOP between the country club moderates who had migrated to Houston and a deeply conservative faction aligned with the John Birch Society. Despite the Bush family's longtime closeness to the Rockefellers, Bush would join his fellow Texans for Barry Goldwater in 1964 and asked his Senator father to withhold his endorsement of Rockefeller.[4]

In the 1964 Republican senate primary, Bush was opposed by Jack Cox, who had made a valiant run as the Republican candidate for Governor in 1962, and by Robert Morris, who served on the chief counsel of the Senate Judiciary Subcommittee on Internal Security through the 1950s. Morris ran for the Republican US Senate nomination in 1964 and 1970 and was defeated both times. Bush defeated Cox in the runoff, 62–38 percent, to win the GOP nomination. Morris endorsed Cox nonetheless.

Bush waged a spirited and peripatetic campaign. To his credit, he refused to write off African American or Mexican American votes. Bush ran to the right: He denounced the United Nations and pledged to vote against Kennedy on civil rights. Like Barry Goldwater, he argued federal enforcement of civil rights was a violation of states' rights. Although Bush got two hundred thousand more votes in the state than Barry Goldwater, more than any Republican ever had, Texans voted the ticket led by their native son Lyndon Johnson. Bush was trounced by Senator Ralph Yarborough.

In 1985, a memo dated November 29, 1963 from FBI director Hoover came to light in which he discussed reactions among Cuban exiles to the JFK assassination. Hoover said, "George Bush of the CIA had been briefed. . . ."

In 1988, reporting for *The Nation*, Joseph McBride asked Vice President George Bush's office for comment. Bush's representatives claimed that he "didn't know what you are talking about." Bush also said it "must be another George Bush."

At first, the CIA said that there was no employee named George Bush at the CIA in 1963. After McBride wrote his story, the CIA would change theirs. There was a George William Bush detailed from another agency in 1963, but the CIA could not find him. McBride didn't have trouble finding him—he was still on the payroll. George William Bush said that he had been detailed only briefly to the agency and denied knowing anything about a briefing regarding anti-Castro elements and what they might do in the wake of Kennedy's murder. In fact, George William Bush was a lowly clerk. Did the CIA plant this George Bush as a "cut-out" to shield the real George Bush?

In 1988, a second FBI document was revealed. In a memo from Houston FBI agent in charge, Graham Kitchel, (whose brother George Kitchel was a Bush political supporter and friend), it was reported that George Bush had called the Houston FBI bureau with a tip on November 22, 1963 at 1:58 p.m., only six minutes after Walter Cronkite would announce to the world that JFK was dead. This memo makes Bush's claim that he could not remember where he was on November 22, 1963 all the more incredible.

Before leaving for Dallas, Bush called the Houston FBI field office at 1:45 p.m. and promptly identified himself and his location in Tyler, Texas. "Bush stated that he wanted [the call] to be kept confidential but wanted to furnish hearsay that he recalled hearing

November 29, 1963

To: Director
        Bureau of Intelligence and Research
        Department of State

From: John Edgar Hoover, Director

Subject: ASSASSINATION OF PRESIDENT JOHN F. KENNEDY
         NOVEMBER 22, 1963

Our Miami, Florida, Office on November 23, 1963, advised
that the Office of Coordinator of Cuban Affairs in Miami advised
that the Department of State feels some misguided anti-Castro
group might capitalize on the present situation and undertake an
unauthorized raid against Cuba, believing that the assassination
of President John F. Kennedy might herald a change in U. S. policy,
which is not true.

Our sources and informants familiar with Cuban matters in
the Miami area advise that the general feeling in the anti-Castro
Cuban community is one of stunned disbelief and, even among those
who did not entirely agree with the President's policy concerning
Cuba, the feeling is that the President's death represents a great
loss not only to the U. S. but to all of Latin America. These
sources knew of no plans for unauthorized action against Cuba.

An informant who has furnished reliable information in
the past and who is close to a small pro-Castro group in Miami
has advised that these individuals are afraid that the assassination
of the President may result in strong repressive measures being
taken against them and, although pro-Castro in their feelings,
regret the assassination.

The substance of the foregoing information was orally
furnished to Mr. George Bush of the Central Intelligence Agency and
Captain William Edward of the Defense Intelligence Agency on
November 23, 1963, by Mr. W. T. Forsyth of this Bureau.

Director of Naval Intelligence

UNITED STATES GOVERNMENT

Memorandum

TO : SAC, HOUSTON   DATE: 11-22-63

FROM : SA GRAHAM W. KITCHEL

SUBJECT: UNKNOWN SUBJECT;
ASSASSINATION OF PRESIDENT
JOHN F. KENNEDY

     At 1:45 p.m. Mr. GEORGE H. W. BUSH, President
of the Zapata Off-shore Drilling Company, Houston, Texas,
residence 5525 Briar, Houston, telephonically furnished
the following information to writer by long distance
telephone call from Tyler, Texas.

     BUSH stated that he wanted to be kept confidential
but wanted to furnish hearsay that he recalled hearing in
recent weeks, the day and source unknown. He stated that
one JAMES PARROTT has been talking of killing the President
when he comes to Houston.

     BUSH stated that PARROTT is possibly a student
at the University of Houston and is active in political
matters in this area. He stated that he felt Mrs. FAWLEY,
telephone number SU 2-5239, or ARLINE SMITH, telephone
number JA 9-9194 of the Harris County Republican Party
Headquarters would be able to furnish additional information regarding the identity of PARROTT.

     BUSH stated that he was proceeding to Dallas, Texas,
would remain in the Sheraton-Dallas Hotel and return to his
residence on 11-23-63. His office telephone number is
CA 2-0395.

GWK:djw.
(2)

ALL INFORMATION CONTAINED
HEREIN IS UNCLASSIFIED
DATE 10-15-93 BY 9803 RPO/KSR
(JFK)

62-2115-6

SEARCHED_____ INDEXED_____
SERIALIZED_____ FILED_____
NOV 18 1963
FBI - HOUSTON

in recent days . . . He stated that one James Milton Parrott has been talking of killing the president when he comes to Houston."

Bush dropped a dime on an unemployed twenty-four-year-old Air Force veteran who had been honorably discharged, albeit upon the recommendation of a psychiatrist. During questioning, Parrott acknowledged that he was a member of the Texas Young Republicans and had been active in picketing members of the Kennedy administration. He also insisted that he had not threatened the president's life.

Parrott was a member of the ultra-rightwing John Birch Society and had vigorously opposed Bush during his campaign for GOP chairman of Harris County—a major offense to Bush running for a minor office, and he never forgot the offender. Parrott had been painting BUSH FOR SENATE? signs when the FBI arrived to question him. Ironically, Parrott would surface again—as a volunteer for George Bush's 1988 Presidential campaign. Was Parrott also a patsy?

Here's how Poppy covered his tracks on that day: George registered himself and Barbara Bush for a two-night stay at the Dallas Sheraton November 21 and 22. On the morning of November 22, after their first night in Dallas, they flew by private plane to Tyler, Texas, about one hundred miles away, where the GOP Senate candidate was to speak at a local Kiwanis Club luncheon.

According to an eyewitness account published in Kitty Kelley's *The Family: The Real Story of the Bush Dynasty*, Bush had just started to speak when news of the shooting reached the club. "I gave the news to the president of the club, Wendell Cherry, and he leaned over to tell George that wires from Dallas confirmed President Kennedy had been assassinated," Aubrey Irby recalled in the book.

"George stopped his speech and told the audience what had happened. 'In view of the president's death,' he said, 'I consider it inappropriate to continue with a political speech at this time. Thank you very much for your attention.' Then he sat down."

Who could forget such a moment? More importantly, why would Bush lie about it? Because he was attempting to cover his trail and make a plausible denial case against personal involvement, just as CIA agents are instructed?

In 1994, Barbara Bush, or "Bar" as she was known, published *Barbara Bush: A Memoir,* in which she revealed the actual "letter" that she had written on the very day, at the very *moment,* that Kennedy was shot. The letter has plenty of details, but curiously does not mention George H. W. Bush's call to Hoover's boys in Houston.

On November 22, 1963, George and I were in the middle of a several-city swing. I was getting my hair done in Tyler, Texas, working on a letter home.

"Dearest family, Wednesday, I took Doris Ulmer out for lunch. They were here from England, and they had been so nice to George in Greece. That night we went to. . . ."

I am writing this at the Beauty Parlor, and the radio says that the president has been shot. Oh Texas—my Texas—my God—let's hope it's not true. I am sick at heart as we all are. Yes, the story is true and the Governor also. How hateful some people are.

Since the beauty parlor, the president has died. We are once again on a plane. This time a commercial plane. Poppy picked me up at the beauty parlor—we went right to the airport, flew to Ft. Worth and dropped Mr. Zeppo off (we were on his plane) and flew back to Dallas. We had to circle the field while the second presidential plane took off. Immediately, Pop got tickets back to Houston, and here we are flying home. We are sick at heart. The tales the radio reporters tell of Jackie Kennedy are the bravest I've ever heard. The rumors are flying about that horrid assassin. We are hoping that it is not some far-right nut, but a "commie" nut. You understand that we know they are both nuts, but just hope that it is not a Texan and not an American at all.

I am amazed by the rapid-fire thinking and planning that has already been done. LBJ has been the president for some time now—two hours at least and it is only 4:30.

My dearest love to you all,
Bar

Exactly to whom this letter was mailed has never been made clear and the original is not known to exist.

Note the jab at LBJ. Bar had no idea. The documents reversing JFK's Vietnam policies were drafted before his death and were executed on November 23.[5]

On the night of November 21, 1963, "Poppy" attended an oil contractors' association meeting in Dallas, and he stayed for drinks afterward. This would seem to preclude his presence at a party at the home of Clint Murchison, which Oliver Stone made iconic in his movie *Nixon*. I believe this Murchison affair did take place, and I believe that Nixon was there but left early. I think LBJ did come late. Jack Ruby would supply the girls to entertain the business and government titans, according to Madeleine Brown.

Barbara said that their friend Zeppo's private plane transported them to Tyler. This was, in fact, oilman Joe Zeppa, partners with Bush friend John Alston Crichton in a private offshore drilling company. Swashbuckling right-wing oilman Jack Crichton had deep ties to Army intelligence and the events of November 22, 1963. Fabian Escalante, the chief of a Cuban counterintelligence unit during the late 1950s and early 1960s, George Bush and Jack Crichton, both Texas oilmen, gathered the necessary funds for the operation to assassinate Castro. In fact, Crichton is woven into the fabric of the Kennedy assassination.

The Bushes' entertaining a spy and his wife is yet another curious agency tie. According to Barbara Bush, she and her husband had lunch with longtime CIA operative Alfred Ulmer and his wife Dorothy during the week of November 22. Thus, George and Barbara were drinking Bloody Marys with an expert on assassination and coup d'état only days before the assassination of JFK. This is particularly curious in view of the fact that Bush would deny any connection to the CIA prior to his becoming director in 1975.

In 1966, Texas Republicans won a surprise victory in court mandating congressional redistricting. A new Houston district was carved for Bush—it was "country club" and heavily Republican.

George H. W. Bush would go to Congress and quickly become a water-carrier for Big Oil, a defender of the oil-depletion allowance and a proponent of the Texas defense contractors. Prescott Bush pulled strings to get his son appointed to the powerful Ways and Means Committee, a key assignment with real fundraising potential for another Senate race.

Bush and his father were major backers of Richard Nixon in his 1968 comeback bid. Together with Texas business associates Hugh Liedke and Robert Mosbacher, the Bushes raised big money for Nixon's bid. Once Nixon was nominated, Bush would mount the first of his drives to be selected for vice president. Although only in Congress four years, George and Prescott Bush orchestrated an effort to get major party figures to urge Nixon to take "Poppy" as his running mate. Prescott Bush would get Tom Dewey, instrumental in Nixon's own selection as vice president, to urge Nixon to take the young Texan on the ticket. Texas Senator John Tower, elected in a special election to fill Johnson's senate seat in 1961, pushed Bush with Nixon. So did the CEOs of Chase Manhattan, J. P. Stevens, and Pennzoil. Of course, Brown Brother Harriman weighed in.

William Middendorf II, a longtime GOP fundraiser for Barry Goldwater, Nixon, Gerald Ford, and Reagan who later served as Secretary of the Navy, claimed that he had worked the 1968 GOP convention to line up support for Bush. On the day after Nixon was nominated, Middendorf said that his associate, New York financier Jerry Milbank, went to Nixon's hotel room to talk about the vice presidential choices. "It was pretty early, I think it was about 7:30, I think it was his bedroom, actually, reading the paper. I said we've got delegates pretty much lined up for George, and it looks like he'd be a very popular choice among the delegates," Middendorf recalled. "That's when he told me that, 'Oh, gee, fellas, I'm going with my man Spiro T. Agnew,'" the little-known governor of Maryland who would later resign in a scandal.[6]

Prescott Bush was furious with Nixon's passing over Poppy for the little-known Agnew; he would share his anger in a letter to Tom Dewey, the Eastern Kingmaker who had "made" Eisenhower.[7]

Warming up for a rematch with Yarborough, Bush courted LBJ on the theory that, once out of office, LBJ would rally the Texas Bourbon Democrats against his hated enemy, Yarborough. In 1969, Bush was the only Republican member of the Texas congressional delegation to see LBJ off at Andrews Air Force Base rather than attend Nixon's inaugural festivities. Bush traveled to the LBJ ranch to seek Johnson's "advice" about leaving his House seat to challenge Yarborough. Johnson would urge him to run, saying that the difference between the House and Senate was like the difference between "chicken salad and chicken shit." After he landed a seat on the House Ways and Means Committee, many of the oil barons who had financed LBJ's career became Bush donors. As he had in 1964, Bush also raised hundreds of thousands from well-connected donors back East.

Bush's election to the Senate in 1970 was considered a cakewalk. The Ways and Means seat brought vast fundraising capability, Texas had moved right, the Republican Party in Texas had grown, and Yarborough was out of step with the new Texas. Bush was again opposed in the Republican Primary by Robert Morris. This time, the primary was a rout. Bush won with 96,806 votes (87.6 percent) to Morris's 13,654 ballots (12.4 percent). Morris would move back to New Jersey where he had already run once in the Republican primary for the Senate in 1958 against Representative Robert W. Kean, veteran congressman and father of future New Jersey governor Tom Kean. Morris ran again in 1982—and lost again—to the stunning Hungarian American mayor of Montclair, Mary Mochary.

Bush had the nomination, but LBJ and his protégé John Connally were lying in wait to sandbag him.

Lloyd Bentsen, a conservative Democrat who served in the House with Johnson and was his neighbor on the Pedernales River, jumped into the Democratic Primary. John Connally made thirty-second TV ads endorsing Bentsen. LBJ told Bush that he was "neutral," but Johnson's friends did his bidding. Yarborough lost the Democratic primary in an upset.

Poppy had prepared for six years for a race against Yarborough. Now, he faced a smooth Bourbon Democrat to his right. An attempt to get Democrat liberals to cross over for Bush fizzled. Bentsen ran well with Mexican Americans and blacks yet held conservative Democrats, who would have deserted Yarborough.

Bush brought in Harry Trealeven who, with the skillful Roger Ailes, remade Nixon's TV image in 1968—no small feat. Trealeven staged the penultimate modern media campaign, showing Bush as handsome, friendly, energetic, and glamorous. This "Kennedyesque" appeal was devoid of substance to attract both pro–Nixon conservatives and liberals upset with the Yarborough loss. Bush's slogan "He Can Do More" boasted of his "connections." Bush was depicted as dashing here and there, jacket slung over his shoulder, playing touch football. He outspent Bentsen—even Nixon sent $100,000 from his secret Townhouse fund. This particular gift would come back to bite "Poppy."

Bush's brother Jonathan Bush said that George was "getting in position to run for president."[8] Peter Roussel, Bush's highly regarded press aide from 1970 to 1974 said "There were high hopes for him in that race. It was one of the premier races of that year, and a lot of people thought, well, Bush is going to win this Senate race, and there's probably a good chance that'll be the stepping stone for him ultimately going to run for president."[9] Bush lost, however.

I attended John Jay High School in Katonah, New York with Marvin Pierce II, or "Peter" Pierce as he was called. I ran with Peter—he was a crazy motherfucker. George H. W. Bush was Peter's uncle—his father, Jim Pierce, was Barbara Bush's brother. I drank a lot of beer, smoked a lot of marijuana, and drove a lot of cars too fast with "Pete," who was a big supporter of his uncle in the 1970 Texas Senate race.

I was volunteering for the New York campaign of Jim Buckley for the Senate at the time, and I recall spending election night with Pete. We were in his car, drinking beer and listening to returns on the radio. I was exultant because Conservative Party nominee Jim Buckley was winning a three-way race with liberal Republican Charles Goodell and Democrat Richard Ottinger. Bill Brock won in Tennessee. J. Glen Beall snagged a Senate seat in Maryland, Lowell Weicker (then a Nixon man) won in Connecticut over Reverend Joe Duffy, a far-left anti-war Democrat, and disgraced incumbent Tom Dodd running as an Independent. Then came the news out of Texas: Bush had lost to Lloyd Bentsen, a creation of LBJ and John Connally.

Peter was inconsolable. "My uncle said LBJ is a prick. Years of kissing his ass, and he decides to settle an old score—and screw George Bush in the mean time," he said. I was a Bush man, too, and had written him a letter telling him that I would come to Texas in the summer to volunteer for his Senate campaign. I got a response from his assistant Tom Lias brushing me off, so instead I did volunteer work for Buckley all summer.

"My uncle is going to be president someday," Pete said. At that time, I doubted he was right. Pete was later badly injured in a car crash in which his female passenger died. He passed away in 2012.

As a victim of two unsuccessful Senate campaigns, Bush's political future was in doubt. For the next eighteen years, he was not in control of his political career. He was well suited to advance his career by serving others in administrative posts, but it seemed a dead end. When Nixon offered him an insignificant job as assistant to the president, Bush made his case for more.

When Bush heard that Nixon Treasury Secretary David Kennedy was leaving, he inquired of the president for the job. He was shocked to learn that his nemesis John Connally would be taking that job. "Bush hated Connally," David Keene, Bush's 1980 political honcho told me at the time. Bush sold Nixon on going to the UN as ambassador. Poppy got to brush up his foreign policy credentials and attend endless cocktail parties. He wrote notes, kept in touch with his friends, and bided his time.

Kissinger and Nixon both considered Bush a lightweight. He was never told of the back channel communiqués with the Communist Chinese. He staked himself out at the UN as a hardliner for Nationalist China and against the Reds. Poppy was kept in the dark about Nixon's visit to China. George and Barbara Bush lived blissfully ignorant in a sumptuous double apartment at the Waldorf Towers, with socialite Mildred Hilson and Mrs. Douglas MacArthur as their neighbors.

Bob Dole served Nixon well as chairman of the Republican National Committee. Day-to-day operations were run by co-chair Thomas B. Evans Jr., later a Delaware Congressman and an important early supporter of Ronald Reagan in 1980. Nixon decided to sack Dole for no good reason other than he had got beaten up for attacking Democrats on behalf of Nixon. The president asked Bush to take Dole's place. "Dole is still pissed about it," Scott Reed, the Kansas senator's 1996 campaign manager, told me in 2013.

Bush mounted his second bid to be chosen for vice president. A boiler room run by Nebraska Republican National Committeeman Richard "Dick" Herman was set up in a suite of rooms at the Statler Hilton Hotel in Washington. There, Richard L. Herman and two assistants began calling through George Bush's deep Rolodex. Senator Howard Baker, Elliot Richardson, Governor William Scranton, Melvin Laird, Senator Bill Brock, Governor Dan Evans, Donald Rumsfeld, Governor Nelson Rockefeller, and Senator Barry Goldwater were all under consideration.

My friend, syndicated Columnist Robert Novak, reported that "as the new president was sworn in, Rockefeller had become a considerably less likely prospect than either Senator Howard Baker of Tennessee or George Bush, the gregarious patrician and transplanted Texan who heads the Republican National Committee." Bush's elevation seemed assured.

On August 10, Ford announced that he would poll Republicans with the Republican National Committee to tabulate the results. Many Republicans who didn't favor Bush didn't want to tell him that, given George and Barbara's reputation for vindictiveness. RNC members and Republican members of the House overwhelmingly supported Poppy. The matter of the poll itself was the subject of a complaint by Delaware Republican National Committeeman Thomas B. Evans Jr., who attacked the poll in the press and also wrote to Ford. Evans, a former RNC co-chair, wrote "no one should campaign for the position, and I offer these thoughts only because of an active campaign that is being conducted on George Bush's behalf, which I do not believe properly reflects Republican opinion. Certainly, one of the major issues confronting our country at this time is the economy and the related problems of inflation, unemployment, and high interest rates. I respectfully suggest that you need someone who can help substantively in these areas. George is great at PR, but he is not as good in substantive matters. This opinion can be confirmed by individuals who held key positions at the National Committee."

Those favoring Rockefeller would counter attack. Webster G. Tarpley and Anton Chaitkin report it in *George Bush: The Unauthorized Biography*.

By August 19, the eve of Ford's expected announcement, the *Washington Post* reported that unnamed White House sources were telling *Newsweek* magazine that Bush's vice presidential bid "had slipped badly because of alleged irregularities in the financing of his 1970 Senate race in Texas." *Newsweek* quoted White House sources that "there was potential embarrassment in reports that the Nixon White House had funneled about $100,000 from a secret fund called the 'Townhouse Operation' into Bush's losing Senate campaign against Democrat Lloyd Bentsen four years ago." *Newsweek* added that $40,000 of this money may not have been properly reported under the election laws. Bush was unavailable for comment that day, and retainers James Bayless and

C. Fred Chambers scrambled to deliver plausible denials, but the issue would not go away.

Bush's special treatment during the 1970 campaign was a subject of acute resentment, especially among senate Republicans whom Ford needed to keep on board. Back in 1970, Senator Mark Hatfield of Oregon had demanded to know why John Tower had given Bush nearly twice as much money as any other Senate Republican. Senator Tower had tried to deny favoritism, but Hatfield and Edward Brooke of Massachusetts had not been placated. Now, there was the threat that, if Bush had to go through lengthy confirmation hearings in the Congress, the entire Townhouse affair might be dredged up once again. According to some accounts, there were as many as eighteen Republican senators who had gotten money from Townhouse but whose names had not been divulged. Any attempt to force Bush through as vice president might lead to the fingering of these senators, and perhaps others, mightily antagonizing those who had figured that they were getting off with a whole coat. Ripping off the scabs of Watergate wounds in this way conflicted with Ford's "healing time" strategy, which was designed to put an hermetic lid on the festering mass of Watergate. Bush was too dangerous to Ford. Bush could not be chosen.

Poppy would become Ford's envoy to China and, recognizing conservative animosity towards Rockefeller, he began focusing on the 1976 vice presidential nomination. That effort was short-circuited by Ford's request that Bush become director of the Central Intelligence Agency. Bush believed that White House Chief of Staff Donald Rumsfeld, soon to become Secretary of Defense, had maneuvered Bush into the CIA post to eliminate him from consideration as Ford's 1976 running mate. Indeed, Senate Democrats sought and received a commitment from Ford that Bush would not be considered as a condition of Senate confirmation. The 1980 Bush operative David Keene—later national chairman of the National Rifle Association—told me "Bush thought Rummy screwed him."

According to Rumsfeld, Bush began grumbling beginning in 1975 that Rumsfeld, then chief of staff to President Gerald Ford, had sent him to run the CIA, so that he wouldn't be in the running to be on Ford's 1976 ticket.

Rumsfeld details the situation in his book *Known and Unknown*. "The circumstances surrounding George H. W. Bush's nomination to be director of the CIA is a particularly stubborn chapter of the myth that I had stage-managed Ford's staff reorganization," he writes, according to *Politico*. "By repeating the myth instead of setting the record straight, Bush in effect endorsed it."

The tension between Rumsfeld and George H. W. Bush was still alive in 2006. *Salon* reported that "Former President George H. W. Bush waged a secret campaign over several months early this year to remove Secretary of Defense Donald Rumsfeld. The elder Bush went so far as to recruit Rumsfeld's potential replacement, personally asking a retired four-star general if he would accept the position, a reliable source close to the general told me. But the former president's effort failed, apparently rebuffed by the current president. When seven retired generals who had been commanders in Iraq demanded Rumsfeld's resignation in April, the younger Bush leapt to his defense. 'I'm the decider, and I decide what's best. And what's best is for Don Rumsfeld to remain,' he said. His endorsement of Rumsfeld was a rebuke not only to the generals but also to his father."

The two memos detailing Bush's connection to the events of November 22 are troubling enough, but in 1978, when Lee Harvey Oswald's "handler" George de Mohrenschildt committed suicide only a day before he was to testify before the House Select Committee on Assassinations, the name and phone number of George "Poppy" Bush was found in de Mohrenschildt's personal phone book.

In fact, Bush had a decades-long friendship with George de Mohrenschildt, a man who was in daily touch with Oswald throughout 1963. De Mohrenschildt and Oswald became acquainted after Oswald had returned from the Soviet Union. In 1977, de Mohrenschildt was interviewed by Edward Jay Epstein, an American investigative journalist and former political science professor at Harvard, UCLA, and MIT, who wrote three controversial books on the Kennedy assassination, eventually collected in *The Assassination Chronicles: Inquest, Counterplot, and Legend*. De Mohrenschildt told Epstein that he had been ordered by CIA operative J. Walton Moore to meet Oswald, and he said that he would not have done so if he had not been ordered to.

More troubling is the letter exchange between de Mohrenschildt and Bush when the latter was the director of Central Intelligence:

> You will excuse this handwritten letter. Maybe you will be able to bring a solution to the hopeless situation I find myself in. My wife and I find ourselves surrounded by some vigilantes; our phone bugged; and we are being followed everywhere. Either the FBI is involved in this, or they do not want to accept my complaints. We are driven to insanity by the situation. I have been behaving like a damn fool ever since my daughter Nadya died [cystic fibrosis] over three years ago. I tried to write, stupidly and unsuccessfully, about Lee H. Oswald and must have angered a lot of people—I do not know. But to punish an elderly man like myself and my highly nervous and sick wife is really too much. Could you do something to remove the net around us? This will be my last request for help, and I will not annoy you anymore. Good luck in your important job. Thank you so much.[10]

George Bush wrote back:

> Let me say first that I know it must have been difficult for you to seek my help in the situation outlined in your letter. I believe I can appreciate your state of mind in view of your daughter's tragic death a few years ago, and the current poor state of your wife's health. I was extremely sorry to hear of these circumstances.

In your situation, I can well imagine how the attentions you described in your letter affect both you and your wife. However, my staff has been unable to find any indication of interest in your activities on the part of federal authorities in recent years. The flurry of interest that attended your testimony before the Warren Commission has long subsided. I can only speculate that you may have become "newsworthy" again in view of the renewed interest in the Kennedy assassination, and thus may be attracting the attention of people in the media. I hope this letter has been of some comfort to you, George, although I realize I am unable to answer your question completely."[11]

House Select Committee on Assassinations investigator Gaeton Fonzi obtained an address book from de Mohrenschildt's briefcase after his death. In the address book was an entry for "Bush, George H. W. (Poppy), 1412 W. Ohio also Zapata Petroleum, Midland." Only intimates called George Bush "Poppy."

Once again, Bush would have a memory lapse. He insisted that he had never asked for CIA files and records on the JFK assassination. "Yet the agency would release eighteen documents (under the Freedom of Information Act) that showed he had, as the director of Central Intelligence, requested information from agency files—not once, but numerous times—on a wide range of questions regarding the Kennedy assassination."

Was George Bush trying to find out if *his* name was in the CIA Kennedy Assassination file?

If Bush's actions on November 22, 1963 are curious, consider the case of his friend and 1964 Republican running mate John Alston Crichton, a former World War II spy, Cold War military intelligence officer, and Big Oil millionaire.

Born in Louisiana in 1916, Crichton served in the Army after graduation and landed in the Office of Strategic Services, the forerunner to the Central Intelligence Agency. Soon after World War II, he used his intelligence and business contacts to build an international network of companies, which were the epitome of "Big Oil" during the era.

By most accounts, Crichton first encountered Poppy Bush in 1964 when he earned the Republican nomination for Governor in an uphill challenge to popular incumbent Democrat Governor John Connally Jr. Bush had the nomination for the Senate—both men went down in defeat. Still, they formed a friendship sharing many political stages across Texas.

Fabian Escalante, the chief of a Cuban counterintelligence unit during the late 1950s and early 1960s, describes in his 1995 book a National Security Council plan called "Operation 40," a CIA assassination squad debuted at the Bay of Pigs. Escalante charges that Vice President Richard Nixon assembled an important group of businessmen headed by George Bush and Jack Crichton to gather the necessary funds for the operation. At the time, Crichton had big investments at stake in Cuban oil rights.

An owner, investor, and board member in innumerable companies, Crichton knew or worked with nearly every player in Texas. A founder of the Dallas Civil Defense, he was a popular figure in Texas's growing right-wing movement. He was also director of Dorchester Gas Producing Co. with D. H. Byrd, who owned the Texas School Book Depository building and was a close friend of Lyndon Johnson. Clint Murchison Sr., a connected oil man who hosted an assassination-eve party at his Dallas mansion, served on a Crichton company board.

Crichton also became commander of the 488th Military Intelligence Detachment in 1956, an Army Reserve unit based in Dallas. According to him, dozens of the men in his unit worked in the Dallas Police Department. Some of them were in Dealey Plaza on November 22.

As we saw earlier, Crichton would actually be involved in the arrangements for President Kennedy's trip to Dallas. His close friend, Deputy Police Chief George L. Lumpkin, a fellow member of the the Dallas Army Intelligence unit that Crichton headed, drove the pilot car of Kennedy's motorcade. Also riding in the car was Lieutenant Colonel George Whitmeyer, commander of all

Army Reserve units in East Texas. Crichton himself was thought to be in a command-center bunker established by Crichton's Army Intelligence unit.

Also, after Oswald's arrest, the Dallas Police Department would contact Crichton to provide an interpreter for a distraught Marina Oswald. According to the Warren Commission report, Ilya Mamanto translated for Oswald during her initial questioning by the Dallas authorities in the hours immediately after her husband had been arrested. According to author Russ Baker in *Family of Secrets*, these "were far from literal translations of her Russian words and had the effect of implicating her husband in Kennedy's death."

Incredibly, Crichton was never questioned by the Warren Commission.

Every way the JFK assassination story turns, you see the specter of the swashbuckling Crichton. A very public man, he died in 2007, a pillar of his community. He was ninety-one years old.

Today, John Alston Crichton's papers are stored at the George Bush Presidential Library in College Station, Texas. They are sealed.

NOTES

1. Interview with Beverly Tipton.
2. Baker, *Family of Secrets*, 12.
3. Brad Steiger and Sherry Hansen, *Conspiracies and Secret Societies: The Complete Dossier* (Canton: Visible Ink Press, 2006), 69.
4. Baker, *Family of Secrets*, 61.
5. NSAM, 273.
6. John William Middendorf, *Potomac Fever: A Memoir of Politics and Public Service* (Annapolis: Naval Institute Press. 2011), 75.
7. Baker, *Family of Secrets*, 161.
8. Ibid., 171.
9. *American Experience: George H. W. Bush*, PBS, 2008
10. Baker, *Family of Secrets*, 268.
11. Ibid., 270.

CHAPTER EIGHTEEN

A FEW GOOD MEN

In 1906, the Good Government Association (GGA), a group formed in Boston to root out and stop unnecessary taxation, expenditures, and corruption, petitioned the state legislature for the authority to investigate Mayor John F. Fitzgerald. For years, the mayor, who was elected under the promise that ward politics and patronage jobs would not be a part of his administration, was repeatedly accused of graft. Fitzgerald was putting major donors under city employ, many in jobs for which they were vastly unqualified. James Doyle, a barkeep who had worked for Fitzgerald's campaign, was named superintendent of streets; another barkeep was appointed to the board of health as a physician.[1] James Nolan, a liquor distributor, was named superintendent of public buildings.[2]

In anticipation of the danger that could come from an independent organization investigating cronyism and fraud in his administration, Fitzgerald sought to cut off the GGA by proposing an independent commission be created by the city. The purpose of the commission would be to launch "a comprehensive inquiry"[3] into the corruption in city hall.

"By making this proposal," wrote Thomas H. O'Connor in *The Boston Irish: A Political History*, "Fitzgerald obviously hoped to sidestep the Republican thrust, co-opt the process, name the members of the commission himself, and manipulate the investigation to show him in the most favorable light."[4]

It is doubtful that Fitzgerald would have found humor in the irony of a commission being formed nearly six decades later under similar pretenses. That this second commission, the Warren Commission, was formed to manipulate the evidence in relation to the death of his grandson, President John F. Kennedy, would no doubt come with less laughter. Fitzgerald would, however, understand the purpose of such a commission.

There would be no trial for Lee Harvey Oswald, but investigations into the assassination being held on federal and state levels would have to be quashed to ensure information contradictory to Oswald's guilt was not found. The lone gunman story was admittedly flimsy.

"We, of course, charged him with the murder of the president," J. Edgar Hoover said to Johnson on the morning after the assassination. "The evidence that they have at the present time is not very, very strong."[5]

Having stolen the presidency, Johnson, with a hand in the killing, and Hoover, with a measurable knowledge and association in the conspiracy, were as thick as thieves.

"Me and you are going to talk just like brothers," Johnson told Hoover.

Both Hoover and Johnson realized the importance of controlling the inquest.

"I think it would be very, very bad to have a rash of investigations on this thing," said Hoover.

"Well, the only way we can stop them is probably to appoint a high-level one to evaluate your report and put somebody that's pretty good on it that I can select,"[6] answered Johnson.

The FBI report on the assassination was clear in its determination of Oswald as the lone gunman and would serve as a blueprint for the Warren Commission. However, a few of the facts present in the report would have to be altered to pin the tail on the donkey.

The bureau report said that two bullets had killed President Kennedy and one wounded Governor Connally. The theory that the president and Connally were wounded by three separate bullets was damaged irreparably by James Tauge, who, standing near the underpass, was injured by a stray bullet while watching the motorcade. The bullet, more than two hundred feet from the fatal Kennedy shot, had hit the curb and deflected bits of concrete, one of which hit Tauge.[7] In the words of Deputy Sheriff Eddy Walthers "the projectile struck so near the underpass, it was, in my opinion, probably the last shot that was fired and apparently went high and above the president's car."[8]

To fit into the time that one assassin could potentially have committed the act, the Commission would turn two bullets into one: a single bullet that caused all the nonfatal injuries to Kennedy and Connally.[9] Another fact that would have to be amended is the discovery of a bullet on the president's stretcher. The FBI report concluded that the bullet must have dropped out of the wound on the upper back of the president, the wound that, according to the report had "no point of exit."[10] Because the path of the bullet had not been not tracked during the official autopsy, the wound could be turned from a penetrating gunshot wound—one that has an entrance but no exit—into a perforating gunshot wound with a track leading from the upper right back up and through the base of the neck.

For the bullet to follow this track, it would have to be twice deflected off of Kennedy's bones. "If the bullet had enough remaining velocity to punch straight through Connally's back, breaking his ribs then shattering his wrist bone before lodging in his thigh, it had too much velocity to be deflected by bones inside Kennedy's body prior to striking Connally," wrote G. Paul Chambers in *Head Shot*. "It would just shatter Kennedy's bones the same way it shattered Connally's and keep right on going along its original path. Unless Kennedy was eating lead for breakfast, or his bones were made of depleted uranium, or he was the bionic man, a full-metal jacket 6.5 mm lead round fired from a military rifle could not bounce around inside his body like a pinball."[11]

For facts to be altered, discarded or invented, the investigation into Kennedy's death would have to take place in a controlled environment.

Johnson used fear of nuclear destruction to validate his halting of independent investigations in all branches of federal and state government and law enforcement.

"We don't want to be testifying," Johnson said to Speaker of the House John McCormack, "and some fellow comes up from Dallas and says, 'I think Khrushchev planned this whole thing, and he got our president assassinated.'. . . You can see what that'll lead us to, right quick. . . . You take care of the House of Representatives for me."

"How am I going to take care of them?" McCormack asked.

"Just keep them from investigating!" was Johnson's decisive answer.[12]

Robert Kennedy's trusted advisor Nicolas Katzenbach wrote into a memo the true purpose of what would become the Warren Commission.

"The public must be satisfied that Oswald was the assassin; that he did not have confederates who are still at large; and that the evidence was such that he would have been convicted at a trial," Katzenbach wrote. "The only other step would be the appointment of a presidential commission of unimpeachable personnel to review and examine the evidence and announce its conclusions. . . . We need something to head off public speculation or congressional hearings of the wrong sort."[13]

The interest of the Commission would be to use and maneuver the available evidence to ensure Oswald's perceived guilt; all other evidence was to be suppressed or ignored.

The seven-member Warren Commission comprised Chief Justice Earl Warren, Senators Richard Russell Jr., and John Sherman Cooper, Congressmen Gerald Ford and Hale Boggs, John McCloy, and, representing the CIA, Allen Dulles.

The talks between Hoover and Johnson to handpick and assign appropriate members to the Warren Commission sounded like mafiosi talking within their ranks. Each faction of the assassination pact within the government would have to be represented: a Johnson company man, a CIA interest, and an FBI confidant. These men would channel information back and forth between their respective agency and the Commission brokering the interests of that particular agency.

Former Director of the CIA Allen Dulles was an asset for the agency on the Commission. He and JFK blamed each other for the failure of the Bay of Pigs invasion and Dulles was dressed down and fired by the president after the disastrous operation. Dulles also held a lingering hatred for Kennedy.

"What do you think about Allen Dulles?" Johnson asked.

"I think he would be a good man,"[14] Hoover answered.

Dulles himself had pushed hard to get on the Commission to help distance the CIA from Oswald and the assassination. He was so active and omnipresent on the Commission that critic Mark Lane commented that it should have been renamed the "Dulles Commission."[15]

"Though no longer on the CIA payroll, the scorned director served as the agency's undercover man on the Commission,"[16] wrote David Talbot in *Brothers*, his sweeping indictment of CIA complicity in the Kennedy assassination.

At the first executive session of the Commission, Dulles issued each member a book which detailed the case that American assassinations were the work of lone, unaided triggermen.[17] The message was clear: Oswald was the CIA's dupe and any connections to him would have to be derided or buried.

"I don't think Allen Dulles ever missed a meeting,"[18] Warren said.

Dulles pushed the preconceived agenda of the Commission, while at the same time privately wiping his hands clean of any wrongdoing in front of the other members. A stenotypist's notes on a private conversation among Dulles, Hale Boggs, and commission general counsel J. Lee Rankin partially revealed his manipulative, faux-naïveté and also several commissioners' willingness to follow the design of the proceedings:

> DULLES: Why would it be in their [the FBI's] interest to say he [Oswald] is clearly the only guilty one?
>
> RANKIN: They would like us to fold up and quit.
>
> BOGGS: This closes the case, you see. Don't you see?
>
> RANKIN: They found the man. There is nothing more to do. The Commission supports their conclusions, and we can go home, and that is the end of it.
>
> BOGGS: I don't even like this being taken down.
>
> DULLES: Yes, I think this record ought to be destroyed.
>
> RANKIN: There is this factor too that. . . . Is somewhat of an issue in this case, and I suppose you are all aware of it. That is that the FBI is very explicit that Oswald is the assassin . . . and they are very explicit that there was no conspiracy, and they are also saying they are continuing their investigation. Now, in my experience of almost nine years, in the first place, it is hard to get them to say when you think you have got a case tight enough to convict somebody, that this is the person who committed the crime. In my experience with the FBI, they don't do that. They claim that they don't evaluate [come to conclusions], and it is my uniform experience that they don't do that. Secondly, they have not run out all kinds of leads in Mexico or in Russia and so forth which they could probably—It is not our business, it is the very . . .
>
> DULLES: Why is that?
>
> RANKIN: They haven't run out all the leads on the information, and they could probably say . . . that isn't our business.
>
> DULLES: Yes.
>
> RANKIN: But they are concluding that there can't be a conspiracy without those being run out. Now, that is not from my experience with the FBI.
>
> DULLES: It is not. You are quite right. I have seen a great many reports.[19]

Revealed in this transcript is the belief of an FBI conspiracy not to investigate the assassination and a defeatist attitude in the decision of the Commission members not to question the Bureau. Reviewing the official FBI report on the assassination, the outline for the Commission, did not set the members any more at ease:

WARREN: Well, gentlemen, to be very frank about it, I have read the FBI report two or three times, and I have not seen anything in there yet that has not been in the press.
BOGGS: . . . Reading the FBI report leaves a million questions.
MCCLOY: Why did the FBI report come out with something that was inconsistent with the autopsy? The bullet business has me confused.
WARREN: It's totally inconclusive.
BOGGS: Well, the FBI report doesn't clear it up.
WARREN: It doesn't do anything.
BOGGS: It raised a lot of new questions in my mind . . . There is still little on this fellow Ruby, including his movements . . . what he was doing, how he got in [the Dallas jail], it's fantastic.[20]

Commission member Gerald Ford took pen in hand and changed the Commission's initial description of where the bullet had entered John F. Kennedy's body when he was killed in Dealey Plaza.

William C. Sullivan, the FBI's number-two man, recounts in his book *The Bureau: My Thirty Years in Hoover's FBI* that "Hoover was delighted when Gerald Ford was named to the Warren Commission. The director wrote in one of his internal memos that the Bureau could expect Ford to 'look after FBI interests,' and he did, keeping us fully advised of what was going on behind closed doors. He was our man, our informant, on the Warren Commission."

Sullivan said that Hoover had been watching Ford from the beginning. "Our agents out in the field kept a watchful eye on local congressional races and advised Hoover whether the winners were friends or enemies. Hoover had a complete file developed on each incoming congressman. He knew their family backgrounds, where they had gone to school, whether or not they played football [Ford played football at Michigan], and any other tidbits he could weave into a subsequent conversation," Sullivan said. "Gerald Ford was a friend of Hoover's, and he first proved it when he made a speech not long after he came to Congress recommending a pay raise for him. He tried to impeach Supreme Court Justice William O. Douglas, a Hoover enemy."

Strangely enough, Sullivan himself would be killed in a "hunting accident" only days before he was to testify before the House Select Committee on Assassinations. He was shot dead near his home in Sugar Hill, New Hampshire, on November 9, 1977. Courts ruled that he had been shot accidentally by fellow hunter Robert Daniels, who was later fined $500 and stripped of his hunting license for ten years.

Conservative Pundit and reporter Robert Novak said in August 2007 "[William Sullivan] told me the last time I saw him—he had lunch at my house—he had been fired by Hoover and he was going into retirement—he said that 'Someday, you will read that I have been killed in an accident, but don't believe it, I've been murdered,' which was a shocking thing to say."[21]

Sullivan was one of six top FBI officials who died in the six months before they were to testify before the House Select Committee in 1977. Others included Alan H. Belmont, special assistant to Hoover; Louis Nicholas, another special assistant and Hoover's liaison with the Warren Commission; James Cadigan, a document expert who handled papers related to the murder of John F. Kennedy; J. M. English, former head of the FBI forensic sciences laboratory where Oswald's rifle and pistol were both tested; and Donald Kaylor, an FBI fingerprint chemist who examined prints from the JFK case.

FBI documents disclosed in 2006 detail even more about Ford's role as the FBI's informant and agent. Assistant FBI Director Cartha "Deke" DeLoach regularly met secretly with Ford to inform the FBI on the status of the Warren Commission investigation. "Ford indicated he would keep me thoroughly advised as to the activities of the Commission," DeLoach wrote in a memo. "He stated this would have to be done on a confidential basis, however he thought it should be done."

The Associated Press reported that DeLoach wrote another FBI memo, which explained "that Ford wanted to take the FBI's confidential assassination report on a ski vacation, but had no way to do so 'in complete safety.' DeLoach recommended lending him a bureau briefcase with a lock. The bottom of the memo contains a handwritten 'OK' over Hoover's distinctive initial 'H,' which he regularly used in commenting on memos." In return for his loyalty, the FBI gave its full blessing to Ford; he was given complete access to whatever he wanted, whenever he wanted it.

The Associated Press also reported that DeLoach wrote a memo on December 17, 1963, about a meeting with Ford in which the deputy director laid out a problem. "Two members of the Commission brought up the fact that they still were not convinced that the president had been shot from the sixth floor window of the Texas Book Depository," DeLoach wrote. "These members failed to understand the trajectory of the slugs that had killed the president. He [Ford] stated he felt this point would be discussed further but, of course, would represent no problem."

Indeed, we shall see what Ford meant by "no problem."

Here, more specifically, is the problem DeLoach described. The initial draft of the Warren Commission report stated, "A bullet had entered his back at a point slightly above the shoulder to the right of the spine." This description matches that of Admiral Burkley's autopsy. Burkley, JFK's personal physician, attended the autopsy at Bethesda Naval Medical center and noted that the wound was "in the upper posterior about even with the third thoracic vertebra."

In fact, autopsy photographs of the back place the wound in the back two to three inches below the base of the neck. A diagram by Burkley included in the Warren Commission's own report confirms this location. The actual physical evidence demonstrates that the first draft of the Warren Commission report was indeed accurate.

Photographs of bullet holes in Kennedy's shirt and suit jacket, almost six inches below the top of the collar, place the wound in the upper right back.

As American history Professor Michael L. Kurtz pointed out in *The JFK Assassination Debates*: "If a bullet fired from the sixth-floor window of the Depository building nearly sixty feet higher than the limousine entered the president's back, with the president sitting in an upright position, it could hardly have exited from his throat at a point just above the Adam's apple, then abruptly change course and drive downward into Governor Connally's back."

Ford did Hoover's bidding. His handwritten edit said, "A bullet had entered the base of the back of his neck slightly to the right of his spine." This change was later revealed in declassified papers kept by the Warren Commission's general counsel accepted in the final report.

"A small change," Ford told the Associated Press when it surfaced decades later in 1997.

Ford, a public supporter of the single-assassin theory, insisted that his edit had intended to clarify meaning, not change history. However, the effect of his alteration is clear: With this "small change," he bolstered the Commission's false conclusion that a single bullet had passed through Kennedy and hit Governor Connally—thus solidifying what is now known as "The Magic Bullet Theory." Indeed, the Associated Press stated that Ford's "small change" became "the crucial element" to determine that Lee Harvey Oswald had been the lone assassin.

Ford's cooperation may have been motivated by other factors. Bobby "Little Lyndon" Baker wrote that Washington lobbyist Fred Black, a crony and secret business partner of Baker and LBJ, had a suite at Washington's Sheraton Carlton Hotel. There, he often arranged for call girls to entertain congressmen and senators. The FBI surreptitiously filmed the action.

According to Baker, Ford was a frequent visitor.

The American public first learned of Ford's alteration in 1997, over three decades after Kennedy's assassination, and this information was only released as a result of the Assassination Records Review Board (ARRB). Interestingly enough, the ARRB was formed as a response to Oliver Stone's film *JFK*. For the first time in generations, the public demanded an in-depth examination to determine what was fact, what was fiction and what was covered up. In 1992, Congress passed the JFK Assassination Records Collection Act to empower the ARRB to declassify JFK assassination records.

Hoover memorialized Ford's role in an internal FBI memo dated 1965 that stated, "Though we did experience some difficulty with all the members of the Warren Commission, Ford was of considerable help to the Bureau."

In a supreme act of irony, in April 2001 in Boston, former President Ford was given the John F. Kennedy Profile in Courage Award from the directors of the Kennedy Library. Was he rewarded for covering up the facts of John F. Kennedy's death?

Tim Miller, the publisher of Ford's 2007 memoir, revealed that although the book contended that Ford had maintained the belief that Oswald had acted alone, in private, the former president believed that Oswald had had help.[22]

"There is no doubt that President Gerald Ford knew more about the JFK death,"[23] Miller said.

Another Commission member who succumbed to the pressure to follow the foundations laid by Johnson and Hoover was Richard Russell, an old mentor of Johnson.

In public, Russell would be a willing participant to its motives and conclusions, but in private, to Johnson and to the Commission, he would voice his concerns. Russell's biggest contention was the "Magic Bullet Theory," on which the Commission's entire case hung.

"Well, what difference does it make which bullet got Connally?" Johnson asked Russell.

"Well, it doesn't *make* much difference. But they said that . . . the Commission believes that the same bullet that hit Kennedy hit Connally. Well, I don't believe it."[24]

The "Magic Bullet Theory" did make a difference, however. More than one bullet causing all the nonfatal wounds to President Kennedy and Governor Connally would have meant that there were at least four shots fired. If true, it was impossible that just one gunman had fired upon the president in the timeframe of the assassination.

"To say that they were hit by separate bullets," a commission lawyer stated, "is synonymous with saying that there were two assassins."[25]

Another shooter meant a conspiracy, which did not fit the Warren Commission narrative.

A handwritten note by Russell in December 1963 further detailed his disenchantment with the Commission. "W. [Warren] & Katzenbach know all about the FBI, and they are apparently through psychiatrists & others planning to show Oswald only one who even considered—this to me is untenable position—I must insist on outside counsel,"[26] Russell wrote.

Before he died in 1970, Russell had given a final interview saying that he "never believed that Lee Harvey Oswald assassinated President Kennedy without at least some encouragement from others. And that's what a majority of the Committee wanted to find. I think someone else worked with him on the planning."[27]

The witnesses to the assassination who were to testify were presupposed to follow the established conclusions set for the Commission. If the witnesses testified contrarily, they were led or coerced to present their case otherwise. If they did not, their account was altered or discarded.

George de Mohrenschildt saw that the testimony he had given, one with positive assessments of Oswald, was purposefully altered in print. "All the favorable facts that we mentioned about Lee were subsequently misinterpreted in the printed edition of the report or not mentioned in it at all," de Mohrenschildt wrote.[28]

De Mohrenschildt also later felt that much of the interviewing conducted by the Commission had intentionally been leading the public to a visceral response, drawing it away from the evidence.

"We wondered why the Commission paid so much attention to the testimonies of people who had known Lee and Marina in Dallas long before the assassination or others who had known him long before that? And the answer was—just to fill up the pages and tranquilize the American populace."[29]

The script had been written, and the Warren Commission was simply looking for actors to fill the roles. Such was the case with the witnesses attesting to the origin of the shots. Of the twenty-five witnesses who gave affidavits attesting to the origin of the shots on the day of and the day following the assassination, twenty-two pointed to the grassy knoll.[30] In the evidence on hand for the Commission from 121 witnesses, fifty-one believed that the shots had come from the area of the grassy knoll; only thirty-two thought that they had come from the Texas School Book Depository.[31] Yet the Warren Report would conclude that "No credible evidence suggests that the shots were fired from the railroad bridge over the Triple Underpass, the nearby railroad yards, or any place other than the Texas School Book Depository."[32] In spite of the majority of eyewitnesses pointing elsewhere, the Book Depository fit the story.

For the Commission, the shots *could not* have originated from anywhere else.

"In what other murder case would the testimony of fifty-one sworn and many other unheard witnesses be dismissed so cavalierly as 'no credible evidence,'"[33] wrote Commission critic Harold Feldman.

Also dismissed were reports from three Dallas Police Department officers—Seymour Weitzman, D. V. Harkness, and Joe Marshall Smith—that they had encountered men disguised as Secret Service agents just following the assassination. Officer Smith, directed to the grassy knoll from a woman who heard the shots, ran into someone who flashed him secret service credentials.[34] This could only have been a counterfeit agent because all the Secret Service agents with the motorcade proceeded instantly to Parkland Hospital. When interviewed by Commission lawyer Wesley Liebeler, Officer Smith maintained his story:

> MR. LIEBELER: There is a parking lot behind this grassy area back from Elm Street toward the railroad tracks, and you went down to the parking lot and looked around?
> MR. SMITH: Yes, sir. I checked all the cars. I looked into all the cars and checked around the bushes. Of course, I wasn't alone. There was some deputy sheriff with me, and I believe one Secret Service man when I got there. I got to make this statement, too. I felt awfully silly, but after the shot and this woman, I pulled my pistol from my holster, and I thought, this is silly, I don't know who I am looking for, and I put it back. Just as I did, he showed me that he was a Secret Service agent.

Gordon Arnold, a man on military leave in Dallas who stopped to watch the presidential motorcade, also saw someone who claimed to be a Secret Service agent behind the fence on the grassy knoll just before the shooting. The pseudo agent flashed a badge and informed Arnold that he didn't belong in that area. Arnold recalled his confrontation with assassination researcher Jim Marrs:

> I said all right and started walking back along the fence. I could feel that he was following me, and we had a few more words. I walked around the front of the fence and found a little mound of dirt to stand on to see the motorcade . . . Just after the car turned onto Elm and started toward me, a shot went off from over my left shoulder. I felt the bullet rather than heard it, and it went right past my left ear. . . . I had just gotten out of basic training. In my mind, live ammunition was being fired. It was being fired over my head. And I hit the dirt.

Arnold's story of an agent was confirmed by a photograph taken by Mary Moorman just as President Kennedy was fatally shot. The photograph shows an image of Arnold wearing an army cap and a service medallion filming the motorcade. The photograph more interestingly showed another figure. Known as the "Badge Man," it provided proof that there was a man behind the fence on the grassy knoll. When analyzed with a photograph taken from a different angle at the same time by assassination witness Orville Nix, Jacques de Langre, a commercial photographer who had also done investigative photography work for the United States Army, said "without question, that the two angles of the subject are from the same person . . . [and] the subject is a man holding an elongated object."[35]

In the 1980s, assassination researchers Gary Mack and Jack White, who studied the photograph and tried to have it better analyzed, attracted the attention of a news organization. The group had the Moorman photo analyzed using computer enhancement at the Massachusetts Institute of Technology. The result: The photo unequivocally showed a figure firing a rifle.[36]

When Arnold was later shown the photograph, he became overwhelmed with emotion as he recollected the moment. "I couldn't understand why I would be standing crooked," Arnold said as he examined the photograph and realized, "if that's a muzzle blast or flash, then whoever is standing there would have been a fool to stand up straight, he would be trying to get away from harm's way is what it boils down to."[37]

Arlen Specter, then serving as an assistant district attorney in Philadelphia, was the sole lawyer brought in to determine the facts of the assassination. Incredibly, before the assassination, Specter had made a fan in Robert Kennedy. He was successfully prosecuting teamsters in Philadelphia, which led Bobby, in 1963, to seek Specter out to help in his Justice Department fight against Teamster President Jimmy Hoffa. Specter declined the offer. Six months later, he would accept a very different offer.

As assistant counsel for the Warren Commission, the "facts" that Specter determined included the "Magic Bullet Theory," the trajectories and origin of the shots, and the sequence of events and number of assassins.[38]

Specter staged an elaborate re-enactment of the assassination in Dealey Plaza but used a different make and model car for the presidential limousine (the presidential limousine was a 1961 Lincoln; for the re-enactment investigators used a 1956 Cadillac). The smaller vehicle had no jump seats and instead had a rear bench more raised than the 1961 Lincoln.[39] The replacement model invalidated the entire re-enactment. Strangely, the role of Governor John Connally in Specter's re-enactment would be played by FBI Deputy Director Mark Felt, who would later be revealed as "Deep Throat" in the Watergate scandal. Felt would be the famous anonymous source for Robert Woodward and Carl Bernstein of the *Washington Post*.

I worked as a consultant in Specter's 1980 US Senate campaign, which sent him to Washington after he had lost election bids for mayor of Philadelphia, district attorney, governor, and a previous race for the Senate in 1976. His perseverance was like Nixon's—The quality that drove him was ambition.

I came to know Specter much better in his Senate days and served as chairman of his 1996 campaign for president. The race was a symbolic gesture meant to argue for a broader, more inclusive Republican Party not dominated by the religious right.

I told the senator that I thought the "Magic Bullet Theory" was bullshit. He always smiled and postponed the debate until cocktail time. Over drinks, he could zealously debate his theory of JFK's death by gunshot. Specter had a zest for political combat and a passion for the details of public policy. He enjoyed campaigning, a brisk game of squash, a slab of roast beef, and an ice-cold martini with a glass of ice on the side. He would nurse it slowly adding ice cubes to keep it ever cold.

Specter was dogged and abrasive; he could be brusque and brutal. He rarely backed down when he pursued a course of action. When Robert Kennedy noticed his relentless pursuit of the teamsters, the Pennsylvania poll was at the height of his energy. Specter's manner was a whirlwind of questions and orders, and he was notoriously rough on his staff. Yet in thirty years of friendship, he never spoke a harsh word to me.

The medical staff who treated President Kennedy following the shooting was also bullied, badgered, or had their testimony discarded. Ronald Jones, a resident physician at Parkland Hospital, upon viewing Kennedy's body, saw what he knew to be an entrance wound in the throat. When this was suggested to Specter, Jones was probed to the accuracy of his statement:

> **DR. JONES:** The hole was very small and relatively clean cut, as you would see in a bullet that is entering rather than exiting from a patient. If this were an exit wound, you would think that it exited at a very low velocity to produce no more damage than this had done, and if this were a missile of high velocity, you would expect more of an explosive type of exit wound, with more tissue destruction than this appeared to have on superficial examination.
> **MR. SPECTER:** Would it be consistent, then, with an exit wound, but of low velocity, as you put it?
> **DR. JONES:** Yes, of very low velocity to the point that you might think that this bullet barely made it through the soft tissues and just enough to drop out of the skin on the opposite side.[40]

The conviction that a bullet fired from behind could only make the small neck wound upon exit if traveling very slowly was not consistent with the "Magic Bullet Theory," in which the bullet upon leaving the president's neck would also have ripped through Governor Connally's chest, through his hand, and have burrowed into his leg. Specter found Jones's testimony disagreeable and consequently asked him to alter it.

Over thirty years later, answering questions in front of the Assassination Records Review Board (ARRB), Jones recounted a meeting with Specter following his Warren Commission testimony:

> When I completed my testimony, Arlen Specter followed me into the hall and said, "I want to tell you something that I don't want you to say anything about," Jones recollected. He said, "We have people who will testify that they saw the president shot from the front." He said, "You can always get people to testify about something." But he said: "We are pretty convinced that he was shot from the back. And that implied, although some of us thought that might initially have been an entrance wound, that, you know, that's the end of the discussion, and we do have people who will testify to that." I don't know whether you construe that as pressure or not, but certainly I was surprised that he said don't say anything about that to anyone. A young resident, thirty-one years old, you're not going to say about that episode to anybody because, at that time, I think we were all— the whole country was—I mean, you didn't joke about anything, and there were jokes going around about what happened at the time of the assassination. But we were serious about that. I thought that was unusual.[41]

Specter bullied Parkland Hospital engineer Darrell Tomlinson, the man who found the magic bullet, into testimony that implied Tomlinson had found the bullet on a stretcher that connected the projectile to Governor Connally. Specter also harassed Jean Hill, who as a witness to the assassination, testified that she had heard more shots fired than were accounted for by the Warren Commission, that the shots had come from multiple locations, and that one of those locations was the grassy knoll

Hill recounted Specter's badgering to assassination researcher Jim Marrs:

He kept trying to get me to change my story, particularly regarding the number of shots. He said that I had been told how many shots there were, and I figured he was talking about what the Secret Service told me right after the assassination. His inflection and attitude were that I knew what I was supposed to be saying, why wouldn't I just say it. I asked him, "Look, do you want the truth or just what you want me to say?" He said he wanted the truth, so I said, "The truth is that I heard between four and six shots." I told him, "I'm not going to lie for you." So he starts talking off the record. He told me about my life, my family, and even mentioned that my marriage was in trouble. I said, "What's the point of interviewing me if you already know everything about me?" He got angrier and angrier and finally told me, "Look, we can make you look as crazy as [Marina] Oswald and everybody knows how crazy she is. We could have you put in a mental institution if you don't cooperate with us."[42]

The harassment was necessary to ensure that the witness testimony had the appearance of a uniform conclusion. In truth, not even the government itself could form a uniform conclusion.

In 1964, Specter would even tell the Philadelphia Bar Association that the FBI disagreed with the "Magic Bullet Theory." While it was common knowledge that the FBI had initially believed Kennedy and Connally were hit by separate shots, documents uncovered concerning the FBI's conclusions found that CE 399, the magic bullet fired into JFK "had entered just below his shoulder to the right of the spinal column at an angle of twenty-five to sixty degrees downward, that there was no point of exit, and that the bullet was not in the body."[43]

Specter later admitted to HSCA and Church Committee investigator Gaeton Fonzi that, after initial denial, the Zapruder film that the Warren Commission had reviewed was "missing frames" in critical sequences. When they looked at the frames together, Fonzi pointed out to Specter that Zapruder film frames 207 to 212 had been spliced. "Boy, you sure got me," Specter said. "207–212? Well, I've got the intervening frames. I don't think there's anything deliberate about that at all. I never knew that. I'm very much surprised...."[44]

When confronted by Fonzi with evidence that the bullet holes in the clothing confirmed that the shot to the upper right back and throat did not line up, Specter seemed equally as absent minded and put forth the inane theory that the impeccably tailored Kennedy's suit jacket and shirt were bunched up high as he was waving when the bullet was fired:

SPECTER: Well, the back hole, when the shirt is laid down, comes...ah...well, I forget exactly where it came, but it certainly wasn't higher, enough higher to ... ah ... understand the ... ah ... the angle of decline which ...

FONZI: Was the hole in the back of the shirt lower than the hole in the front of the neck of the shirt? [The president had a throat wound made by a bullet that had pierced his tie and made a hole in the front of the shirt at the throat.]

SPECTER: Well, I think, that ... that if you took the shirt without allowing for it being pulled up, that it would either have been in line or somewhat lower.

FONZI: Somewhat lower?

SPECTER: Perhaps, I ... I don't want to say because I don't really remember. I got to take a look at that shirt.

Specter also admitted to Fonzi that the Commission had not been interested in seeing the autopsy photographs and X-rays and would not say whether or not he had asked to see the important evidence.

"Have I dodged your question?" Specter asked. "Yes, I have dodged your question."[45]

What Specter could not evade was the lack of credible eyewitnesses to testify that the same bullet that struck Kennedy also wounded Connally. It was a theory that forensic pathologist Cyril H. Wecht called "an asinine, pseudoscientific sham at best."[46]

Oddly, Wecht's career would intersect with Specter's on a few occasions. He served on the staff of St. Francis Hospital in Pittsburgh before becoming deputy coroner of Allegheny County in 1965. He was elected Allegheny County coroner four years later, where he served from 1970 to 1980 and again from 1996 to 2006.

In 1978, he was elected chairman of the Allegheny County Democratic Party. One year later, he was elected to the Allegheny County Board of Commissioners. In 1982, he was the Democratic Party's nominee to oppose Senator John Heinz, who won a seat by defeating Arlen Specter in the Republican Primary six years earlier. Heinz won the election with 59 percent of the vote.

In 1978, Wecht was the lone dissenter on a nine-member forensic pathology panel before the HSCA re-examining the assassination of John F. Kennedy, which had concurred with the Warren Commission conclusions and "Magic Bullet Theory." Out of the four official examinations into the Kennedy assassination, Wecht is the only forensic pathologist who has disagreed with the conclusion that both the "Magic Bullet Theory" and Kennedy's head wounds are mutually consistent.

Wecht, after studying the clothes of the victims, the alleged rifle of the shooter, X-rays, and photographs from the autopsy and the actual bullet itself, came to the undeniable conclusion that the path the bullet had taken in the "Magic Bullet Theory" was a scientific impossibility.[47]

"Give me one bullet, in one case, just one from hundreds of thousands of cases . . . that has done this. Nobody has ever produced one,"[48] Wecht said. As with almost all of the researchers, he realized that the theory was necessary to string together the Commission's faulty conclusions. "Without the single bullet theory, there cannot be one assassin, whether it is Oswald or anybody else,"[49] said Wecht.

John Connally himself testified that he had been hit with a separate bullet. "They talk about the 'one-bullet' or 'two-bullet theory,' but as far as I am concerned, there is no 'theory,'" Connally said. "There is my absolute knowledge, and Nellie's too, that one bullet caused the president's first wound, and that an entirely separate shot struck me."[50] Connally though, ever the ardent Johnson man, concluded that he had been satisfied with the final judgments of the Warren Commission.

"Connally has stated that he is satisfied with the conclusions of the Warren Commission," said assassination researcher Penn Jones. "This is insanity. By persisting that he was hit by a separate shot, Connally destroys the Warren Report completely. How can he then state that he has no quarrel with the Commission's findings?"[51]

More damaging to the theory was Commission Exhibit 399, the recovered bullet that the Commission linked to it. The problem with the projectile found is that it was completely intact, without a mark on it. Still, Specter stood by his theory. When Oliver Stone's film *JFK* was released, Specter expressed the opinion that it might only bolster the Commission's findings. "In a curious way, this absurd movie, which no one is taking seriously once acquainted with the facts, may lead people to read and accept the extensive factual analysis and sound conclusions of the Warren Commission's Report," Specter said.[52]

After releasing his memoirs, Specter was even more emboldened. "I now call it the Single-Bullet Conclusion," Specter absurdly wrote in 2000. "It began as a theory, but when a theory is established by the facts, it deserves to be called a conclusion."[53]

Another arduous task of the Commission was proving that Oswald fired the shots. No nitrates [contained in powders in gases when a weapon is discharged] were found on Oswald's cheek when a paraffin test was conducted following his arrest.

"Since the paraffin wax seeps deep down in to the pores, it is a very sensitive test," wrote G. Paul Chambers in his scientific approach to the assassination, *Head Shot*. "Even washing one's face prior to the test will not remove all presence of nitrates. As someone who has worked extensively with ball powders, I can tell you that reacted powders have a very distinctive odor, which is difficult to get out of your skin and clothes. The presence of nitrates on Oswald's hands may indicate that he had fired a revolver, for instance (he was accused of shooting Officer Tippet on the same day as the assassination), however, nitrates could also have gotten on his hands from other sources, such as paper or ink. The absence of nitrates on his cheek is court-admissible evidence, however, that he had not fired a rifle that day."[54]

Another discrepancy in the Oswald story is the weapon found on the sixth floor of the Depository: It was initially reported by police to be a 7.65 German Mauser, a gun that bore a passing resemblance to the Mannlicher-Carcano 6.5 Italian carbine, which Oswald owned and allegedly fired. Seymour Weitzman, the deputy constable who, along with Deputy Sheriff Eugene Boone, found the rifle on the sixth floor, told the Commission that in regards to firearms, he was "fairly familiar because I was in the sporting goods business awhile."[55]

An affidavit filled out by Weitzman a day after the assassination details his claim of finding the Mauser. "We were in the Northwest corner of the sixth floor when Deputy Boone and myself spotted the rifle about the same time," Weitzman wrote. "This rifle was a 7.65 Mauser bolt action equipped with a 4/18 scope, a thick leather brownish-black sling on it."[56]

This description was verified and repeated by officers on the scene, including Deputy Dallas Sheriff Roger Craig:

> Deputy Constable Seymour Weitzman had joined us. Weitzman was a gun buff, he had a sporting goods store at one time, and he was very good with weapons. He said it looked like a Mauser, and he walked over to Fritz. Captain Fritz was holding the rifle up in the air and I was standing next to Weitzman, who was standing next to Fritz, and we weren't any more than six to eight inches from the rifle and stamped right on the barrel of the rifle was '7.65 Mauser.' That's when Weitzman said "It is a Mauser" and pointed to the '7.65 Mauser' stamp on the barrel.[57]

Craig, an officer on the scene, who voiced many contrary viewpoints that challenged the official story, was one of the many witnesses involved intimately with the assassination who died mysteriously—another death from a supposed self-inflicted gunshot wound.[58]

When assassination researcher Mark Lane appeared before the Warren Commission, he asked to examine the weapon that had been found on the sixth floor of the Depository. The markings stamped on the side of the rifle clearly identified it with the words "MADE IN ITALY" and "CAL. 6.5"[59]

Only one witness claimed to have seen Oswald in the sixth floor window with the rifle. The witness, Howard L. Brennan, saw a man standing at the window and firing. The shooter could not have been standing because the window was open only slightly. It was determined by the Commission that "Although Brennan testified that the man in the window had been standing when he fired the shots, most probably he had been either sitting or kneeling."[60]

The identification by Brennan was used by the Dallas Police Department to identify Oswald as the suspect: "A white male, approximately thirty years of age, approximately six feet tall, approximately 165 pounds, wearing a white shirt and khaki pants."[61]

The description, which was wholly inaccurate in describing Oswald's attire, led to his capture within an hour.

"He was *not* wearing a white shirt and khaki pants," said assassination researcher Mary Ferrell. "He was wearing a dark reddish-brown shirt—I've held it in my hands at the Archives. It had a slight—a reddish thread, and a gold thread, kind of a plaid—but it was very dark. And he wasn't wearing khaki trousers. He was wearing brown wool trousers."[62]

Another failure of the Commission was proving that Oswald could have gotten off three shots accurately in the 5.6 seconds that were alleged.

Three professional marksmen with a rank of Master given by the National Rifle Association were appropriated with the purpose of recreating the shots made by Oswald.[63]

In comparison to the professionals, Oswald seemed to have poor hand-eye coordination and trouble with dexterous tasks. He showed incompetence when handling firearms, once as a Marine dropping a loaded pistol inside a barracks, causing it to fire.[64] Oswald registered as a "rather poor shot" in his last rifle test prior to the assassination.[65] He could not drive a motor vehicle and was fired from a job at a graphic arts plant in Dallas earlier in the year of the assassination for ineptness.

"He just couldn't see to do anything right," stated his employer. "Oswald seemed to have trouble producing the exact sizes called for."[66]

Yet Oswald had allegedly hit President Kennedy once through the head and once through the throat in 5.6 seconds with a rifle deemed poor in terms of accuracy with a scope not properly sighted when discovered by Dallas police. The expert marksmen, in turn, each firing two series of shots with three shots apiece, could not once hit the neck or head on a stationary target.[67] Additionally, only one of the marksmen could get the shots off in the minimum time alleged.[68]

These results did not deter the findings of the Commission, which concluded that "The various tests showed that the Mannlicher-Carcano was an accurate rifle and that the use of a four-power scope was a substantial aid to rapid, accurate firing.... Oswald had the capability to fire three shots, with two hits, within 4.8 and 5.6 seconds."[69]

The results of the Warren Commission rifle tests compounded with the failure of all subsequent attempts to recreate the shooting further embolden the illusion of Oswald as the lone gunman. A CBS recreation of the shooting was attempted in 1967 using eleven expert marksmen. Not one of them was able to score two hits on the moving target on the first attempt, and only four of the eleven scored two hits on further attempts.[70]

The Discovery Channel show *Mythbusters* attempted to validate the "Magic Bullet Theory." In a recreation, two replica torsos of President Kennedy and Governor Connally were created by Anatomical Surrogates Technology, a company that creates life-like body parts containing artificial bones and flesh. Marks were made on the bodies where the shots had entered, Kennedy's on the right upper back and Connally in the right back range underneath his armpit. The replica torsos were lined up and positioned as they were in the presidential limousine. A gel-block embedded with artificial wrist bones and a similar thigh block represented Connally's arm and leg.

The shot fired in the test, on a non-moving target, went through Kennedy's back, through Connally and his wrist, bouncing off the thigh block. It was proclaimed a success by the *Mythbusters* team.

"Our shot has almost exactly duplicated the path of the magic bullet," stated narrator Robert Lee.[71]

In reality, the recreation did more to debunk the theory than to prove it. Setting aside that the bullet did not embed in the thigh block, the projectile was bent and mangled following the test, much different than the pristine shape of Commission Exhibit 399. The path of the bullet on the *Mythbusters* re-creation was also much different from the one advanced by the Warren Commission. The *Mythbusters* bullet entered Kennedy in the upper-right portion of the back from the angle and distance of the Book Depository sniper's nest and exited in the front middle of his chest, nowhere near the neck—a path consistent with reality.

Mark Fuhrman, the former Los Angeles Police Department detective who rose to prominence with his investigations in relation to the O. J. Simpson trial, in his book *A Simple Act of Murder*, noted its impossibility and dismissed the "Magic Bullet Theory" completely. In Fuhrman's opinion, three bullets hit the occupants of the limousine.[72]

The convoluted Warren Commission had been called a failure for the ages, but in truth, it couldn't have been more of a success. The bending of facts, disposal of evidence, and disregard of the truth had distorted the reality of the assassination, allowing the true culprits of the crime not to slip away but to stay precisely where they were, in the highest reaches of government.

President Nixon would also doubt the findings of the Commission. He called the FBI on May 15, 1972, after Alabama Governor George Wallace had been shot by a deranged gunman in Maryland. The FBI's number-two man Mark Felt answered the president's call:

"Bremer, the assailant is in good physical shape," Felt said. "He's got some cuts and bruises, and—'Good!'" said Nixon. "I hope they worked him over a little more than that."

Felt laughed. "Anyway, the psychiatrist has examined him," he said, adding, "We've got a mental problem here with this guy."

Nixon wanted to make one thing perfectly clear. "Be sure we don't go through the thing we went through with the Kennedy assassination, where we didn't really follow up adequately. You know?"[73]

Mark Lane, one of the original investigators of the assassination and a critic of the Warren Commission, cut to the core of its faulty proceedings in his second testimony in front of it. He addressed general counsel Rankin:

> There are 180 million Americans in this country. I am perhaps the only one who is a private citizen who has taken off the last six months to devote all of his efforts to securing whatever information can be found and to making that known to this Commission, and publicly to the people of this country at great personal cost in terms of the harassment that I have suffered, in terms of the terrible financial losses that I have suffered. And to sit here today, after six months of this work, which I have given all to this Commission, voluntarily, and again have come here again today voluntarily to give you this information, and to hear you say that I am not cooperating with the Commission, and I am going to do harm to the country by not making information available to you astonishes me. You have hundreds of agents of the FBI running all over the Dallas area—agents of the Secret Service, Dallas policemen. Are you telling me that in one trip to Dallas where I spent something like two days, I uncovered information which the whole police force of this nation has not yet in six months been able to secure? I cannot believe that is a valid assessment of this situation. I cannot, Mr. Rankin.[74]

NOTES

1. Thomas H. O'Connor, *The Boston Irish: A Political History* (Boston: Northeastern University Press, 1995), 170.
2. Ibid.
3. Ibid., 176.
4. Ibid.
5. Beschloss, *Taking Charge*, 22.
6. Ibid., 51.
7. Marrs, *Crossfire*, 61.
8. Ibid.
9. "Commission Document - FBI Summary Report," *Warren Commission Documents* (March, 2012), maryferrell.org/mffweb/archive/viewer/showDoc.do?docId=10402; 1.
10. Ibid., 18.
11. Chambers, *Head Shot*, 154–55.
12. Beschloss, *Taking Charge*, 62.
13. Kelin, *Praise from a Future Generation*, 5.
14. Beschloss, *Taking Charge*, 52.
15. Talbot, *Brothers*, 274.
16. Ibid.
17. Janney, *Mary's Mosaic*, 301.
18. Talbot, *Brothers*, 274.
19. North, *Act of Treason*, 508–9.
20. Gentry, *J. Edgar Hoover: The Man and his Secrets*, 553–54.
21. Novak, *The Prince of Darkness*, 210–211.
22. PR News Channel, "Book Publisher: President Ford Knew of CIA Coverup in Kennedy Assassination" (November 27, 2007), www.prnewschannel.com/absolutenm/templates/?a=141.
23. Ibid.
24. Ibid., 560.
25. Epstein, *Inquest*, 38.
26. Nelson, *The Mastermind of the JFK Assassination*, 443.
27. Talbot, *Brothers*, 282.
28. De Mohrenschildt, "I am a Patsy!, I am a Patsy!"
29. Ibid.
30. Lane, *Rush To Judgement*, 39.
31. Kelin, *Praise From a Future Generation*, 213.
32. Ibid., 215.
33. Ibid.

34. Ibid., 238.
35. Kelin, *Praise from a Future Generation*, 365.
36. Marrs, *Crossfire*, 80.
37. Nigel Turner, The Men Who Killed Kennedy, Episode 9, October 25, 1988, Central Television (ITV Network), UK.
38. Epstein, *Inquest*, 60.
39. Fuhrman, *A Simple Act of Murder*, pg. 125.
40. Warren Commission testimony of Ronald Jones.
41. Assassination Records Review Board, Examination of Ronald Jones.
42. Marrs, *Crossfire*, 483.
43. Kelin, *Praise from a Future Generation*, 274.
44. Ibid., 299.
45. Ibid., 300.
46. Michael A. Fuoco, "40 Years On, Arlen Specter and Cyril Wecht Still Don't Agree How JFK Died," *Pittsburgh Post-Gazette* (November 16, 2003).
47. Ibid.
48. Ibid.
49. Fuhrman, *A Simple Act of Murder*, 179.
50. Ibid., 157.
51. Kelin, *Praise from a Future Generation*, 355.
52. Ibid., 469.
53. Ibid., 473.
54. Chambers, *Head Shot*, 171-72.
55. Warren Commission testimony of Seymour Weitzman.
56. Affidavit of Seymour Weitzman, jfk.ci.dallas.tx.us/04/0433-001.gif.
57. Mark Lane, "Two Men in Dallas," *Ustream* (February 22, 2010), ustream, tv/recorded/4919473.
58. "Autopsy Report of Roger Craig," mcadams.posc.mu.edu/craig_autopsy. htm.
59. Lane, *Rush to Judgment*, 115.
60. Kelin, *Praise from a Future Generation*, 108.
61. Ibid.
62. Ibid.
63. Lane, *Rush to Judgment*, 126.
64. North, *Act of Treason*, 212.
65. Lane, *Rush to Judgment*, 126.
66. North, *Act of Treason*, 212.
67. Lane, *Rush to Judgment*, 127.

68. Ibid.
69. Ibid., 128.
70. Michael T. Griffith, "How Long Would the Lone Gunman Have Had to Fire?" (May, 2012), mtgriffith.com/web_documents/howlong.htm.
71. "JFK Assassination Magic Bullet Test (Part 2)," posted by Nelson Smith (July 25, 2009), www.youtube.com/watch?v=PZRUNYZY71g.
72. Fuhrman, *A Simple Act of Murder*, 207–9.
73. Tim Weiner, *Enemies: A History of the FBI* (New York: Random House. 2012), 308.
74. Warren Commission testimony of Mark Lane.

CHAPTER NINETEEN

AT LAND'S END

It was just past 5:30 in the late afternoon of the president's death, and former First Brother Bobby Kennedy was waiting for Air Force One. Kennedy, who had arrived at Andrews Air Force Base a short time before, had isolated himself in the back of a canvas-covered US Army transport truck close to the runway but far enough away from the reporters, legislators, and military personnel littering the base. Kennedy was alone, waiting for Jackie and what remained of his brother.

"Kennedys never cry" was a hard lesson his father, Joe Sr., had extolled to his children when they were growing up. For Bobby, the most temperamental of the brothers, this was particularly tough. In his lifetime, the younger Kennedy had suffered the loss of his older brother Joe Jr. and his sister Kathleen, both in tragic plane accidents, both of which could have been avoided with more thoughtful planning. His sister Rosemary was alive in body alone, her mind permanently regressed to that of a five-year-old due to an ill-advised frontal lobotomy. John's death was different: Bobby felt responsible. He had made it his goal as attorney general to fight the forces that he considered evil: organized crime, FBI director J. Edgar Hoover, the CIA, and his nemesis Lyndon Johnson. Bobby's endgame was not only to battle these forces but to vanquish them. In the end, it was a game of survival at all costs.

"I thought they would get one of us," Bobby had told his aide Ed Guthman shortly after the assassination. "But Jack, after all he'd been through, never worried about it. I thought it would be me."[1]

Bobby no doubt felt tremendous guilt over the death of his brother.

"My own feeling was that Bobby was worried that there might be some conspiracy, and that it might be his fault," RFK's man Katzenbach said. "I think the idea that he could be responsible for his brother's death might be the most terrible idea imaginable. It might very well have been that he was worried that the investigation would somehow point back to him."[2]

At 6:00 p.m., Air Force One descended onto the runway, ending the 1,300-mile journey from Dallas. Bobby removed himself from his cloistered safe haven in the back of the truck and made his way to the aircraft as it landed. With the mobile stairway in place, he frantically made his way up and into the plane.

Lyndon Johnson, noticing Bobby making his way to the rear of the plane, extended his hand and his sympathies.

"Bob,"[3] Johnson said with his hand outstretched.

Bobby moved right past the president without a handshake or recognition of his new boss, his emotions guiding him to his brother and Jackie. Johnson, unsympathetic to the toughest day in Bobby's life, was outraged by Kennedy's perceived rebuff.

"He ran, so that he would not have to pause and recognize the new president,"[4] Johnson said.

This slight would later add fuel to the embittered rivalry between Kennedy and Johnson, but at that moment, Bobby was not concerned with the jilted feelings of his new commander-in-chief.

"Politics is a noble adventure,"[5] were the last words John had said to Bobby before leaving for Dallas. Bobby had begun the day of his brother's death with such intentions.

He spent the morning as he had spent many as attorney general: planning the dissolution of organized crime. The meeting of the organized crime section took place in Bobby's office and covered the types of corruption that the Justice Department was looking to end: Mafia-infiltrated labor unions, illegal gambling, and private businesses. The meeting also covered the innovative methods that the department was using to round up those suspected of crookedness.

"Most cases, there are kickbacks," said prosecutor Henry Peterson. "We're arresting cops on the scene at some of the raids. Where we can, we're including conspiracy, bribery, and tax evasion counts to bring in police, district attorneys, city officials, legislators on the take."[6]

Attorney Ronald Goldfarb, in his book *Perfect Villains, Imperfect Heroes*, recounted the extreme methods of pursuing indictment:

> Criminalizing the making of false statements to law enforcement officials and increasing the use of the hard-to-prove perjury laws were tough cases to make, but we'd have to resort to them. Both laws provided opportunities to close investigatory circles and pressure witnesses to cooperate or incriminate themselves. The false statement statute, for example, S.1001 of the federal penal code, made it a crime to lie in certain documents. We would snag racketeers for doing so on home improvement loans, naturalization documents, FAA loans, FCC radio- and telephone-operator license applications, IRS tax documents, and Small Business Administration and Veterans Administration loans. These were not the laws we preferred to use, but they were the ones on the books at the time.[7]

The attorney general ended the session before noon, so that he could travel back to Hickory Hill for a planned lunch with Robert Morgenthau and Silvio Mollo to discuss the future of the Justice Department. The rumor on Capitol Hill was that Morgenthau might have been Robert Kennedy's replacement in the department while Kennedy went back to work as his brother's campaign manager. Before Bobby left, he talked with Ronald Goldfarb about the indictment of a notable mobster using the dubious tactic of estate tax laws.

"Let's break early," Bobby said. "I'll think about it. We'll decide this afternoon."[8] It was the last time the group would meet.

That afternoon, Bobby was sitting by the pool with Morgenthau and Mollo awaiting the verdict in *The United States v. Carlos Marcello*. It was two years since the New Orleans Mafia chieftain had been deported, and now the government was trying to oust Marcello permanently on charges that he had re-entered the United States illegally.

A conviction of the mob boss would be another solid victory for Bobby's war on organized crime.

The phone call that afternoon would effectively end that crusade. It would also end the attorney general's probes into matters of the CIA and his war to extricate and possibly incarcerate the vice president.

The call came at 1:43 p.m. It was Hoover.

The director of the FBI told Bobby that his brother, the president, when riding through Dallas, had been fired upon and was hit.

"I think it's serious,"[9] Hoover said.

"Jack's been shot," Kennedy told his guests, unable to face them. "It may be fatal."[10]

In the follow-up call from Hoover, at 2:10 p.m., it would be Bobby relaying the horrid details to the director.

"I called the attorney general to advise him that the president was in a very, very critical condition," Hoover later wrote. "The attorney general then told me the president had died."[11]

The death of President Kennedy signified the death of Bobby's effectiveness in the Justice Department and a stay of execution for Hoover as the director of the FBI. Hoover's tradition of going over the head of the attorney general and directly to the president, which had gone unimpeded until the Kennedys took office, would now continue. Lyndon Johnson, as president, would open the lines of communication with Hoover almost immediately after the death of President Kennedy. The pressing order of business would be to convince the public of a lone gunman.

The FBI, "starting at 1:10 on November 22," one Justice Department staffer recalled, "began pissing on the attorney general." Almost immediately, "we stopped getting information from the FBI on the Bobby Baker investigation. Within a month, the FBI men in the field wouldn't tell us anything. We started running out of gas."[12]

Also dissipated was the hunt to end organized crime. The access that Bobby had enjoyed with the CIA would also be revoked; Johnson made sure of this by ordering CIA director John McCone to let the attorney general know his presence was no longer wanted, needed, or allowed.

With Johnson as the president, Bobby tumbled down the ladder of power. He was no longer the second most powerful man in the country, nor the third. And probably not the fourth.

"Suddenly it occurred to me," said Justice Department attorney Bob Blakely, "it all depended on Robert Kennedy. And Robert Kennedy depended on John Kennedy. And the day the assassination went down, all that was over."[13]

The morning after JFK's assassination, Robert Kennedy was exposed to a scene that demonstrated just how quickly the paradigm in the Capitol had shifted. Upon entering the White House at 9:00 a.m. to gather up some of his brother's personal items, Bobby came into contact with a distraught Evelyn Lincoln. When Lyndon Johnson had arrived at the White House as president that morning, he made a special point to expedite the removal of JFK's secretary in an unemotional fashion.

"I have a meeting at 9:30 and would like you to clear your things out of your office by then so my own girls can come in,"[14] Johnson said to Lincoln. Kennedy interceded on Lincoln's behalf. Johnson, offering a minor concession, gave Lincoln until noon to vacate her office. Lincoln later formed her own views on the assassination. In a letter dated October 7, 1994, she expressed her belief that the "five conspirators, in my opinion, were Lyndon B. Johnson, J. Edgar Hoover, the Mafia, the CIA, and the Cubans in Florida."[15]

Other reminders of the Kennedy administration were also quickly moved. Kennedy's rocking chair, which the president had used to ease the debilitating pain in his back, was overturned in the hallway, making room for the Oval Office carpets to be cleaned. The red rug in the office, installed shortly before the Dallas trip, was quickly removed as well.

"It reminded him of the president being assassinated, and he put another rug in the Oval Office with the presidential seal on it,"[16] Cartha DeLoach said.

DeLoach, the FBI's liaison to the Johnson administration would later, in 1967, notify top FBI officials that some White House aides privately questioned the official conclusion that Lee Harvey Oswald had been the lone assassin. DeLoach wrote in a memo: "In this connection, Marvin Watson [LBJ's chief of staff] called me late last night and stated that the president had told him, in an off moment, that he was now convinced that there was a plot in connection with the assassination. Watson stated the president felt that [the] CIA had had something to do with plot."[17] It was a move that Johnson would use on several occasions as president, always with a new "group" that he guessed was connected to the plot.

On December 31, 1963, at the Driskill Hotel in Austin, shortly after the death of John Kennedy, President Johnson would tell Madeleine Brown that the assassination was pulled off by "Texas oil and those fucking renegade intelligence bastards in Washington."[18] Johnson's daily schedule confirms his stay at the Driskill that New Years Eve, thus confirming Brown's memory.

Author Alfred Steinberg also places LBJ at the Driskill that night: "On New Year's Eve [1963], with his first presidential vacation almost over, Johnson paid a surprise visit to the drinking party that Washington reporters away from home were holding at the hotel. He had done handsomely for some of them during the vacation, and they were excited to see him now."

LBJ's presidential schedule lists the event at the Driskill as "White House Press." He often trysted with his girlfriends at the Driskill.

In the dawn of his presidency, Johnson was making a quick transition to solidify power because he still feared a Bobby Kennedy coup.

"During all of that period," Johnson said, "I think [Bobby] seriously considered whether he would let me be president, whether he should really take the position [that] the vice president didn't automatically move in. I thought that was on his mind every time I saw him in the first few days."[19]

Kennedy was merely trying to cope in those early months, his countenance a combination of fatigue, irritation, and anguish.

"I was upset about what had happened on the plane and the fact that [Johnson] came into the [Oval] office," said Kennedy. "So by this time I was rather fed up with him." In late December, Bobby, in an attempt at normalcy, threw a party at the Justice Department to celebrate the proficiency of the past three years. Hoover, normally not one to attend work functions, made an appearance. On arriving, the director was badgered by a still-game Ethel Kennedy, who teased him by speculating who might be the replacement for the director when he retired. She suggested a man on the Los Angeles Police Force whom she knew Hoover hated.[20]

However, retirement was not in the cards for Hoover. With Johnson in office, the mandatory retirement age was waived, and the director remained as head of the FBI in perpetuity. His position secure, Hoover began to show Kennedy hints of a renaissance of power.

"These people don't work for us anymore," Kennedy said. He was talking about Hoover and the FBI.[21]

The attorney general's buzzer was removed from the director's desk. Many employees hired during the Kennedy administration were fired, including Courtney Evans, the go-between from the director to the White House. Evans's replacement would be Cartha DeLoach, a Johnson man.

With John Kennedy alive, Hoover was constantly wary of the whereabouts of the ubiquitous attorney general. "This certainly proves the point we have been stressing," Hoover wrote early in Kennedy's reign. "Our employees should always be busy; engage in no horse play and be properly attired. No one knows when and where A.G. may appear."[22]

Kennedy was now, like his purpose, disappearing. In a cruel twist of fate, it was now Johnson in power, Hoover re-animated, and Robert Kennedy sidelined and ineffectual.

Hoover now openly gloated about brushing the attorney general off in the office and at functions. "For that matter, he ceased communicating with Bobby, reporting instead directly to LBJ," said Kenny O' Donnell.[23]

Bobby lasted only ten months as attorney general after his brother's murder. In his final months in office, he was a shadow of his former self.

"He was a walking zombie in the Department of Justice from the day of the assassination to the day he left," Blakely said. "I remember vividly the day I went up to say goodbye to him. Looking at him was like looking right through him to the wall. When we shook hands, his hand was limp."[24]

The position of power did not matter to Bobby, for in losing his brother, he had lost himself. Bobby turned introspective in the months following his brother's assassination, losing touch with public service and public life. His first appearance to the American people following the assassination was on *The Jack Paar Program* on March 13, 1964. On the show, Bobby was reserved, solemnly sitting facing Paar, with hands carefully folded in his lap. Fielding a question concerning his brother's legacy, Kennedy answered slowly, many times staring into blank space, careful not to let the emotion, so close to the surface, from bubbling over.

"Well, I think really he made," Kennedy said, stammering, "Americans feel young again. I think that . . . I think that he gave all of us more confidence in the country, more confidence that struggles involved in externally and internally would be successful. More confidence. . . in our . . . efforts . . . with those that are opposed to us. Also, he gave great confidence to people who lived in . . . other countries, great confidence in the United States and in its leadership and that we were dedicated to serve the principles and ideals and that we would live up to them and if necessary . . . fight for them. I think it changed over a period of years, our own feelings, as well as the feelings of peoples around the world."[25]

In order to preserve the legacy of President Kennedy, Bobby, against his beliefs, would not challenge the conclusions of the Warren Commission.

With John Kennedy dead and out of power, Hoover's trump card was more valuable. Information connecting the late president to Sam Giancana through Frank Sinatra and his former lover Judith Campbell could destroy the fond recollection of Camelot, which had been built up by the press. Hoover not only had information in his files detailing countless brushes with John and female admirers, he now had dirt on Bobby as well.

In late 1961, JFK began an affair with Marilyn Monroe, which lasted until the spring of 1962, when he sent out his brother to end things between the president and the blonde bombshell. Delivering the message, Bobby himself became entangled with her.

"It wasn't Bobby's intention," actor Peter Lawford, brother-in-law to the Kennedys, recalled, "but they became lovers and spent the night in our guest bedroom. Almost immediately, the affair got heavy. It was as if she could no longer tell the difference between Bobby and Jack."[26]

The director could tell the difference, and from time to time would remind Kennedy that the intelligence could be leaked at any moment. In July 1964, Hoover let Bobby know that information regarding the scandal had been circulated and would be released. The writings would "make reference to your alleged friendship with the late Miss Marilyn Monroe," warned Hoover. "He will indicate in his book that you and Miss Monroe were intimate, and that you were in Miss Monroe's home at the time of her death."[27]

Bobby was hogtied. Gun to the head, he issued the view that "There is no question that he [Oswald] did it on his own and by himself. He was not a member of a right-wing organization. He was a confessed Communist, but even the Communists would not have anything to do with him. Ideology, in my opinion, did not motivate his act. It was a single act of an individual protesting against society."[28]

In the words of biographer Evan Thomas, though Bobby "gave lip service to the single-gunman explanation, he never quieted his own doubts."[29]

For the duration of his remaining years, Bobby held the belief that it was an inside job. Following his brother's death, he unhesitatingly followed his instincts in an attempt to flesh out his suspicions. The story was further developed in David Talbot's story about Bobby's private investigation, *Brothers*.

Shortly following the assassination, Bobby went to the Director of the CIA John McCone fueled by the information that he already had regarding a CIA/Mafia partnership.

"You know, at the time, I asked McCone," Bobby said later, "if they had killed my brother, and I asked him in a way that he couldn't lie to me, and they hadn't."[30]

In Talbot's analysis, Kennedy knew that the information concerning his brother's assassins would not be available to many, especially in an agency of secret affairs that compartmentalized specific activities, making them knowledgeable to a select few in the ranks. McCone, who became director following the abrupt firing of Allen Dulles, was not privy to information concerning the existence of CIA-Mafia collusion. This was confirmed in testimony by, among others, Bill Harvey, Richard Helms, and McCone himself.

"A mansion has many rooms," said Counterintelligence Chief James Angleton. "I'm not privy to who struck John."[31]

This did not halt Bobby's belief in a conspiracy, which he privately confided to close associates. Bobby confided in Dick Goodwin, an advisor to the president, who believed as he did.

"We know the CIA was involved, and the Mafia. We all know that," Goodwin said. "But [exactly] how you link those to the assassination, I don't know."[32]

Though Bobby trusted Goodwin, he still spoke to him about the assassination in cryptic tones. The subject hit too close to home.

"About that other thing," Bobby said to Goodwin at the tail-end of a late night conversation. "I never thought it was the Cubans. If anyone was involved, it was organized crime. But there's nothing I can do about it. Not now."[33]

In his time as senator, Bobby continued his search for knowledge on the death of his brother. In a recent interview, Robert F. Kennedy Jr. said that his father had believed the Warren Commission report to be a "shoddy piece of craftsmanship," and that investigators hired by Bobby had found that Ruby's and Oswald's phone records prior to the assassination "were like an inventory" of Mafia figures.[34]

Bobby maintained a safe view on the assassination publicly throughout his tenure as a senator in the mid–1960s and while he was running for president in 1968. In *Brothers*, Talbot recounts a speech that Kennedy made at San Fernando Valley State College on March 25, 1968. He finished his declaration and entered into a question and answer session. After fielding questions concerning his feelings about troop de-escalation in Vietnam and peace initiatives in different parts of the world, the queries shifted to the death of his brother. A question was raised concerning the archives related to President Kennedy's death, which remained hidden from public view.

"Who killed John Kennedy? We want to know," cried a female student. Other students screamed in the background. "The archives! When will the archives be opened?"

After a long pause, Bobby answered sharply, "Your manner is overwhelming." Clearly miffed by the presentation of the question, Bobby still felt the need to respond.

"Could I just say that . . . and I haven't answered this question before . . . but there would be nobody more interested in all of
these matters as to who was responsible for the uh . . . uh," Bobby
stopped, hesitating for a moment to speak his most private words
aloud to the public and changed direction to a more sterile, safe
place ". . . death of President Kennedy . . . than I would. I have seen
all matters in the archives. If I became president of the United States,
I would not . . . I would not reopen the Warren Commission report.
I stand by the Warren Commission report. I have seen everything in
the archives, and it will be available at the appropriate time."[35]

Privately, Bobby felt differently, and it certainly was hard to
mouth words he didn't believe. At a later campaign event only
days before his own assassination, he said just the opposite,
according to his former Press Secretary Frank Mankiewicz. When
asked if he would reopen the investigation into his brother's death,
he answered with a simple, one-word answer: "Yes." Mankiewicz
recalled "I remember that I was stunned by the answer. It was
either like he was suddenly blurting out the truth, or it was a way
to shut down the questioning—you know, 'Yes, now let's move
on.'"

Kennedy knew that only the powers that come with winning
the presidency could provide the perception needed to figure out
the assassination. Bobby could also attempt to fix the problems of
the war in Vietnam and civil unrest in America if elected president.

Johnson, who no doubt saw the value of a president-appointed
commission with the Warren Commission, attempted to sway
the American public opinion on the problems in American cities
with the President's Special Commission on Civil Disorders.
Johnson had expected the findings of the Commission to support
the administration's strides to aid urban communities. When the
Commission report was released, it ran contrary to Johnson's
expectations, finding the federal government giving a less-than-
sufficient effort to mend inner-city turmoil. If something was
not done, the report found, the result would be the "continuing

polarization of the American community and, ultimately, the destruction of basic democratic values."[36] Johnson did not endorse the Commission report and sent Vice President Hubert H. Humphrey out, nearly a week after the release of the findings, to openly question them.

"This means," Bobby said, "that he's not going to do anything about the war, and he's not going to do anything about the cities either."[37] The findings of the report and President Johnson's unwillingness to acknowledge them further bolstered Bobby's decision to run for president.

Johnson's fears of Bobby taking the presidency from him had returned. To steer Bobby from the course of candidacy, he suggested yet another commission: this one to explore the country's course in Vietnam. Both men entertained the idea, but neither did so seriously. Kennedy, suspicious of the motives of the proposed commission, felt that "if it were more than a public-relations gimmick, if both the president's announcement of the commission and its membership signaled a clear-cut willingness to seek a wider path to peace in Vietnam, then my declaration of candidacy would no longer be necessary. Ending the bloodshed in Vietnam is far more important to me than starting a presidential campaign."[38]

Bobby Kennedy knew that Johnson had money and interest in Vietnam, which went far beyond what public sentiments or the findings of a commission could dictate. The prospective candidate felt that it was "unmistakably clear that, so long as Lyndon B. Johnson was President, our Vietnam policy would consist of only more war, more troops, more killing, and more senseless destruction of the country we were supposedly there to save."[39]

On March 16, 1968, Robert Kennedy announced his candidacy. It was more than Lyndon Johnson could handle. Wracked with guilt over the assassination of JFK as well as war policies that he was forced to employ and recognizing the cruel joke of being bookended by Kennedys, Johnson announced his decision to not run for re-election fifteen days later.

"I'm tired," Johnson privately confided. "I'm tired of feeling rejected by the American people. I'm tired of waking up in the middle of the night worrying about the war. I'm tired of all these personal attacks on me."[40]

With Johnson out of the picture, Kennedy now had a clear path to the presidency, a path that would afford him a deeper look into the death of his brother.

Nixon foresaw RFK's death. He watched Kennedy's announcement from a hotel room in Portland, Oregon, where the former vice president was campaigning for the 1968 Republican presidential nomination. John Ehrlichman, one of several aides in the room with Nixon, later wrote, "When it was over and the hotel room TV was turned off, Nixon sat and looked at the blank screen for a long time, saying nothing. Finally, he shook his head slowly. 'We've just seen some very terrible forces unleashed,' he said. 'Something bad is going to come of this.' He pointed at the screen, 'God knows where this is going to lead.'"

William Sullivan, then the number-four man at the FBI, in his posthumously published memoir *The Bureau: My Thirty Years in Hoover's FBI*, describes a high-level FBI meeting in the spring of 1968. "Hoover was not present, and Clyde Tolson [FBI's number-two man] was presiding in his absence. I was one of eight men who heard Tolson respond to the mention of [RFK's] name by saying 'I hope someone shoots and kills the son of a bitch.'"

Ironically, a researcher of the Kennedy assassination tried to bring evidence of a conspiracy to kill JFK to Robert Kennedy's attention in May, 1967. For years, assassination researcher Ray Marcus had been trying to get public officials interested in the Kennedy assassination. Marcus got in contact with RFK Press Secretary Frank Mankiewicz and succeeded in scheduling a meeting with Mankiewicz.[41]

At the meeting, Marcus showed the Moorman photograph of the "Badge Man" shooter on the grassy knoll. At the conclusion of the meeting, Mankiewicz invited Marcus to show the photo to Kennedy aide Adam Walinsky. Both Mankiewicz and Walinsky confirmed their belief that these were images of men on the grassy knoll at the time of the assassination. When Marcus expressed his belief that Robert Kennedy should publicly dispute the Warren Report, Walinsky was dismissive.[42]

"What good will it do the country for Robert Kennedy to stand up and say, 'I don't believe the Warren Report,'" Walinsky asked.

Mankiewicz, though, promised Marcus that he would bring the photograph to Robert Kennedy's attention. As we know, he became an eyewitness to RFK's startling disclosure that he would reopen the investigation into his brother's death, but whether or not Kennedy saw the photo will never be known.

Bobby was shot and killed a little more than a year later, on June 5, 1968, following a speech in the Embassy Room at the Ambassador Hotel in Los Angeles. He had just claimed victory in the California primary. The message from the candidate that night reflected his brother's, and ran contrary to those whose particular interests led to those of his brother death, who made their money from destruction and violence.

"The country wants to move in a different direction," Bobby said. "We want to deal with our own problems within our own country, and we want peace in Vietnam."[43]

Despite the death of his brother five years earlier, Bobby wanted to continue the initiatives of peace and equality that John had championed during his presidency. Though they had cut off the head of the dog, the tail was still wagging.

"He was an activist," wrote Frank Mankiewicz for *Look* magazine, "and those who disliked him were not concerned that if he got power, he wouldn't do what he said; they feared that indeed he would."[44]

Bobby finished his speech and took a shortcut through the hotel kitchen on his way to the Colonial Room for a news conference. In the crowded kitchen area, shots rang out. Much like the death of his brother, Bobby's slaying was attributed to the work of a lone gunman, Sirhan Sirhan. Similar to the evidence incriminating Lee Harvey Oswald, the evidence of Bobby's death pointed away from Sirhan as the killer.

The official truth in Robert Kennedy's death, much like his brother's, would be reached by distorting facts, destroying evidence, devaluing contrary testimony, and harassing naysayers.

When County Coroner Dr. Thomas T. Noguchi performed Bobby's autopsy, he found that the three bullets that had hit Kennedy had entered from the rear.[45] Sirhan fired his .22-caliber, eight-shot revolver a few feet in front of Kennedy, yet the fatal shot was fired from "less than one inch from Kennedy's head, behind his right ear."[46] Noguchi also found that the bullets had entered Senator Kennedy at an upward angle.

Noguchi's autopsy confirmed that it would have been impossible for Sirhan, who was standing to the front of Kennedy and whom not a single witness would testify was shooting any closer than one-and-a-half to two feet away from Kennedy, to have fired any shot, never mind the fatal shot with the gun barrel nearly pressed to the back of the senator's head. One of the closest witnesses to the shooting, busboy Juan Romero, saw the gun of Sirhan "approximately one yard from Senator Kennedy's head."[47]

Investigators responded to Noguchi's autopsy evidence by slandering the doctor. Law enforcement officers investigating the assassination accused the doctor of intentionally cooking up the autopsy report for self-promotion.

"I hope he dies because if he dies, then my international reputation will be established,"[48] Noguchi was reported to have exclaimed with Kennedy on his deathbed. He was also alleged to have been a drug user, who displayed "erratic behavior" and danced around Kennedy's corpse with apparent delight.[49] His reputation was damaged, and he was temporarily fired due to the allegations.

"Some people believe that the problems I had resulted from my work on the Kennedy case," Noguchi later said. "One of the charges was that the Kennedy autopsy was 'botched up.' The first thing they did was withdraw that particular charge. There were sixty-four charges in all. They were prepared to show a shock value. They didn't expect me to fight back. And I was fully vindicated in the end."[50]

Investigators also had to control witness testimony. One witness, Sandra Serrano, who was the co-chairwoman of youth for Kennedy in the Pasadena–Altadena area at the time of Bobby's assassination, had been standing outside of the Ambassador on the terrace during Kennedy's victory speech when "this girl came running down the stairs and said, 'We've shot him!' 'Who did you shoot?' And she said, 'We've shot Senator Kennedy.'" Serrano went on to describe a woman with light skin, dark hair, a funny nose, and a white dress with polka dots.

Despite the intricate description of the woman by Serrano and the corroboration of other witnesses of seeing the same woman, including a couple who immediately reported the incident to LAPD Sergeant Paul Shangara, Serrano's testimony was distorted and dismissed. Shangara, who was in the area, was responding to an "ambulance shooting" call and quickly made his way to the Ambassador. There, he encountered a frantic exodus of people pouring out of the hotel. An older couple saw Shangara and raced up to him. They described the same woman, wearing the same dress, shouting the same pronouncements about shooting Kennedy.[51]

Shangara was told by Detective Inspector John Powers to drop the description of the suspects. "We don't want to make a federal case out of it," Powers told him. "We've already got the suspect in custody."[52]

Sandra Serrano, who stuck to her story, was treated much less professionally than was Shangara. She was bullied and badgered by investigator Enrique Hernandez during a polygraph examination:

HERNANDEZ: I think you owe it to Senator Kennedy, the late Senator Kennedy, to come forth, be a woman about this. If he, and you don't know and I don't know whether he's a witness right now in the room watching what we're doing in here. Don't shame his death by keeping this thing up. I have compassion for you. I want to know why. I want to know why you did what you did. This is a very serious thing.

SERRANO: I've seen those people!

HERNANDEZ: No, no, no, no, no, Sandy. Remember what I told you about that: You can't say you saw something when you didn't see it. . . .

SERRANO: Well, I don't feel I'm doing anything wrong. . . . I remember seeing the girl!

HERNANDEZ: No, I'm talking about what you have told her about seeing a person tell you, 'We have shot Kennedy.' And that's wrong.

SERRANO: That's what she said.

HERNANDEZ: No, it isn't, Sandy.

SERRANO: No! That's what she said.

HERNANDEZ: Look it! Look it! I love this man!

SERRANO: So do I.

HERNANDEZ: And you're shaming [him]!

SERRANO: Don't shout at me.

HERNANDEZ: Well, I'm trying not to shout, but this is a very emotional thing for me, too. . . . If you love the man, the least you owe him is the courtesy of letting him rest in peace.[53]

Serrano and Shangara were not the only witnesses who brought forth the story of the woman in the white dress with the polka dots. Booker Griffin, at the hotel to support Kennedy, also saw her but inside the hotel and in the company of a man later identified as Sirhan.[54] Susanne Locke, a Kennedy campaign worker, also saw the woman inside the hotel, as did Cathy Sue Fulmer.[55] Thomas Vincent DiPierro, a college student, saw the woman with Sirhan in the pantry kitchen area seconds before Kennedy had been shot.[56]

The statements of many in attendance of the Kennedy speech synched with the description of a Sirhan accomplice.

These witnesses did not fit the official narrative, which claimed that Sirhan had no accomplice. Certainly not Thane Eugene Cesar, a security guard who was escorting Kennedy through the kitchen. Cesar was in the right position to have caused the wounds to Kennedy and had been carrying a gun, which was not examined by police. Witnesses said that Cesar had fired shots, but their testimonies were neglected. Years later, Cesar intimated to investigators that he was not carrying the type of gun that killed Kennedy. He did say that he had owned the type, a .22 caliber, but had sold it four months before the assassination.[57] It was later discovered that Cesar sold the gun three months *after* the killing of Kennedy. It mattered not. Law enforcement had their man.

Audio expert Philip Van Praag also found an audiotape of the shooting to indicate at least thirteen gunshots[58]; Sirhan could only have gotten off a maximum of eight. Sirhan, like Oswald, was a minor player in a major plot.

"Sirhan was set up to be the distracting actor, while the shooter bent down close to Bob [Kennedy] and fired close and upward, with four bullets hitting the senator's body or passing through his clothing,"[59] said Sirhan attorney William Pepper.

Recently, another witness to the murder of Bobby Kennedy has come forward with her claim that there was more than one shooter, strengthening available evidence. Nina Rhodes-Hughes contends that she heard twelve to fourteen shots fired and that the FBI altered her account.[60]

"What has to come out is that there was another shooter to my right," Rhodes-Hughes said. "The truth has got to be told. No more cover-ups."[61]

Vincent Bugliosi, a fixed critic against conspiracy theories in the deaths of both Kennedys, helped analysts of the Bobby Kennedy assassination find too many bullet holes and wounds for only one gun to have fired. Bugliosi offered this statement in 1978, in much contradiction to his staunch beliefs:

> "I have no way of knowing for sure whether or not more than one gun was fired at the assassination scene. And I have formed no opinion at this point. What I will say is this: The signed statements given me perhaps can be explained away, but in the absence of a logical explanation, these statements, by simple arithmetic, add up to too many bullets and therefore, the *probability* of a second gun."[62]

Both brothers died in an attempt to purge their country and their family of the enemy within. The words of Ted Kennedy, then a senator, at his brother Bobby's eulogy, could have easily been applied to John as well.

"My brother need not be idealized," Kennedy said, "or enlarged in death beyond what he was in life, to be remembered simply as a good and decent man, who saw wrong and tried to right it, saw suffering and tried to heal it, saw war and tried to stop it."[63]

NOTES

1. Goldfarb, *Perfect Villains, Imperfect Heroes*, 256–57.
2. Talbot, *Brothers*, 277.
3. Smith, *Bad Blood*, 7.
4. Ibid.
5. Talbot, *Brothers*, 244.
6. Goldfarb, *Perfect Villains, Imperfect Heroes*, 248.
7. Ibid., 58.
8. Ibid., 255.
9. Heymann, *RFK*, 346.
10. Ibid.
11. Ibid.
12. Hersh, *Bobby and J. Edgar*, 448.
13. Goldfarb, *Perfect Villains, Imperfect Heroes*, 256.
14. Shesol, *Mutual Contempt*, 118.

15. Fetzer, *Assassination Science*, 372.
16. Talbot, *Brothers*, 283.
17. Rob Caprio to JFK Assassination Forum, August 3, 2012, www.jfkassassinationforum.com/index.php?topic=6785.0.
18. Brown, *Texas in the Morning*, 189.
19. Talbot, *Brothers*, 119.
20. Hersh, *Bobby and J. Edgar*, 448.
21. Ibid.
22. Ibid., 220.
23. Heymann, *RFK*, 368.
24. Goldfarb, *Perfect Villains, Imperfect Heroes*, 302.
25. "Bobby Kennedy Appears on Jack Paar Show," YouTube video, 2:14, posted by "thousandrobots" (December 23, 2006), www.youtube.com/watch?v=01tTeOzPuZQ.
26. Hersh, *Bobby and J. Edgar*, 322.
27. Gentry, *J Edgar Hoover: The Man and his Secrets*, 562.
28. Talbot, *Brothers*, 279.
29. Thomas, *Robert Kennedy: His Life*, 284.
30. Talbot, *Brothers*, 6.
31. *New York Times*, December 26, 1974.
32. Talbot, *Brothers*, 303.
33. Ibid., 305.
34. Jamie Stengle, "RFK Jr.: 'Very Convincing' Evidence That JFK Wasn't Killed by Lone Gunman," NBCNEWS.com (January 11, 2013).
35. "Robert F. Kennedy At San Fernando Valley State College." *Pacifica Radio Archives* (May, 2012), archive.org/details/RobertFKennedyAtSanFernandoValleyStateCollege.
36. John Herbers, "Panel on Civil Disorders Calls for Drastic Action To Avoid 2-Nation Society," *The New York Times* (March 1, 1968).
37. Shesol, *Mutual Contempt*, 415.
38. Jules Witcover, *85 Days: The Last Campaign of Robert Kennedy* (New York: Putnam, 1969), 77.
39. Shesol, *Mutual Contempt*, 424.
40. Ibid., 437–38.
41. Kelin, *Praise From a Future Generation*, 452.
42. Ibid., 452.
43. "RFK part 2 Last Speech Ambassador Hotel," YouTube video, 9:57, posted by "JFK1963," September 5, 2006, www.youtube.com/watch?v=ae7H0aWFWNY&feature=relmfu

44. Witcover, *85 Days*, 332.
45. William Turner and Jonn Christian, *The Assassination of Robert F. Kennedy* (New York: Carroll and Graf, 1978), 162.
46. Michael Taylor, "40 Years After RFK's Death, Questions Linger," *San Francisco Chronicle* (June 3, 2008).
47. Moldea, *The Killing of Robert F. Kennedy*, 96.
48. Ibid., 160.
49. Ibid.
50. Ibid.
51. Turner and Christian, *The Assassination of Robert F. Kennedy*, 67.
52. Ibid., 74.
53. Moldea, *The Killing of Robert F. Kennedy*, 113–14.
54. Turner and Christian, *The Assassination of Robert F. Kennedy*, 68.
55. Ibid., 69.
56. Ibid., 72.
57. Ibid., 165.
58. Michael Martinez and Brad Johnson, "Attorneys for RFK Convicted Killer Sirhan Push 'Second Gunman' Argument," CNN (March 12, 2012).
59. Ibid.
60. Michael Martinez and Brad Johnson, "RFK Assassination Witness Tells CNN: There Was a Second Shooter." CNN (April 28, 2012).
61. Ibid.
62. Turner and Christian, *The Assassination of Robert F. Kennedy*, 185–86.
63. Witcover, *85 Days*, 306.

CHAPTER TWENTY

CUI BONO

Cui prodest scelus, is fecit

The one who derives advantage from the crime is the one who committed it.

Out of respect for John F. Kennedy, who had been treated in Trauma Room One, Lee Harvey Oswald was wheeled into Trauma Room Two at Parkland Hospital after he was mortally wounded by Jack Ruby. Similar to the life-saving efforts performed on Kennedy, the effort expended on Oswald by the medical staff at Parkland was fruitless. The bullet had cut through vital organs, and Oswald had severe internal bleeding. The rescue attempt was, to Dr. Charles Crenshaw, similar to "preventing a boat from sinking when it's taking on water, with part of the crew bailing and others plugging holes." Looking on during the emergency operation was a man in a scrub suit whom no one in the room recognized. He had a gun protruding from his back pocket.[1]

As Dr. Crenshaw continued the operation in vain, an important call came in to the hospital. Crenshaw recalls the phone conversation in his book, *Trauma Room One*:

"This is Dr. Crenshaw, may I help you?"
"This is President Lyndon B. Johnson," the voice thundered.
"Dr. Crenshaw, how is the accused assassin?"
I couldn't believe what I was hearing. The very first thought that I had was, how did he know when to call?
"Mr. President, he's holding his own at the moment," I reported.

"Would you mind taking a message to the operating surgeon?" he asked in a manner that sounded more like an order.

"Dr. Shires is very busy right now, but I will convey your
message."

"Dr. Crenshaw, I want a death-bed confession from the
accused assassin. There's a man in the operating room who will
take the statement. I will expect full cooperation in this matter,"
he said firmly."

"Yes, sir," I replied, and the telephone went dead."[2]

It is suspicious that the president of the United States would personally call a hospital to ask for a confession from a dying alleged
assassin. It is implausible that Johnson would have armed muscle
at Parkland to take the confession. Still, the call and the armed visitor are proven facts, backed up by several employees at Parkland
Hospital that day.

"I vividly remember someone said . . . the White House is
calling, and President Johnson wants to know what the status of
Oswald is," recalled Dallas neurosurgeon Phillip E. Williams. "I
heard the statement in the operating room, and it was not Dr. Crenshaw's book or anyone else who revived my thoughts about this
because I have said this for years."[3]

Phyllis Bartlett, the chief telephone operator at Parkland Hospi-
tal that day, took the call and transferred it to the operating room.
She stated that the man had a loud voice and said he was Lyndon
Johnson.[4]

The armed visitor presiding over the operation was a federal
agent. Dr. Paul Peters, present at the operation, remembered the
presence of multiple agents vividly. "There were Secret Service men
intermingled with the operating room personnel . . . some were
dressed in green clothes as the surgeons . . . two or three shouted in
his ear, 'Did you do it? Did you do it?'"

Johnson's desperate attempt to force or coerce a statement out of a
dying man was clearly the move of someone trying to tie loose ends,
pin all guilt on Oswald, and separate himself further from the crime.

Over the years, some of those still alive and connected to the assassination have come forward or have been routed out of hiding. Slowly, Johnson's connections to the event have made their way to the surface.

* * *

I had the opportunity to see Richard Nixon up close because I was the youngest senior staff member of his 1972 election campaign. As a political director in Ronald Reagan's 1980 and 1984 campaigns, I carried Nixon's messages on strategy and tactics to the Reagan high command. I did his political chores in Washington in his post-presidential years. I learned politics at Nixon's knee.

Nixon told me that former Supreme Court Justice Tom Clark had told him that LBJ had asked him to head a Texas state inquiry into Kennedy's death and that "Clark wanted no part of it" fearing the public outcry over containing the investigation. Nixon intimated that "Johnson's people convinced him a Texas-based investigation wouldn't fly."

Over the years, Nixon would make veiled references to Johnson's complicity in the Kennedy assassination. One of the more notable references was an off-the-cuff remark during the famed Frost–Nixon interviews of 1977. Nixon was touching on a comment made by Johnson's Press Secretary George E. Christian regarding Nixon's escalation of bombing in Vietnam.

"We were meeting in the Oval Office, I saw the morning news report, and I just happened to catch it, and I mentioned it to George. I said, 'Well I'll betcha that President Johnson is gonna be real pleased when he finds that now they're calling me the number-one.' George Christian said, 'Oh, don't be too sure, you know LBJ. He never likes to be number two.'"[5]

At the end of the anecdote, Nixon's smile curls into a knowing grin.

In addition to his admission are the many witnesses in recent years who have come forth linking President Johnson to the murder of John F. Kennedy and others.

The family of Martin Luther King Jr. is publicly on record saying that Lyndon Johnson was part of the plot to murder Dr. King, the most revered civil rights leader of his time.

Dexter Scott King, Dr. King's son, told ABC News that President Lyndon B. Johnson must have been part of a military and governmental conspiracy to kill his father.

"Based on the evidence that I've been shown, I would think that it would be very difficult for something of that magnitude to occur on his watch and he not be privy to it," he said on the ABC News program *Turning Point*.

A possible motive for LBJ? Johnson knew how pivotal King had been in the election of JFK in 1960. He feared that Robert F. Kennedy would challenge him for the 1968 Democratic presidential nomination and that King would back such a move. King and Bobby Kennedy had both emerged as critics of LBJ's policies in Vietnam.[6]

Johnson's mistress, Madeleine Brown, and Murchison family maid, May Newman, confirmed the secret party thrown with heads of government and Big Oil leaders on the eve of the assassination. Texas Governor Allan Shivers accused Johnson of murdering Sam Smithwick who had written to Coke Stevenson and said that he was ready to talk about the 1948 voting fraud that had given LBJ the Democratic nomination over Stevenson.

Before Stevenson could make it to the prison to interview the man, Smithwick was found dead and hanging in his cell. LBJ later told journalist Ronnie Dugger, "Shivers charged me with murder. Shivers said I was a murderer!"

The first person to call Lyndon Johnson a murderer was not a JFK assassination researcher or an 1960s anti-war protester. It was a Tory Democrat governor of Texas who knew Lyndon Johnson and his deformed character and utter ruthlessness quite well.

Johnson associate Billy Sol Estes, in a letter to the Department of Justice, connected Johnson with the deaths of eight people including John F. Kennedy. Texas Ranger Clint Peoples had knowledge of Johnson with his hand in a number of murders. George de

Mohrenschildt was a link between Johnson, his Texas cronies, and the CIA. Before his death, E. Howard Hunt also helped provide links between Johnson and the CIA.

All of the groups involved benefited tremendously from the assassination. Johnson avoided political exile and incarceration; the CIA had their war in Vietnam; Big Oil had a politician in office to legislate in their favor; and the mob had someone to call off the dogs. Indeed, J. Edgar Hoover had his mandatory retirement waived by Johnson and was declared director of the FBI for life.

Although Johnson avoided punishment for his actions, the presidency would be his penance. His power, which he had long sought, was an illusion. Johnson was now accountable to those groups that had helped him capture the office. The war in Vietnam did not belong to Johnson—it belonged to the CIA and Texas businessmen. And Johnson was a figurehead. Although he profited greatly from Vietnam, it tore his spirit to pieces. He was crucified by the public for the war and spent his post-presidential years at the LBJ ranch racked with mental and physical maladies.

He died before the war ended.

The destruction of the Kennedys would "bring to the foreground two vice presidents who had never been more than the shadows of other shadows," wrote James Hepburn in *Farewell America*, referring to Nixon and Johnson. "For four years, Lyndon Johnson ran the country as his background and obligations required, concealing his conservatism beneath minor racial and social reforms."

Kennedy's murder would clear the way for LBJ to 1600 Pennsylvania Avenue. It also paved the road there for his rival Richard Nixon.

The assassination, noted Hepburn, was "rooted in a system that had produced a senator named Lyndon Johnson, and it was suppressed by the same system, now presided over by the same Lyndon Johnson."

Companies such as Brown and Root, Bell Helicopter, and oil tycoons such as Clint Murchison, H. L. Hunt, and D. H. Byrd had used Johnson to get favorable government contracts. And Johnson used them to get elected. With him as president, the oil-depletion allowance was allowed to continue untouched, and no one company in the country would benefit more from Vietnam than Brown and Root. Decades later, merging with Halliburton, they continued to reap wartime profits in Iraq.

The obstruction blocking the truth had been the Warren Commission, a clever dog-and-pony show set up to obfuscate the facts and connections involved. Nevertheless, some facts have come into view.

The following are all facts: Mac Wallace killed John Kinser. Mac Wallace knew Lyndon Johnson. Johnson's attorney, John Cofer, the same lawyer who represented Johnson in 1948 and Billy Sol Estes in 1962, got Wallace a suspended sentence for the murder of Kinser. That sentence was eventually dismissed. Following the suspension of the case, Wallace acquired a job with Dallas defense contractor Temco, owned by D. H. Byrd, who also owned the Texas School Book Depository building.

While investigating Wallace's acquisition of the job at Temco, a Navy intelligence officer told Texas Ranger Clint Peoples that "the vice president"[7] got Wallace clearance for the government contractors. Following the assassination of Kennedy, the fingerprints of Wallace were found on a cardboard box in the snipers nest and identified by an expert as indisputable.

The CIA's recruitment of Mafia chieftains to help dispose of Cuban Prime Minister Fidel Castro sounds imagined, but it is also a part of American history. Both the CIA and the Mafia relied on each other for survival in the face of the Kennedy administration.

Lyndon Johnson, whose freedom and future were also threatened by the Kennedys, looked to allies in the FBI, CIA, and Mafia to help him. Big Oil, which had a tangible connection to the CIA through Johnson and Oswald's handler, George de Mohrenschildt, was already in the bag for Johnson and vice versa.

Inasmuch as Johnson needed elements from the government and the underworld to help him actuate the plan, they needed him.

Johnson is the key to the Kennedy assassination. Johnson, and only Johnson, had the means to bury the facts.

It is also astounding how many witnesses and those believed intimately connected to the Kennedy assassination met untimely and abnormal deaths. In his recent work, *Hit List*, which contextualized the many bizarre circumstances of deaths surrounding the assassination, Richard Belzer estimated that in the fourteen years following the incident, out of the approximately 1,400 witnesses, seventy have died unnaturally.[8] The odds of this happening has been mathematically calculated as 1 in 715 million trillion trillion.[9] Lyndon Johnson, as a psychopathic serial murderer, is not a pleasant topic to think about for establishment liberals who like to think of him as a belated champion of civil rights, voting rights, and a slew of Great Society programs. In fact, acknowledging the JFK assassination for what it was—a coup d'état—is discrediting to the narrative of the United States as a beacon of democracy, freedom, and justice, as well as a place that is morally superior to banana republics and third-world dictatorships. Establishment conservatives, just like the liberals, choke on that bone in unison.

Historians have found themselves in a prime position to bury the facts. Mac Wallace is absent from the exhaustive four-volume biography of Lyndon Johnson by Robert Caro. Wallace, such an integral piece of the Johnson story, does not get as much as a mention in any of the books. Also missing is any information from Madeleine Brown, Johnson's mistress, who made herself readily available for assassination research over the years. Supplied by Billy Sol Estes, who accused Johnson of eight murders. The phone call Johnson made to Parkland Hospital during the Oswald operation is unaccounted for or simply overlooked.

Even today, the cover-up continues. The newest Nixon tapes are rife with deletions—segments censored by the US government for "national security" reasons. Most of these edits occurred during discussions involving the Bay of Pigs, E. Howard Hunt, and John F. Kennedy. On the White House tape, recorded in May of 1972,

Nixon told White House counsel, "Why don't we play the game a bit smarter for a change. They pinned the assassination of Kennedy on the right wing, the Birchers. It was done by a communist, and it was the greatest hoax that has ever been perpetuated." Nixon is clearly talking about the Warren Commission's conclusion that Oswald was a communist. The Left had tried to blame the Right until the government laid out the "Oswald was a Red" line. Nixon had known since 1963 that Oswald was not a communist but a CIA pawn in the grand conspiracy yoked by Lyndon Johnson and abetted by the mob.

Books like those written by Gerald Posner and Vincent Bugliosi are as threatening to the truth as the Warren Commission. They distort the official record, lay out brass tacks, and throw on a layer of varnish. In a way, Posner and Bugliosi have not only taken the safe but also the smart road. Anyone who asks probing questions, no matter how sound, are dismissed as crackpots. Courageous Americans who have dedicated their lives to seeking the facts of the assassination—citizens like Mark Lane, Vincent Salandria, Robert Morrow, Raymond Marcus, and Mary Ferrell—have earned this flaky distinction. Many who questioned the official story were branded as treasonous. Today, years later, they are tagged by some in the mainstream media as just plain nuts.

It is no wonder Caro chose not to interview important people in Johnson's life, who held convictions and information connecting him to the assassination. Caro was certainly correct in following this avenue if his goals were respect and profit—he has earned both from the literary community. But in terms of spine and veracity, Caro fails.

Bill O'Reilly put up a similar smokescreen in his recent interpretation of the assassination, *Killing Kennedy*.

"This is a fact-based book, so we don't chase any conspiracy theories," O'Reilly said during the book's promotion.[10]

Mr. O'Reilly, pegging Oswald as the lone assassin, knows that the facts are not on his side, so he dodges them. He doesn't register that Oswald was deemed a "rather poor shot" in his last rifle test before the assassination. In the O'Reilly book, Oswald, as a former Marine Corps sharpshooter, "knows how to clean, maintain, load, and aim the weapon."[11] Reinforcing Oswald as a professional marksman, O'Reilly's Oswald shows up at the Sports Drome Rifle Range a week prior to the assassination for target practice, and Sterling Wood, a thirteen-year-old boy, identifies him later to the Warren Commission. O'Reilly uses this testimony to build a case for Oswald's presence at the range.

The testimony of Malcolm Howard Price, however, is absent from O'Reilly's account. Price, a retiree, who sometimes helped out at the rifle range, saw the man who resembled Oswald show up on several occasions. The man whom Price saw drove an old Ford; the real Oswald could not drive a car. Price also testified that he had seen the man show up at the range following the assassination:

MR. PRICE: That's right, I was down there for the turkey shoot we had.
MR. LIEBELER: You saw him at the rifle range that day?
MR. PRICE: Yes.
MR. LIEBELER: Well, the last Sunday before Thanksgiving was after the assassination.
MR. PRICE: It was after?
MR. LIEBELER: Yes. And you saw this man at the rifle range, you saw Oswald at the rifle range after the assassination?
MR. PRICE: I believe I did because that was the last time I went down there.[12]

For reasons unknown, O'Reilly includes Wood's recollection of the Oswald look-alike gathering the bullet casings after each round and putting them in his pocket, a move indicative of a methodical planner. Contrarily, the bullet casings on the sixth floor of the Book Depository were haphazardly left behind.

O'Reilly neglects to mention the paraffin test, which came back negative on the cheek of Oswald and does not mention that the recreations of the shooting with expert marksmen were unsuccessful. The Magic Bullet Theory, which defies logic, science, and sworn testimony, is blindly accepted in *Killing Kennedy*. The book concludes that only three shots were fired in Dealey Plaza—the HSCA's Dictabelt recording test proved that at least six shots had been fired.

Killing Kennedy paints Oswald as frantic following the shooting. "He races to get out of the depository,"[13] writes O'Reilly. This depiction is at odds with every eyewitness who saw Oswald on his way out of the building. When Roy Truly and Officer Marrion L. Baker first confront Oswald immediately after the assassination, Oswald is not on his way out—he is in the second floor cafeteria drinking a soda. When Mrs. Robert Reid later confronts him on the second floor, Oswald is "moving at a very slow pace,"[14] and not racing anywhere.

O'Reilly's version of the assassination mirrors that of the Warren Commission. Both reach faulty conclusions.

"There was not another gunman," O'Reilly recently opined on the talk show, *The View*. "He [Oswald] was the gunman."[15] This assessment is completely erroneous. At least one shot was proven by the HSCA to have come from the grassy knoll.

It is difficult for O'Reilly to assemble the impaired facts of the assassination to support his thesis. It is even harder for him to find a motive for Oswald to kill the president. O'Reilly's Oswald devours literature on Kennedy, likes the president, and wants to be like him. The reasoning that O'Reilly provides for Oswald's actions are an unharmonious home life and a longing to "be a great man."

The real Oswald had credible links to both the CIA and the Mafia, but those would lead to a palpable conspiracy in a pop culture book, which does not want to follow leads. The lack of any plausible reason or evidence that Oswald was about to kill the president leaves O'Reilly with the task of filling in a book with details that lend context to Kennedy's life. We learn about Kennedy as a father, a playboy, and a politician. We learn about his wife Jackie as a fashion idol, an interior decorator, and a jilted wife. We learn nothing about the policies and pacts that led to Kennedy's death.

It is baffling, but *Killing Kennedy* actually develops conspiratorial figures. Lyndon Johnson, whom we know had the motive, means, and opportunity to pull off the assassination, is painted as a ruthless figure by O'Reilly.

"The loneliest man in Camelot wants to be president of the United States," O'Reilly writes of Johnson, correctly assessing him as a desperate man sapped of power.

"What Lyndon wants, above all else, is a return to power," he continues. "He adores power. And he will endure anything to know that heady sensation once again. Anything."[16]

The endurance that O'Reilly refers to is not the important role that the vice president played in the conduct and cover-up of the assassination; it is a speaking engagement in St. Augustine, Florida, to celebrate the founding of the nation's oldest city. This is the power play that O'Reilly believes could help put the power back into LBJ's hands. That is preposterous.

O'Reilly further declaws the vice president by incorrectly assessing his demeanor abroad as an ambassador. To O'Reilly, Johnson enjoys his assignment and begins to accept his designation as vice president:

"In Washington, his craving for authority has many in the White House referring to him as Seward, a reference to Abraham Lincoln's power-hungry secretary of state," writes O'Reilly. "But on the road, Johnson truly does have power. He speaks for the president, but just as often veers off message to speak his own mind, which are moments he relishes."[17]

In fact, Johnson hated the diplomatic missions. Loaded on Cutty Sark, flying from country to country, he begrudgingly accepted what little power was afforded him. He would remember his vice presidency "filled with trips . . . chauffeurs, men saluting, people clapping . . . in the end, it is nothing."[18]

O'Reilly admits that Johnson was also likely to be dropped from the ticket in 1964—and then promptly leaves this Texas-sized insult as if it would not torture Johnson to his dying breath.

Like Caro, O'Reilly does not begin to connect the dots between Johnson's associates and the ways they benefited or survived due to the assassination. Hoover, who had been Johnson's neighbor and friend in Washington for decades, was able to retain his employment as director of the FBI. O'Reilly accurately described the director as a believer in the conspiracy. Of course he was—he knew the plot. O'Reilly actually seizes Hoover's and Johnson's roles in the assassination as an opportunity to cover up the cover-up.

"J. Edgar Hoover said 'I want this investigation,'" O'Reilly said recently. "So, he went to LBJ, then just sworn in as president, and said, 'There's a conspiracy.' Hoover was the first conspiratorialist because he wanted to control the investigation, and if there were a conspiracy to kill the president, that's a federal crime. LBJ gave him the investigation."[19]

In fact, the investigation was brought under federal control to prevent anyone from thinking outside the government's narrative. Hoover and Johnson both needed control over a singular investigation in order to guide the outcome. In a telephone conversation with his attorney, Abe Fortas, in the days following the assassination, Johnson questioned the legality of the Commission and attempted to give its intent a patriotic spin:

LBJ: Let's think along that line now. Can we do this by executive order?

FORTAS: Yes, sir.

LBJ: Do we infringe upon the Congress in any way in doing it? Reflect on them in any way?

FORTAS: No, sir. I think on the contrary, you know all these editorials are saying this would be a shame to have all these investigations. I think the country will think the Congress had started acting wisely for a change.[20]

O'Reilly does not bother to touch on recordings of Hoover and Johnson talking on the telephone about multiple Oswald sightings in Mexico City while they were collecting evidence to convince America that Oswald had worked alone. Even though Hoover knows there is a conspiracy, he also knows it is a part of his job to quash any mention of it.

O'Reilly also acknowledges the connection between the Kennedys and organized crime, but passes off the Mafia's campaign contribution pact as "rumors." In reality, there is more substantial evidence to back up the claim of a Kennedy-Mafia pact than there is to convict Oswald as the killer.

O'Reilly writes as if he knew that there is more to the story, that Oswald was a stooge. In his assessment of Oswald's "friend" George de Mohrenschildt, O'Reilly pegs him as a man who "may" have CIA connections. George de Mohrenschildt was a close friend of George H. W. Bush.

In promoting the book, O'Reilly admitted that de Mohrenschildt in fact *did* have CIA connections. "We couldn't find out this man George de Mohrenschildt with CIA contacts, what he was doing with Oswald," O'Reilly said. "Oswald as I said, loser, lowest rung. This guy [de Mohrenschildt] is an aristocratic Russian with CIA connections. Why was he around? We couldn't really nail that down."[21]

De Mohrenschildt himself admittedly was friendly with and did freelance work for the agency.

O'Reilly also admits to de Mohrenschildt's helping Oswald get a job at Jaggars-Chiles-Stovall, a company that did photographic work for the US government, particularly in relation to photographs taken by U-2 spy planes. This was a topic familiar to Oswald. As a radar technician in the Marine Corps, at Atsugi Naval Air Station in Japan, Oswald was privy to many covert CIA U-2 spy missions.[22]

O'Reilly also neglects to mention de Mohrenschildt's connections to Johnson and several Texas businessmen. Again, the dots are not connected.

Speaking in Budapest, eminent American linguist Noam Chomsky fielded questions about conspiracy theories. When his answer touched upon the energy which, over the years, has gone into finding out who had killed President Kennedy, Chomsky was dismissive.

"Who knows and who cares," he replied. "Plenty of people get killed all the time. Why does it matter that one of them happened to be John F. Kennedy? If there was some reason to believe there was a high-level conspiracy, it might be interesting, but the evidence against that is overwhelming. And after that, it's just a matter of if it happened to be a jealous husband or the Mafia or someone else, what difference does it make? It's just taking energy away from serious issues to the ones that don't matter."[23]

Chomsky mentions overwhelming evidence against a high-level conspiracy, but supplies no evidence to back it up. He fleetingly mentions the Mafia as a potential tie to the assassination—the same Mafia that had, in fact, connected interests with the CIA and many ties to Jack Ruby, the assassin of Lee Harvey Oswald. Oswald had an extensive file, the contents of which were manipulated, maneuvered, and hidden throughout the CIA.

It is important to ask "Why?" when looking into the Kennedy assassination. Why did John and Bobby Kennedy, after living a privileged life, raised by a father who knew how the game was played, suddenly, when power was acquired, attempt to change the game? This question leads to significant events: The firing of Dulles, the crusade against organized crime, the attempt to unseat and neutralize Hoover, the attempt to dismantle the CIA, the initiatives taken against the oil-depletion allowance, the pursuit of unseating Vice President Johnson through the multiple charges brought against him.

Why care about a murder that happened fifty years ago? The Kennedy assassination goes hand-in-hand with the popular distrust of the government that sprung up in the late 1960s. The assassination of Kennedy dug the foundation of distrust; the lies that landed us in Vietnam War and the Watergate break-in cemented it.

In order to win back the trust of the people, it is the government's responsibility to come clean.

When speaking about the Warren Commission, Bobby Kennedy maintained that the conclusions didn't matter. "He said he didn't give a damn whether there was any investigation," Nicholas Katzenbach said. "'What's the difference? My brother's dead.' That's what he would say to me."[24]

Bobby had handed a similar line to news producer Don Hewitt, but the notion that Kennedy didn't care was easily dismissed.

"I never believed that Bobby believed 'What difference does it make?'" Hewitt said. "I've always believed that he knew something he didn't want to share with me or anyone else."[25]

Bobby Kennedy was tortured. He knew that in his attempt to reform the CIA and the FBI, while attempting to disable the Mafia and Lyndon Johnson, something went terribly wrong. Because of Bobby's crusade, his brother was shot and killed in Dallas. Because of the crusade, Bobby himself was killed five years later.

"History is hard to know," wrote Hunter S. Thompson, reflecting on the sixties, "because of all the hired bullshit, but even without being sure of 'history,' it seems entirely reasonable to think that every now and then, the energy of a whole generation comes to a head in a long fine flash, for reasons that nobody really understands at the time—and which never explain, in retrospect, what actually happened."[26]

Comedian Mort Sahl also articulates the spirit of the sixties. Sahl, who worked as a joke writer for John F. Kennedy and later became a Warren Commission critic, had perhaps the best forum to express his opinions: a national television show.

"It isn't any fun to awaken America now," Sahl said on *The Mort Sahl Show*. "It's like walking into a party—everybody's been drunk for 175 years, and you're getting the tab for the liquor. But we've gotta keep this thing going. As I always remind you . . . America is at stake."[27]

NOTES

1. Crenshaw, *Trauma Room One*, 131–32.
2. Ibid., 132–33.
3. Crenshaw, *Assassination Science*, 41.
4. Ibid.
5. "Richard Nixon Jokes About LBJ Killing JFK." February 7, 2012, youtube.com/watch?v=oqTMELBh23g.
6. "King's Son Accuses LBJ of Conspiracy," ChicagoTribune.com (June 20, 1997).
7. Collom and Sample, *The Men On the Sixth Floor*, 167.
8. Belzer, *Hit List*, 279.
9. Ibid.
10. Don Imus, *Imus In the Morning*, October 2, 2012.
11. Bill O'Reilly and Martin Dugard, *Killing Kennedy: The End of Camelot* (New York: Henry Holt and Company, 2012), 152.
12. Warren Commission testimony of Malcolm Howard Price Jr.
13. O'Reilly, *Killing Kennedy*, 265.
14. North, *Act of Treason*, 390.
15. *The View*, October 9, 2012.
16. O'Reilly, *Killing Kennedy*, 145.
17. Ibid., 92.
18. Robert Caro, "The Transition" *The New Yorker* (April 2, 2012).
19. Don Imus, *Imus In the Morning*, October 2, 2012.
20. Beschloss, *Taking Charge*, 50.
21. *The View*, October 9, 2012.
22. Newman, *Oswald and the CIA*, 3–42.
23. "Noam Chomsky Debunks 9/11 and JFK Murder" posted by Adam Phoenix, April 12, 2008, youtube.com/watch?v=m7SPm-HFYLo.
24. Talbot, *Brothers*, 277.
25. Ibid, pg. 308.
26. Hunter S. Thompson, *Fear and Loathing in Las Vegas: A Savage Journey to the Heart of the American Dream* (New York: Vintage, 1998), 67.
27. Kelin, *Praise from a Future Generation*, 328.

CHAPTER TWENTY-ONE

SINKING *LIBERTY*

The JFK assassination opened the door to an even greater crime by Lyndon Johnson, which might be his most egregious: the orchestration of the attack on the *USS Liberty* on June 8, 1967, in which 34 Americans were murdered and 171 others were wounded. It was an attempted murder of 294 Americans and is the type of a crime that puts Lyndon Johnson justifiably in the same league with Adolf Hitler and Joseph Stalin. In fact, McGeorge Bundy would say that in his last days of working at the White House, Lyndon Johnson specifically reminded him of Joseph Stalin.[1]

In a nutshell, Lyndon Johnson coordinated with the Israeli Defense Forces, in particular Israeli military leader Moshe Dayan, to attack an American intelligence ship the *USS Liberty*, sink it, and murder all 294 Americans on board in order to engineer a false-flag pretext, an action made to appear as if it were perpetrated by Egypt. Blaming the attack on Egypt would have given the US cover to attack, bomb, and remove Egypt's Gamal Abdel Nasser, who had drifted into the Soviet camp over the preceding ten years.

In order to understand the attack on the *USS Liberty*, you must first understand "Operation Northwoods," an incredible Joint Chiefs of Staff (JCS) proposal rejected by JFK in 1962 as it reveals the mentality of the Joint Chiefs of Staff in the 1960s.

Operation Northwoods was a diabolical proposal presented to John Kennedy in the spring of 1962. It called for a series of false flag attacks and self-inflicted acts of terrorism by the CIA or the US military which would then be blamed on Cuba that would give the US a pretext to invade Cuba and take out Fidel Castro. In other words, Operation Northwoods called for deceiving the American people into a war with Cuba.

The Northwoods documents are astounding and give deep insight into the Machiavellian thinking of high-level American military brass and intelligence. The National Security papers are revealing:

1. Start rumors (many). Use clandestine radio.
2. Land friendly Cubans in uniform "over-the-fence" to stage attack on base.
3. Capture Cuban (friendly) saboteurs inside the base.
4. Start riots near the base main gate (friendly Cubans).
5. Blow up ammunition inside the base; start fires.
6. Burn aircraft on air base (sabotage).
7. Lob mortar shells from outside of base into base. Some damage to installations.
8. Capture assault teams approaching from the sea or vicinity of Guantanamo City.
9. Capture militia group which storms the base.
10. Sabotage ship in harbor; large fires—naphthalene.
11. Sink ship near harbor entrance. Conduct funerals for mock-victims (may be in lieu of #10).
    a.   We could blow up a U.S. ship in Guantanamo Bay and blame Cuba.
    b.   We could blow up a drone (unmanned) vessel anywhere in the Cuban waters. We could arrange to cause such incident in the vicinity of Havana or Santiago as a spectacular result of Cuban attack from the air or sea, or both. The presence of Cuban planes or ships merely investigating the intent of the vessel could be fairly compelling evidence that the ship was taken under attack. The nearness to Havana or Santiago would add credibility especially to those people that might have heard the blast or have seen the

fire. The United States could follow up with an air/sea rescue operation covered by U.S. fighters to "evacuate" remaining members of the non-existent crew. Casualty lists in U.S. newspapers would cause a helpful wave of national indignation.

Operation Northwoods, which was approved by the entire JCS, even called for creating a terror campaign in the Miami area or even sinking a boatload of actual Cuban refugees!:

"We could develop a Communist Cuban terror campaign in the Miami area, in other Florida cities and even in Washington.

The terror campaign could be pointed at refugees seeking haven in the United States. We could sink a boatload of Cubans en route to Florida (real or simulated). We could foster attempts on lives of Cuban refugees in the United States even to the extent of wounding in instances to be widely publicized. Exploding a few plastic bombs in carefully chosen spots, the arrest of Cuban agents and the release of prepared documents substantiating Cuban involvement, also would be helpful in projecting the idea of an irresponsible government."[2]

Author James Bamford summarized just how deplorable Operation Northwoods was:

"Operation Northwoods, which had the written approval of the Chairman and every member of the Joint Chiefs of Staff, called for innocent people to be shot on American streets; for boats carrying refugees fleeing Cuba to be sunk on the high seas; for a wave of violent terrorism to be launched in Washington, D.C., Miami, and elsewhere. People would be framed for bombings they did not commit; planes would be hijacked. Using phony evidence, all of it would be blamed on Castro, thus giving [General] Lemnitzer and his cabal the excuse, as well as the public and international backing, they needed to launch their war."[3]

Lyndon Johnson's mentality precisely mirrored that of the Machiavellians in the JCS and CIA. LBJ, a master of deception and dirty machinations, would often say that behind every great success was a great crime. It was a motto that he lived his life by.[4]

Peter Hounam, the author of the book *Operation Cyanide: Why the Bombing of the USS Liberty Nearly Caused WWIII* provided evidence that Israel was fully aware that the *USS Liberty* was an American ship and went to great lengths attempting to murder every one of the 294 Americans on the *Liberty*. There is absolutely no way Israel would have intentionally committed this heinous crime against American life and property unless the Israeli Defense Forces had been *given explicit orders from the President of the United States Lyndon Johnson to commit such a crime.*[5]

Hounam demonstrates that the US Strategic Air Command going on full alert *before* Israel attacked the *USS Liberty* at 1:58 p.m. Israeli time, (6:58 a.m. Eastern time, 3:58 a.m. Pacific time) is the smoking gun that proves that the US was fully aware of the impending Israeli attack on the *Liberty* on June, 8, 1967.

Hounam interviewed a retired Air Force pilot, Jim Nanjo, who told him that his strategic (i.e. nuclear) air wing went on full alert sometime between 2 a.m. and 4 p.m. Pacific time, in other words one or two hours *before* Israel attacked the *USS Liberty* at 4 a.m. Pacific (or 7 a.m. Eastern, or 2 p.m. Israeli time). Nanjo said he was awakened by the alarm klaxons "early, early" in the morning.[6]

Nanjo, at the time, was a thirty-year-old pilot in the elite 744 Bomb Squadron of the 456 Strategic Air Wing at Beale Air Force Base which is located near Sacramento, California. He confirmed to Peter Hounam that his plane's nuclear payload was thermonuclear weapons, also known as hydrogen bombs. His unit of six B-52 bombers supported by a group of KC-135 tanker planes meant they could drop their payload pretty much anywhere in the world— Russia being a top target.[7]

Nanjo also said that US strategic (nuclear) airbases were on high alert around the world in places such as Guam, Britain, Spain and other strategic bases in American cities. Nanjo was asked was it a World War III nuclear situation.[8]

"'It was. Yes. Yes,' he said. 'The only thing we were looking for was the go-code, authorized by the National Command Authority. The aircraft commander and myself were the only people [who were authorized] to authenticate the message. We were both waiting for this message to come, which never came.'[9]

"Having arrived at his plane between 2 a.m. and 4 a.m., Nanjo taxied to the end of the runway, where the squadron waited loaded with hydrogen bomb payloads with engines running. Nanjo cannot remember whether they sat for four hours, six hours or even longer, but it was well into the morning before a coded message came through ordering everyone to stand down."[10]

Only the President of the United States could have ordered the strategic air wings to go on high alert all around the world at the same time, and apparently Johnson gave those orders one to two hours before Israel attacked the USS Liberty. In other words, LBJ had to know the attack on the USS Liberty was coming.

Another key incident that indicts Lyndon Johnson in the attack is the incriminating behavior he displayed after being informed that Israel was attacking the ship. The Liberty had miraculously sent out an SOS, known as an emergency flash bulletin, within ten to twelve minutes of being attacked.

The Sixth Fleet in the Mediterranean, after getting the SOS flash bulletin, immediately sent out two separate squadrons of fighter jets to give assistance to the ship. On both occasions the rescue planes were called back. It is documented that on one of the occasions, during a conversation between Defense Secretary Robert McNamara and the Sixth Fleet Commander, Johnson personally got on the radio and roared, "We will not embarrass an ally [Israel]," and ordered the planes turned back.[11]

Miraculously, the Liberty did not sink despite being bombed, napalmed, torpedoed, and machine gunned by the Israelis. Some Israeli pilots, knowing the ship was a well-marked American vessel, dropped their ordinance into the ocean or refused to continue bombing. They were in open insubordination to their Israeli Air

Force superiors and baffled about why they were being asked to sink an American ship.[12]

The *Liberty* suffered a direct hit from a torpedo courtesy of the Israeli Navy but miraculously still did not sink. James Ennes, a *Liberty* survivor and an expert on the subject, estimates that the whole attack lasted an hour and fifteen minutes. Because the *Liberty* had been able to send out an SOS flash bulletin, the world became aware quickly that an American ship was under attack.[13] The attack stopped just before Israel was going to drop commandos onto the *Liberty* and "finish the job," i.e. kill everyone still alive.

The Israeli attack on the Liberty came to an end but did not precipitate a direct attack on Cairo.

LBJ was ready to launch a nuclear attack on Cairo and almost did so, notwithstanding the *Liberty* not sinking. In a 2002 interview with *Liberty* survivor Moe Shafer, Peter Hounam wrote:

> Before the attack he was cleaning the moon-bounce dish and watched as an Israeli plane flew low over the ship taking photographs. He had a direct view of cameras slung from an opening on the underside of the plane and it was confirmation of the testimony of other eyewitnesses that Israel was well aware of the ship's presence.
>
> The second memory from after the attack was much more significant. Moe said he was hurt by shrapnel during the assault.... Unlike most of the injured who had already been taken away to the USS America, he was loaded into a helicopter and flown to the USS Davis, the flagship of Sixth Fleet commander Admiral Martin. The next morning he was sitting on his bunk with two or three other injured men when Martin came in to see them.
>
> Shafer said he seemed to want to tell someone about what had happened before he would be obliged through pressure from above to clam up: 'Not only did Admiral Martin tell me that four jets were on their way to the Liberty with conventional weapons [and were recalled]; he stated that four were on their way to Cairo loaded with nuclear weapons. He stated they were three minutes from bombing them [the Egyptians]. He also said

that the jets could not land back on the carrier with nuclear arms and they had had to land in Athens. He stated this from my bedside while on the Little Rock [the codename of the flagship] after the attack.[14]

Ronnie Dugger in his book *The Life and Times of Lyndon Johnson* tells the story about LBJ having a long and deep conversation with Austrian ambassador, Dr. Ernst Lemberger. LBJ told Lemberger that he was being visited by God in the White House. Dugger:

"Didn't the ambassador think, Johnson asked him, that the Holy Ghost might visit the leader of a very powerful country now that we had nuclear weapons? The ambassador still did not think so, and he told the president he did not. With that, the president told him that he knew the Holy Ghost [God] was making such visitations, because the Holy Ghost was visiting him.

"Really!" the ambassador said, displaying amazement in a manner that conveyed acceptance.

Yes, President Johnson told the ambassador, the Holy Ghost was visiting him around two or three o'clock in the morning at about the time he received reports from Vietnam."[15]

Ambassador Lemberger was quite rattled after talking with LBJ. "He said, What if this got to the Russians, and they decided he was crazy, and they are afraid he's unstable and go into a pre-emptive strike?" reported Clyda Gugenberger, a friend of the ambassador's. Lemberger told her, "If the Soviets think he's completely crazy, they might be forced into doing something."[16]

Keep in mind the above anecdote when examining LBJ's behavior and his approval of the Israeli attack on the *Liberty*. LBJ was playing with nuclear hellfire and his mental instabilities were well known to people who had intimate dealings with him.

Maybe that is why Defense Secretary Robert McNamara—like Bundy considered a "Whiz Kid" and a man of acute intelligence—developed a curious case of amnesia when it came to the *Liberty* "incident." McNamara did not mention the attack in his memoirs or that the Russians had to use the "hotline" with the Americans three times that day. June 8, 1967, was one of the most dangerous and intense days in US military history, yet McNamara would not mention it. According to Peter Hounam: "When I interviewed [McNamara] for a BBC TV documentary and for [my] book, what he said was unbelievable. 'Don't have . . . anything about the *Liberty* on the tape,' he told me after we finished recording, 'because I don't know what the hell happened and I haven't taken the time to find out."[17]

Both Bundy and McNamara were fully aware of how mentally unstable LBJ was and how reckless he was during the Six Day War. Both men knew that nuclear war was on the table at the time of attack on the *Liberty*. Think of Slim Pickens waving his 10-gallon cowboy hat while riding the nuclear bomb down in the movie *Dr. Strangelove*, and one can imagine Lyndon Johnson in his stead.

At the very height of the Cuban Missile Crisis, on Sunday, October 28, 1962, the very day before it was settled, Lyndon Johnson forcefully allied himself with the majority hawks on ExComm (the Executive Committee of the National Security Council), a body of United States government officials assembled to advise the President during the crisis, and told Jack Kennedy that he should bomb, attack or invade Cuba. LBJ favored war with Cuba just hours before Kennedy accepted Khrushchev's offer that resulted in the crisis being resolved without bloodshed. For decades historians have understood just how close the US came to nuclear war with Cuba and Russia. Any US invasion or bombing campaign against Cuba—as LBJ and Curtis LeMay and the war hawks on the Joint Chiefs staff were pushing for—would almost certainly have been met with a nuclear response from the Russians.

If Cuba had launched a nuclear attack on even one American city, then under the "Single Integrated Operational Plan" the USA would have responded with a retaliatory nuclear strike against

Cuba and much of the USSR. LBJ favored a course of actions that would have led to a catastrophic nuclear Armageddon .

Author Peter Hounam also details Lyndon Johnson's mindset in the run-up to the attack on the *Liberty*. Israeli diplomat Eppie Evron, who was close to Lyndon Johnson (who was pro-Israel in the extreme), met with him on May 26, 1967 just before the Six Day War. Evron said:

"Then he went on to say, 'I, Lyndon Johnson, have to get congressional approval if I want to act as President of the United States. Otherwise, I'm just a six-foot-four Texan friend of Israel.' (That description stuck in my memory.) 'But you and I, the two most powerful people in Washington, are going to get Congress to pass another Tonkin resolution.'. . . . I thought, 'He's telling me that Congress is never going to give him permission to use military force.'"[18]

The notations on LBJ's presidential diary for the LBJ-Evron meeting (which lasted from 7:15 p.m. to 8:40 p.m.) on 5/26/67 are notated as "STRICTLY OFF RECORD" (all caps in the diary).

The Gulf of Tonkin was the pretext to get America into a war with Vietnam. The attack on the *USS Liberty*, if it had been successful, was LBJ's pretext to get Congress to justify American military intervention in the Six Day War on the side of Israel. More importantly, Lyndon Johnson wanted to topple Nasser, who had drifted into the Soviet camp, once and for all. Toppling Nasser and controlling all of Egypt was a pill too hard to swallow for Israel alone: LBJ wanted American intervention.

A final side note: within ten days of the attack on the *USS Liberty*, a US Navy Court of Inquiry issued a report on the incident that declared it had all been a tragic case of mistaken identity and that Israel thought it was attacking an Egyptian ship that carried horses. The man who issued this whitewash report was Admiral John S. McCain Jr., the father of current Arizona Senator John McCain. The report was the equivalent of the now discredited Warren Commission report on the JFK assassination; in other words, a cover-up.

It is not enough to rely on only the word of Author James Bamford. He also supplies a list of high-level players who were convinced that Israel *intentionally* attacked the *USS Liberty* with LBJ's approval:

- Lieutenant General Marshall S. Carter, director of the National Security Agency at the time: "There was no other answer than it was deliberate."
- Dr. Louis Tordella, the deputy director of NSA at the time: "I believed the attack might have been ordered by some senior commander on the Sinai Peninsula [where the massacres were taking place] who wrongly suspected that the *Liberty* was monitoring his activities." Tordella also scrawled across the top page of the formal Israeli "mistake" report, "A nice whitewash."
- Major General John Morrison, NSA deputy director of Operations at the time: "Nobody believes that explanation. The only conjecture that we ever made that made any near sense is that the Israelis did not want us to intercept their communications at that time."
- Walter Deeley, the senior NSA official who conducted an internal NSA investigation of the incident: "There is no way that they didn't know that the *Liberty* was American."
- Admiral Thomas H. Moorer, former Chairman of the Joint Chiefs of Staff: "I have to conclude that it was Israel's intent to sink the Liberty and leave as few survivors as possible. Israel knew perfectly well that the ship was American."
- Captain William L. McGonnagle, the *Liberty's* commander: "After many years I finally believe that the attack was deliberate."
- Phillip F. Tourney, president of the *USS Liberty* Veterans Association and a survivor of the attack: "The Israelis got by with cold-blooded, premeditated murder of Americans."
- Richard Helms, Director of Central Intelligence at the time: "Your chapter on the *Liberty* was exactly right."
- George Christian, press secretary to President Johnson at the time: "I became convinced that an accident of this magnitude was too much to swallow."

- Paul C. Warnke, Under Secretary of the Navy at the time: "I found it hard to believe that it was, in fact, an honest mistake on the part of the Israeli air force units. . . . I suspect that in the heat of battle they figured that the presence of this American ship was inimical to their interests."
- Dean Rusk, Secretary of State at the time: "The *Liberty* was flying an American flag. It was not all that difficult to identify, and my judgment was that somewhere along the line some fairly senior Israeli official gave the go-ahead for these attacks."
- David G. Nes, the deputy head of the American mission in Cairo at the time: "I don't think that there's any doubt that it was deliberate. . . . [It is] one of the great cover-ups of our military history."
- George Ball, Under Secretary of State at the time: "American leaders did not have the courage to punish Israel for the blatant murder of its citizens."[19]

The assault on the *USS Liberty* was likely Lyndon Johnson's greatest crime and the blood of the 34 Americans murdered and 171 wounded that day is on LBJ's hands.

NOTES

1. Schlesinger, Arthur M. *Journals:1952-2000*. Pg. 333
2. http://www2.gwu.edu/~nsarchiv/news/20010430/northwoods. pdf. Pretexts to Justify US Intervention in Cuba
3. Bamford, *Body of Secrets*, 82.
4. Brown, Madeleine. *Texas in the Morning*. 92
5. Hounam, *Operation Cyanide*, 7.
6. Ibid.
7. Ibid.
8. Ibid., 11.
9. Ibid.
10. Ibid.

THE MAN WHO KILLED KENNEDY

11. http://hnn.us/article/191
12. https://www.lewrockwell.com/2001/05/eric-margolis/the-uss-liberty-americas-most-shameful-secret/
13. http://www.youtube.com/watch?v=t-ZJEhDfono
14. Hounam, *Operation Cyanide*, 221.
15. Dugger, *The Life and Times of Lyndon Johnson*, 161–62.
16. Ibid., 163.
17. Hounam, *Operation Cyanide*, 16-17.
18. Ibid., 267.
19. James Bamford, response to Steve Aftergood, July 25, 2001, https://www.fas.org/sgp/eprint/bamford.html.

AFTERWORD

When *The Man Who Killed Kennedy: The Case Against LBJ* was published in early November 2013, shortly before the fiftieth anniversary of President John Kennedy's assassination, I underestimated the mainstream media's intention to continue to promulgate the now ridiculous idea that Lee Harvey Oswald was simply a "communist nut" acting alone in the murder of the president. I also underestimated the intention of many in the media to continue to whitewash Lyndon Johnson's background as an amoral lunatic whose depravity and corruption knew no limits.

If anything, *The Man Who Killed Kennedy* understated the case that Lyndon Baines Johnson was a psychopathic killer who may have been responsible for as many as fifty-one deaths. LBJ aide Cliff Carter told LBJ intimate Billy Sol Estes that Johnson was responsible for as many as seventeen murders, including murders to cover-up electoral fraud and corruption. You can add the thirty-four servicemen killed on the *USS Liberty* when it was attacked by the Israeli air force in a military operation in which LBJ authorized an attack on American assets. That LBJ would callously order the death of American servicemen demonstrates the monster that he was. Many would also add the 50,000 Americans killed in Vietnam to the death toll.

At this late date, it's hard for me to believe that anyone with intelligence or objectivity can continue to believe the Warren Commission's ludicrous claim that President Kennedy was assassinated by a lone gunman named Lee Harvey Oswald, and that no conspiracy existed. We now know that Oswald was a US intelligence asset who had worked for both the CIA and FBI and that both agencies lied to the Warren Commission about their previous knowledge of him and his activities.

Important to note are the systematic seizing of witnesses whose testimony bolstered the Commission's conclusions while at the same time ignoring multiple witnesses who contradicted the Commission's version of events. These witnesses provided evidence additional to the fingerprint evidence which tied Johnson's gunman Wallace to the crime, i.e. multiple witnesses described a man who *fit the description* of Wallace, heavyset, and bespeckled, wearing a brown sports coat. It adds to the evidence that Lee Harvey Oswald was not the shooter from the sixth floor of the Texas School Book Depository building; Malcolm Wallace, LBJ's longtime hitman, was.

A witness testimony buried deep within the twenty-six volumes of the Warren Commission report shows why the Warren Commission conclusion that it was possible for Oswald to fire three gunshots from the sixth floor, have *time to hide the rifle and run down four flights of stairs*, only to be seen in the second floor lunchroom of the Texas School Book Depository building approximately 75 seconds after the shooting, is wrong. The letter found in the twenty-six volumes of the Warren Commission report demonstrates why this was impossible. Victoria Adams, a twenty-three-year-old woman who worked on the fourth floor of the building, from where she and co-workers Sandra Styles, Elsie Dorman, and Dorothy May Garner were watching the motorcade, was on the wooden staircase running to the first floor entrance immediately after the shooting and neither saw nor heard Oswald. It is important to note that Adams was running down the stairs in three-inch heels,[1] an impediment to her pace, and that she saw Book Depository superintendent Roy Truly and Dallas police officer Marion L. Baker running up the stairs. Truly and Baker would immediately encounter a calm Oswald in the second floor lunchroom calmly sipping a Coke. The

Warren Commission's depiction of Oswald's hasty flight from the sixth floor to the second was impossible.

When Adams told her story, which negated Oswald's flight from the sixth floor, she was met with resistance. "I do not believe a word you are saying," David Belin, an assistant counsel on the Warren Commission, told Adams dismissively.[2] Years later, Styles and May Garner, who were not called to testify for the Warren Commission, would have corroborated Adams's story.

The Man Who Killed Kennedy has come under fire from several places. Joan Mellen, a professor and proponent of CIA involvement in the assassination of JFK, called my book "absurd." She issues this tag to all the books that find LBJ culpable in the assassination. "I have to say that when you look at all those books, one thing they have in common is the CIA is never mentioned at all."[3] It is clear to me that Professor Mellen has not bothered to read my addition to the Kennedy assassination research canon and has not taken the time to consider that the theories are not mutually exclusive.

Professor Mellen is also in denial about the complex relationship between LBJ and his personal hitman, Malcolm "Mac" Wallace. Mellen believes that the Wallace-Johnson connection was a delusion concocted and solely held by Texas wheeler-dealer, Billy Sol Estes. "I'm talking about self-described Texas wheeler-dealer and con man Billie Sol Estes, who is the source and the only source that I could discover, for the claim that Mac Wallace had been a hit man, henchman, and serial killer under the command of Lyndon Johnson, first as a US senator, and then as a vice president," Mellen said late last year at the annual "November in Dallas" JFK Lancer Group meeting.[4]

Mellen also seeks to discredit LBJ crony Billie Sol Estes who testified under oath and under threat of perjury that he, LBJ, and LBJ Aide Cliff Carter planned the murder of US Agriculture Henry Marshall. Estes also testified that Carter knew of at least seventeen murders LBJ had ordered to cover up voter fraud or corruption. Estes lawyer Douglas Caddy wrote the Justice Department for Estes to testify as to LBJ's direct involvement with eight specific murders including that of John F. Kennedy. Estes *did this after serving his time in prison and after LBJ's death, when there was no conceivable benefit to him.*

I would direct Professor Mellen to the research tying Wallace to LBJ. Respected Texas lawman and Texas Ranger Clint Peoples. The well-regarded Peoples, a detective and former deputy county sheriff, gained a reputation as a man who was fearless and incorruptible. In 1969, Peoples was promoted to Senior Ranger Captain for the Texas Rangers. In 1974, Peoples would be appointed US Marshall for the Northern District of Texas by President Richard Nixon.[5]

Peoples tracked Wallace to his job at a major defense contracting company owned by an LBJ crony. Peoples learned from a Naval intelligence officer that Wallace, three months after receiving a suspended sentence for cold-blooded murder, had received a top security clearance for a new job at Temco, a company that, at the same time of Wallace's initial employment, received a huge defense contract from Lyndon Johnson. Temco, was owned by Lyndon Johnson crony, Texas School Book Depository owner, D. H. Byrd.[6] In Peoples' own words: "I asked who could be so strong and powerful in politics that he could get a clearance for a man like this, and he said 'the Vice President (Lyndon Johnson).'"[7]

Mellen should also examine the words of Austin police investigator Marion Lee, one of the officers who arrested Wallace for the murder. Wallace, who at the time was an economist working a cushy political patronage job at the Department of Agriculture secured for him by LBJ, told Lee that "he was working for Mr. Johnson and [that's why] he had to get back to Washington."[8]

Lucianne Goldberg, an LBJ campaign worker in 1960, had seen Wallace at least three times hanging around LBJ's Presidential Campaign Headquarters at the Mayflower Hotel in Washington, DC, always in the company of LBJ aide and murder conspirator, Cliff Carter.[9] LBJ mistress Madeleine Brown also corroborated the claims of Billy Sol Estes, and added many of her own more intimate details.[10]

Mellen choose to ignore much eyewitness and fingerprint evidence tying Wallace to the sixth floor of the Texas Schoolbook Depository Building. As a JFK researcher, Professor Mellen is either dangerously uninformed or naively ignorant.

* * *

The mainstream media's commitment to the Warren Commission conclusions and the cleaned-up image of LBJ run deep. When CNN booked me for their popular show *Crossfire*, as well as *The Erin Burnet Show*, both shows were quickly canceled under pressure from CNN president emeritus Tom Johnson, who is not coincidently a member of the LBJ Library Board. When I was booked to discuss my book on *Fox and Friends*, Johnson went so far as to call a top executive at Fox to argue that my appearance should be cancelled.[11]

I am gratified at the attention that my book has gotten. I think it is vital that readers whose notion about the period are vague or are interested in ascertaining the truth about Lyndon Johnson and his role in the events of November 22, 1963, review the facts. When Emmy winner Bryan Cranston agreed to make the easy transition from playing murderous, narcissist meth-dealer Walter White on the television hit *Breaking Bad* to portray murderous, narcissist President Lyndon Johnson on Broadway in a one-man play called "All The Way," he told the *New York Times* Sunday Book Review that the book he was most interested in reading was *The Man Who Killed Kennedy: The Case Against LBJ*;[12] this despite the *New York Times* decision not to review the book or include it in the *Times Roundup* along with other JFK fiftieth anniversary literature.

Fox and Friends welcomed me to talk about the book, as did Sean Hannity, Larry King and Glenn Beck. I am convinced the late night radio program *Coast to Coast* allowed me and my coauthor to reach thousands of readers interested in the truth despite a mainstream media blackout. Talk radio has changed the face of political communications because it makes it possible to reach open-minded listeners without having to rely on the big television networks and, say, the *New York Times*. Thank god for Larry Kudlow, Wilcow, the Mancow, Curtis Sliwa, and hundreds of other radio talk show hosts and their producers who have let me make my case about how and why LBJ orchestrated the murder of JFK to a broader audience. The Internet today really makes government cover-ups more difficult, if not impossible. The free flow of researcher evidence and greater access to previously classified federal documents, as well as documents obtained from the Soviet Union after the collapse of the USSR, have also fueled debate about our history and the facts that surround it. Churchill wrote "history is written by the winners." The "winners", i.e. those interests that control our federal government, who set the narrative for the tragic events of November 22, 1963, can now be fairly and reasonably challenged. Thank god for David Freedlander of the *Daily Beast* and Patrick Howley of the *Daily Caller*, *Newsmax*, and dozens of others whose blogs and websites were open-minded enough to help make this book a *New York Times* bestseller and continued to raise questions about President Johnson's legitimacy. I can't help but think that the public relations campaign launched by the LBJ Library is in response to the many reasonable questions that involve Lyndon Johnson, the assassination of John Kennedy, and other questionable historical material regarding LBJ. The noose tightens. So in 2013 the LBJ Presidential Library would launch a PR blitz in which we are asked to forget LBJ's role (and self-dealing) in Vietnam and focus on civil rights legislation that LBJ passed only for political gain rather than principle, as we shall see. The facade that is the public image of Lyndon Johnson is crumbling.

It is easy for elites to dismiss the impact of the supermarket tabloids like the *National Enquirer*, the *Examiner*, and the *Globe* that reach millions of readers each week. Their readers tend to be African Americans, Hispanics, and working class whites. This is elitist error. These people vote and, I can tell you, many buy books.

The *National Enquirer* broke the John Edwards scandal while the mainstream media was oblivious or dismissive. *The National Enquirer's* reporting on the many vulnerabilities of Hillary Clinton as America goes into the 2016 presidential election will foreshadow major issues surrounding Hillary, Bill, and their past in the 2016 contest.

I also suspect that sales of the book were helped by the popularity of Netflix's hit show *House of Cards* in which actor Kevin Spacey plays devious, scheming, evil Vice President Frank Underwood, whose drawl and lust for power are clearly based on LBJ.

* * *

From the beginning of my investigation, I have based the allegations against Lyndon Johnson using the standard law enforcement requirements of motive, means, and opportunity. Lyndon Johnson was fully aware of the fact that Time-Life had a veritable SWAT team of investigative reporters on the ground in Central Texas digging into his ill-gotten and vast financial holdings, as well as his relationship with Texas wheeler-dealer Billy Sol Estes.[13] The LBJ exposé was scheduled for the December 1 cover story of *Life* magazine. Johnson knew the information that nine investigative reporters on the ground were working on had been leaked from the Justice Department of Attorney General Robert Kennedy. The piece, which would have been a death blow for Vice President Johnson, would be spiked by Time-Life owner Henry Luce the minute Johnson became president and the magazine would step in to buy all rights to the Zapruder film and lock it away for eleven years as a favor to the government. The *Time-Life* magazines also began promoting LBJ right after he became president. The Time-Life corporation would vigorously promote the conclusions of the Warren Commission as well.

I have since learned that Johnson faced even more imminent and perhaps dangerous public exposure only *two days* after the assassination. On Sunday, November 24, within 48 hours of the assassination, Drew Pearson, perhaps the most influential newspaperman of his day, had a column due to hit doorsteps up and down the East Coast. The report, a "devastating story" in the words of Pearson, would tie Johnson and his right-hand man Bobby Baker to a $7 billion fighter-jet contract doled out to the Texas firm, General Dynamics.[14] Pearson's column appeared in over 700 newspapers, including his flagship column in the *Washington Post*.

Pearson was breaking the story that on the very morning of the assassination, Baker associate Don Reynolds, in testimony to the Senate Rules Committee, admitted he had seen Baker delivering a suitcase containing $100,000 to Lyndon Johnson, a payoff for steering the defense contract to General Dynamics.[15] Johnson would pressure the Air Force and the Pentagon to take the contract from Boeing and deliver it to his cronies at the General Dynamics headquarters in Fort Worth.[16] Lyndon Johnson actually skated within hours of political and personal annihilation. Pearson would also spike his column and become one of Johnson's biggest presidential boosters.

While it is my assertion that LBJ was the lynchpin of a plot that included the CIA, military intelligence, organized crime, and big Texas oil, none of the plotters' concerns were as immediate as LBJ, who was facing not only removal from the 1964 ticket, but public humiliation, federal prosecution, and, most likely, jail.

* * *

Many fine books have outlined the CIA's animosity towards John Kennedy in the wake of the failed Bay of Pigs invasion and what they viewed as the young president's mishandling of the Cuban Missile Crisis. Overlooked however was Lyndon Johnson's seminal role in the formation of the CIA and his ongoing role throughout the 1950s as the chief congressional appropriator for both the Central Intelligence Agency and the military industrial complex.

Senator Harry Byrd, cousin of LBJ oil crony D. H. Byrd, and Johnson were two of the earliest congressional overseers of the CIA. This unique tie gave Johnson unfettered access and valuable contacts within the agency. As a Senator, Johnson became chair of the Committee on Aeronautical and Space Science. The appointment gave Johnson additional access to the CIA and also military access, chairing both the Senate Preparedness Subcommittee and Aeronautical and Space Science.

Johnson's military ties are well covered by George Michael Evica in *A Certain Arrogance*:

> Throughout the Eisenhower Administration, Senator Johnson was the crucial ally of the military/intelligence coalition as it collected its funding from inside the Pentagon budget, especially after the heavily publicized threats of Soviet space and missile programs. The softest entry for the U.S. intelligence's black budget operations then became the hot areas of "air" and "space," specifically through the U.S. Air Force's programs in research and development, and then through NASA; hence Johnson's 1959–1960 Senatorial pressure on the Eisenhower White House that was topped by his 1960 Senate hearings.

What followed were the "research and analysis" contracts (with their significant intelligence dimensions) for aircraft and space companies and think-tank/development corporations funded by the Pentagon, all of them ostensibly working for the Air Force and the US "aerospace" program. For LBJ and Texas, following his collaboration with the USAF, aerospace research and development (both in the government and business), the Budget Bureau, and with covert intelligence operations hidden inside persistent Pentagon funding appeals, the payoff was staggering: "As President, [LBJ] . . . helped engineer the greatest Pentagon raid on the [US] treasury since World War II. Among other results was a gigantic defense-industry boom for his home state, Texas."

Johnson had elected to join the Budget Bureau/Pentagon/black budget intelligence team in the early 1950s, collecting senatorial power and privilege; then as Vice President he acquired more potency for US space and missile programs, the only areas that really mattered to him and Texas, until he "rode the tiger of military [and covert intelligence] spending into the White House . . . [and] it rode him out."[17]

In *The Man Who Killed Kennedy* I detailed Johnson's financial windfall with Bell Helicopter (a company Lady Bird Johnson's trust held considerable stock in)[18] and the company's defense contracts in the Vietnam War. I have since learned from former Kaman Aircraft employee John Tollenaere that Kaman had *signed* a contract for the procurement of 220 helicopters that was submitted and approved by Congress in 1963. However, as soon as LBJ got into office, the contract was nullified and re-awarded to Bell Helicopter, the US involvement in Vietnam was escalated, and rival Bell thrived.

"Within five days after the assassination of President Kennedy and the succession of Lyndon B. Johnson to the Presidency, the program for procuring UH-2's from Kaman was dropped by the Department of Defense," wrote Kaman Corporation founder, Charles H. Kaman. "Politics had reared its ugly head in a very certain way. The days of the reign of technical proficiency as the primary consideration in aircraft procurements were over."[19]

* * *

Overlooked historically have been Lyndon Johnson's unique relationships with organized crime. Johnson had been the recipient of large campaign contributions from Carlos Marcello, the mob boss who controlled organized crime in both Texas and Louisiana and who the House Select Committee on Assassination's Final Report said was a plotter in John Kennedy's murder. According to author and former Secretary of State and Arizona Governor Richard D. Mahoney in his definitive book *The Kennedy Brothers*, Marcello and his Dallas underboss Joe Civello, had delivered at least $500,000 to LBJ, a transaction handled by Jack Halfen, a convicted tax evader and bagman for the Texas mob.[20]

LBJ was paid as much as $50,000 a year to protect the mob's illegal gambling operations from Johnson-controlled US attorneys in Houston, Dallas, and San Antonio.[21] Given the mob's closeness to Johnson, wiretapped conversations ordered by Attorney General Kennedy in which mob bosses Carlos Marcello and Santos Trafficante, the Florida mob boss, claim responsibility for the Kennedy murder are not inconsistent with Johnson's involvement. Halfen, who delivered cash to LBJ throughout the 1950s and '60s, would later receive a pardon for tax evasion by Johnson. It is not a coincidence that Johnson ordered termination of all wiretaps on organized crime figures put in place by Attorney General Robert Kennedy shortly after taking office.[22]

* * *

It was widely viewed that Lyndon Johnson was steeped in corruption. Billie Sol Estes would later tell his lawyer Doug Caddy that LBJ would do absolutely anything if you gave him enough money.[23] Far beyond mere bribes and kickbacks, LBJ had perfected the art of using the federal government to make himself money. No major defense contract, no major federal appropriation would get through the United States Senate without a bribe to Lyndon Johnson. Sometimes he wanted money for various campaign committees but most of the time he wanted cash. Numerous special interests were required to pay the Johnson-owned radio station inflated prices for radio "advertising" that never really ran. Bobby Baker associate Don Reynolds said that on any given day there were "men bringing suitcases of cash into the Senate Majority Leader's office."

An accomplished attorney in Palm Beach County, Florida put me in touch with a man in suburban Maryland whose veracity the attorney vouched for. The man told me a story his father, a defense contractor, told him. "If you wanted a contract, it was $25,000 just for the meeting to discuss it. My dad met LBJ and Bobby Baker at the Carousel Motel in Ocean City, which Baker (and probably Johnson) owned. Baker warned him in advance that LBJ would not speak. Johnson did not offer his hand and the man didn't shake it. Baker did all the talking. LBJ would deliver a small defense contract to his firm for which Johnson got a $50,000 kickback. Larceny was in Lyndon Johnson's blood."[24]

LBJ and his crony in corruption Bobby Baker would spend their money wisely. Larry Stern, the deputy managing editor of the *Washington Post* in the early 1960s told one of his "leg men" reporters Sterling Seagrave, now a respected author and historian, that "LBJ and Bobby Baker owned an abortion clinic in Puerto Rico called the San Jorge Clinic where they sent congressional secretary staff who got pregnant, posing as "holidays."[25]

An even more stunning example of LBJ's criminality and greed is the story of gold theft from Victorio Peak in New Mexico by the military, President Johnson and, years later, President Richard Nixon. Incredibly, LBJ would steal millions of dollars in "dory" gold bullion that was flown first to Mexico, then to Vancouver for smelting and ultimately to the LBJ ranch. Men loyal to Johnson moved the gold surreptitiously over a period of time.

The huge cache of gold was first discovered by Doc and Ova Noss on November 7, 1937, at Victorio Peak in southern New Mexico, a location now known as the White Sands Missile Range. Most of the gold was old dory bars, crude bars that were made on site. The origin of the wealth might have been Spanish conquistador gold stolen from the Aztecs, Apache gold stolen from Wells Fargo couriers, or Mexican bandito gold caches. Regardless of its history, the US military would soon learn that there were literally billions of dollars in gold in these caverns in New Mexico.

At Victorio Peak there were multiple caverns and multiple sources of gold. The largest cache was huge amounts of gold bricks stacked like firewood. Told he would be given a title to the claim if he made the cache more easily accessible, Doc Noss accidentally dynamited the passageway to the fortune shut.[26] Following Doc's murder at the hands of a disgruntled business partner who was helping finance the removal of the treasure, an underfunded Ova Noss spent years trying to recover the find. By 1955, the US military had learned about the gold cache and forcibly removed her from her claim.

The military found some of the gold bar cache and started to extract it in 1961 while publicly denying that the cache existed. The gold thefts flowed right into the pockets of the generals supervising the extraction and engaging the cover-up of this crime. Major General John Shinkle is reputed to have stolen 700 gold bars from the site.[27] It appears knowledge of the gold was limited to the military until the early '60s when it came to the attention of the Executive Branch. President John F. Kennedy and his attorney general brother Robert F. Kennedy, accompanied by Vice President Lyndon Johnson and LBJ protégé and Texas Governor John Connally would personally inspect the gold on June 5 in 1963. The president's appointment book for June 5th showed that he, Johnson, and Connally arrived at El Paso's Cortez Hotel at 6:30 p.m. "No further activity this date," the appointment log revealed.[28] The public story for the trip was for JFK and LBJ to watch a test firing of missiles at White Sands Missile Range. Their real appointment was with the Victorio Peak gold treasure.

Lyndon Johnson, with his close ties to the military as congressional appropriator for the military industrial complex in the 1950s, was first to learn about the gold in 1963. LBJ was a man very close to top military brass, defense industry lobbyists and defense contractors and was one of just a handful of early congressional CIA overseers; if there were massive amounts of gold to be stolen from military-controlled property, Lyndon Johnson was a man ideally suited to do it.

Tom Whittle had originally researched this incredibly revealing story in a series of superb articles for *Freedom Magazine*. In those articles, Whittle expanded upon what he had unearthed about Lyndon Johnson and other figures central to what appears to be one of the greatest cases of Presidential misconduct in history. In his two-part story, he wrote the following account:

> Lyndon Johnson's name loomed large . . . with various sources claiming that the president was instrumental in the planning and the execution of the removal of the gold.[29]

One of Whittle's informants told him that Johnson and Governor John Connally "headed a team which brought in sophisticated excavation equipment to remove gold. They even brought their own security guards." Another source Whittle located claimed "he had personally interviewed several men who had brought a large load of the Peak's gold to Johnson's [Mexican] ranch." The articles by Whittle documented what many people associated with the history of Victorio Peak had long suspected.[30]

Historian John Clarence states that most of the gold at Victorio Peak was stolen by Lyndon Johnson in the sixties with an additional cache of thirty-seven tons stolen by Richard Nixon over Thanksgiving weekend 1973.[31]

Clarence, in his book *The Gold House: The True Story of the Victorio Peak Treasure: The Lies, The Thefts*, meticulously recreates the great gold heist with extensive sourcing: security guards there at the time; a pilot who flew much of the gold from Mexico to Vancouver where it was re-smelted to erase markers of its origin. Clarence hit the mother lode of documentation when he came in contact with Betty Tucker, the wife of CIA man Lloyd Tucker who had helped LBJ launder the stolen gold. Betty had many documents that confirmed LBJ's role in the massive gold heist at Victorio Peak.

One of the key people Clarence interviewed was a retired CIA agent who was very close to the Kennedys and referred to as "Mr. H." Mr. H. was an ex-Marine who had been recruited into the CIA in the 1950s and was assigned to protect and look after John and Robert Kennedy. Mr. H. did advance work on key Kennedy trips and also served as a CIA assassin. His upline superior was Tracy Barnes, who Mr. H. said supervised "many, many, many" assassinations.[32]

Mr. H. is important because he was assigned to do advance work at Victorio Peak before the Kennedys and LBJ went there on June 5, 1963. Mr. H. had arrived three days earlier to familiarize himself with the scene and assess any security threats. When he got to the Gold Cavern, Mr. H. said, "I saw massive amounts of gold bars, two different sizes."[33] He said they were not shiny gold bars, but rather looked like volcanic ash, consistent with the description of dory gold.

Mr. H. would describe the meeting between the president, the vice president, and the attorney general. He said that those present at the Gold Cavern on June 5, 1963, also included some other members of the Kennedy entourage. "All we have to do is just take it. Bobby, what are you going to do with your share?" LBJ said to Robert Kennedy, according to Mr. H. Bobby replied he didn't need it and didn't want it.

Was the ability to steal the gold an added motive for LBJ to get President Kennedy and his brother out of the way? That Johnson and both Kennedys visited the gold caverns in New Mexico is indisputable. That Johnson could not steal the gold as long as John Kennedy was president is a fact. Incredibly, Johnson was unable to remove all of the gold to Texas and his successor, Richard Nixon, would be able to extract $37 million in gold bullion after becoming president.[34]

Mr. H. said that there was another meeting at Victorio Peak sometime between the June meeting and the JFK assassination in November 1963. Following the assassination, Mr. H. stayed with the CIA until December 1965, and had additional dealings with Lyndon Johnson. In his book, Clarence sheds more light on the curious relationship between LBJ and Mr. H. LBJ had actually directed Mr. H to murder his arch-enemy from the liberal wing of the Texas Democratic Party that would ultimately take control of the Democratic Party from the "Bourbon" Conservative Democrats and hasten their exit to a new born Texas Republican Party by the 1980s. Senator Ralph Yarborough would rally liberals, Mexican and African Americans with the state's weak unions to oppose LBJ and Governor John Connally within the Democratic Party. Indeed JFK's visit to Dallas only weeks later was for the purpose of healing the rift between the Johnson-Connally forces on the right of the Democratic Party, essentially its big business wing and the liberal wing headed by the populist Yarborough. Johnson detested Yarborough.

Mr. H. was asked if there was a time after Kennedy's murder when he spoke to Connally or Johnson about the treasure. He said there was not and that he had done his job and there wasn't anything else he was "asked to perform." He was asked if he had any talks with Johnson while he was president regarding any assignments Johnson asked him to perform. Mr. H. said there were but "none were connected to the Peak." He was asked if Johnson had given him a specific assignment.

> **MR. H:** Yes he did.
> **CLARENCE:** What was that?
> **MR. H:** He wanted me to remove Senator Yarborough.
> **CLARENCE:** When you say remove him . . . ?
> **MR. H:** He wanted Yarborough dead. This was just after the second visit I made to the Peak.
> **CLARENCE:** It wasn't long after that then?
> **MR. H:** That's correct.
> **CLARENCE:** Why did he want Yarborough dead?
> **MR. H:** He said Yarborough had been a thorn in his side forever.
> **CLARENCE:** How did he feel about Connally?
> **MR. H:** Connally was his protégé. He brought him along, schooled him to that point.
> **CLARENCE:** How and when did he want you to remove Yarborough?
> **MR. H:** How and when was my choice.
> **CLARENCE:** But you intended not to?
> **MR. H:** That's correct. I told him I would, though.

Mr. H. was asked why he told Johnson he would do the job when he intended not to do it. He said that he hated Johnson because he suspected that he had something to do with Kennedy's murder and he felt Johnson needed something to worry about, meaning not knowing when he was going to "do" Yarborough, or him for that matter. When the events of the interview were recapped, Mr. H revealed and confirmed that he was with the Central Intelligence Agency and that he left the agency in December 1965. He was asked if he had received orders from the Kennedys during that time period, but before President Kennedy was murdered.

CLARENCE: The second time that you were in the basin did Johnson say anything about what he wanted to do with the gold?
MR. H: Johnson had planned to take this gold, what amount I had no idea how much he planned to take out at that point. He said he was taking that to his domain. Johnson had mentioned his domain many times in the past as his ranch.
CLARENCE: Is his ranch in Texas?
MR. H: Yes, it is . . . Johnson City.
CLARENCE: Did Connally say anything during that day?
MR. H: Very little. Connally was like a little boy following his dad around.
CLARENCE: This thing that Johnson asked you to do [murdering Sen. Ralph Yarborough]; did Yarborough ever become aware of it?
MR. H: No, he did not . . . to my knowledge.

Mr. H. said that he had informed the agency about Johnson's request to have him assassinate Senator Yarborough. He said that he had advised Tracy Barnes. He said, "Tracy was my immediate." The subject of the conversation between Mr. H. and Johnson involving Yarborough was on the interview videotape, but not all of that particular conversation. Later, Mr. H. said that when Johnson asked him to kill Yarborough, he replied, "You are the President, my President, and your wish is my command." Mr. H. claimed that he liked Yarborough and he had no intention of harming him. During the same conversation he claimed that Johnson said, "Bobby Baker has been part of the family since we were kids, but that son-of-a-bitch could bury me. You might as well include him."[35]

Betty Tucker, wife of CIA man Lloyd Tucker, said that her husband was a close friend of Lyndon Johnson. LBJ in 1969 was seen by a security guard camping for about ten days at Victorio Peak and with the finest excavation equipment. Note this is after LBJ had left the presidency. Lloyd told his wife that LBJ had made dozens of trips to Victorio Peak; other witnesses have described visits by John Connally and Lady Bird Johnson there. Lloyd Tucker's job was to help Lyndon Johnson launder perhaps billions in stolen gold.[36]

Others mentioned as helping LBJ with his gold extraction project were Cliff Carter, a very key longtime LBJ aide who was his political director and important bag man and also Congressman Earle Cabell, who had been the mayor of Dallas at the time of the JFK assassination. Earle Cabell was the brother of Gen. Charles Cabell, one of the CIA men fired by JFK after the Bay of Pigs fiasco. In addition to being CIA, Gen. Cabell was an Air Force general who nurtured a fabulous hatred of the Kennedys. The Cabell brothers were hardcore Texas "Bourbon" Democrats and longtime LBJ loyalists.

In his successful effort to steal and launder the Victorio Peak gold, Lyndon Johnson set up a corporation called the LaRue Corporation. A prominent El Paso attorney Ray Pearson set up the corporation for LBJ and John Connally.[37] The incorporation date of the LaRue Corporation was December 5, 1967, the same time period that very unpopular President Lyndon Johnson was seriously considering not running for re-election (announced on March 31, 1968).

In his stunning book, John Clarence includes an affidavit from investigator Charles Berg, dated 8/28/81, of a Mexican man who had knowledge of LBJ's gold theft operation which continued after LBJ left the presidency:

According to [deleted], former President Lyndon B. Johnson bought a very large ranch named "Las Pampas" from Miguel Aleman, a former president of Mexico. [Deleted] said that occurred while LBJ was President.

The ranch was in the state of Chihuahua, near the towns of Camargo and Jimenez. [Deleted] said that Johnson bought the ranch in order to secure a very large amount of gold he brought in from the United States.

The gold was flown in, [deleted] stated two months after LBJ ended his term of office. He described the aircraft used as a big airplane, with four engines. He said it was propeller-driven.

[Deleted] said he was from that area and had spent much time there. He said the fact of the gold being brought there was common knowledge in the area around Camaro.[38]

* * *

Many have questioned how Lyndon Johnson could have put his closest protégé and right hand man John Connally in mortal danger by having him ride with JFK in the presidential limousine in the Dallas motorcade . Indeed, Johnson maneuvered desperately to get Connally moved to the vice-presidential car and substitute his archenemy Yarborough in the presidential vehicle. Senator George Smathers said in his memoirs that JFK complained to him prior to the trip about an effort by LBJ to get first lady Jacqueline Kennedy to ride in the vice presidential car, an idea JFK flatly rejected.[39] Shortly before Kennedy's death in the motorcade LBJ would visit the president's hotel room and try again to convince him to have Connally and Yarborough swap places. Again, JFK refused, and Johnson stormed from the room after a shouting match.[40] The outburst was so loud that first lady Jacqueline Kennedy expressed to her husband that Johnson "sounded mad."[41]

Perhaps this explains LBJ's taciturn behavior from the moment the presidential motorcade left Love Field for Dealey Plaza. An earlier rain had subsided, giving way to sunny skies. The crowds were large and friendly, yet LBJ stared straight ahead and never cracked a smile or waved to the crowds as did Lady Bird, Senator Yarborough, the Connallys, and the Kennedys. LBJ would actually tell Robert Kennedy, "of all things in life, this [campaigning] is what I enjoy most."[42] Normally, the gregarious Johnson would wave his hat, pose and wave to the crowd and shout "howdy," but on this day he seemed non-expressive and focused.

New 3-D imaging analysis and more sophisticated photographic analysis now show without question that LBJ ducked to the floor of his limousine before the first shots were fired.[43]

* * *

As I have traveled the country talking about this book, many have asked me how "respected" historians like Robert Caro, Robert Dallek, Douglas Brinkley and Doris Kearns Goodwin could have missed both Johnson's ties to his longtime hit man Malcolm "Mac" Wallace and Johnson's complicity in the murder of JFK. In fact, I have learned that these historians have all served as paid consultants to the LBJ Presidential Library. All were named as "consultants" in a press release from the LBJ Presidential Library.[44] A call to the public information officer at the LBJ Library in Austin confirmed that all four "consultants" were compensated for their contribution to the LBJ Library renovation project.[45] How can someone be an objective biographer of Lyndon Johnson when they are on the payroll of a taxpayer-financed institution whose mission it is to burnish Johnson's image and erase his many misdeeds and excesses? At what point does an "author" come a "historian," particularly absent any degree in the subject? Doris Kearns Goodwin most likely had an adulterous affair with Lyndon Johnson.[46] LBJ asked Goodwin to marry him and expressed jealously about her other suitors.[47] How can she be expected to give us an objective view of the man Attorney General Robert Kennedy called "mean, bitter, vicious, an animal in many ways?"[48]

It is indisputable that President Lyndon Johnson turned to exchange winks with his longtime crony, Congressman Albert Thomas, only seconds after being sworn in aboard Air Force One. Lady Bird Johnson broke into a broad grin as LBJ repeated the final words of the oath. Indeed, the famous photograph of Johnson and Thomas exchanging winks was found in the archives of the LBJ Library, with the notation "never to be released" written on the reverse.[49]

* * *

Rather than speculation or conjecture, I have tied LBJ to the murder of John Kennedy through the fingerprint of Johnson's longtime hitman Mac Wallace. Wallace's ties to Johnson beginning in the early 1950s are undeniable. Johnson cronies would bail Wallace out of jail when he was indicted for first degree murder and Johnson's personal attorney John Cofer would defend Wallace in the murder trial. Federal records show that Senator and later Vice President Lyndon Johnson would arrange for political appointee-status patronage jobs for Wallace at the US Agriculture Department and Texas Ranger Clint Peoples would confirm that Johnson would arrange the Wallace employment at Temco, the defense contractor owned by oilman and Johnson crony D. H. Byrd. As reported previously, Wallace inconveniently left a 34-point match fingerprint on a cardboard box in the hastily fashioned snipers nest on the sixth floor of the Texas School Book Depository building. Eyewitness testimony also tied Wallace to the sixth floor both before and immediately after the shooting. One man would describe seeing someone matching the description of Wallace including his "horn-rimmed glasses" both in the window on the sixth floor and later bolting the building for a late model Rambler.

On November 22, 1963, forty-five-year-old amateur photographer Charles Bronson stood atop a concrete pedestal on the southwest corner of Dallas's Main and Houston Streets. As Bronson awaited the motorcade, he accidentally filmed video of three figures moving in the windows of the depository building six minutes before the assassination.[50] Robert Hughes also captured the same figures.[51] Other witnesses added detail to these figures. Richard Carr, a steelworker, was on the seventh floor of the new courthouse building under construction on the corner of Houston Street in Dealey Plaza. From his vantage point, Carr had a clear view of the depository, located just south and west of the new courthouse building, and of the motorcade's passage onto Elm Street.

As the presidential motorcade approached, Carr noticed someone moving on the sixth floor. The man, who Carr initially thought was an agent of the Secret Service or the FBI, wore a brown sports coat, a tie, and heavy, horn-rimmed glasses.[52] Mrs. Carolyn Walther, watching the motorcade from Houston Street close to the Elm Street turn, also saw the man. Walther, who could not see the man's face due to his height and her vantage point, noticed he was in the company of another individual. The other man, wearing a white shirt, was holding a rifle.[53] Ruby Henderson, standing on Elm Street, also saw the two men, one wearing a dark shirt, one wearing a white shirt. Henderson would later tell the FBI that the man wearing the white shirt "had dark hair and was possibly a Mexican, but could have been a Negro as he appeared to be dark-complexioned." Henderson noticed that the man in the dark shirt was taller than the other individual.[54] Arnold Rowland, given the opportunity to tell his story to the Warren commission also *saw the dark-skinned man* and the man with the rifle. Rowland told the Commission's junior counsel Arlen Specter that the FBI had intentionally omitted references in his statement of the dark-skinned man and "they didn't pursue it. I mean, I just mentioned that I saw him in that window. They didn't ask me, you know, if this was at the same time or such. They just didn't seem very interested in that at all." It is important to also note that Specter's early questioning of Rowland, focused on his education, eyesight, and employment was geared towards discrediting Rowland.[55]

Johnny Powell, serving three days at the Dallas County Jail, had a clear view of the sixth floor, where he and other inmates also saw the *dark skinned man and the man with the rifle.*[56] According to Stanley Kaufman, a lawyer of Jack Ruby who also had a client jailed at the time of the assassination, the inmates were told by the jailers that the motorcade would be passing by and many were watching from the windows.[57] "I did tell Mrs. Stroud [Martha Joe Stroud, assistant US attorney] that I thought it might be helpful to the Commission to know that there were people in jail who saw the actual killing," Kaufman said in testimony to the Warren Commission.[58] No inmates were called to testify.

Shots rang out in Dealey Plaza as the presidential motorcade made its way down Elm. Richard Carr heard one shot from "small arms, a pistol" followed by "three shots in succession" which came from the picket fence on the grassy knoll. From his experience with the Fifth Ranger Battalion in World War II, he recognized the shots as from a high-powered rifle.[59]

Following the gunfire, James Worrell, who had hitchhiked to Love Field earlier in the day to see the president's arrival and then stood at the corner of Elm and Houston, made his way to the rear of the Depository. Worrell saw the man wearing the brown sports coat fleeing from the back door. The man ran with his back to Worrell, who did not see the man's face.[60]

Richard Carr also saw the man with the brown coat fleeing from the depository in the company of two other men, one *"real dark-complected."* The men got into a blue and white Nash Rambler station wagon and started north down Houston.

Dallas Deputy Sheriff Roger Craig saw the Rambler turn onto Elm from Houston. The driver of the rambler was "very dark complected, had real dark short hair, and was wearing a thin white-looking jacket." Craig heard someone whistle and witnessed a white male in his mid-twenties run down from the area of the depository and get into the Rambler.[61] Ironically, one of the first to dig the FBI reports out of the twenty-six volumes of the Warren

Commission documents was James T. Tague, who reported them in his book *LBJ and the Kennedy Killing*. Tague was the man whose cheek was grazed by a stray bullet in Dealey Plaza on November 22, 1963, and whose exposure of that fact forced the government to concoct the so-called "Single-bullet theory." Tague, who was a straight-shooting Texan of uncommon integrity, decency, and patriotism, would die on February 28, 2014.

That five different witnesses would all say they saw a dark-complected man in the window of the sixth floor would become far more significant when Loy Factor's story became known. Loy Factor was a Chickasaw Indian and a crack shot recruited for the assassination compact by Mac Wallace and paid $10,000 for his services.

In their compelling book, *The Men on Sixth Floor* Glen Sample and Mark Collom report that Factor verified the descriptions of the two men in the window of the depository; he was one of them, the dark complexioned man in the white shirt.[62] Mac Wallace was the man in the brown sports coat with the horn-rimmed glasses. Factor validated his story with three startling, detailed revelations. One was that the shooters escaped through the loading dock at the back of the depository. The loading dock, later removed, was the same from which James Worrell saw Wallace fleeing. Factor also said that the shooters used a station wagon as their mode of transportation, mirroring the claims of at least four witnesses.

In his third and most revealing recollection, Factor gave the odd detail of a table saw stationed on the sixth floor. The random memory of the table saw was verified by Harold Norman, an employee of the Depository. Loy's recollections were compelling because they did not come from a man looking for money or recognition; they were issued from an old man, a diabetic amputee wracked with maladies, for the most part confined to a bed, whose admissions were issued as a dying man's penance. Loy Factor was particularly dark complexioned for a Native American.

Other witnesses added evidence to the case that Wallace was the shooter. Marvin Robinson, driving his Cadillac westbound on

Elm, also saw the "light-colored station wagon" and the "white male" who "came down the grass-covered incline between the Depository building and the street and entered the station wagon."[63] Robinson's employee, Roy Cooper, backed up Craig and Robinson's claim of the Rambler and the man running down the incline from the building.[64]

Many witnesses of the assassination, including Richard Carr, Ruby Henderson, Carolyn Walthers, Johnny L. Powell and Charles I. Bronson, were not called to testify before the Commission. Carr, who lived his life on the run due to multiple threats and attempts on his life, was never at peace in his mission to spread the truth about the assassination. Immediately after telling the FBI what he had witnessed, Carr reported multiple anonymous phone calls telling him to "get out of town." Terrified, Carr fled to Montana where, on one occasion, he would find dynamite wired to the ignition of his car. A subsequent attempt to shoot him in Montana was thwarted by a local policeman. When called to testify for New Orleans District Attorney Jim Garrison, two assailants would attack him in the Crescent City. Although suffering from a stab wound, Carr was armed and killed one of the two assailants, shooting him three times. The other attacker fled. Richard R. Carr was the man who could ID Malcolm "Mac" Wallace.[65]

* * *

The Man Who Killed Kennedy linked LBJ to the assassination of President Kennedy as well as ten other *well-documented* murders enacted to protect his Senate seat, cover up corruption, and hide his greed and his adulterous, debauched lifestyle. These do not include the additional murders that LBJ aide Cliff Carter told Johnson intimate Billy Sol Estes that Johnson was responsible for or the thirty-four American servicemen who died on the *U.S.S. Liberty*. If Lyndon Johnson perceived someone was a threat to him, he would order a murder like you or I would order a ham sandwich. I have since learned of additional butchery that can be tied to the mad Texan.

Dr. George Cimochowski is a retired open heart surgeon who has held academic and/or clinic positions at the Medical College of Virginia, University of Chicago, Harbor-UCLA Medical Center and Cornell University Medical Center. Last year, he was honored as Penn State University's Alumni of the Year.

In 1968, Dr. Cimochowski was starting his medical career, working as an intern at DC General Hospital. During one night shift, Secret Service agents entered the hospital pushing a stretcher on which a shapely, young blonde woman lay. Dr. Cimochowski, who was working alone with the help of a black female nurse, was summoned by one of the agents. "Come here," the agent said. "I need you to go over there and pronounce that woman dead."

However, the agents would not let Dr. Cimochowski within 30 feet of the stretcher. Curious about the cause of her death, he began asking questions. "Don't ask questions," an agent fired back. "Listen to me. I'll have you fired by sun-up if you don't pronounce her dead."

Dr. Cimochowski, noting the anger and serious intention of the agent, signed the paperwork. The agents then took the woman and the paperwork away.

"There was no evidence that she was ever there," Dr. Cimochowski said. "But I was told that there was some relation between the dead woman and Lyndon Johnson."[66]

* * *

Some readers found my depiction of Lyndon Johnson the man as stunning. Johnson was a course, crude, loudmouthed bully with an insatiable appetite for cigarettes, alcohol, and women. Far from the civil rights-crusading statesman that the media likes to portray, Johnson was epically corrupt, greedy, vain, manipulative, ambitious, vindictive, and nasty. LBJ was a sadist who enjoyed the discomfort of the people who worked for him and reveled in being viciously abusive to his rabidly loyal staff. Richard Nixon captured this description during a commercial break while he was a guest on the television program *Crossfire* with Pat Buchanan in 1982:

> **BUCHANAN:** I think maybe we can get through LBJ in that period.
> **NIXON:** Oh yes, I can do that.
> **BUCHANAN:** Ok
> **NIXON:** You know there is this terrible book out on him, this Caro book.
> **BUCHANAN:** I know it, by . . . uh . . . George Reedy. Is it Reedy's book?
> **NIXON:** No
> **BUCHANAN:** Oh, no, this new Caro book.
> **NIXON:** It gets a rave review by Clifton Fadiman in Book-of-the-Month. Unbelievable. Shit, it makes him feel like a goddamn . . . animal. Of course . . . *He was.*[67]

Noted researcher Jon Hopwood knows a ninety-year old African American man who worked in the White House in the 1960s. The employee told Hopwood about the time he went into the Oval Office and "LBJ was banging a woman in the closet. When I [Hopwood] expressed astonishment, he looked at me like I was incredibly naive. I got the FEELING that this wasn't out of the ordinary. . . . He didn't go into any details. What could he say? I think the door was open to the closet, whatever "closet" means. . . . I was astonished that LBJ would be screwing with doors unlocked, and he [the former White House employee] looked at me like I was a foolish boy."[68]

A Capitol Hill police officer in the late-fifties and early sixties who preferred to remain anonymous but for purposes of this story we will call "Ed," has many memories of Senator Lyndon Johnson's primordial behavior. Johnson "was a tough guy, was a bull," said Ed and added that LBJ "walked like a bull, big long steps" with behavior and manners reminiscent of "Genghis Khan."

One night in 1959, Ed and another Capitol Hill police officer, while on patrol, walked into a Capitol office and discovered Lyndon Johnson on top of his secretary, screwing her missionary style on a couch. "Get the fuck out!" screamed Johnson.

"Ed" said months later, probably in 1959 or early 1960, LBJ was suffering from heart attack symptoms. Because LBJ did not want the public spectacle of an ambulance picking him up, the cop, his partner, and Lady Bird had to steady a shaky LBJ while riding down a senator-only elevator to LBJ's Lincoln car that was waiting outside. LBJ, remembering the secretary incident, said to the cop "You again, Ed!"—the cop laughed recounting the story five decades later. Ed recalled that every time he ran into Johnson after the incident, he was met with an evil eye. [69]

Johnson even found a way to desecrate the USS *Sequoia* a presidential yacht that serviced Presidents from Herbert Hoover to Jimmy Carter, with masturbatory excess: "Lyndon Johnson would put a film projector on this table and come up here and watch certain risqué movies," said boat owner Gary Silversmith, "reportedly in a robe and in his underwear so he was relaxed and alone, and they would sail to Mount Vernon."[70]

The devil's handshake aside, even LBJ's motives in pushing a civil rights agenda after becoming president were formed with malice. Johnson had been the leader of the segregationist "Southern Block" in the Senate until 1957. That year he led the Senate to pass a watered-down civil rights bill to which LBJ would add a poison pill; citizens who violated the law would be tried before state, not federal, juries. No all-white jury in the South would convict a white man of violating this new law. The thus toothless bill was passed to burnish LBJ credentials for the 1960 Presidential race and ease opposition to him from Northern liberals and the growing Negro element in the Democratic party. Eleanor Roosevelt herself would denounce LBJ's ploy as "fakery."[71]

Johnson's ultimate embrace of civil rights is a classic example of a man doing the right thing for the wrong reasons. Johnson, upon seizing the presidency quickly became convinced that Attorney General Robert Kennedy would challenge him for the 1964 Democratic nomination. "I believe that Bobby is having his governors jump on me," LBJ can be heard plaintively wailing to his attorney Abe Fortas in his White House tapes, "and he's having his mayors, and he's having his nigras, and he's having his Catholics. And he's having them just systematically, one after the other, each day."[72] Johnson's embrace of civil rights was meant to blunt this challenge as well as giving him cover for his rapid expansion of the Vietnam War. It also helped end some of the messy details regarding what had happened in Dallas. Johnson's embrace of civil rights was not a moral question; it was a crude political calculation. What Johnson would tell his cronies was simple: "I'll have them niggers voting Democratic for two hundred years."[73]

"That was the reason he was pushing the bill," said Robert MacMillan, an Air Force steward who was present during the conversation. "Not because he wanted equality for everyone. It was strictly a political ploy for the Democratic Party. He was phony from the word go."[74]

Johnson had no personal empathy or regard for African Americans. In a White House meeting with Alabama Governor George Wallace, LBJ would order the bantam governor to "make those G--damned niggers act right and calm the hell down!"[75]

Nor was Johnson's family particularly sensitive to the issue of race. *New York Times* bestselling author Ronald Kessler, who has broken multiple national stories regarding political use of the Secret Service, reported on the actions of LBJ's seventeen-year old daughter while campaigning for her father in 1964. On one stopover in Florida, Luci Baines Johnson was having a tantrum because she could not find her manservant during a crowded airport landing. She turned on MacMillan, an Air Force steward, with a vengeance. "She said, 'Damn you. You go find my nigger right now,'" MacMillan said. Playing dumb, Macmillan asked for a description of the man.

She screamed again. 'Find my nigger.' People around were smiling. She drew her hand back as if she was going to slap me. I said, 'Miss Johnson, I don't think that would be a good idea.' She said, 'Dammit, I'll find him myself.' This was the attitude of those people who were championing civil rights."

This is the same Luci Baines Johnson who would, according to The *New York Times*, spearhead a campaign by the LBJ Presidential Library in 2014 to reappraise the Johnson presidency but for the Vietnam War. Asked how her father would ultimately be judged, Luci Baines responded: "I think that's something the historians will look at. But can you think of where we would be without Lyndon Johnson? If we had not passed a civil rights bill? Think of what we would be like if Daddy hadn't signed that bill."[76] Clearly, Ms. Johnson is more sensitive about civil rights and the equality and dignity of black people than she was in 1964.

Johnson pushed the bill, but in reality, he had little to do with drafting the legislation. Unlike the puffed up, baloney-filled revisionist history by Robert Caro, which places LBJ on the front lines, strategizing and plotting morning to night on the Civil Rights agenda, LBJ put little more than pen to paper once the legislation was ready to sign. "We did give him regular reports on the progress of civil rights over at the Tuesday morning breakfasts," said Hubert Humphrey. "But the president was not put on the spot. He was not enlisted in the battle particularly. I understand he did contact some of the senators, but not at our insistence."[77]

In April of 2014, the Lyndon Baines Johnson Presidential Library would host a "Civil Rights Summit" which President Barack Obama would attend along with former Presidents George Bush and Jimmy Carter. The purpose of the so called "summit" was to divert attention from Johnson's disastrous escalation of the Vietnam war in which 50,000 Americans would die and emphasize LBJ's passage of the 1964 Civil Rights Bill, despite the fact that LBJ had led the opposition in the Congress to every civil rights bill from 1937 to 1957. Indeed Lyndon Johnson spent much of his congressional career ruthlessly killing one civil rights and anti-lynching bill after another with an efficiency very similar to the way he murdered witnesses to his epic corruption. It was only in 1957 when Lyndon Johnson was pointedly told by *Washington Post* publisher Phil Graham and aide Jim Rowe that he, LBJ, had better pass some sort of civil rights bill if he was going to have even a shot at being acceptable to northern liberals as the Democratic nominee for president in 1960, something that LBJ had been lusting after for decades. LBJ wanted the White House so bad "his tongue was hanging out," said a top LBJ aide.[78] They said that it was "Armageddon for LBJ": either pass a civil rights bill or you will never be palatable to the Democratic nominating base. In 1957, LBJ was not acting out of a Mother Theresa-like concern for the well being of black citizens. In 1960, Johnson would tour the South attacking GOP nominee Richard Nixon for being a member of the NAACP and for supporting Eisenhower's bayonet-point integration of the schools in Little Rock, Arkansas. While Kennedy would court Black voters in the north, LBJ would assure white southerners that JFK was serious about civil rights. At the same time many of the Texas oil men whose politics were closer to Nixon's knew LBJ would still be Senate Majority Leader if the Kennedy-Johnson ticket lost and could be most vindictive about their cherished oil depletion allowance. At about the time of the LBJ Libraries Civil Rights Summit Katie Couric aired an interview in which the grown daughters of President Johnson claimed that if LBJ was alive today he would care about the ban on gay marriage as a "civil rights issue" because "he believed deeply in social justice."[79] This is pure hokum, part of a misguided PR effort to burnish Johnson's public image. In fact, documents reveal that LBJ had his aide Bill Moyers order the FBI to investigate whether his other top aide Jack Valenti was gay, and have the FBI seek to identify gays on the staff of his 1964 Republican opponent Barry Goldwater so they could be outed because LBJ's own Chief of Staff Walter Jenkins had been arrested in a Washington DC men's room for lewd conduct with another man.[80]

* * *

Johnson particularly enjoyed abusing, humiliating, and embarrassing those who worked for him. Indeed, his National Security Advisor, Mac Bundy, likened Johnson to Hitler and Stalin.[81] Even Bill Moyers confided to other Johnson aides that he thought his boss was mentally ill.[82]

A troubling aspect of LBJ's personality was his taste for sadism. A speechwriter for Vice President Hubert Humphrey, Norman Sherman, recalled this behavior for the *Washington Post.* "In 1967, he invited Humphrey, then his vice president, to his ranch. He insisted they hunt deer, which Humphrey disliked. When they spotted a buck, Johnson gave Humphrey a rifle and ordered him to shoot. The president than taunted Humphrey, "Bobby Kennedy got two." He found a second deer and directed Humphrey to kill again. Later, he sent deer sausage and antlers to Humphrey, knowing that the antlers were not likely to be mounted nor the sausage eaten. That is not greatness. It is not even decency."

Nowhere can Johnson's depravity be better seen than in the tape recording of his telephone call to newly widowed Jackie Kennedy. LBJ actually said he wanted to be the "daddy" to the two children whose father he has just murdered. The incident is covered well in Randall Wood's *LBJ: Architect of American Ambition:*

During his first five weeks in office, Johnson called Jackie numerous times. Instinctively, awkwardly, he attempted to make what Hubert Humphrey referred to as "cowboy love" to her. A conversation the first week in December was typical: "Your picture was gorgeous. Now you had that chin up and that chest out and you looked so pretty marching in the front page of the *New York Daily News* . . . well," LBJ said, "I just came, sat in my desk and started signing a log of long things, and I decided to I wanted to flirt with you a little bit. . . . Darling, you know what I said to the Congress

—I'd give anything in the world if I wasn't here today. . . . Tell Caroline and John-John I'd like to be their daddy!"[83]

Ironically, both Lyndon Johnson and his 1960 presidential competitor Richard Nixon would attempt to bed the glamorous Jackie, although Nixon would try to do so before Kennedy's death.[84]

Critics of the Warren Commission like to single out Arlen Specter as a particular target of abuse. Specter, an extremely intelligent, tough, and abrasive prosecutor, was essentially handed the conclusions of the FBI (three shots, all from behind, with Lee Harvey Oswald as the only participant) and told to justify them. Specter's mission was complicated by a fourth bullet, which indisputably hit the curb next to twenty-seven-year-old car salesman James Tague. Specter now had an extra bullet to account for, which gave rise to the cockamamie 'Single Bullet Theory' in which Specter now argued that one bullet hit the curb, one bullet caused seven, nonfatal wounds in both Kennedy and Governor John Connally, and one bullet fatally hit Kennedy in the head. What is not known is that Specter pressed for copies of the X-rays and photos taken at Parkland Hospital and the Bethesda Medical Center but was overruled by the full Commission. Specter also sought to question President Lyndon Johnson under oath and was again overruled by Commission Chairman Earl Warren.

* * *

One cannot examine the actions of the Secret Service on November 22, 1963, without concluding that the Service stood down on protecting President Kennedy. Indeed, the 120-degree turn into Dealey Plaza violates Secret Service procedures, because it required the presidential limousine to come to a virtual stop. The reduction of the president's motorcycle escort from six police motorcycles to two and the order for those two officers to ride *behind* the presidential limousine also violates standard Secret Service procedure. The failure to empty and secure the tall buildings on either side of the motorcade route through Dealey Plaza likewise violates formal procedure, as does the lack of any agents dispersed through the crowd gathered in Dealey Plaza. Readers who are interested in a comprehensive analysis of the Secret Service's multiple failures and the conspicuous violation of longstanding Secret Service policies regarding the movement and protection of the president on November 22, 1963, should read Vince Palamara's *Survivor's Guilt: The Secret Service and the Failure to Protect.* The difference in JFK Secret Service protection and its adherence to the services standard required procedures in Chicago and Miami would be starkly different from the arrangements for Dallas.

Palamara established that Agent Emory Roberts worked overtime to help both orchestrate the assassination and cover up the unusual actions of the Secret Service in the aftermath. Roberts was commander of the follow-up car trailing the presidential limousine. Roberts covered up the escapades of his fellow secret servicemen at The Cellar, a club in downtown Ft. Worth, where agents, some directly responsible for the safety of President Kennedy during the motorcade, drank until dawn on November 22. He also ordered a perplexed agent Donald Lawton off the back of the presidential limousine while at Love Field, thus giving the assassins clearer, more direct shots and more time to get them off. Also, although Roberts recognized rifle fire being discharged in Dealey Plaza, he neglected to mobilize any of the agents under his watch to act. To mask the inactivity of his agents, Roberts, in sworn testimony, falsely increased the speed of the cars (from 9–11 mph to 20–25 mph) and the distance between them (from five feet to 20–25 feet).[85]

No analysis of the Secret Service's actions on the day of the assassination can be complete without mentioning that Secret Service director James Rowley was a former FBI agent and close ally of FBI Director J. Edgar Hoover, as well as a crony of Lyndon Johnson. Hoover was one of Johnson's closest associates. The FBI Director would take the unusual step of flying to Dallas for a victory celebration in 1948 when Johnson illegally stole his Senate seat through election fraud. Johnson and Hoover were neighbors in the Foxhall Road area of the District of Columbia. Hoover's budget would virtually triple during the years LBJ dominated the appropriations process as Senate Majority Leader. Rowley was a protégé of the director and one of the few men who left the FBI on good terms with Hoover. Rowley's first public service job in the Roosevelt administration was arranged for him by LBJ. The neglect of assigning even one Secret Service agent to secure Dealey Plaza, as well as cleaning blood and other relatable pieces of evidence from the presidential limousine immediately following the assassination, seizing Kennedy's body from Parkland Hospital to prevent a proper, well-documented autopsy, failing to record Oswald's interrogation—all were important pieces of the assassination deftly executed by Rowley.

*　*　*

Many Americans wonder why Robert Kennedy took no action against Lyndon Johnson if he suspected the vice president's complicity in the murder of his brother. In fact, we now know that Johnson was concerned that Robert Kennedy would object to his immediate ascendancy to the presidency. The very fact that Johnson would worry about something so constitutionally preordained virtually proved Johnson's fear that Kennedy would see through his role in the murder. I now believe that Johnson's call to Robert Kennedy to obtain the wording of the presidential oath was an act of obsequiousness to test Kennedy as well as an opportunity to twist the knife in Johnson's bitter rival. We now know that the "oath" aboard Air Force One was purely symbolic; the US Constitution elevates the vice president to the presidency automatically upon the death of the president. Johnson's carefully arranged ceremony in which he insisted that Jackie Kennedy be present was to put his imprimatur and that of the Kennedys, on his presidency. Additionally, Judge Sarah T. Hughes, who administered the oath, had recently been blocked from elevation on the federal bench by

Attorney General Robert Kennedy. This impediment would be removed under President Lyndon Johnson.

Robert Kennedy knew his brother was murdered by a domestic conspiracy and, at a minimum, suspected that Lyndon Johnson was complicit. Kennedy would tell his aide Richard Goodwin, "there's nothing I can do about it. Not now."[86] In essence, Kennedy understood that with both the FBI and the Justice Department under the control of Lyndon Johnson and Kennedy nemesis J. Edgar Hoover, there was, indeed, nothing he could do immediately. While numerous biographers describe RFK as being shattered by the murder of his brother, Robert Kennedy was not so bereaved that it prevented him from seeking to maneuver his way onto the 1964 ticket as vice president. Indeed, RFK had Jackie Kennedy call Johnson to lobby for Bobby's selection. Johnson declined, far too cunning to put Bobby in the exact position that he had maneuvered John Kennedy into three years previous.

Robert Kennedy knew that only by becoming president could he avenge his brother's death. After lukewarm endorsements of the Warren Commission's conclusions between 1963 and 1968, while campaigning in the California primary, RFK would be asked about his brother's murder. In the morning, he mumbled half-hearted support for the Warren Commission conclusions but asked the same question that afternoon he would tell a student audience in Northern California that if elected he would reopen the investigation into his brother's murder. Kennedy's highly regarded press secretary Frank Mankiewicz would say he was "shocked" by RFK's comment because he had never said anything like it publicly before. Mankiewicz and Robert Kennedy aide Adam Walinsky would ultimately conclude that JFK had been murdered by a conspiracy, but to my knowledge, neither understood the full involvement of LBJ. Only days after Robert Kennedy said he would release all the records of the Kennedy assassination, the New York Senator would be killed in an assassination eerily similar to his brother's, in which there are disputes, even today, about the number of shooters and the number of shots.

The morning after Robert Kennedy was murdered a distraught Jacqueline Kennedy called close friend New York socialite Carter Burden, and said "They got Bobby, too," leaving little doubt that she recognized that the same people who killed her husband also killed her brother in law.[87]

* * *

A number of readers have asked why Lyndon Johnson would decide not to run in 1968 after seizing power in 1963. In fact, Johnson *did* run, only to be nicked badly in the New Hampshire presidential primary by Senator Eugene McCarthy. Johnson withdrew only when White House-commissioned polling showed he would suffer a chain of ignominious defeats in the Democratic primaries, fueled by opposition to the Vietnam War. That McCarthy would demonstrate Johnson's weakness was a blow to the president but Robert Kennedy's decision to join the race drove Johnson wild. It was bad enough that he was giving up the crown, but he hated the idea of handing it over to the usurper. McCarthy's strong showing brought RFK into the race where they would split the anti-war vote. LBJ maneuvered to secure the nomination for his Vice President Hubert Humphrey, nailing down most of the big city machines and utilizing the power of federal patronage to secure the delegates Humphrey needed. After Robert Kennedy's murder, Johnson even toyed with the idea of reentering the 1968 presidential contest, contemplating a surprise helicopter landing to seize the nomination at the 1968 Democratic Convention in Chicago. LBJ would jettison this plan only when Chicago Mayor Richard M. Daley told the president that he doubted he could maintain order in such an event.[88]

As I traveled the country promoting my book, I was asked by many people, 'What are you trying to prove here? Lyndon Johnson is dead. He can't be prosecuted. What is the point of this other than an academic exercise?' Here is the point: The government does not always tell us the truth. In fact, the government seldom tells us the truth. If *ONE* citizen understands by reading my book that everything the government says must be regarded with a healthy dose of skepticism, then I will have achieved my goal.

Perhaps the best analysis comes from former federal prosecutor and US Attorney David Marston, who wrote to me, "You have viewed the JFK assassination through the prism of a murder investigator's first question, *cui bono* (who benefits)? The shocking answer is that the primary suspect has been hiding in plain sight for fifty years: LBJ."

NOTES

1. Warren Commission testimony of Victoria Elizabeth Adams.
2. Tague, James. *LBJ and the Kennedy Killing,* 215.
3. Vimeo.com/85810171. "Webster Tarpley and Joan Mellen Break the Set On Trendy CIA-Sponsored Conspiracy Theories."
4. http://joanmellen.com/wordpress/2013/12/03/speech-delivered-by-joan-mellen-at-the-annual-meeting-of-november-in-dallas-for-the-jfk-lancer-group-november-23-2013/#more-562
5. Simkin, John. "Clint Peoples" *Spartacus, http://www.spartacus. schoolnet.co.uk/JFKpeoples.htm*
6. Collum and Sample, *The Men On the Sixth Floor,* 167.
7. Ibid.
8. *Dallas Times Herald,* April 6, 1984, n.p.
9. Adler, "The Killing of Henry Marshall," 236.
10. Brown, Texas in the Morning, 120.
11. Conversation with top FOX executive, by the author.
12. "Bryan Cranston: By the Book," *The New York Times* (December 5, 2013).
13. Janney, Peter. *Mary's Mosaic,* 307.

14. Shenon, Philip. *A Cruel and Shocking Act: The Secret History of the Kennedy Assassination*, 43–44.

15. Lasky, Victor. *It Didn't Start With Watergate*, 144.

16. Janney, Peter. *Mary's Mosaic*, 307.

17. Evica, George Michael. *A Certain Arrogance: U.S. Intelligence's Manipulation of Religious Groups and Individuals in Two World Wars and the Cold War and the Sacrificing of Lee Harvey Oswald*, 215.

18. Livingston, *The Radical Right*, 37.

19. Kaman, Charles. *Kaman: Our Early Years*, 159–160.

20. Mahoney, Richard D. *The Kennedy Brothers: The Rise and Fall of Jack and Bobby*, 39.

21. Shaw, Mark. *The Poison Patriarch*, 199.

22. Earley, Pete. *Witsec: Inside the Federal Witness Protection Program*, 47.

23. Email exchange with Douglas Caddy, November 2013

24. Interview with author.

25. Sterling Seagrave, email to Robert Morrow, April 17, 2014.

26. Guy Garcia, "In Search of a Legend," *People* 38, no. 11 (September 14, 1992).

27. Clarence, John. *The Gold House: The True Story of the Victorio Peak Treasure, Volume II The Lies, the Thefts*, 180.

28. http://spot.acorn.net/jfkplace../09/fp.back_issues/32nd_Issue/jfk_texas.html

29. Whittle, Tom. *Freedom Magazine*, June, 1986, 29.

30. Clarence and Whittle, *The Gold House Volume III*, xviii.

31. Clarence and Whittle, "Jim McKee and LBJ's $2.2 Billion Windfall," chap. 29 in vol. 3 of *The Gold House*.

32. Robert Morrow, interview with "Mr. H," October, 2013.

33. Clarence and Whittle, *The Gold House*, 193.

34. Chapters 21–25 in vol. 2, "The Lies, the Thefts," in Clarence and Whittle, *The Gold House*.

35. Clarence and Whittle, *The Gold House Volume II*, 198–99.

36. Ibid., 200.

37. Ibid., 252.

38. Ibid., 254.

39. Nelson, *LBJ: The Mastermind of the JFK Assassination*, 373.

40. Zirbel, *The Texas Connection*, 191.
41. Manchesteer, *Death of a President*, 82.
42. Smith, *Bad Blood*, 180.
43. Edward Baker, "LBJ Dallas 3D Analysis," http://www.youtube.com/watch?v=DIOChRBrkrI.
44. "LBJ Presidential Library Re-Opening After $10 Million Renovation," *PRNewswire* (December 19, 2012).
45. Author conversation with Public Information Officer. February, 2014.
46. This can be concluded after reading the article by Sally Quinn, "A Tale of Hearts and Minds," *Washington Post* (August 25, 1975). Privately she has admitted this to friends.
47. Ibid.
48. Shesol, *Mutual Contempt*, 3.
49. Interview with Robert Morrow.
50. Tague, *LBJ and the Kennedy Killing*, 366.
51. Ibid.
52. Clay Shaw trial testimony of William Carr.
53. FBI report of Carolyn Walther.
54. FBI report of Ruby Henderson.
55. Warren Commission testimony of Arnold Rowland.
56. Tague, *LBJ and the Kennedy Killing*, 366.
57. Ibid.
58. Warren Commission testimony of Stanley Kaufmann.
59. Clay Shaw trial testimony of William Carr.
60. Warren Commission testimony of James Worrell.
61. Warren Commission testimony of Roger Craig.
62. Collom and Sample, *The Men on the Sixth Floor*, 54–68.
63. Bugliosi, *Reclaiming History*, 890.
64. Ibid.
65. Tague, *LBJ and the Kennedy Killing*, 36.
66. Interview with Dr. George Cimochowski.
67. *Crossfire*, CNN, November, 1982.
68. Interview with Jon Hopwood.
69. Interview with "Ed."
70. Gavin, Patrick. "LBJ Watched 'Risque' Films." *Politico*. November 18, 2010 http://www.politico.com/click/stories/1011/lbj_watched_risqu_fi lms.html

71. Shesol, Jeff. *Mutual Contempt*, 14.
72. Ibid., 361.
73. Walsh, Kenneth T. *Air Force One: A History of the Presidents and Their Planes*, 81.
74. Ibid.
75. Letter from Warren Trammell (son of Alabama political operative/George Wallace right-hand man, Seymore Trammell to Robert Morrow. Aug 28, 2013.
76. Nagourney, Adam. "Rescuing a Vietnam Casualty: Johnson's Legacy." Feb. 15, 2014.
77. Clay Risen, "The Shrinking of Lyndon Johnson," New Republic, *http://www.newrepublic.com/article/116404/lbjs-civil-rights-act-arm-twisting-was-myth?a&utm_campaign=tnr-daily-newsletter&utm_source=hs_email&utm_medium=email&utm_content=11893031*
78. Smith, Jeffrey. *Bad Blood*, 54.
79. "LBJ's Daughters on Civil Rights Act at 50," interview of Lucy Baines Johnson and Lynda Bird Johnson Robb by Katie Couric, April 11, 2014.
80. Jack Shafer, "The Intolerable Smugness of Bill Moyers," *Slate. com*, February 20, 2009.
81. Schlesinger, Arthur M. *Journals: 1952–2000*, 333.
82. Renshon, Stanley Allen. *The Psychological Assessment of Political Candidates*, 102.
83. Woods, Randall. *LBJ: Architect of American Ambition*, 423.
84. Gardner, David. "Jackie AND Bobby Kennedy 'BOTH had affairs with ballet dancer Rudolf Nureyev', new book based on interviews with Jackie's 'closest confidantes' claims." *Daily Mail*. January 15, 2014.
85. Written testimony of Emory Roberts.
86. Talbot, *Brothers*, 303.
87. Interview with Amanda Burden.
88. http://www.nbcchicago.com/blogs/ward-room/LBJ-Planned-To-Fly-To-Chicago-To-Seize-1968-Nomination-199870531.html

BIBLIOGRAPHY

Books

Andersen, Christopher P. *Jackie After Jack: Portrait of the Lady*. New York: William Morrow, 1998.

Azzoni, Meg, John F. Kennedy Jr. to Meg Azzoni, *11 Letters: Memories of Kennedys & Reflections on His Quest*, p. 52.

Baker, Bobby, and Larry L. King. *Wheeling and Dealing: Confessions of a Capitol Hill Operator*. New York: Norton, 1978.

Baker, Russell. *Family of Secrets*. New York: Bloomsbury, 2009.

Bamford, James. "USS Liberty: Cover up." July 19, 2002. http://hnn.us/article/191

Belzer, Richard. *Hit List*. New York: Skyhorse Publishing, 2013.

Beschloss, Michael R. *Reaching for Glory: Lyndon Johnson's Secret White House Tapes, 1964–1965*. New York: Simon & Schuster, 2001.

Beschloss, Michael R. *Taking Charge: The Johnson White House Tapes, 1963–1964*. New York: Simon & Schuster, 1997.

Bonanno, Bill. *Bound by Honor: A Mafioso's Story*. New York: St. Martin's Press, 1999.

Briody, Dan. *The Halliburton Agenda: The Politics of Oil and Money*. Hoboken: John Wiley & Sons, 2004.

Brown, Madeleine. *Texas in the Morning: The Love Story of Madeleine Brown and President Lyndon Baines Johnson*. Baltimore: Conservatory, 1997.

Bryce, Robert. *Cronies: Oil, the Bushes, and the Rise of Texas, America's Superstate*. New York: PublicAffairs, 2004.

Bugliosi, Vincent. *Reclaiming History: The Assassination of President John F. Kennedy*. New York: W. W. Norton & Company, 2007.

Caro, Robert A. *Master of the Senate: The Years of Lyndon Johnson*. New York: Alfred A. Knopf, 2002.

Caro, Robert A. *Means of Ascent*. New York: Alfred A. Knopf, 1990.

Caro, Robert A. *The Passage of Power*. New York: Alfred A. Knopf, 2012.

Chambers, G. Paul. *Head Shot: The Science Behind the JFK Assassination*. Amherst: Prometheus, 2010.

Chatterjee, Pratap. *Halliburton's Army: How a Well-Connected Texas Oil Company Revolutionized the Way America Makes War*. New York: Nation, 2009.

Clarence John. Whittle, Tom. *The Gold House Trilogy: Volume II*. Soledad Publishing; 2013

Clark, John E. and George Berham Parr. *The Fall of the Duke of Duval*. Austin: Eakin, 1995.

Collier, Peter, and David Horowitz. *The Kennedys: An American Drama*. New York: Summit, 1984.

Collom, Mark and Glen Sample. *The Men on the Sixth Floor*. Garden Grove: Sample Graphics, 1997.

Crenshaw, Charles A. *Trauma Room One: The JFK Medical Coverup Exposed*. New York: Paraview, 2001.

Dallek, Robert. *Lone Star Rising: Lyndon Johnson and His Times, 1908–1960*. New York: Oxford University Press, 1991.

Dallek, Robert. *Flawed Giant: Lyndon Johnson and His Times, 1961–1973*. Oxford, UK. Oxford University Press; 1999

Davis, John H. *The Kennedys: Dynasty and Disaster*. New York: Shapolsky, 1992.

Davis, John H. *Mafia Kingfish: Carlos Marcello and the Assassination of John F. Kennedy*. New York: McGraw-Hill, 1989.

Day, James M. *Captain Clint Peoples: Texas Ranger*. Waco: Texian, 1980.

Deitche, Scott M. *The Silent Don: The Criminal Underworld of Santo Traffi-cante Jr*. Fort Lee: Barricade, 2007.

Douglass, James W. *JFK and the Unspeakable: Why He Died and Why It Matters*. New York: Touchstone, 2008.

Dugger, Ronnie. *The Politician: The Life and Times of Lyndon Johnson*, New York. Norton & Co; 1984

Earley, Pete. *Witsec: Inside the Federal Witness Protection Program*, New York, Bantam Books; 2003

Epstein, Edward Jay. *Inquest: The Warren Commission and the Establishment of Truth*. New York: Viking, 1966.

Estes, Pam. *Billy Sol King of Texas Wheeler-Dealers*. N.p.: Noble Craft, 1983.

Evica, George Michael. *A Certain Arrogance*. Indiana, Xlibris; 2006

Fetzer, James H. *Assassination Science: Experts Speak out on the Death of JFK.* Chicago: Catfeet, 1998.

Fuhrman, Mark. *A Simple Act of Murder*, New York, HarperCollins; 2008

Fulsom, Don. "Richard Nixon's Greatest Coverup: His Ties to the Assassination of President Kennedy." *Crime Magazine.* October 15, 2003

Fulsom, Don. *Nixon's Darkest Secrets.* New York: St. Martin's Press, 2012.

Gentry, Curt. *J. Edgar Hoover: The Man and His Secrets.* New York: Norton, 1991.

Giancana, Antoinette, John R. Hughes, and Thomas H. Jobe. *JFK and Sam: The Connection between the Giancana and Kennedy Assassinations.* Nashville: Cumberland House, 2005.

Giancana, Sam and Chuck Giancana. *Double Cross.* New York: Warner, 1993.

Giancana, Sam. *Mafia: The Government's Secret File on Organized Crime.* New York: Collins, 2007.

Gilbride, Richard. *Matrix for Assassination: The JFK Conspiracy.* Bloomington: Trafford Publishing, 2009.

Gillon, Steven M. *The Kennedy Assassination—24 Hours After: Lyndon B. Johnson's Pivotal First Day as President.* New York: Basic, 2009.

Goldfarb, Ronald L. *Perfect Villains, Imperfect Heroes: Robert F. Kennedy's War Against Organized Crime.* New York: Random House, 1995.

Goulden, Joseph C. *Truth Is the First Casualty: The Gulf of Tonkin Affair: Illusion and Reality.* Chicago: Rand McNally, 1969.

Green, George Norris. *The Establishment in Texas Politics: The Primitive Years, 1939–1957.* Norman: University of Oklahoma, 1984.

Haldeman, H. R., *The Ends of Power.* New York: Dell Publishing, 1978.

Haley, J. Evetts. *A Texan Looks at Lyndon: A Study in Illegitimate Power.* Canyon, Texas: Palo Duro Press, 1964.

Kaman, Charles. *Kaman: Our Early Years.* Penn. Curtis Publishing, 1985

Hepburn, James G. *Farewell America.* [Vaduz]: Frontiers, 1968.

Hersh, Burton. *Bobby and J. Edgar: The Historic Face-Off Between the Kennedys and J. Edgar Hoover That Transformed America.* New York: Carroll & Graf, 2007.

Hersh, Seymour. *The Dark Side of Camelot*, New York. Back Bay Books; 1997

Heymann, C. David. *RFK*, New York: Penguin Books; 1998.

Hilty, James W. *Robert Kennedy: Brother Protector.* Philadelphia: Temple University Press, 1997.

Janney, Peter. *Mary's Mosaic: The CIA Conspiracy to Murder John F. Kennedy, Mary Pinchot Meyer, and Their Vision for World Peace*. New York: Skyhorse Publishing, 2012.

Kantor, Seth. *The Ruby Cover-up*. New York: Kensington Publishing, 1978.

Kelin, John. *Praise from a Future Generation: The Assassination of John F. Kennedy and the First Generation Critics of the Warren Report*. San Antonio: Wings, 2007.

Kennedy, Robert F. *The Enemy Within*. New York: Harper, 1960.

Kessler, Ronald. *Inside the White House*. New York. Pocket Books; 1995

Kessler, Ronald. *The Sins of the Father: Joseph P. Kennedy and the Dynasty He Founded*. New York: Warner, 1996.

Lane, Mark. *Rush to Judgment: A Critique of the Warren Commission's Inquiry*. Greenwich: Fawcett Publications, 1967.

Lasky, Victor. *It Didn't Start With Watergate*. New York, E.P. Dutton; 1997

Leamer, Laurence. *The Kennedy Women: The Saga of an American Family*. New York: Villard, 1994.

Lincoln, Evelyn. *Kennedy and Johnson*. New York: Holt, Rinehart and Winston, 1968.

Livingstone, Harrison Edward and Robert J. Groden. *High Treason: The Assassination of JFK & the Case for Conspiracy*. New York: Carroll & Graf, 1998.

Livingstone, Harrison. *The Radical Right And The Murder of John F. Kennedy*, Indiana, Trafford; 2006

Mahoney, Richard. *The Kennedy Brothers: The Rise and Fall of Jack and Bobby*. New York, Arcade Publishing; 1999

Manchester, William. *The Death of a President*. New York: Harper & Row, 1963.

Marrs, Jim. *Crossfire: The Plot That Killed Kennedy*. New York: Basic Books, 1989.

Margolis, Jay. *Marilyn Monroe: A Case for Murder*. Bloomington: iUniverse, 2011.

Martin, Ralph. *Seeds of Destruction*, New York: Putnam Publishing Group; 1995

McClellan, Barr. *Blood, Money & Power: How L.B.J. Killed J.F.K*. New York, New York: Skyhorse Publishing, 2011.

McClelland, Edward. "LBJ Planned to Fly to Chicago to Seize 1968 Nomination." *NBC 5 Chicago*. March 25, 2013

McPherson, Harry. *A Political Education*. Boston: Little, Brown and Company, 1972.

Middendorf, John William. *Potomac Fever: A Memoir of Politics and Public Service*. Annapolis: Naval Institute Press. 2011.

Miller, David. *The JFK Conspiracy*. Indiana, iuniverse; 2002

Moldea, Dan E. *The Hoffa Wars: The Rise and Fall of Jimmy Hoffa*. New York: Shapolsky, 1993.

Moldea, Dan E. *The Killing of Robert F. Kennedy*. New York: W. W. Norton & Company, 1995.

Morrow, Lance. *The Best Year of Their Lives: Kennedy, Johnson, and Nixon in 1948, Learning the Secrets of Power*. New York: Basic, 2005.

Nellor, Edward K. *Washington's Wheeler Dealers: Broads, Booze & Bobby Baker!* New York: Bee-Line, 1967.

Nelson, Phillip F. *LBJ: The Mastermind of the JFK Assassination*. New York: Skyhorse Publishing, 2011.

Newcomb, Fred T. and Perry Adams. *Murder from Within: Lyndon Johnson's Plot Against President Kennedy*. Bloomington: AuthorHouse, 2011.

Newman, John M. *Oswald and the CIA*. New York: Carroll & Graf, 1995.

North, Mark. *Act of Treason: The Role of J. Edgar Hoover in the Assassination of President Kennedy*. New York: Carroll & Graf, 1991.

Novak, Robert, *The Prince of Darkness*, New York, Three Rivers Press; 2008

O'Connor, Thomas H. *The Boston Irish: A Political History*. Boston: Northeastern University Press, 1995.

O'Donnell, Kenneth P. and David F. Powers. *"Johnny, We Hardly Knew Ye": Memories of John Fitzgerald Kennedy*. Boston: Little, Brown and Company, 1972.

O'Neill, Gerard. *Rogues and Redeemers: When Politics Was King in Irish Boston*. New York: Crown, 2012.

O'Reilly, Bill and Martin Dugard. *Killing Kennedy: The End of Camelot*. New York: Henry Holt and Company, 2012.

Phipps, Joe. *Summer Stock: Behind the Scenes with LBJ in '48*. Fort Worth: Texas Christian University Press, 1992.

Pietrusza, David. *LBJ vs. JFK vs. Nixon: The Epic Campaign That Forged Three Presidencies*. New York: Union Square Press, 2008.

Ragano, Frank and Selwyn Raab. *Mob Lawyer*. New York: Scribners, 1994.

Rappleye, Charles, and Ed Becker. *All American Mafioso: The Johnny Rosselli Story*. New York: Doubleday, 1991.

Renshon, Stanley Allen. *The Psychological Assessment of Presidential Candidates*, New York. Routledge; 1998

Royko, Michael. *Boss: Richard J. Daley of Chicago*. New York: Dutton, 1971.

Russo, Gus. *The Outfit: The Role of Chicago's Underworld in the Shaping of Modern America*. New York: Bloomsbury, 2001.

Schlesinger, Arthur M. *Robert Kennedy and His times*. Boston: Houghton Mifflin, 1978.

Schlesinger, Arthur. *Journals: 1952–2000*. New York. Penguin; 2007

Schwarz, Ted. *Joseph P. Kennedy: The Mogul, the Mob, the Statesman, and the Making of an American Myth*. Hoboken: John Wiley & Sons, 2003.

Scott, Peter Dale. *Deep Politics and the Death of JFK*. California. University of California Press; 1996

Shaw, Mark. *The Poison Patriarch*, New York, Skyhorse Publishing; 2013

Shenon, Philip. *A Cruel and Shocking Act: The Secret History of the Kennedy Assassination*, New York, Henry Holt and Company. 2013

Shesol, Jeff. *Mutual Contempt: Lyndon Johnson, Robert Kennedy, and the Feud That Defined a Decade*. New York: W. W. Norton, 1997.

Smith, Jeffery K. *Bad Blood: Lyndon B. Johnson, Robert F. Kennedy, and the Tumultuous 1960s*. Bloomington: AuthorHouse, 2010.

Stans, Maurice. *The Terrors of Justice*. New York, Everest House; 1978

Steiger, Brad and Sherry Hansen. *Conspiracies and Secret Societies: The Complete Dossier*. Canton: Visible Ink Press. 2006.

Stockton, Bayard. *Flawed Patriot: The Rise and Fall of CIA Legend Bill Harvey*. Washington: Potomac, 2006.

Summers, Anthony. *The Arrogance of Power: The Secret World of Richard Nixon*. New York: Penguin, 2000.

Summers, Anthony. *Official and Confidential: The Secret LIfe of J. Edgar Hoover*, New York. G.P. Putnam's Sons; 1993

Tague, James. *LBJ and the Kennedy Killing*, Trine Day publishing; 2013

Talbot, David. *Brothers: The Hidden History of the Kennedy Years*. New York: Free, 2007.

Thomas, Evan. *Robert Kennedy: His Life*. New York: Simon & Schuster, 2000.

Thompson, Hunter S. *Fear and Loathing in Las Vegas: A Savage Journey to the Heart of the American Dream*. New York: Vintage, 1998.

Tosches, Nick. *Dino: Living High in the Dirty Business of Dreams*. New York: Doubleday, 1992.

Turner, William and Jonn Christian. *The Assassination of Robert F. Kennedy*. New York: Carroll and Graf, 1978.

Ventura, Jesse. *American Conspiracies: Lies, Lies and More Dirty Lies That that the Government Tells Us*. New York: Skyhorse Publishing, 2010.

Waldron, Lamar and Thom Hartmann. *Legacy of Secrecy: The Long Shadow of the JFK Assassination*. New York: Counterpoint Press, 2008. Print.

Waldron, Lamar and Thom Hartmann. *Ultimate Sacrifice: John and Robert Kennedy, the Plan for a Coup in Cuba, and the Murder of JFK*. New York: Carroll & Graf, 2005.

Waldron, Lamar. *Watergate: The Hidden History*, Berkeley: Counterpoint, 2012.

Walsh, Kenneth. *Air Force One: A History of the Presidents and Their Planes*. New York. Hyperion Books, 2004

Wasserman, Jack and Paul L. Winings. *Carlos Marcello, Petitioner, v. Robert F. Kennedy, Attorney General of the United States, et al. U.S. Supreme Court Transcript of Record with Supporting Pleadings*. N.p.: Making of the Modern Law Print Edition, n.d.

Weiner, Tim. *Enemies: A History of the FBI*. New York: Random House. 2012.

Wills, Garry and Ovid Demaris. *Jack Ruby*. New York: New American Library, 1968.

Witcover, Jules. *85 Days: The Last Campaign of Robert Kennedy*. New York: Putnam, 1969.

Woods, Randall. *LBJ: Architect of American Ambition*. Massachusetts. Harvard University Press; 2007

Zirbel, Craig I. *The Texas Connection: The Assassination of John F. Kennedy*. Scottsdale: Wright & 1991.

Newspaper and Magazine

Adler, Bill. "The Killing of Henry Marshall." *Texas Observer* (November 7, 1986).

Anderson, Jack. *The Washington Post* (September 7, 1976).

Black, Edwin. "The Plot to Kill JFK in Chicago." *Chicago Independent* (November, 1975).

Caro, Robert. "The Transition." *New Yorker* (April 2, 2012).

Clendinen, Dudley. "J. Edgar Hoover, 'Sex Deviates' and My Godfather." *New York Times* (November 25, 2011).

Cronkite, Walter. "'Hell' Pictured as Flying Forts Raid Germany." *Los Angeles Times* (February 27, 1943).

Dallas Morning News (November 22, 1963): n.p.

Dallas Times Herald (April 6, 1984): n.p.

Dallek, Robert. "The Medical Ordeals of JFK." *Atlantic* (December 2002).

Daniel, Jean. "Unofficial Envoy: An Historic Report from Two Capitals." *New Republic* (December 14, 1963): 15–20.

Daytona Beach News-Journal (July 31, 1977): n.p.

Demaret, Kent. "Billie Sol Estes May Face New Fraud Charges, but He's Never Up the Creek Without a Paddle." *People* (April 23, 1979).

Fisher, Dan. "U.S. Far Off on Troop Estimates in Cuba Crisis." *Los Angeles Times* (January 30, 1989).

"Ford Made Key Change In Kennedy Death Report." *New York Times* (July 3, 1997).

Fuoco, Michael A. "40 Years on, Arlen Specter and Cyril Wecht Still Don't Agree How JFK Died." *Pittsburgh Post-Gazette* (November 16, 2003).

Gettysburg Times (January 13, 1964).

Glynn, Don. "Area Delegates Attended Mob Convention." *Niagara Gazette* (November 11, 2007).

Gonzalez, John. "1962 Death of Estes' Accountant to Be Probed." *The Dallas Morning News* (March 29, 1984).

Herbers, John. "Panel on Civil Disorders Calls for Drastic Action To Avoid 2-Nation Society." *New York Times* (March 1, 1968).

Horwitz, Jane. "She Hopes 'MacBird' Flies in a New Era." *The Washington Post* (September 5, 2006).

Houston Chronicle (August 4, 2003).

"Investigations: Decline and Fall." *Time* (May 25, 1962).

Janos, Leo. "The Last Days of the President." *Atlantic* (July 1973): 35–41 Web.

Kelley, Kitty. "The Dark Side of Camelot." *People* (February 29, 1988)

Kuempel, George. "Suicide Ruling Changed to Murder." *Dallas Morning News* (August 14, 1985).

Levin, Hillel. "How the Outfit Killed JFK." *Playboy* (November 22, 2011).

Loeb, Vernon. "Soviets Knew Date of Cuba Attack." *Washington Post* (April 29, 2000).

Martinez, Michael and Brad Johnson. "Attorneys for RFK Convicted Killer Sirhan Push 'Second Gunman' Argument." *CNN* (March 12, 2012).

Martinez, Michael and Brad Johnson. "RFK Assassination Witness Tells CNN: There Was a Second Shooter." *CNN* (April 28, 2012).

Nagourney, Adam. "Rescuing a Vietnam Casualty: Johnson's Legacy." *New York Times*. Feb. 15, 2014

Sarasota HeraldTribune (December 31, 1975).

Schendel, Gordon. "Something Is Rotten in the State of Texas." *Collier's Weekly* 9 (June 1951): 13–15.

Severo, Richard. "John Connally of Texas, a Power in 2 Political Parties, Dies at 76." *New York Times* (June 16, 1993).

Shields, Gerard. "Mechanic Tells Of Role in Joe Kennedy's Last Flight— Stripped Navy Plane Was Turned Into 'Bomb'" *Seattle Times* (April 22, 1996).

Taylor, Michael. "40 Years After RFK's Death, Questions Linger." *San Francisco Chronicle* (June 3, 2008).

News and Courier. [Charleston, SC] (September 27, 1978): 14-D.

Reading Eagle. [Reading, PA] (March 30, 1984).

Tri City Herald [Kennewick, WA] (September 26, 1976): n.p.

Truman, Harry. "Limit CIA Role To Intelligence." *The Washington Post* (December 22, 1963).

Valley Morning Star [Harlingen, TX] (April 17, 1952): n.p.

Watson, Paul Joseph. "Son of JFK Conspirator Drops New Bombshell Revelations." *Prison Planet* (May 3, 2009).

Weber, Bruce. "Moyer and Others Want History Channel Inquiry Over Film That Accuses Johnson." *New York Times*, February 5, 2004.

Television, Internet, and Radio

Aguilar, Gary L. MD, "The HSCA and JFK's Skull Wound", March 30,1995. http://spot.acorn.net/jfkplace/09/fp.back_issues/05th_Issue/hsca_med.html

American Experience: George H. W. Bush, PBS, 2008

"Autopsy Report of Roger Craig." mcadams.posc.mu.edu/craig_autopsy.htm.

"AARC Public Library - Interim Report: Alleged Assassination Plots Involving Foreign Leaders." *AARC Public Library - Interim Report: Alleged Assassination Plots Involving Foreign Leaders* (April 10, 2012), aarclibrary.org/publib/contents/church/contents_church_reports_ir.htm.

"Bobby Kennedy and Other Mixed Blessings." *Firing Line,* June 6, 1966.

"Book Publisher: President Ford Knew of CIA Coverup in Kennedy Assassination." *PR News Channel* (September 2012), prnewschannel.com/absolutenm/templates/?a=141.

"Commission Document 1 - FBI Summary Report." *Warren Commission Documents* (March 2012), maryferrell.org/mffweb/archive/viewer/showDoc.do?docId=10402.

De Mohrenschildt, George. "I Am a Patsy! I Am a Patsy!" jfkassassination.net/russ/jfkinfo4/jfk12/hscapatsy.htm.

Dreamslaughter2. "Jack Ruby Talks." (January 25, 2011), youtube.com/watch?v=omnpQBa1Euc.

Education Forum Q&A with Douglas Caddy, educationforum.ipbhost.com/index.php?showtopic=18833&st=0&gopid=247779.

The Alex Jones Channel, "Exclusive Interview with E. Howard Hunt; The JFK Cover-Up," youtube.com/watch?v=DbD_u7nUB_c.

"Family Jewels." *Central Intelligence Agency*, foia.cia.gov/docs/DOC_0001451843/DOC_0001451843.pdf.

"FBI Memo Reveals a Lot," www.jfkassassinationforum.com/index.php?topic=6785.0.

FederalJacktube6. "Richard Nixon Jokes About LBJ Killing JFK." (February 7, 2012), youtube.com/watch?v=oqTMELBh23g.

Gavin, Patrick. "LBJ Watched 'Risque' Films." *Politico*. November 18, 2010 http://www.politico.com/click/stories/1011/lbj_watched_risqu_films.html

Griffith, Michael T. "How Long Would the Lone Gunman Have Had to Fire?" (May 2012), mtgriffith.com/web_documents/howlong.htm.

"Henry Marshall Bio." *Spartacus Educational* (April 2012), spartacus.schoolnet.co.uk/JFKmarshallH.htm.

"HSCA Final Assassinations Report." *History Matters* (June 2012), history-matters.com/archive/contents/hsca/contents_hsca_report.htm.

"HSCA Report, Volume IV: Testimony of Jack Reville." (September 2012), maryferrell.org/mffweb/archive/getToc.do;jsessionid=87D7313922396B042793DFE14EBC0095?docId=957.

"HSCA Testimony of John and Nellie Connally." (June 2012), jfkassassination.net/russ/m_j_russ/hscacon.htm.

"HSCA Testimony of Santos Trafficante." *AARC Public Library - HSCA Hearings - Volume V*, (May 10, 2012), aarclibrary.org/publib/contents/hsca/contents_hsca_vol5.htm.

Hughes, Bill, LCDR Ennes: "It Was a Deliberate Attack...on USS Liberty!" June 9, 2007. http://www.youtube.com/watch?v=t-ZJEhDfono

Imus, Don. *Imus in the Morning*, (October 2, 2012). Radio.

"Inspector General's Survey of the Cuban Operation and Associated Documents." *The George Washington University* (1997), gwu.edu/~nsarchiv/NSAEBB/NSAEBB341/IGrpt1.pdf.

"JFK Asaassination Witness Page." (May 10, 2012), jfkassassination.net/russ/wit.htm.

JFK1963. "RFK Part 2 Last Speech Ambassador Hotel." (September 5, 2005), youtube.com/watch?v=ae7H0aWFWNY.

"Kennedy Assassination Chronicles, vol. 3, issue 3 Current Section: Cuban Missile Crisis: 35 Years Ago JFK on Tape." *Mary Ferrell Foundation.* (April-May 2012), maryferrell.org/mffweb/archive/viewer/showDoc.do?absPageId=222680.

"Kennedy-Khrushchev Exchanges." *U.S. Department of State* (June-July 2012), state.gov/www/about_state/history/volume_vi/exchanges.html.

"King's Son Accuses LBJ of Conspiracy," ChicagoTribune.com (June 20, 1997).

Lane, Mark. "Two Men in Dallas." *Ustream,* (February 22, 2010), ustream.tv/recorded/4919473.

"'The Last Words of Lee Harvey Oswald,' compiled by Mae Brussell." (May 2012) ratical.org/ratville/JFK/LHO.html.

"LBJ Library: NSAM 273." (May 2012) lbjlib.utexas.edu/johnson/archives.hom/nsams/nsam273.asp.

"Mary Rattan Affidavit." jfk.ci.dallas.tx.us/04/0433-001.gif.

Margolis, Eric. "The USS Liberty: America's Most Shameful Secret," May 2, 2001. https://www.lewrockwell.com/2001/05/eric-margolis/the-uss-liberty-americas-most-shameful-secret/

Morley, Jefferson. "What Jane Roman Said" (August 10, 2012), history-matters.com/essays/frameup/WhatJaneRomanSaid/WhatJaneRomanSaid_1.htm.

Turner, Nigel. "The Men Who Killed Kennedy." History Channel.

Onedeaddj. "LBJ's Mistress Blows Whistle On JFK Assassination." (November 2006) www.youtube.com/watch?v=79lOKs0Kr_Y.

"Parkland Doctors ARRB Testimony." (July 2012) jfkassassination.net/russ/testimony/arrbpark.htm.

Phoenix, Adam. "Noam Chomsky Debunks 9/11 and JFK Murder." *YouTube,* April 12, 2008, youtube.com/watch?v=m7SPm-HFYLo.

"Poll: Continued Belief in JFK Conpiracy." *CBSNEWS.com.* (May 11, 2013).

"Politics and Presidential Protection: The Motorcade." Staff Report of the Select Committee on Assassinations." (May 10, 2012) karws.gso.uri.edu/Marsh/HSCA/MOTORCAD.TXT.

"Radio and Television Address to the American People on the Nuclear Test Ban Treaty, July 26, 1963." *John F. Kennedy Presidential Library & Museum* (March-April 2012) jfklibrary.org/Research/Ready-Reference/

JFK-Speeches/Radio-and-Television-Address-to-the-American-People-on-the-Nuclear-Test-Ban-Treaty-July-26-1963.aspx.

"Remarks Prepared for Delivery at the Trade Mart in Dallas, November 22, 1963." *John F. Kennedy Presidential Library & Museum* (March–April 2012) jfklibrary.org/Research/Ready-Reference/JFK-Speeches/Remarks-Prepared-for-Delivery-at-the-Trade-Mart-in-Dallas-November-22-1963. aspx.

"Report on Plots to Assassinate Fidel Castro (1967 Inspector General's Report)" *HSCA Segregated CIA Collection* (microfilm) November 10, 2012) maryferrell.org/mffweb/archive/viewer/showDoc.do?docId=9983.

"Robert F. Kennedy at San Fernando Valley State College." *Pacifica Radio Archives* (May 2012) archive.org/details/RobertFKennedyAtSan FernandoValleyStateCollege.

"Selections from Lady Bird's Diary on the Assassination." (June 10, 2012) pbs.org/ladybird/epicenter/epicenter_doc_diary.html.

"Shari Angel Interview" www.jfklink.com/articles/Shari.html.

Smith, Nelson. "MythBusters. JFK Assassination Magic Bullet Test (Part 2)." (July 25, 2009) www.youtube.com/watch?v=PZRUNYZY71g.

Stengle, Jamie. "RFK Jr. 'Very Convincing' Evidence That JFK Wasn't Killed by Lone Gunman." *NBCNEWS.com* (January 11, 2013).

"Testimony of William K. Harvey." *Church Committee Boxed Files* (April 10, 2012) maryferrell.org/mffweb/archive/viewer/showDoc.do?docId= 33933.

Tonight Starring Jack Paar (March 13, 1964).

Turner, Nigel. "The Men Who Killed Kennedy." History Channel.

Urantianow. "James Files Confesses in JFK Assassination." (May 15, 2009) youtube.com/watch?v=XTVH—eqWg4.

The View, October 9, 2012.

"Vincent Bugliosi in San Francisco." *FORA.tv.* (June 2012) fora. tv/2007/05/29/Vincent_Bugliosi_in_San_Francisco/Oswald_Not_ Involved_in_JFK_Assassination.

"Warren Commission Hearings, Volume VI." *Warren Commission Hearings and Exhibits.* (November 10, 2012) maryferrell.org/mffweb/archive/ getToc.do;jsessionid=6DB181E237F530AEB6CAE0864742D6B7?doc Id=35.

"The Clint Murchison Meeting," YouTube video, 1:21:24, posted by "Se7ensenses," (May 26, 2011) youtube.com/watch?v=POmdd6HQsus.

http://www.mackwhite.com/lbj.html

INDEX

INDEX

Cold War and, 112
coverup, 169
JFK, briefings to, 10–12
JFK and, 116, 150
JFK's false signals to, 10
LBJ and, 375
Marcello and, 177
McCord and, 164
mob and, 146, 149, 155, 163
Nixon and, 159, 161, 169
NSC 10/2, 112–13, 151
Operation 40, 149–150, 152, 156, 159, 298–99, 316
Oswald and, 265, 267, 286
Rosselli and, 143
Truman op-ed, 125–26
Vallee and, 272
in Vietnam, 2, 3–4
Watergate, 161
Zapata and, 298
Cesar, Thane Eugene, 367
Chaitkin, Anton, 311
Chamberlain, Neville, 61, 77
Chambers, C. Fred, 312
Chambers, G. Paul, 240, 321, 340–41
Chapin, Dwight, 231
Chase Manhattan Bank, 306
Cheney, Dick, 193
Chennault, Anna, 230
Chennault, Claire, 230
Cheramie, Rose, 282
Cherry, Wendell, 303
Chicago plot, 272
Chicago Tribune, 283
Chicago Waste Handlers Union, 283
Chomsky, Noam, 384
Chotiner, Murray, 18, 133

Christian, George E., 373
Chudars, Jim, 45
Church Committee, 126, 151, 156
Churchill Farms, 175
CIA. see Central Intelligence Agency (CIA)
Civello, Joseph, 95, 284
Civil Air Patrol, 121, 176
civil rights, 8–9, 16, 299
Civil Rights Act, 33
Clark, Ed, 47, 47–48, 49, 186, 189
Clark, John E,, 49
Clark, Tom, 373
Clifford, Clark, 80–81, 126
Cofer, John, 206, 210, 376
Cohen, Mickey, 133, 134
Cohn, Harry, 131
Cohn, Roy M., Esq., 178–79, F
Cold War, 10
Collateral Loan Company, 57
Collier's Weekly, 38
Collom, Mark, 13, 211
Colson, Charles, 164
Columbia Pictures, 131
Columbia Trust, 55
Commercial Solvents, 201
Commission Exhibit. see CE
Commission on Civil Disorders, 360–61
Committee of Equal Employment Opportunity, 85
Committee to Re-elect the President (CREEP), 1, 163, 167
Commodoro, 67
Connally, John
  Bentsen and, 307–8
  bullets, hit by, 237–38
  bullets, separate, 339–340
  Bush and, 309

457

Good Neighbor Commission, 42
Goodell, Charles, 309
Goodfellow's Grotto, 133
Goodson, Clyde F., 280
Goodwin, Richard, 11, 12, 31, 359
Goodwin, Doris Kearns, 31
Gore Dean, Mary, 6
grassy knoll, 238–40, 331–32, 333, 362–63, 380
Green, Petey, 40–41
Greer, Walter H., 39
Griffin, Booker, 366
Griffin, Burt, 289–90
Griffin, Nolan, 204
Grober, Bert "Wingy," 135
Gruzik, Jake, 130
Guatemala, 155, 173
Guevara, Che, 155
Guilty Men, The (TV special), 234
Gulf of Tonkin Incident, 192
Gulf Oil, 47

H
Haiti, 155
Haldeman, H. R., 161, 162, 231
Halfen, John, 172
Halliburton, 34, 47, 192, 193, 246, 376
Hamer, Frank, 50
Hardeman, D. P., 228
Harkness, D. V., 331
Harris, Betty, 233
Harrison, W. J., 287–88, 289, 290
Harvey, Bill
  Berlin Tunnel operation, 150
  Church Committee, 151, 156
  Hunt named, 169
  JFK and, 150
  LBJ and, 152
  on McCone, 358

Operation 40, 149–50, 155
  Rosselli and, 150–51, 151–52
Hatfield, Mark, 312
Hauser, Joseph, 177
Hayden, Stone, and Company, 58
Head Shot, 240, 321, 340
Heinz, John, 339
helicopters, 45–46
Helms, Richard, 156–57, 161, 162, 164, 358
Hepburn, James, 221, 375
Herman, Richard, 310
Hernandez, Enrique, 365–66
Hersh, Burton, 99, 132, 174
Hersh, Seymour, 80, 89–90
Hess, Stephen, 229
Hess and Eisenhart, 249
Hewitt, Don, 160
Heymann, C. David, 153, 257
Hickory Hill, 87, 351
"High Hopes" (song), 129–30
Hill, Jean, 336–37
Hill, Ralph, 197
Hilter, Adolf, 61, 77, 105
History Channel, 234
Hit List, 377
Hoff, Jeffrey, 126
Hoffa, Jimmy, 19, 132, 333
Hoffman, Ed, 239
Hole in the Head, A (film), 129
Holland, S.M., 239
Holloway, Pat, 34, 246
"Honey Fitz." see Fitzgerald, John F.
Hooker, Eddie, 270
Hoover, J. Edgar
  Attorney Generals and, 102–3
  authoritarian, 98
  blackmail, 103–5, 357–58